Contents

Figures and tables

About the editors

Olivia Kyriakidou   Olivia Kyriakidou studied philosophy and psychology at Aristotle University of Thessaloniki, Greece, before specializing in the study of identity, completing a PhD in organizational psychology. Her research programme to date pursues a long term interest in the application of psychology to organizational issues, with particular interest in conceptualizing and managing the interface between macro, meso and micro perspectives. Her current interest focuses on the relationality of organizational life. Examples of her research include enacting organizational change, identity orientations and identity change, knowledge sharing and networks, virtual teams and the creation of virtual working environments, careers and social capital, European HRM and diversity management. Finally, Olivia practices consultancy work on the design and implementation of HR and training solutions to organizational problems in a wide range of different business contexts. For further details: o.kyriakidou@aegean.gr

Mustafa F. Özbilgin   Mustafa F. Özbilgin is a Senior Lecturer in Employment Relations at the School of Business and Management, Queen Mary, University of London. He holds a BA in Business Administration from Bosphorus University (Turkey), an MA in Human Resource Management and Development from Marmara University (Turkey) and a PhD in Social Sciences from the University of Bristol (UK). He has previously worked at the University of Hertfordshire (UK) and University of Surrey (UK) as a lecturer, and at CEPS-INSTEAD (Luxembourg), Cornell University, School of Industrial and Labor Relations (USA) and the Japan Institute of Labour Policy and Training (Japan) as visiting fellow. His research focuses on equality, diversity, and fairness in employment as well as career 'choice' from comparative, relational and international perspectives. His publications are available via his personal web site at http://www.ozbilgin.net. For more information: m.ozbilgin@qmul.ac.uk

Contributors

Blake E. Ashforth Blake Ashforth is the Jerry and Mary Ann Chapman Professor of Business in the W.P. Carey School of Business, Arizona State University. He received his PhD from the University of Toronto. His research focuses on identity and identification in organizational settings, socialization and newcomer work adjustment, the dysfunctions of organizational structures and processes, and the links among individual-, group-, and organization-level phenomena. Blake is the author of *Role Transitions in Organizational Life: An Identity-Based Perspective*, published by Lawrence Erlbaum Associates in 2001. Blake can be contacted at: blake.ashforth@asu.edu

M. Turan Ayvaz M. Turan Ayvaz is an ABD Doctoral Candidate in the Human and Organizational Studies Program at the George Washington University. His research interests include knowledge creation, organizational knowing, epistemology of knowledge, complexity and organizational change, cognitive maps, cross-cultural collective sense-making, and collective and distributed cognition. For more information contact: ayvaz@gwu.edu

Julie Battilana Julie Battilana is a PhD candidate in organizational behaviour at INSEAD. She holds a Masters of Science from INSEAD and École Normale Supérieure de Cachan with a focus in sociology and a MBA from HEC. Her dissertation examines the role of individuals in institutional change. Her research focuses on interactions between actors (be they organizations or individuals) and their institutional environment. Julie is a research associate with INSEAD's Health Care Management Initiative where she is a principle investigator on a study about leading change in the English National Health Service. To contact Julie: julie.battilana@insead.edu

Laura A. Costanzo Laura A. Costanzo is a lecturer in strategic management at the School of Management, University of Surrey. She obtained her PhD from the University of Leeds where she was formerly a research fellow in financial services within the International Institute of Banking and Financial Services. Her paper 'Avoiding the Myopia of Adaptive Learning' was among the top ten finalist best papers presented at the 23rd Annual Conference of the Strategic Management Society, Baltimore. Her current research interests are in the area of strategic innovation, innovation management, strategy process and innovative forms of organizations in high-velocity environments. Laura can be contacted at: l.costanzo@surrey.ac.uk

Margaret D. Gorman   Margaret D. Gorman is the director of the Center for the Study of Learning and the Executive Leadership Doctoral Program at the George Washington University. Dr Gorman's teaching and research areas of interest focus on organizational learning and leadership, collective knowledge creation, chaos theory, sociological approaches to organizational change and development, and use of mix methodologies in applied research. For more information: mgorman@gwu.edu

Jody Hoffer Gittel   Jody Hoffer Gittell is assistant professor of management at The Heller School for Social Policy and Management, Brandeis University. Her research explores the communication and relationship patterns through which front-line employees coordinate their work, and how these patterns are shaped by organizational practices. She has developed a theory of relational coordination, and has demonstrated its performance effects and how organizations can foster it. She received her PhD in 1995 from the MIT Sloan School of Management, and recently authored a book based on her dissertation, titled *The Southwest Airlines Way: Using the Power of Relationships to Achieve High Performance* (McGraw-Hill, 2003). To contact Jody: jgittell@brandeis.edu

Dian Marie Hosking   Dian Marie Hosking is a Professor of Relational Processes. Dian studied sociology, psychology and law at Sheffield University (UK). She won a scholarship to study for an MSc in Social and Industrial Psychology at Hull University. Her PhD (Warwick) combined psychological literatures, the sociology of organizations, political science and interactionist traditions from many fields in a study of leadership. She has lived and worked in Australia (as Visiting Fellow in the Social Sciences, Flinders University), California (Visiting Fellow, USC), and Switzerland – where she was guest professor at the University of St Gallen. In 2001, Dian was appointed full professor at Tilburg University in Organisational Development and Change. In 2004 she moved to the Utrecht School of Governance. Her personal website is: http://www.geocities.com/dian_marie_hosking, or you can email her at, d.hosking@usg.uu.nl

Mine Karataş-Özkan   Mine Karataş-Özkan is a Lecturer in Entrepreneurship at the Institute for Entrepreneurship, School of Management, University of Southampton, UK. Her research interests include nascent entrepreneurship, entrepreneurial learning, enterprise education, gender and technology entrepreneurship, diversity in venture teams and venture performance, social entrepreneurship and entrepreneurial careers. She has published a number of research articles in these areas in entrepreneurship as well as organization studies journals. To contact Mine: mko@soton.ac.uk

Edward J. Lawler Edward J. Lawler is Martin P. Catherwood Professor of Industrial and Labor Relations and Professor of Sociology at Cornell University. He co-authored (with Samuel B. Bacharach) *Politics in Organizations* (1980) and *Bargaining* (1981). He co-edits (with Shane Thye) volumes of the series *Advances in Group Processes*, and he served as Editor of *Social Psychology Quarterly* (1992–96). His current research deals with the role of emotional/affective processes in social exchange. In 2001 he received the Cooley-Mead Award for career achievement from the Social Psychology Section of the American Sociological Association. His paper, 'An Affect Theory of Social Exchange' won the 2002 Theory Section Prize. For more information: ej13@cornell.edu

Ayala Malach Pines Professor Ayala Malach Pines is a clinical, social and organizational psychologist and the head of the Department of Business Administration at the Ben-Gurion University School of Management in Israel. Professor Pines is one of the pioneers in the study of burnout and has published extensively on the subject including numerous research articles, book chapters and a book entitled *Career Burnout: Causes and Cures* co-authored with Elliot Aronson. Altogether she has had ten books, twenty book chapters and over eighty research articles published. Her books have been translated into many languages including Hebrew, French, German, Spanish, Hungarian, Greek, Turkish, Korean, Japanese and Chinese. She can be contacted at: pinesa@zahav.net.il

William D. Murphy William Murphy is the School Research Manager and Senior Research Fellow at the Derbyshire Business School, University of Derby, UK. His research focuses on the themes of organizational behaviour and organizational control with particular reference to public sector financial management and public sector management. Other work with research degree students involves learning in venturing; best value; production planning and control in small firms; modelling impacts of strategic decisions on efficiency measures; risk management. He has published in quality management, marketing, operational research and entrepreneurship journals as well as accounting and accounting education. To contact William: w.d.murphy@derby.ac.uk

Cecilia L. Ridgeway   Cecilia L. Ridgeway is Lucie Stern Professor in the Social Sciences and a member of the Sociology Department at Stanford University, USA. She is particularly interested in the role that social hierarchies in everyday interaction play in the larger processes of stratification and inequality in a society. Current projects include empirical tests of status construction theory, which is a theory about the power of interactional contexts to create and spread status beliefs about social differences. Other work addresses the role of interactional processes in preserving gender inequality despite major changes in the socio-economic organization of society. Contact Cecilia at: ridgeway@stanford.edu

Yoshimichi Sato   Yoshimichi Sato is a professor of sociology and the director of the Center for the Study of Social Stratification and Inequality at Tohoku University. He has studied trust using rational choice theory and also conducted empirical studies of social stratification. He is currently interested in building agent-based models of the emergence of inequality. His recent publications include 'Market, trust, and inequality: an agent-based model of effect of market attractiveness on trusting behavior and inequality', in *Sociological Theory and Methods* and 'Trust, cooperation, and market formation in the US and Japan', in *Proceedings of the National Academy of Sciences* (with Michael W. Macy). He can be contacted at: ysato@sal.tohoku.ac.jp

David R. Schwandt   David R. Schwandt is Professor of Human and Organizational Studies at the George Washington University. His current research centres on organizational issues that relate to collective cognition. Specific areas of inquiry include organizational learning, strategy development and implementation, collective sense-making and culture, and organizational development. For more information: drschwandt@msn.com

Metin Sengul   Metin Sengul is a PhD student in Strategic Management at INSEAD. His current research interests lie in competitive dynamics and strategic behaviour of multinationals. He has written on the role of organizational structure, cognitive categorization, and institutional factors in firm behavior and performance. Contact Metin at: metin.sengul@insead.edu

David M. Sluss   David M. Sluss is a PhD candidate at Arizona State University. David's research interests focus on the issues of identity and identification within the contexts of the newcomer adjustment process and within a wide array of professions such as knowledge workers, temporary workers, and dirty work. David is particularly interested in how work role-relationships influence identification with the organization, occupation, and other salient work relationships. He can be contacted at: david.sluss@ asu.edu

Thomas A. Wright   Thomas A. Wright is a Professor of Organizational Behavior at the University of Nevada, Reno. He received his PhD in organizational behavior and industrial relations from the University of California, Berkeley. Similar to the Claude Rains character from the classic movie, Casablanca, he has published his work in many of the 'usual suspects' including the *Academy of Management Review, Journal of Applied Psychology, Psychometrika, Journal of Organizational Behavior, Journal of Management, Organizational Dynamics* and the *Journal of Management Inquiry*. Included among his personal interests are spending time with his wife (Kay) and family, and competitively lifting weights with other aging gym fanatics. Contact him at: taw@unr.nevada.edu

Jeongkoo Yoon   Jeongkoo Yoon is Professor in the OB and HRM Department of the School of Business Administration at Ajou University, South Korea. In collaboration with Ed Lawler and Shane Thye, he has developed the research program of relational cohesion in power and exchange relations (*American Sociological Review*, 1993, 1996, 1998; *American Journal of Sociology*, 2000). He has also applied the program and theory to understand key organizational behaviour topics such as empowerment, leadership, organizational commitment, and change management (*Human Relations*, 1994, 1999; *Social Psychology Quarterly*, 2001; *Work & Occupations*, 2002). Jeongkoo can be contacted at: jy26@cornell.edu

1 Introduction

Olivia Kyriakidou and Mustafa F. Özbilgin

Organizational theorists are faced with a fundamental dilemma: whether to conceive of the social world as consisting in substances or in processes, in static 'things' or in dynamic, unfolding relations. They take as their point of departure the notion that it is static, preformed (Emirbayer, 1997) entities (structures, organizations, groups, individuals) that constitute the fundamental units of all inquiry without being modified internally by their interrelationships and dynamic processes. This theoretical stance has led large parts of the organizational community to study implicitly or explicitly organizational phenomena either from a micro or macro perspective without depicting organizational reality in dynamic, continuous and processual terms. Unfortunately, while there is an increasing interest in incorporating both micro and macro perspectives in the same theoretical formulation or research design, there are no systematic attempts underpinned by a coherent framework to synthesize micro and macro organizational processes. The thesis of the present book is that organizational phenomena ranging from the behaviors, thoughts and emotions of organization members to the collective actions of organizations occur at several levels of analysis which are in some way linked. It is our argument that micro and macro processes cannot be treated separately and then added up to understand behavior in, or behavior of organizations. We argue for a relational perspective to foster integration of micro and macro organizational perspectives and to provide a framework in which organizational phenomena could be studied in dynamic and processual terms.

Entrepreneurial venturing, in Chapter 7, could provide a case point. Mine Karataş-Özkan and William Murphy, locating entrepreneurial processes in a contextual framework, recognize that they occur within a larger context – a framework of events, circumstances, situations, settings and niches. Entrepreneurs interpret these situations and coordinate their actions. In this sense, they report that entrepreneurial actors are active participants in entrepreneurial processes which occur in a historical and cultural context. In this way, they place particular emphasis on the processual, relational and creative qualities of entrepreneurial practices undertaken by these actors as and when they are engaged together in developing the venture on an everyday basis.

Therefore to understand venturing it is necessary to examine how organizational structure and settings (macro) foster interactions between individual actors (micro) and how individuals make sense of settings and interactions. Thus both macro and micro variables are needed to explain theoretically and account for entrepreneurial venturing. Further, the relationships among these variables, and the relationships between these variables and venturing, are specified. The specification of the relevant variables, their relationships and the dynamic nature of these relationships constitute a relational approach to entrepreneurial venturing.

Moreover several phenomena are unique to, and occur, only in organizations. For example, consider organizational learning and knowledge creation (Chapter 4), stress and burnout (Chapter 6), organizational health (Chapter 2), coordination (Chapter 5), organizational commitment (Chapter 8), interorganizational cooperation (Chapter 11), networking (Chapter 3), knowledge integration (Chapter 12) and inequality (Chapter 10). The units of analysis involved in the study of these organizational phenomena occur naturally at several levels: individual, dyad, informal groups, subdivisions of organizations such as work units, departments or divisions, organizations, and networks of organizations. Ayala Malach Pines (Chapter 6) for example develops a perspective of burnout (previously analyzed from an individualistic perspective) that does not treat individuals as functioning independently, but rather in terms of their interconnections and dynamic relations with other individuals and social systems, namely their work team, their organization, their culture and their global village. In this sense, the way employees interact with each other and their service recipients and the kinds of relationships they form in and out of the organization are critical to the way they experience, express and cope with burnout. In this sense, the relational perspective develops the ability to study how organizational settings and organizational members influence each other and are influenced in turn. Consequently, a relational perspective in organization studies could address effectively the complexities of the relationships between the units at different levels of analysis that comprise organizations.

Micro, macro and the relational perspective

Micro approaches viewed from a relational perspective
The micro perspective begins with rational calculating individuals as the elementary unit of organizational contexts (Emirbayer, 1997) but assumes the fixity of various identities, interests, goals and preferences. It takes norm-following individuals, and the inner forces driving them, as its basic unit of analysis. It depicts individuals as self-subsistent entities that pursue

internalized norms given in advance and fixed for the duration of the action under investigation.

Fundamentally opposed to these approaches is the relational perspective, where aspects of action are not attributed to individuals isolated from their interrelations. Blake Ashforth and Davis Sluss in Chapter 2, developing the concept of relational identities, argue that individual identities and interests are not preconstituted and they do not enter into mutual interactions with their attributes already given. Rather, identities are constituted within communities including cultural values and networks of interpersonal, social relationships. One's sense of identity therefore may also vary as a function of relations with others. Social interaction involves a complex process of negotiation (Stryker & Statham, 1985) whereby individuals mutually define each other's roles and the situation they are in, and on the basis of role expectations, the patterns of interaction that are therefore appropriate.

What is distinct about the relational approach is that it sees relations between structures and individuals as dynamic in nature, as unfolding, ongoing processes rather than as static ties among their constituent elements. Olivia Kyriakidou, in Chapter 3, argues for the concept of relational identity orientations bringing a renewed interest in the social and relational aspects of knowledge transfer, learning and change within network arrangements. Central to this perspective is the idea that identity processes play a central role in the dynamics that unfold in organizational networks in order to facilitate knowledge transfer, learning and change. In this context, she argues that new approaches in organizational network research should incorporate modes of thinking about relationality and identity, and especially encourage those that conceptualize identities as relational and dynamic, adopt multiple levels of analysis and promote a relational and multilevel discourse about organizations.

Moreover there are some micro phenomena that are uniquely organizational in nature, such as coordination (Chapter 5), learning and knowledge creation (Chapter 4), organizational commitment (Chapter 8) (among others such as recruiting, socialization, management development, organizational citizenship, team behavior and so on). Because microorganizational issues only emerge in the context of organizations, it is necessary to think organizationally, in terms of organizational processes, as well as behaviorally.

The image most often employed when speaking of the relational perspective is that of complex joint action, in which it makes no sense to envision constituent elements apart from the processes within which they are involved. Based on this image, David Schwandt, M. Turan Ayvaz and Margaret Gorman, in Chapter 4, argue against the disassociation of knowledge from its dependence on a value context and its social relational origins.

They propose instead, that understanding the dynamics of learning, knowledge creation and collective cognition requires an analytic framework that takes into consideration both micro and macro, subjective and objective concepts, such as structuration, institutionalization and implications for interactions of actors into an analytical framework based on a functional action theory that will enable the understanding of individual actions and judgements.

Jody Hoffer Gittell, in Chapter 5, develops a relational perspective of coordination where micro, meso and macro processes are integrated to articulate how organizational contextual variables and micro processes influence each other. She explores the micro dynamics of coordination in work processes that are highly interdependent, uncertain and time-constrained and argues that effective coordination is carried out through relationships of shared knowledge, shared goals and mutual respect. In this way, she generates unique insights and knowledge about coordination, over and above that contributed by micro- and macro-level research and theory alone. She argues that for effective coordination shared knowledge is not sufficient, a finding which was supported by theories of task interdependence (Thompson, 1967). If effective coordination is to occur, participants must be connected by relationships of shared goals and mutual respect because together they form the basis for collective identity and for coordinated collective action.

Macro approaches viewed from a relational perspective
The macro perspective on the other hand finds its way into organizational thought by means of 'structuralisms' that posit not individuals but self-subsistent 'societies' and 'structures' as the unit of analysis. Macro theory has the tendency to make predictions of market and organizational functioning and performance while treating individuals and groups as 'black boxes' whose functioning they do not explain, based on the assumption that durable, coherent structures possess properties not reducible to the discrete elements of which they consist. A reading of most of the macro literature would lead one to believe that there is no role for human agency in macro organizational processes.

Yet there is evidence that individuals and groups substantially influence macro-organizational phenomena. Individuals carve out jobs and therefore influence structure (Miner, 1987). Individuals enact environments (Weick, 1991). Traditional macro theorists have ignored many of the behavioral processes by which situations evolve. Jeongkoo Yoon and Edward Lawler, in Chapter 8, developed the relational cohesion theory in order to question the instrumental explanation of commitment in exchange and rational choice theories. These theories do not explain why actors remain in commitment relations in the face of better alternatives, competitive bidding and changing incentives in the environment. On the other hand, they attempt to solve the problem by embedding a variety of incentive configurations in social structures. However Yoon and Lawler, by emphasizing the process of emotional experience triggered by human action and social interaction, expand the instrumentally oriented approaches and add explanatory power to the concept of organizational commitment by putting emphasis on emotions, cognition and agency. In this sense, commitment is not attributed to independent structures or individuals isolated from their interrelations. On the contrary, they examine the relationships between organizational contexts and behavior of components and they evaluate how these relationships shape outcomes, such as organizational commitment.

In a similar vein, Yoshimichi Sato in Chapter 9, in his analysis of trust and commitment in the market, integrates micro-behavioral processes to more fully account for the predictions of transaction and opportunity cost theories. Based on their assumptions, it is predicted that commitment relationships become more difficult to maintain as the market becomes more attractive, since commitment relationships incur high opportunity costs if the market is very attractive. In this way, at the most macro level, the market is often interpreted as an autonomous, internally organized, self-sustaining system. However when the behavioral processes of the agents are explored, the mechanism behind the development of commitment and trust relationships in the market is revealed: it is the diffusion through imitation of behaviors of committed people that creates the possibility of fixing a certain behavioral pattern, such as commitment, in society.

One more distinctive competence of the relational perspective is the ability to study behavior in context. Context refers to the whole structure of connections between components that gives components their meaning. To take something out of context is to remove it from its relationship to other parts, the larger whole, and the setting in which it operates. In this sense, the relational perspective develops the ability to study how contexts, settings and individuals influence each other, and are influenced in turn. Cecilia Ridgeway, in Chapter 10, explores the relationship between social relational contexts in which people coordinate and shape their behavior in relation to others, and the construction of inequality. She argues that self-organizing inequalities are bottom-up processes of contingent, mutually reinforcing events that result in systematic structures of inequality between actors and/or social groups. Social relational contexts act as a taken-for-granted micro-engine of inequality that is missed by purely macro approaches to social inequality that focus entirely on processes at the institutional or socio-economic level. Missing this micro engine, she argues, limits the ability of such macro approaches to explain how some forms of inequality sustain themselves over major transformations in the macro-level, socio-economic processes that sustain them.

The relational perspective argues for the development of a number of linking propositions that outline the processes by which different levels of analysis are related. In this sense, Julie Battilana and Metin Sengul, in Chapter 11, expand the conceptualizations of interorganizational cooperation by integrating a number of relational characteristics and behavioral processes at different levels of analysis to explain the choice of more or less integrative forms of cooperation. In Chapter 12, Laura Costanzo relates the embedded relationality of the firm to its strategic choices and capabilities of knowledge integration, arguing that such dynamic capabilities are the firms' real competitive advantage in turbulent environments. In this sense, change is the joint result of managerial intentionality and environmental effects. In this context, the evolving process of strategic renewal is conceptualized as a recursive process, which occurs in a context of direct interactions with individuals, other firms and responses from the rest of the population.

From relational perspectives to relational methods
Three chapters in this volume examine relational methods in organizational studies. An explosion has been witnessed in the range of approaches to organizational research methods that are termed as relational methods. Tracing the historical development of relational ontology in organizational studies, in Chapter 13, Mustafa F. Özbilgin examines the epistemological and methodological approaches to relationality in this literature. The most promising of these relational methodologies, he argues, are the ones that seek to bridge the agentic, social structural and contextual dimensions of organizational life with a sense of situatedness in time and space, often adopting a pluralism rather than purism in choice of techniques and methods. Özbilgin places relational methods in various typologies by content and context in this chapter. Taking the discussion on relationality to a more philosophical level and drawing on evidence from educational settings, in Chapter 14, Dian Marie Hosking presents three discourses of relationality in which she identifies the nature, context and content of relational thinking and arrives at a relational reality reified in her depiction of critical relational constructionism (CRC).

Finally, drawing on evidence from educational settings, in Chapter 15, Thomas Wright presents a relational method, CPR (committed-to-participant-research method) which has the mighty promise of recognizing and facilitating human capacity to self-regulate and make reflective decisions through relational engagement. The method promises to transcend the reactive models of human agency for a dynamic understanding of agency in relational context.

Concluding comments

The chapters in this book are diverse. Nevertheless, they reflect some common themes that may identify directions for future research. Some of these overlapping themes might include (1) understanding of inequality in organizations; (2) recognition that organizations are multifaceted regarding the provision of identities for members, and of the need to understand the impact of different identity orientations and the tensions they create within an organization; (3) study of new organizational structures that support relational coordination and rely on groups; (4) analysis of discourses of relationality and hierarchical relations of power within groups; (5) the role of relationships in organizational commitment and organizational learning and the mediational role of relationality between norms and the extent to which relationships within and between groups and organizations are cooperative and trusting or not; (6) organizational change, networks, entrepreneurship and organizational strategy in high-speed environments.

The chapters in this book point, we feel, to a promising future for the development of a truly relational perspective around organizational issues. This articulation will identify conceptual and empirical lacunae and thus highlight new directions for future research. Our understanding of relationality and basic relational processes will advance, as will our understanding of contemporary organizations in dynamic, continuous and processual terms. We argue that conducting research that breaks out of the traditional single-level micro or macro framework provides a more comprehensive and more realistic way of thinking about organizations and people in them. By realizing the potential of the relational perspective we can begin to develop more integrated theories of behavior in and of organizations.

References

Emirbayer, M. (1997), Manifesto for a rational sociology, *American Journal of Sociology*, **103**, 281–317.

Miner, A.S. (1987), Idiosyncratic jobs in formalized organizations, *Administrative Science Quarterly*, **32**, 327–51.

Stryker, S. & Statham, A. (1985), Symbolic interaction and role theory, in Lindzey, G. and Aronson, E. (eds), *Handbook of Social Psychology*, 3rd edn, Vol. 1, New York: Random House, pp. 311–78.

Thompson, J. (1967), *Organizations in Action: Social Science Bases of Administrative Theory*, New York: McGraw-Hill.

Weick, K.E. (1991), The nontraditional quality of organizational learning, *Organizational Science*, **2**, 116–24.

2 Relational identities in organizations: healthy versus unhealthy
Blake E. Ashforth and David M. Sluss

Introduction

Most of the vast literature on organizational behavior focuses on the individual, the group, and/or the organization, effectively marginalizing interpersonal relationships. This is a curious development, given the fundamental embeddedness of individuals in dense networks of interpersonal relationships and the rich role that such relationships play in the experience and performance of work and in subsequent attitudes toward an organization. To be sure, research in such areas as mentoring, role theory, leader–member exchange, trust in organizations, and social networks has yielded rich insights into specific aspects of interpersonal connections, but these efforts have not coalesced into an integrative framework of organization-based relationships per se. Fortunately however there appears to be growing interest in the central role of interpersonal relationships in organizational life (for example Dutton, 2003; Fletcher, 2004; Kahn, 1998; Wrzesniewski et al., 2003).

Our chapter focuses on how the identities that individuals derive from their various role-based interpersonal relationships – their 'relational identities' – may affect the 'health' of the relationships (defined below). We argue that healthy relationships may easily tip into unhealthy relationships and that means of redressing the latter are difficult to enact. We begin by defining our key terms, relational identity and relational health. We then examine how relational health may be put at risk by three common manifestations of relational identities: (1) multiplex relationships; (2) relational overidentification and underidentification; and (3) relational identity transference. We close by considering the implications of our arguments for future research.

What is a relational identity?

Individuals in organizations exist in a network of positions, jobs or, more generally, roles (Katz & Kahn, 1978), such that: (1) roles are fundamentally relational; and (2) interpersonal relationships are necessarily predicated on role-relationships (for example Susan the supervisor *vis-à-vis* Frank the subordinate; Amy the co-worker *vis-à-vis* Balaji the co-worker). Our focus here is on the identities that role occupants derive from their role-relationships – their relational identities. A relational identity is the nature of one's role-relationship with either a particular individual (for example Amy the co-worker) or a more generalized conception of individuals (for example with one's co-workers); it 'is how role occupants enact their respective roles *vis-à-vis* each other' (Sluss & Ashforth, 2006: 6). A relational identity consists of the goals, values, norms and so on of the respective roles as well as the more or less unique ways in which the individuals enact the roles. For example two co-workers might enact their task interdependence in a supportive and friendly manner, whereas two others do so in a more reserved and perfunctory manner.

Relational identities are socially constructed. Individuals bring their initial expectations to bear on a relationship and through interaction, negotiation, feedback and other well-known social processes (Stryker & Statham, 1985), come to an explicit or implicit understanding with their partner about the relationship. Although the partners may not completely agree on the nature of their relational identity, research on personal relationships indicates that individuals tend to strive for agreement and that agreement predicts relationship satisfaction and stability (Hardin & Conley, 2001; Hinde, 1997).

In sum, a relational identity necessarily implicates both parties to an interpersonal role-relationship; the term refers to the socially constructed nature of the relationship.

What is relational health (within organizations)?
The literature on role-relationships generally conceptualizes relational health under the rubric of relationship quality (for example Fincham et al., 2002; Hassebrauck & Fehr, 2002; Liden et al., 1997; Settoon & Mossholder, 2002; Sümer & Cozzarelli, 2004).

Relationship quality has been conceptualized as: (1) an individually focused evaluation (for example 'All in all, I am satisfied with my relationship' – Sümer & Cozzarelli, 2004); (2) an overall evaluation of the relationship (for example 'We have a good relationship' – Fincham et al., 2002), and (3) a multidimensional construct consisting of interpersonal issues such as trust, intimacy and support (Rook, 1998; Settoon & Mossholder, 2002). As noted, role-relationships and their subsequent relational identities are socially constructed – becoming more than just a sum of individual dispositions and role expectations (Sluss & Ashforth, 2006). Thus we follow the last of the three conceptualizations to argue that relational health is also more than the sum of its parts and should be defined as a multidimensional and interpersonal construct.

Current literature gives ample direction for both healthy and unhealthy relational dimensions. Rook (1998), in a review of the personal relationship literature, proposes that positive relationships consist of intimacy, emotional support and shared activities, whereas negative relationships consist of rejection, criticism and denial of support. Other qualities that have been proposed include open communication, liking, agreement, forgiveness and conflict resolution (Bartholomew & Horowitz, 1991; Hassebrauck, 1997; Hassebrauck & Fehr, 2002; Kurdek & Schmitt, 1986a, 1986b; Worthington & Scherer, 2004). Similarly, in the management literature, healthy relationships are said to experience support, trust, perspective-taking, empathetic concern and loyalty, whereas unhealthy relationships are devoid of these qualities (for example Liden et al., 1997; Settoon & Mossholder, 2002). Thus we propose that organizational role-relationships consisting of positive interpersonal qualities (such as trust, intimacy and shared activities) be considered as healthy whereas role-relationships consisting of negative interpersonal qualities (such as rejection, unconstructive criticism and denial) be considered as unhealthy.[1]

However relational health within organizations requires more than a focus on relationship quality. As noted, relationships within organizations are necessarily predicated on work roles and draw on both the people and the roles involved (Sluss & Ashforth, 2006). The fulfillment of role expectations influences organizationally significant outputs such as project success, problem-solving, and decision-making. Thus a definition of relational health within organizations should be broadened to include the relationship's in-role performance, defined by Hui et al. (1999) as 'work behaviors that are prescribed by formal job roles' (p. 4).[2]

In sum, we conceptualize a role-relationship as healthy (or unhealthy) when it engenders positive (or negative) relationship qualities and positive (or negative) in-role performance. Given that our definition of relational health includes two criteria – relationship qualities and in-role performance – one could question at what point a relationship becomes unhealthy (for example do both criteria have to be negative for the relationship to be considered unhealthy?). Because of the corrosive nature of negative relationship qualities, it seems likely that such qualities would eventually undermine in-role performance (cf. Rook, 1998). Likewise, negative in-role performance may wear down an otherwise positive relationship, kindling negative interpersonal patterns (cf. Olson & Zanna, 1993). Specifically, negative in-role performance curtails the extrinsic and intrinsic rewards that positive performance normally affords. Following expectancy theory, a decrease in rewards tends to decrease satisfaction derived from the relationship and the work implicated in the relationship (Porter & Lawler, 1968). This relational dissatisfaction may weaken the previously enjoyed relational qualities such as patience, open communication and intimacy, giving way to negative relational qualities such as frustration, blaming and rejection. Thus we argue that a role-relationship may be considered unhealthy when either relationship qualities or in-role performance are negative, given that spill-over between the two relational components appears probable.

As a final note, we recognize that certain relationships may be structurally cast as adversarial (for example two managers competing for resources; a prosecuting lawyer interacting with a defense lawyer), resulting in a poten-tially different view of relational health. However our analysis assumes a generally positive interdependence (that is, cooperation as opposed to com-petition) between the relationship partners. Thus relational health in adver-sarial relationships is outside the purview of this chapter – although an interesting direction for future research.

With the definitions of relational identity and relational health as a foundation, we now turn to three ways in which relational health may easily become jeopardized in organizational contexts.

Multiplex relationships

> For a policeman there are incredible benefits to being raised and living in a town . . . You know everybody . . . you have a sense of the town. But it can be very difficult. If Joe's my next-door neighbor and we sit in the backyard on Saturday afternoon at a barbecue and next Saturday I have to go to Joe's house because he's beating his wife, it's tough . . . [I]t's 'Tom and Joe,' and I'm really stressed because Joe's my buddy. I'm the responding officer and I'm going to do what I have to do, but . . .
>
> (A police chief, Lefkowitz, 1998: 51)

A growing literature exists on what are termed dual, multiple or multiplex relationships (hereafter, multiplex; for example Bersoff, 2003; Herlihy & Corey, 1997; Valcour, 2002). A multiplex relationship exists between two individuals when they each play two or more roles *vis-à-vis* one another, whether simultaneously or sequentially. In organizational settings, the individuals may have either two or more work-based roles (for example an individual chairs a committee that includes her co-worker) or one or more work-based roles and one or more personal roles (for example two co-workers become friends).

The literature suggests that multiplex relationships are virtually inevitable and therefore common. Examples include family businesses where family members are also co-workers, occupations in rural communities where clients are often neighbors, workplace romances, volunteer organizations and cooperatives where co-workers are also customers, and members of helping professions in total institutions such as prisons and the military who are also expected to be agents of control (Daniels, 1975; Kaslow & Kaslow, 1992; Mainiero, 1989; Schank & Skovholt, 1997; Valcour, 2002). But perhaps the most common multiplex relationship is where a work-role based relationship gives rise to a friendship: workplaces are associated with a host of contextual and individual factors that facilitate the development of friendships, such as physical proximity, shared activities and interpersonal similarities (Sias & Cahill, 1998).

Healthy vs. unhealthy?
Just as no two snowflakes are alike, no two relational identities are alike, and their juxtaposition in a multiplex relationship (for example manager and friend) typically raises questions as to which identity should prevail or how the identities should be blended. And just as the most common multiplex relationship may be the work–friend duality, so too may it be among the most benign, at least if the friends are workplace peers. Work peer friendships may provide instrumental and emotional support, an avenue for social and belongingness needs, a source of intrinsic reward, and a reservoir of goodwill to buffer against workplace frictions (for example Kram & Isabella, 1985). In terms of our definition of relational health, the personalized quality of friendships (Sias & Cahill, 1998) may facilitate openness, intimacy and so on, which may in turn facilitate in-role performance (for example Albrecht & Hall, 1991; Fine, 1996). More generally, the rich relational knowledge gained from any role-relationship may enhance the development and conduct of other role-relationships.

However even in relatively benign multiplex role-relationships, the threats to relational health are very real. The major threat that *any* multiplex relationship presents to relational health is that the relational identities usually – although not inevitably – involve contradictions, variously termed interrole conflicts, conflicts of interest and dialectical tensions. In the case of work–friend multiplex relationships, Bridge and Baxter (1992; see also Zorn, 1995) found evidence for five dialectical tensions: (1) impartiality–favoritism, where workplace norms for equal treatment conflict with friendship norms for preferential treatment; (2) judgement–acceptance, where workplace norms of evaluation contradict friendship norms of total acceptance; (3) connection–autonomy, where ongoing workplace relationships may threaten friendships through excessive connection; (4) inequality–equality, where workplace status and other differences conflict with the friendship norm of equality; and (5) closedness–openness, where workplace norms of confidentiality and caution may contradict friendship norms of openness and honesty. Thus, the enactment of one role-relationship may undermine the other role-relationship.

Other multiplex relationships are susceptible to more pernicious contradictions, particularly where the work-roles involve a fiduciary relationship and/or marked power and status differentials. Indeed most of the literature

on multiplex relationships stems from the helping professions, where scholars and practitioners focus on the potential for abuse of clients and patients
(Herlihy & Corey, 1997; Reamer, 2003).[3] Although this literature centers on
the helping professions, the concerns can apply to any role-relationship
involving a fiduciary relationship and power or status differentials: the
more powerful party may be tempted to exploit the dependency for personal gain, may have his or her professional objectivity compromised by
another role-relationship, may confuse the less powerful party as to which
role-relationship prevails in a given context, may render taboo topics that
could threaten the second role-relationship, and may have an adverse
impact on the professional work environment as colleagues witness such
effects (Plaut, 1997; Pope, 1991; Powell & Foley, 1999). Individuals who are
relatively dependent and therefore vulnerable may not be capable of providing true consent to a second role-relationship (Kitchener, 1988; Plaut,
1997). Moreover individuals in positions of power appear to be very adept
at rationalizing their involvement in conflicted multiplex relationships
(Pope & Vasquez, 1991).

The difficulty of mitigating unhealthy multiplexity
In the helping professions, codes of ethics routinely caution practitioners
about the dangers of multiplex relationships. Many scholarly prescriptions
for mitigating potentially problematic multiplexity center on boundary
management, that is, on erecting and maintaining temporal (for example
not discussing personal issues during the workday), physical (for example
confining socializing to off-site locations), social (for example not accepting large gifts from clients), and symbolic (for example language, demeanor,
dress) boundaries around role-relationships such that multiplexity is more
or less compartmentalized or forestalled (for example Herlihy & Corey,
1997; Peterson, 1992; Plaut, 1997).

Bridge and Baxter (1992) offer a more inclusive typology. They found that
individuals attempted to cope with the dialectical tensions of workplace
friendships by not only (1) compartmentalizing the roles via boundary
management, but also by (2) privileging one role-relationship over the other
in a given situation (for example 'What Sally and I would always do is I'd
say "All right, I'm talking to you Sally-friend not Sally-supervisor",' Zorn,
1995: 136) or by (3) integrating the role-relationships. However all three
tactics may be quite difficult to enact (particularly in role-relationships that
appear relatively benign to the partners, such as workplace friendships).
First, regarding boundary management, because multiplex relationships
often emerge spontaneously from the same context as the original work-
based relationship (for example interdependent tasks breed a friendship; a
committee assignment causes overlapping work-role relationships), it may

be difficult not only to forestall the emergence of multiplexity but also to compartmentalize the respective role-relationships *post hoc*. Once a multiplex role-relationship emerges, activating one role-relationship may more or less automatically cue the other. It thus becomes difficult to undo or sequester the relationship without ill effects – particularly if the denied role-relationship is a personal one (Sias et al., 2004).

Second, regarding privileging one role, the more valued each role-relationship is, the more difficult it is to deny one relationship – even if only temporarily. Sias et al. (2004) report that when a supervisor reprimanded his subordinate–friend and attempted to compartmentalize the role-relationships ('This has nothing to do with friendship', p. 330), the friend nonetheless felt betrayed. The common denominator of our counterarguments to boundary management and privileging is that a role-relationship sequestered or put on hold is often seen as a role-relationship violated. Ironically, even the termination of a role-relationship may not solve the problem because of lingering memories of the terminated relationship and perhaps resentment caused by the termination (for example Sias et al., 2004). Relationships can be ended, but they are seldom forgotten and the residual may continue to influence future interactions (for example Ashforth, 2001; Mainiero, 1989).

Third, regarding integration, the greater the inherent contradictions between two or more role-relationships, the more difficult is meaningful integration of the relationships. Valcour (2002) discusses teachers in a parent-run cooperative nursery school who had to juggle three role-relationships *vis-à-vis* parents: service provider–client, employee–owner and manager–volunteer worker. The role-relationships often bled into one another such that teachers faced de facto integrations (for example as owners, parent volunteers were often less willing to be directed by the teacher or to listen to negative feedback; parent volunteers often responded to their own needy children, enacting their client role). Teachers responded by enacting the manager–volunteer relationship with lower expectations and great tact. In short, given the contradictions between the role relationships, 'integration' amounted to a watering down of the teachers' manager–volunteer role-relationship.

In sum, while multiplex relationships may be inevitable, the contradictions they often present may prove intractable.

Relational overidentification and underidentification

Relational identification refers to 'the extent to which one defines oneself in terms of a given role-relationship' (Sluss & Ashforth, 2006: 6). A person may have a clear sense of what it means to be a co-worker of Bob's (that is, a perceived relational identity), but nonetheless resist internalizing that identity as a reflection of self; conversely, she may identify with her role-relationship with Jill because of its friendliness and mutual support. Relational identification is generally thought to be psychologically healthy because it involves 'self-expansion' – a broadening of the self to include another person and what the role-relationship is perceived to mean (Aron & Aron, 2000; Josselson, 1992). And to the extent that the investment of self in the relationship facilitates in-role performance, identification is also likely to meet the second criterion for relational health. However our contention in this section is that relational identification has the potential to tip easily into either overidentification or underidentification.

Relational overidentification
Relational overidentification occurs when identification is so strong that the relational identity remains chronically activated in many situations (relevant or irrelevant), such that other pertinent identities become subjugated or forgotten (Sluss & Ashforth, 2006). We argued elsewhere that over-identification is most likely to occur in relationships with a significant power difference (for example manager–employee) and when the less powerful individual is less certain about role expectations and his or her own capabilities (for example being new to an organization, role or the relationship; Sluss & Ashforth, 2006). Given that organizations are built partly on hierarchical role-relationships, overidentification may not be uncommon. Additionally, not only are organizations increasingly fluid and dynamic, causing frequent changes in the make up of role-relationships and their subsequent relational identities, but individuals are increasingly switching jobs and organizations (Ashforth, 2001). These repeated transitions create 'identity deficits' where an individual in the midst of change is temporarily without a basis for his or her own work identity, engendering a high need for relational identification (cf. Baumeister et al., 1985).

One particularly problematic outcome of overidentification is codependency (Sluss & Ashforth, 2006), defined as 'a dependence on another's approval and is designed to find a sense of safety, identity, and self-worth' (Springer et al., 1998: 141). Codependency is a meaningful concept for understanding interactions not only within alcoholic families but also within dysfunctional relationships in general (Stafford, 2001; Wright & Wright, 1995). Although originally proposed as an intra-psychological construct, we argue, similar to Wright and Wright (1995), that codependency is more useful (especially within organizations) when construed at the relational level as codependent relating. Codependent relating is a relational process in which A enacts 'enmeshed caretaking' (that is, overidentification) within the role-relationship *vis-à-vis* B, where B is usually somewhat 'exploitative, irresponsible, or destructive' (Wright &

Wright, 1995: 126). Interestingly, codependent relating predicts that the 'enmeshed caretaker', although seemingly subservient, will covertly control the relationship in order to maintain the relational identity's consistency (Le Poire et al., 1998). Through overidentification, the relational identity becomes integral to the enmeshed caretaker's sense of self such that any change threatens the self. Thus the caretaker attempts to maintain the relational identity even if it has a negative influence on self-esteem. In short, self-consistency tends to become more important than self-enhancement (Swann, 1987).

Codependent relating has various negative influences on relational health. First, it may appear that codependent relating would create a high level of intimacy and openness (at least from the codependent toward the partner) – an ostensibly positive relational quality. However as the codependent filters or subjugates other potentially relevant identities, the resulting intimacy is likely to be superficial and incomplete. For example the alcoholism counseling literature indicates that codependent couples experience unhealthy levels of intimacy due to codependents' inability to separate (that is, individuate) their self-concept from the relationship (Smalley & Coleman, 1987). Second, codependent relating may create a vicious circle in that the partner (especially if exploitive or abusive) denies interpersonal support yet the codependent enacts enmeshed caretaking, thereby creating an unhealthy tug-of-war between rejecting and enabling. Third, codependent relating can create a relational environment in which open communication and constructive feedback is sacrificed to maintain the extant relational identity (for example a codependent employee not giving important feedback on a manager's decision), thereby impairing in-role performance.

We should note that, while less common and most likely a result of individual differences, it is possible that overidentification can also occur in relatively high-power positions (for example an overidentifying manager in a manager–employee relationship). For example Hall (1992) argues that managers from dysfunctional families may have codependent tendencies and thus overidentify with their employees, resulting in unhealthy relationships. Indeed the unhealthy effects may be more menacing in that the manager has a greater impact on organizational functioning and the relationships within his or her group (for example causing competing factions; Schriesheim et al., 1999).

Overidentification also has the potential to foster passive-aggressiveness, defined as a 'pervasive pattern of passive resistance to demands for adequate social and occupational performances' (McIlduff & Coghlan, 2000: 717). The definition assumes that the demands will be perceived as controlling and negative, thus eliciting the passive aggressive behavior (McCann, 1988). McIlduff and Coghlan (2000) argue that the passive or covert nature of the aggression is what makes this behavior pattern particularly damaging to relationships: the aggression is ever-present yet implicit enough so as to avoid confrontation, thereby prolonging the situation indefinitely. The DSM-III (*Diagnostic and Statistical Manual of Mental Disorders*, American Psychiatric Association, 1987) provides a vivid picture of the unhealthy effects on role-relationships. For example, the passive-aggressor tends to procrastinate, become argumentative when delegated tasks, do poor work, and rail against constructive criticism. Passive-aggressiveness, as will be shown, may emanate from either the overidentifying focal individual or his or her relational partner.

Overidentifying individuals may enact passive-aggressiveness when the relationship includes an exploitative partner (McCann, 1988), as the overidentifier struggles with the constant tug between passively accepting the exploitation and aggressively responding to it (cf. Kets de Vries, 1989). Similarly, overidentifiers may experience the same tug-of-war when the partner is perceived as only distantly engaging in the relationship (cf. unrequited love; Bratslavsky et al., 1998). The overidentifier may indirectly aggress toward the relationship in an unconscious effort to generate a more intense (yet potentially negative) connection with the partner.

Although passive-aggressiveness is more likely in subordinates than superordinates (Kets de Vries, 1989), the latter are not immune. As mentioned, overidentification leads individuals to attempt to control the relationship because of their desire to maintain relational consistency. Thus, a non-exploitative manager, when experiencing controlling behaviors from an overidentifying subordinate, may resent the social demands yet feel constrained (for example feel guilty) from showing direct aggression due to the overidentifying subordinate also enacting caretaking behaviors. As a result, the manager may (whether consciously or not) enact passive-aggressive behaviors toward the subordinate.

Finally, it should be noted that because relational identities tend to be context-specific (for example manager–employee in the work domain, husband–wife in the family domain), tendencies toward overidentification may not spill over to other social domains or change the person as a whole (that is, become so enduring as to be diagnosed as a personality disorder; see DSM-IV, American Psychiatric Association, 1995). Thus one may experience healthy relationships in one relational context and unhealthy relationships in another.

Relational underidentification

Just as relational identification can easily tip forward into overidentification, so can it easily tip backward into underidentification. Relational underidentification occurs when an individual defines him or herself only slightly or not at all in terms of a given role-relationship, regarding it with more or less indifference. Underidentification is likely a function of the salience – the situational relevance and subjective importance (Ashforth, 2001) – of the role-relationship. Regarding situational relevance, a role-relationship that has little bearing on one's organizational life (for example low task interdependence with a co-worker) is less likely to stimulate an investment of self in the relationship. Given the lack of situational relevance, relational underidentification is not problematic. Regarding subjective importance however, a role-relationship that fails to spark a personal affinity (for example a co-worker that one fails to 'click' with) may also not stimulate an investment of self – in spite of the situational relevance. In other words, a lack of subjective importance may offset situational relevance such that the role-relationship is viewed with indifference.

Similar to the relationships of autistic children, relational indifference results in a lack of connection and intimacy (cf. Dukerich et al., 1998). As a result, the relationship will have little basis for open communication, conflict resolution and task-relevant consensus while setting the groundwork for unhealthy relational qualities such as denial of support and rejection. Underidentifying partners may still meet basic performance standards, basing their interactions more on their shared organizational membership than any personal and relational connection (cf. depersonalized trust; Brewer, 1981). However in situations that require intense cooperation, the lack of intimacy may negatively influence in-role performance.

Indifference may also convert into active antipathy. Indifference involves showing little or no interest in or sympathy toward the target – in short, an absence of identification. We speculate that, given frequent interaction, it is difficult to remain wholly indifferent to a role-relationship, and that the indifference tends to gravitate toward either identification or antipathy (cf. disidentification; Elsbach, 1999; Kreiner & Ashforth, 2004). However because some degree of identification is normatively expected, perceiving that one's relational partner is indifferent – particularly after the relationship becomes more personalized – may foster negative interpersonal feelings. This negativity may in turn poison the relationship such that indifference slides into antipathy.

Relational identity transference
Similar to psychoanalytic notions of transference (for example Ellman, 2001; Frank, 2000), the social-cognitive model of transference holds that an encounter with a new person may trigger a mental representation of a significant other such that one perceives and interacts with the new person in light of the representation (Andersen & Glassman, 1996; Chen & Andersen, 1999; cf. stimulus generalization, van Osselaer et al., 2004). For

example a new manager may remind one of one's parent, triggering certain assumptions, expectations, emotions, attitudes and behaviors, thereby influencing how one interacts with the manager. Indeed these preconceptions may be viewed in normative terms – as the way one *ought* to interact, including the standards one ought to attain (Andersen & Chen, 2002). In short, for better and for worse, the parent–child relational identity is projected onto the manager–subordinate relationship. It is important to note that transference involves not only seeing the new person through the prism of a prior relationship (my manager is like my father), but the perceiver 'becoming who they are when with the significant other [i.e., in the prior relationship] in relating to the new person' (Anderson & Berenson, 2001: 245): the perceiver essentially acts out the transferred relational identity.

Given the profound importance of relationships and the diverse repertoire of rich relational identities that individuals typically have, Andersen and Chen (2002) argue that transference is quite common. Indeed Kets de Vries and Miller (1984) go so far as to say that 'transference is present in all meaningful relationships' (p. 74). Transference is primed by the chronic accessibility of the other (that is, by the frequency of prior activations of the mental representation, where significant others are more likely to be salient and thus accessible) and by transient cues that remind one of the other. Transient cues typically come from the new person (for example appearance, mannerisms) and the local context (for example symbols of hierarchical status may trigger authority-based relational identities, such as parent–child).

The transference of prior relational identities in organizations can facilitate adjustment to the new role-relationship and thereby relational health by suggesting what to expect and how to interact and by stimulating positive affect in the case of positively-viewed significant others. However transference is potentially problematic in at least four respects.

First, it is very unlikely that the preconceptions associated with a rich pre-existing relational identity will perfectly match the new relationship – particularly if the social context differs (for example work vs. home). After all, in transference, the perceiver goes well beyond the information at hand, filling in blanks by projecting a relational identity on the relationship with the new person.

Second, although individuals are certainly capable of transcending their initial projections as they come to know the new person, there is a bias toward confirmation rather than disconfirmation. Research on labeling theory suggests that individuals tend to discount contradictory information and interpret ambiguous information as supporting their preconceptions (Ashforth & Humphrey, 1995). Given the richness of relational identities, it is often easy to find some matches between the new relationship and the projection. Thus the perceiver may persist in enacting a prior relational identity even if the objective match between the new relationship and the relationship with a significant other is dubious. As a result, transference tends to be associated with unjustified confidence in the validity of the projection (Anderson & Berenson, 2001).

Third, transference often occurs without conscious effort such that one may unwittingly project a relational identity that one would consider to be unfair – if one were aware of the transference (Andersen & Berenson, 2001). However in the absence of awareness, it becomes difficult to see past one's preconceptions and interact with the new person as the unique individual he or she is. And, as the saying goes, one who 'forgets' the past is doomed to repeat it, thus becoming entrapped in recurring relational patterns (Fein, 1990).

Finally, research on labeling theory and behavioral confirmation suggests that once the new relationship is labeled, the perceiver tends to act toward the person in such a way that the label *becomes* valid (Ashforth & Humphrey, 1995; Snyder, 1992). For example if one perceives a new co-worker as reminiscent of a previous, distrusted co-worker, one may behave coldly toward the new co-worker, thereby engendering a cold and self-fulfilling response (Berk & Andersen, 2000). Moreover if the relational identity leads to unrealistic positive expectations, then the new person may come to be seen quite negatively when he or she is unable to live up to them (Andersen & Berenson, 2001). Thus the new person may be damned whether the relational identity is positive or negative.

Pierce's (1995) discussion of 'mothering paralegals' provides a good example of these problematic tendencies. The paralegals, who were generally female, tended to enact the traditional roles of wife and mother *vis-à-vis* the lawyers, who were generally male. As a traditional wife, the paralegals provided a highly personalized relationship, deferred to the lawyers' authority, affirmed the lawyers' status by submitting to and then soothing over their angry outbursts, took care of the mundane chores, provided unconditional emotional support, and accepted that the lawyers did not reciprocate the attention and caring. Similarly, as a traditional mother, they put the needs of the lawyers above their own and were expected to be cheerful and reassuring, to express appreciation of the lawyers to others, and to serve as the emotional go-between in the lawyers' relationships with others. Given the notion of self-fulfilling labels, it isn't surprising that both the paralegals and the lawyers came to think of their relationship in similar domestic terms. Interestingly, Pierce notes that this transference was not confined to isolated paralegal–lawyer pairings; it was a cultural expectation in the two organizations she studied, such that the personnel directors preferred to hire female paralegals and the organizational context evoked and tacitly supported the wife–husband and mother–son transference.

Although the social-cognitive model of transference focuses on particularized representations of a role-relationship (for example my wife/husband), Pierce's (1995) study suggests that transference may also involve a more generalized representation of a role-relationship (a traditional wife/husband). Sluss and Ashforth (2006) argue that relational identities exist in a hierarchy ranging from actual and therefore concrete role-relationships to generalized and therefore abstract role-relationships. The generalized and particularized are reciprocally related as abstract beliefs inform initial interactions with concrete exemplars, and experiences with exemplars are aggregated and shape abstract beliefs. It seems likely that, just as situational and personal cues may trigger a particularized transference (for example you're like my child), so too may they trigger a more generalized transference (for example you're like *a* child; see Kahn, 1998, for an example of generalized parent–child transference in a social service agency).

Pierce's (1995) study also highlights the importance of our dyadic-level definition of relational health. At the individual level, the lawyers and even some of the paralegals would likely report a sense of satisfaction with the relationship: after all, the lawyers are 'mothered' and the paralegals may feel some maternal or spousal pride. However it is questionable whether a relationship predicated on transference – in this case, where the nurturing flows one way, the paralegals are often invisible to the lawyers, constructive feedback is not welcomed by the lawyers, and so on – meets the criteria outlined earlier for relational health (cf. false consciousness, Duncombe & Marsden, 1995).

Discussion
Interpersonal relationships are deservedly getting more attention in the organizational literature. Given that organizations are patterned role networks, interpersonal relationships are typically predicated on role interdependencies. As such, interpersonal relationships and their associated relational identities help ground the individual in the organizational context, embedding him or her in a fabric of embodied role-relationships and providing a sense of connection and belonging.

However our analysis suggests that relational ties influence relational health in complex ways, where healthy relationships are comprised of positive interactional qualities (for example trust, intimacy, shared activities) and in-role performance. Specifically: (1) although multiplex relationships may permit a nuanced knowledge and appreciation of a role partner, they may contradict one another such that the enactment of each relationship is impaired; (2) although relational identification broadens the self to include those facets of another individual that are implicated in the role-relationship, it may easily tip into either overidentification (threatening other facets of the self) or underidentification (threatening connection and intimacy); and (3) although relational identity transference may suggest what to expect in a new role-relationship, such expectations tend to be unrealistic and artificially constraining.

The prescriptions suggested by these threats to relational health vary widely but are alike in that they are difficult to enact. As noted, a commonly prescribed remedy to multiplex relationships is boundary management, where the role-relationships are buffered or even suppressed. However the same work setting that engenders multiplexity makes it hard to then compartmentalize relationships. A common prescription for over- and underidentification, borrowed from the helping professions, is to view partners with 'detached concern' (Lief & Fox, 1963; see Halpern, 2001, for a contrary view); the 'concern' negating underidentification while the 'detachment' protects against overidentification. However the literature also suggests that it is very difficult to tread the roof peak that is identification, avoiding the dual slopes that can easily lead to over- or underidentification. Finally, a prescription for transference is to be aware of one's unconscious tendency to project the familiar on the unfamiliar and to view such projections as little more than provisional hypotheses, subject to disconfirmation as a new role-relationship is perceived on its own merits. It remains difficult however to consciously regulate a reflexive habit.

Our analysis thus suggests an important direction for future research: to investigate the extent to which individuals in various kinds of role-relationships (for example co-worker–co-worker, manager–subordinate, company representative–client) are aware of the above threats to relational health and, if so, how they attempt to cope with each of them – and with what efficacy. Are concepts like boundary management and detached concern laudable ideals that, although difficult to realize in practice, are nevertheless worth pursuing? Similarly, a common default assumption in organizations is that such threats are the *individual's* problem to resolve rather than the systemic problem they truly are. Accordingly, what can organizations do to mitigate threats to relational health and, more generally, to encourage the development of healthy role-relationships?

Another direction for research involves particularized versus generalized relational identities. We defined a relational identity as the nature of one's role-relationship with either a specific role-incumbent (for example Kathryn, the co-worker) or a generalized conception of the set of role-incumbents (for example co-workers). Most of the discussion however focused on the former. Given that organizations are first and foremost places of work, when do individuals prefer and not prefer to personalize their role-relationships – and with what impact on relational health? Do the dynamics of multiplex relationships, relational over- and underidentification, and relational identity transference – and their impact on relational health – change as relational identities become more abstract (generalized)? For example we speculate that it is easier to recommend prescriptions for coping with multiplexity and transference at the general level than it is when real, flesh-and-blood individuals and complex and possibly equivocal role-relationships are involved. A counselor may agree that meeting patients outside the office is inadvisable, but find it difficult to deny a patient who wants the counselor to attend his wedding.

Finally, because role-relationships are embedded in role networks, an intriguing issue for future research is the links between relational health and 'network health'. For example how might the health of one role-relationship affect or spill over onto other role-relationships? A supervisor who develops a strained relationship with a popular subordinate may find that her relationships with other subordinates become strained as well. To what extent does a network develop a 'relational culture' (cf. Kahn, 1998) – where role-relationships become defined in similar terms and have similar influences on relational health – and what predicts the strength of such cultures (that is, how widely shared and deeply felt a culture is)? Pierce's (1995) analysis of mothering paralegals, described earlier, provides an example of a relatively strong relational culture. And how might the concept of role modeling – where the focus is on learning a given position – apply to role-relationships *vis-à-vis* a network? Ibarra (1999), for instance, describes how neophyte consultants and investment bankers learned how to interact with clients by observing their mentors while on assignments. What kinds and aspects of relationships are most amenable to modeling, and how much variety in relational identities for a given role-relationship is advisable?

In closing, relational identities are a fundamental building block of organizations, underscoring the importance of further theorizing and research on the relationships that individuals form with their various role partners.

Notes

1. Our list is illustrative rather than exhaustive. We suspect that the specific nature and rank order of characteristics may fluctuate based on the roles and the organizational context within which the relationships are situated.
2. Note that extra-role performance is outside the definition of relational health. Consequently, we do not include extra-role performance in the analysis. We speculate that extra-role performance results *from* relational health (rather than being a defining quality of relational health; cf. Settoon & Mossholder, 2002).
3. However, it should be noted that there is a range of opinion about the ethics of multiplex relationships in the helping professions, with some regarding such relationships as not only benign but potentially therapeutically constructive (for example Lazarus & Zur, 2002).

References

Albrecht , T.L. & Hall, B. (1991), Facilitating talk about new ideas: the role of personal relationships in organizational innovation, *Communication Monographs*, **58**, 273–88.

American Psychiatric Association (1987), *Diagnostic and Statistical Manual of Mental Disorders: DSM-III-R*, 3rd edn, Washington, DC: American Psychiatric Association.

American Psychiatric Association (1995), *Diagnostic and Statistical Manual of Mental Disorders*, 4th edn, *Primary Care Version*, Washington, DC: American Psychiatric Association.

Andersen, S.M. & Berenson, K.R. (2001), Perceiving, feeling, and wanting: experiencing prior relationships in present-day interpersonal relations, in Forgas, J.P., Williams, K.D. and Wheeler, L. (eds), *The Social Mind: Cognitive and Motivational Aspects of Interpersonal Behavior*, Cambridge: Cambridge University Press, pp. 231–56.

Andersen, S.M. & Chen, S. (2002), The relational self: an interpersonal social-cognitive theory, *Psychological Review*, **109**, 619–45.

Andersen, S.M. & Glassman, N.S. (1996), Responding to significant others when they are not there: effects on interpersonal interference, motivation, and affect, in Sorrentino, R.M. and Higgins, E.T. (eds), *Handbook of Motivation and Cognition*, Vol. 3, *Interpersonal Context*, New York: Guilford Press, pp. 262–321.

Aron, A. & Aron, E.N. (2000), Self-expansion motivation and including other in the self, in Ickes, W. and Duck, S. (eds), *The Social Psychology of Personal Relationships*, Chichester: Wiley, pp. 109–28.

Ashforth, B.E. (2001), *Role Transitions in Organizational Life: An Identity-Based Perspective*, Mahwah, NJ: Erlbaum.

Ashforth, B.E. & Humphrey, R.H. (1995), Labeling processes in the organization: constructing the individual, in Cummings, L.L. and Staw, B.M. (eds), *Research in Organizational Behavior*, Vol. 17, Greenwich, CT: JAI Press, pp. 413–61.

Bartholomew, K. & Horowitz, L.M. (1991), Attachment styles among young adults: a test of the four-category model, *Journal of Personality and Social Psychology*, **61**, 226–44.

Baumeister, R.F., Shapiro, J.P. & Tice, D.M. (1985), Two kinds of identity crisis, *Journal of Personality*, **53**, 407–24.

Berk, M.S. & Andersen, S.M. (2000), The impact of past relationships on interpersonal behavior: behavioral confirmation in the social-cognitive process of transference, *Journal of Personality and Social Psychology*, **79**, 546–62.

Bersoff, D.N. (ed.) (2003), *Ethical Conflicts in Psychology*, 3rd edn, Washington, DC: American Psychological Association.

Bratslavsky, E., Baumeister, R.F. & Sommer, K.L. (1998), To love or be loved in vain: the trials and tribulations of unrequited love, in Spitzberg, B.H. & Cupach, W.R. (eds), *The Dark Side of Close Relationships*, 2nd edn, Mahwah, NJ: Lawrence Erlbaum, pp. 307–26.

Brewer, M.B. (1981), Ethnocentrism and its role in interpersonal trust, in Brewer, M.B. & Collins, B.E. (eds), *Scientific Inquiry and the Social Sciences: A Volume in Honor of Donald T. Campbell*, San Francisco, CA: Jossey-Bass, pp. 345–60.

Bridge, K. & Baxter, L.A. (1992), Blended relationships: friends as work associates, *Western Journal of Communication*, **56**, 200–25.

Chen, S. & Andersen, S.M. (1999), Relationships from the past in the present: significant-other representations and transference in interpersonal life, in Zanna, M.P. (ed.), *Advances in Experimental Social Psychology*, Vol. 31, San Diego: Academic Press, pp. 123–90.

Daniels, A.K. (1975), Advisory and coercive functions in psychiatry, *Sociology of Work and Occupations*, **2**, 55–78.

Dukerich, J.M., Kramer, R. & McLean Parks, J. (1998), The dark side of organizational identification, in Whetten, D.A. and Godfrey, P.C. (eds), *Identity in Organizations: Building Theory Through Conversations*, Thousand Oaks, CA: Sage, pp. 245–56.

Duncombe, J. & Marsden, D. (1995), 'Workaholics' and 'whingeing women': theorising intimacy and emotion work – the last frontier of gender inequality?, *Sociological Review*, **43**, 150–69.

Dutton, J.E. (2003), *Energize your Workplace: How to Create and Sustain High-Quality Connections at Work*, San Francisco, CA: Jossey-Bass.

Ellman, S. (2001), Modern revisions of Freud's concept of transference, in Scharff, D.E. (ed.), *The Psychoanalytic Century: Freud's Legacy for the Future*, New York: Other Press, pp. 89–102.

Elsbach, K.D. (1999), An expanded model of organizational identification, in Sutton, R.I. and Staw, B.M. (eds), *Research in Organizational Behavior*, Vol. 21, Greenwich, CT: JAI Press, pp. 163–200.

Fein, M.L. (1990), *Role Change: A Resocialization Perspective*, New York: Praeger.

Fincham, F.D., Paleari, F.G. & Regalia, C. (2002), Forgiveness in marriage: the role of relationship quality, attributions, and empathy, *Personal Relationships*, **9**, 27–37.

Fine, G.A. (1996), *Kitchens: The Culture of Restaurant Work*, Berkeley, CA: University of California Press.

Fletcher, J.K. (2004), Relational theory in the workplace, in Jordan, J.V., Walker, M. and Hartling, L.M. (eds), *The Complexity of Connection: Writings from the Stone Center's Jean Baker Miller Training Institute*, New York: Guilford Press, pp. 270–98.

Frank, G. (2000), Transference revisited/transference revisioned, *Psychoanalysis and Contemporary Thought*, **23**, 459–78.

Hall, F.S. (1992), Dysfunctional managers: the next human resource challenge, *Organizational Dynamics*, **20** (2), 48–57.

Halpern, J. (2001), *From Detached Concern to Empathy: Humanizing Medical Practice*, Oxford: Oxford University Press.

Hardin, C.D. & Conley, T.D. (2001), A relational approach to cognition: shared experience and relationship affirmation in social cognition, in Moskowitz, G.B. (ed.), *Cognitive Social Psychology: The Princeton Symposium on the Legacy and Future of Social Cognition*, Mahwah, NJ: Erlbaum, pp. 3–17.

Hassebrauck, M. (1997), Cognitions of relationship quality: a prototype analysis of their structure and consequences, *Personal Relationships*, **4**, 163–85.

Hassebrauck, M. & Fehr, B. (2002), Dimensions of relationship quality, *Personal Relationships*, **9**, 253–70.

Herlihy, B. & Corey, G. (1997), *Boundary Issues in Counseling: Multiple Roles and Responsibilities*, Alexandria, VA: American Counseling Association.

Hinde, R.A. (1997), *Relationships: A Dialectical Perspective*, Hove, UK: Psychology Press.

Hui, C., Law, K.S. & Chen, Z.X. (1999), A structural equation model of the effects of negative affectivity, leader–member exchange, and perceived job mobility on in-role and extra-role performance: a Chinese case, *Organizational Behavior and Human Decision Processes*, **77**, 3–21.

Ibarra, H. (1999), Provisional selves: experimenting with image and identity in professional adaptation, *Administrative Science Quarterly*, **44**, 764–91.

Josselson, R. (1992), *The Space Between Us: Exploring the Dimensions of Human Relationships*, San Francisco, CA: Jossey-Bass.

Kahn, W.A. (1998), Relational systems at work, in Staw, B.M. and Cummings, L.L. (eds), *Research in Organizational Behavior*, Vol. 20, Greenwich, CT: JAI Press, pp. 39–76.

Kaslow, F.W. & Kaslow, S. (1992), The family that works together: special problems of family businesses, in Zedeck, S. (ed.), *Work, Families, and Organizations*, San Francisco, CA: Jossey-Bass, pp. 312–61.

Katz, D. & Kahn, R.L. (1978), *The Social Psychology of Organizations*, 2nd edn, New York: Wiley.

Kets de Vries, M.F.R. (1989), *Prisoners of Leadership: Overcoming Counterproductive Styles of Management*, New York: Wiley.

Kets de Vries, M.F.R. & Miller, D. (1984), *The Neurotic Organization: Diagnosing and Changing Counterproductive Styles of Management*, San Francisco, CA: Jossey-Bass.

Kitchener, K.S. (1988), Dual role relationships: what makes them so problematic?, *Journal of Counseling and Development*, **67**, 217–21.

Kram, K.E. & Isabella, L.A. (1985), Mentoring alternatives: the role of peer relationships in career development, *Academy of Management Journal*, **28**, 110–32.

Kreiner, G.E. & Ashforth, B.E. (2004), Evidence toward an expanded model of organizational identification, *Journal of Organizational Behavior*, **25**, 1–27.

Kurdek, L.A. & Schmitt, J.P. (1986a), Early development of relationship quality in heterosexual married, heterosexual cohabiting, gay, and lesbian couples, *Developmental Psychology*, **22**, 305–9.

Kurdek, L.A. & Schmitt, J.P. (1986b), Relationship quality of partners in heterosexual married, heterosexual cohabiting, and gay and lesbian relationships, *Journal of Personality and Social Psychology*, **51**, 711–20.

Lazarus, A.A. & Zur, O. (eds) (2002), *Dual Relationships and Psychotherapy*, New York: Springer.

Lefkowitz, B. (1998), *Our Guys: The Glen Ridge Rape and the Secret Life of the Perfect Suburb*, New York: Vintage Books.

Le Poire, B.A., Hallett, J.S. & Giles, H. (1998), Codependence: the paradoxical nature of the functional-afflicted relationship, in Spitzberg, B.H. and Cupach, W.R. (eds), *The Dark Side of Close Relationships*, 2nd edn, Mahwah, NJ: Erlbaum, pp. 153–76.

Liden, R.C., Sparrowe, R.T. & Wayne, S.J. (1997), Leader–member exchange theory: the past and potential for the future, in Ferris, G.R. (ed.), *Research in Personnel and Human Resources Management*, Vol. 15, Greenwich, CT: JAI Press, pp. 47–119.

Lief, H.I. & Fox, R.C. (1963), Training for 'detached concern' in medical students, in Lief, H.I., Lief, V.F. and Lief, N.R. (eds), *The Psychological Bases of Medical Practice*, New York: Harper & Row, pp. 12–35.

Mainiero, L.A. (1989), *Office Romance: Love, Power, and Sex in the Workplace*, New York: Rawson Associates.

McCann, J.T. (1988), Passive-aggressive personality disorder – a review, *Journal of Personality Disorders*, **2**, 170–9.

McIlduff, E. & Coghlan, D. (2000), Understanding and contending with passive-aggressive behaviour in teams and organizations, *Journal of Managerial Psychology*, **15**, 716–32.

Olson, J.M. & Zanna, M.P. (1993), Attitudes and attitude change, in Porter, L.W. and Rosenzweig, M.R. (eds), *Annual Review of Psychology*, Vol. 44, Palo Alto, CA: Annual Reviews, pp. 117–54.

Peterson, M.R. (1992), *At Personal Risk: Boundary Violations in Professional–Client Relationships*, New York: W.W. Norton.

Pierce, J.L. (1995), *Gender Trials: Emotional Lives in Contemporary Law Firms*, Berkeley, CA: University of California Press.

Plaut, S.M. (1997), Boundary violations in professional–client relationships: overview and guidelines for prevention, *Sexual and Marital Therapy*, **12**, 77–94.

Pope, K.S. (1991), Dual relationships in psychotherapy, *Ethics and Behavior*, **1**, 21–34.

Pope, K.S. & Vasquez, M.J.T. (1991), *Ethics in Psychotherapy and Counseling: A Practical Guide for Psychologists*, San Francisco, CA: Jossey-Bass.

Porter, L.W. & Lawler, E.E., III. (1968), *Managerial Attitudes and Performance*, Homewood, IL: Irwin.

Powell, G.N. & Foley, S. (1999), Romantic relationships in organizational settings: something to talk about, in Powell, G.N. (ed.), *Handbook of Gender and Work*, Thousand Oaks, CA: Sage, pp. 281–304.

Reamer, F.G. (2003), Boundary issues in social work: managing dual relationships, *Social Work*, **48**, 121–33.

Rook, K.S. (1998), Investigating the positive and negative sides of personal relationships: through a lens darkly?, in Spitzberg, B.H. and Cupach, W.R. (eds), *The Dark Side of Close Relationships*, 2nd edn, Mahwah, NJ: Erlbaum, pp. 369–93.

Schank, J.A. & Skovholt, T.M. (1997), Dual-relationship dilemmas of rural and small-community psychologists, *Professional Psychology: Research and Practice*, **28**, 44–9.

Schriesheim, C.A., Castro, S.L. & Cogliser, C.C. (1999), Leader–member exchange (LMX) research: a comprehensive review of theory, measurement, and data-analytic practices, *Leadership Quarterly*, **10**, 63–113.

Settoon, R.P. & Mossholder, K.W. (2002), Relationship quality and relationship context as antecedents of person- and task-focused interpersonal citizenship behavior, *Journal of Applied Psychology*, **87**, 255–67.

Sias, P.M. & Cahill, D.J. (1998), From co-workers to friends: the development of peer friendships in the workplace, *Western Journal of Communication*, **62**, 273–99.

Sias, P.M., Heath, R.G., Perry, T., Silva, D. & Fix, B. (2004), Narratives of workplace friendship deterioration, *Journal of Social and Personal Relationships*, **21**, 321–40.

Sluss, D.M. & Ashforth, B.E. (2006), Relational identity and identification: defining ourselves through work relationships, *Academy of Management Review*, in press.

Smalley, S. & Coleman, E. (1987), Treating intimacy dysfunctions in dyadic relationships among chemically dependent and codependent clients, *Journal of Chemical Dependency Treatment*, **1**, 229–43.

Snyder, M. (1992), Motivational foundations of behavioral confirmation, in Zanna, M.P. (ed.), *Advances in Experimental Social Psychology*, Vol. 25, San Diego, CA: Academic Press, pp. 67–114.

Springer, C.A., Britt, T.W. & Schlenker, B.R. (1998), Codependency: clarifying the construct, *Journal of Mental Health Counseling*, **20**, 141–58.

Stafford, L.L. (2001), Is codependency a meaningful concept?, *Issues in Mental Health Nursing*, **22**, 273–86.

Stryker, S. & Statham, A. (1985), Symbolic interaction and role theory, in Lindzey, G. and Aronson, E. (eds), *Handbook of Social Psychology*, 3rd edn, Vol. 1, New York: Random House, pp. 311–78.

Sümer, N. & Cozzarelli, C. (2004), The impact of adult attachment on partner and self-attributions and relationship quality, *Personal Relationships*, **11**, 355–71.

Swann, W.B., Jr. (1987), Identity negotiation: where two roads meet, *Journal of Personality and Social Psychology*, **53**, 1038–51.

Valcour, P.M. (2002), Managerial behavior in a multiplex role system, *Human Relations*, **55**, 1163–88.

van Osselaer, S.M.J., Janiszewski, C. & Cunha, M., Jr. (2004), Stimulus generalization in two associative learning processes, *Journal of Experimental Psychology: Learning, Memory, and Cognition*, **30**, 626–38.

Worthington, E.J., Jr. & Scherer, M. (2004), Forgiveness is an emotion-focused coping strategy that can reduce health risks and promote health resilience: theory, review, and hypotheses, *Psychology and Health*, **19**, 385–405.

Wright, P.H. & Wright, K.D. (1995), Codependency: personality syndrome or relational process?, in Duck, S. and Wood, J.T. (eds), *Confronting Relationship Challenges*, Thousand Oaks, CA: Sage, pp. 109–28.

Wrzesniewski, A., Dutton, J.E. & Debebe, G. (2003), Interpersonal sense-making and the meaning of work, in Kramer, R.M. and Staw, B.M. (eds), *Research in Organizational Behavior*, Vol. 25, Amsterdam: Elsevier, pp. 93–135.

Zorn, T.E. (1995), Bosses and buddies: constructing and performing simultaneously hierarchical and close friendship relationships, in Wood, J.T. and Duck, S. (eds), *Under-studied Relationships: Off the Beaten Track*, Thousand Oaks, CA: Sage, pp. 122–47.

3 Identity orientation and networking: a relational framework for understanding attitudes toward change implementation
Olivia Kyriakidou

Introduction

Strategic change involves either a redefinition of organizational mission and purpose or a substantial shift in overall priorities and goals to reflect new emphases or direction (Gioia et al., 1994). It is usually accompanied by significant changes in patterns of resource allocation and/or alterations in organizational structure and processes to meet changing environmental demands. As Ginsberg (1988) notes, strategic change has been discussed in terms of changes in strategy content as well as transformations in strategy process. Strategic change however could also be conceptualized as a virtuous circle in which new information is used to challenge existing ideas and develop new perspectives of the future and new action routines implemented through 'organizational dialogue' (Brown & Starkey, 2000) – 'talk that reveals our meaning structures to each other' (Dixon, 1994: 83). Several scholars have argued for the pursuit of cooperative strategies outside the firm's boundaries as a means of creating new knowledge and skills in the setting of new standards that will facilitate strategic organizational change (for example Badaracco, 1991; Hamel, 1991; Lyles, 1994; Prahalad & Hamel, 1990; Tsai, 2001; Tsai & Ghoshal, 1998). According to Vicari et al. (1996) strategic change involves the transfer of knowledge among different organizational units mainly through interorganizational cooperation that stimulates the creation of new knowledge and contributes to the organization's ability to innovate and change (Tsai, 2001). Moreover a growing number of organization theorists taking a network perspective have emphasized how ongoing social ties between organizational actors and decision-makers and the social processes that occur within them (such as communication, cooperation, social comparison and social learning) enable them to design their strategic intentions, modify their existing routines, gain critical competencies and challenge their collective definitions of their organization's identity (Dutton & Dukerich, 1991; Gioia & Thomas, 1996; Granovetter, 1985; Nohria & Eccles, 1992; Powell et al., 1996; Walker et al., 1997; Uzzi, 1996).

Yet despite this recognition that networks influence the direction and outcomes of strategic change, there is much that is not understood about this aspect of strategic change process. In the social networks literature a debate has arisen over the form of network structures that can appropriately be regarded as beneficial in affecting the organization's capacity for change. According to the strength of weak ties perspective (Burt, 1982; Granovetter, 1973), large networks composed of heterogeneous, distant and infrequent relationships (that is, weak ties) are especially valuable, because they provide access to novel information by bridging otherwise disconnected groups and individuals inside and outside an organization. Strong ties, in contrast, are likely to lead to redundant information because they tend to occur among a small group of actors and decision-makers in which everyone knows what the others know. The alternative view emphasizes the strength of strong ties in promoting change due to their characteristics of frequent interaction, in-depth two-way communication, extended history and mutual confiding between actors (Granovetter, 1982). Strong ties may not maximize decision-makers' awareness of new and foreign ideas and insights since they are formed with socially similar actors; however, they are more valuable than weak ties in helping them to decipher the implications of external threats and to evaluate potential responses to these threats. Further, the trust and mutual identification that are likely to exist when ties are strong make it more likely both that decision-makers from different units will share valuable information with one another and that the information provided will be taken into account and acted upon (Uzzi, 1996). The question thus arises whether it is strong or weak relationships between actors in different organizational sub-units and different organizations that lead to creative strategic renewal. However, the discrepancy between the strong and weak tie perspective may be partly due to different foci. Hansen (1999) argues that weak ties may help actors search for useful information but impede the transfer of complex knowledge, which tends to require a strong tie between the actors to a transfer. However, this discrepancy is addressed within the boundaries and assumptions of structural theories, ignoring the social-psychological reality of organizations. The objective of this study, then, was to address this issue, examining the interactive contribution of structural (that is, strong and weak ties) and social-psychological processes to various strategic organizational outcomes.

Although several social network scholars have argued that weak ties provide information benefits under certain conditions and are less beneficial than strong ties in providing socio-emotional support and solving conflict (Krackhardt, 1992; Nelson, 1989; Podolny & Baron, 1997; Wegener, 1991), social network research has largely remained agnostic with respect to socio-psychological processes that determine the transfer of knowledge within intra- and inter-organizational networks, enabling change. Strategic change strongly depends not only on decision-makers' ability to access information outside the organization's boundaries, but also on their ability to make sense and assimilate the information into their cognitive structures and existing mental models in order to alter them. Organizational identity, as the organization's cognitive and sense-making model, becomes important since it determines its members' attitudes and behaviors towards the 'alter' and the sense-making and interpretation of information provided from individuals outside the organizational or unit boundaries. A strong collective identity may motivate individuals to bask in the successes of their organization and justify its failure, and consequently feel threatened by and resist any information that questions the organizational cognitive system. As a result, a strong collective identity may impede strategic renewal, restricting decision-makers from utilizing the advantages that come with a differentiated network of companies. In this sense, an approach is needed that will introduce a framework that comprises formal, structural and informal social-psychological processes. Hence, an objective of this study was to link the formal, structural and informal socio-psychological processes as a means to understand better how different patterns of social relationships relate to indicators of creative strategic renewal.

An identity framework for understanding attitudes towards strategic renewal
Although many approaches to understanding the impact of networks on organizational life have emerged, research suggests that a network's social capital is partly determined by the identity resources of its employees (Kyriakidou, 2002) which may facilitate or hinder interaction even in the absence of conflict. In this sense, networks could be defined as a mixture of people with different group and organizational identities within the same social system (that is, the network) arguing for the incorporation of identity into the very conceptualization of social networks. Three main intergroup relations theories in psychology that explore the socio-psychological dynamics inherent in the functioning of networks are the contact hypothesis, social identity and social categorization theory. In general, they all argue that identification processes play a central role in the dynamics that unfold in the network of alliances and relationships within a workforce that contribute to, amongst other things, the degree of sharing and sense-making of information necessary for strategic change.

Contact hypothesis theorists (Allport, 1954) propose that intergroup and interorganizational interaction within social networks can be improved via contact between individuals from different groups. Although a large body of literature demonstrates the positive effects of applying contact hypothesis principles in organizational settings for improving intergroup interaction (for example Miller & Davidson-Podgorny, 1987), there are three major criticisms. First, Krackhardt and Stern (1988) and Nelson (1989) used social network analysis to show the positive effects of strong interpersonal relationships across groups. However, as researchers have learnt, interpersonal interactions are not always positive and negative inter-action can create or exacerbate intergroup conflict. Second, as Brickson (2000) argues, the contact hypothesis cannot account for spillover effects (Keenan & Carnevale, 1989) suggesting that positive interpersonal rela-tionships between two individuals with different group identities will spill over into a positive relationship between the different groups. Finally, the overall approach does not take into consideration the social psychological dynamics behind information and knowledge sharing and diffusion or implementation of knowledge.

Social identity theory has also been influential in organizational behav-ior (for example Ashforth & Mael, 1989, 1996; Dutton et al., 1994; Ellemers et al., 1998; van Knippenberg, 2000; Veenstra & Haslam, 2000), providing cognitive (for example positive self-esteem, continuity, distinctiveness; Tajfel, 1969) and motivational (Tajfel & Turner, 1979) mechanisms that fre-quently define what is appropriate and inappropriate for the organization and what the strategic future direction should be. Organizational identities as collective and self-fulfilling systems of meaning and self-definition evoke interorganizational comparisons that provide the figure-ground contrast for crystallizing and articulating a unique identity (Ashforth & Mael, 1996) and establish clear interorganizational boundaries. The existence of bound-aries preserves the self-fulfilling nature of identities that creates a sense of 'we' as different from 'them' and underscores the differences between ingroup and outgroups. When collective organizational identities are salient within networks of relationships, individuals are found to act in ways that serve to advance the organization interests, often at the expense of their own personal organizational and network interests. In this sense, they strive to make their organization better than, and different from, salient outgroups (as represented by their prototypical members through interpersonal interaction), possibly developing negative intergroup rela-tions and minimizing interpersonal and intergroup contact.

Finally, self-categorization theory (Turner, 1985; Turner et al., 1987) pro-poses that the functioning of the self-concept is the cognitive mechanism that underpins social behavior. The psychological process that underpins collective organizational identity salience was referred to by Turner (1982) as depersonalization. This is a process of self-stereotyping through which the self comes to be perceived as categorically interchangeable with other ingroup members. So when a collective organizational identity is salient within networks of relationships, it is predicted that individuals come to see other in-network members as part of the self (redefining the self as 'network-we' rather than 'I'). Through this process, individuals perceive similarities between their previously idiosyncratic perceptions, motivations, values and goals and perceive each other through the cognitive lenses of a homogeneous social and organizational (Oakes el al., 1995) and possibly network profile. In this sense, when people who define themselves in terms of the same social identity disagree, they seek actively to reconcile discordant perspectives, attitudes and actions in order to maintain a homogeneous cognitive profile. Through this process, individuals within networks of relationships are more likely to see each other as valid sources of social influence who are qualified to provide valid information about identity-relevant issues of social reality (Turner, 1991).

At this end, introducing an identity framework in the conceptualization of networks has several effects for the understanding of strategic renewal. First, the creation and structure of organizational networks may facilitate the creation and elaboration of more widened boundaries and the incorporation of the 'alter' into the organizational cognitive system. In this way, different perspectives are developed that enable different aspects of the environment and different responses to get noticed and considered. Second, as a densely interlocked set of self-sealing beliefs, values and ways of doing things, a strong organizational identity can impede comprehension of issues that exceed its bounds (Ashforth & Mael, 1996; Reger et al., 1994). Through the creation of networks, comprehension of distinct perspectives and attitudes is enhanced through the extension of the organization's cognitive lenses. Finally, the perceived extension of the ingroup (group or organization) through the creation of networks may reduce feelings of threat when a facet of the old organizational identity is going to change. Incorporating network identity elements into existing organizational identities may satisfy the organizational need for consistency in order to strive for organizational enhancement through the generation of strategic renewal.

However, Brewer and Gardner (1996) and Brickson (2000) provided a breakthrough for understanding interorganizational relations, as they challenged an explicit assumption in the social identity literature: the notion that there are only two forms of identity – one personal and one collective.[1] They added a third locus of self-definition, the self as an interpersonal being, which gives rise to a relational identity orientation with distinct social motivations, types of significant self-knowledge and sources of self-worth other than the collective organizational identity (Brickson, 2000). A salient relational identity orientation motivates individuals to procure benefits for the others, since they conceive of themselves predominantly in terms of their roles in relation to significant others, and they evaluate themselves based on the adeptness with which they perform interpersonal roles with those others (Brickson, 2000; Markus & Kitayama, 1991). Moreover a salient relational identity may encourage the sharing of ideas, information and perspectives across fluid relationship structures and networks since it promotes interpersonal cooperation and integration as the focus for self-definition and self-evaluation. Indeed the objective here is to place a unique emphasis on the role of forces at the interpersonal level of analysis and stress the role of interactions enabling individuals to move beyond their collective organizational identities in order to utilize the advantages of social networks within and especially across group and organizational boundaries.

Effects of networking on strategic change through collective identity orientation

Social relationships, or network ties, can be described in a number of ways; however central and basic to social network theories is the concept of tie strength (Granovetter, 1973). The strength of the relationship depends on the amount of interaction, emotional intensity and reciprocity that takes place between two individuals (Granovetter, 1973). According to Granovetter's (1973) 'strength of weak ties' perspective, weak ties are more likely to be non-redundant connections between dense social circles (Perry-Smith & Shalley, 2003), creating structural bridges between two social circles, where no other direct or indirect ties connect the two groups. As a result of their structural properties, weak ties are likely to connect different actors because they are not immersed in the same interconnected web of relationships, shaped, to some extent, by similarities (Ibarra, 1992; Perry-Smith & Shalley, 2003). Therefore, weaker ties are more likely to connect people with diverse perspectives, different outlooks and diverse approaches to problems. Researchers have captured these differences in terms of status, levels in the organizational hierarchy, functional areas and demographics (Ibarra, 1992; Lin et al., 1981; Lincoln & Miller, 1979). In this sense, weaker connections provide access to a wider array of people and more non-redundant information (Burt, 1997), potentially inoculating against network inertia. Strongly tied networks are likely to force their members to stay within their existing network relations because they are familiar and include close contacts to whom they can easily turn. Because of this lack of immersion, the access to more non-redundant information outside established channels and diverse social circles facilitates a variety of processes helpful for developing positive attitudes towards strategic renewal. First, access to a wider breadth of knowledge gives decision-makers the opportunity to validate potential responses used by others in their network of relationships. Second, exposure to different approaches and perspectives to a problem may cause one to pursue directions previously unexplored in the industry or integrate new ideas in a novel and innovative way through cooperative and experimental learning (Granovetter, 1982).

The presence of weak ties however, even though this facilitates access to non-redundant information and diverse groups, may not guarantee the exchange and transfer of diverse perspectives and knowledge, since it may at the same time underscore the perceived differences between the prototypical representatives of the various organizations and groups in the network and activate distinctions between ingroup and outgroups. In this sense, the existence of heterogeneous and transient ties may coexist with strong and impermeable boundaries between individuals in the network with strong collective identity orientations, which confine the necessary affective investment and trust for cooperation and interactive experimentation. Besides, it is this affective investment that permits the collapse of organizational boundaries and creates a climate of security when considering organizational change.

When individuals within network relationships are perceived to belong to distinct and salient outgroups, affective reactions may be negative and individuals' and organizations' separation from others is more significant than their integration with others (Brickson, 2000). Given such an identity orientation, organizational members may rely more on themselves and their organization than on network relationships or network members for such resources as information and support. Limited interaction and negative affective reactions will restrict social cognition processes (Fiske & Neuberg, 1990) to rely upon automatic categorizations of the 'alter' and information coming from it rather than actual exploration of the information provided by individuals with salient outgroup identities connected through weak ties. Consequently, diverse information that comes from the network may not enter the existing cognitive organizational schemas and may remain unnoticed. However, assuming the outcomes of the individuals in the network are perceived to be interdependent, people may go beyond automatically processing the information. Since this interdependence is prone to being competitive in nature, affective investment and trust will be limited, which may strain the incorporation of new knowledge and information into the existing system. Competition may evoke feelings of insecurity and anxiety, as well as the desire to control others' outcomes (Brickson, 2000), further reducing one's motivation to create cooperative relationships in which to initiate experimentation and change.

Moreover, a strong collective identity orientation will arguably also motivate individuals to bask in their organization's successes and to justify its failures (Tesser, 1988), producing system-justifying myths (Ashforth & Mael, 1996) that lead to inertia and resistance to change. For example, when an organization is successful, participants prefer to see the system as justifiable and right and maximize the difference between ingroup and out-group, maximizing ingroup advantage (Tajfel, 1970). When organizations are less successful, they will feel threatened by the 'alter', which is also linked to inertia as the other organizations will be excluded from information networks (Gautam, 2000).

Summarizing, it is predicted that the cognitive profiles of individuals in social networks with strong collective identity orientations are heterogeneous and individuals tend not to bracket the information provided by the weak ties of their network. Consequently, information may not be accessible to the assigning of meaning by all individuals and fragmentary meaning is developed. As a result, inertia may be the outcome of such a network structure when organizations desire their members and decision-makers to develop strong collective identities.

Hypothesis 1. For individuals with strong collective identity orientations, weak network ties will be strongly linked to inertia.

Strong ties are less likely to fulfil the structural role of a bridge, because two individuals connected with a strong relationship will come to know the individuals in each other's network (Granovetter, 1973). This arises because of the frequency of interaction and the tendency for similarity between strongly tied actors. Moreover it is expected that stronger ties will result in less innovative attitudes towards strategic renewal since they tend to be created among similar individuals, where most of the actors have some type of connection to one another (that is, density; Granovetter, 1973). As a result, information and perspectives can circulate quickly and are likely to be redundant. Ultimately, 'contagion by cohesion' results (Perry-Smith & Shalley, 2003), which involves shared attitudes, opinions and beliefs that form among strongly connected groups (Burt, 1991). On the other hand however, a growing body of work emphasizes the exchange of know-how, shared norms and trust facilitated by dense networks (Hansen et al., 1999; Podolny & Baron, 1997; Uzzi, 1997). Entrepreneurs successful in bridging different organizational communities often initiate a sustained collaboration that ultimately reflects a dense social network (Hansen et al., 1999).

Moreover, the existence of strong ties assumes the development of inter-personal interdependence, affective investment and trust which may limit automatic categorization of prototypicality attributions as well as the cognitive replacement of network collectivities by organizational ones. This means that a heterogeneous cognitive network profile may be developed that will facilitate complex social cognition, supporting the generation and exchange of diverse perspectives and information in a trusting and affective climate that can enable organizational change. However complex social cognition is rare (Brickson, 2000). A strong collective identity orientation may result in perceiving all network members, including the existing organizational self, as belonging in a superordinate and shared network-organizational category (for example Turner & Oakes, 1989). Perceptions of similarity and sharedness however may lead to conformity due to social influence pressures (Krackhardt, 1992), which leaves little chance for helpful diverse information to surface from other cliques (Hansen, 1999).

When individuals are perceived to belong to the same superordinate network identity, the effect of this on them will be more positive, as long as they subscribe to the same organizational norms. But even assuming complete similarity between the network organizations, it is doubtful that all organizations will be represented in the salient network group. In this sense, boundaries may become salient and subgroupings may arise between the different network organizations within the same superordinate network group (Lau & Murnighan, 1998). Furthermore, even when assumptions of similarity of the distinct network organizations are developed, the existent but non-salient distinct characteristics may create perceptions of competition and negative affective reactions between organizational groups that need to be cooperatively interdependent (Johnson et al., 1984).

In summary, the development of trust and affective investment that facilitates change necessitates perceptions of similarity and subscription to the same organizational norms. However, this necessitates at the same time pressures for assimilation of organizational differences and distinctions necessary for the generation of change through the assimilation of the 'alter' into the existing cognitive structures. In this case, it is predicted that even though the cognitive profile is heterogeneous, pressure for assimilation tries to develop a homogeneous cognitive profile that does not generate change.

Hypothesis 2. For individuals with strong collective identity orientations, strong network ties will be strongly linked to assimilation.

Effects of networking on strategic change through relational identity orientation

As has been argued by the traditional network structure theories, the existence of weak ties broadens the organization's awareness of organizational trends and information from far and wide, introducing fundamentally new and foreign ideas and insights. However, weak ties are accompanied by limited interaction, trust and affective investment which could impede sharing and the transfer of diverse know-how. The development of a relational identity orientation more than collective orientations counterbalances these disadvantages by facilitating the exchange of detailed diverse information and perspectives and their complex cognitive understanding, maximizing decision-makers' awareness and understanding of potential trends and diverse responses. Complex cognitive processing helps in the detailed understanding of the differences between the partners and the implications of the information and knowledge they generate. Moreover as individuals are motivated by the welfare of their partners in the network, both affective investment and trust are more likely evoked, resulting in cooperation rather than competition, which leads to deeper cognitive understanding (Batson, 1998; Lanzetta & Englis, 1989) and facilitates the collapse of organizational boundaries and the assimilation of the new in the existing cognitive structures.

Furthermore, a relational orientation may also promote the extension of empathy and positive affect, even beyond the interactants in the network relationships, to other targets and perceivers and to the organization as a whole (Brickson, 2000). Wright et al.'s (1997) extended contact effect and Keenan and Carnevale's (1989) spillover hypothesis argue that meaningful interpersonal relationships between individuals from different organizations in the network will spill over into positive attitudes and relationships with perceivers who had no direct contact with these individuals. Merely knowing that an organizational member has had significant interactions with a member from a distant part of the network leads to improved attitudes toward members of that part (Brickson, 2000). This characteristic of the relational identity orientation ensures the gradual adoption of the generated knowledge and information and its results by the organization as a whole, that could lead to the generation of organizational change.

In this way, learning networks may be created with the ability to experiment in order to create new knowledge which goes beyond existing distinctions. It may also create entirely new strategic responses to environmental and political demands for institutional change (Fox-Wolfgramm et al., 1998; Prahalad & Hamel, 1994). It may create the context that facilitates cooperative experimentation in the form of an exploratory discovery process through which decision-makers advance their knowledge level and their set of possible responses. Learning contributes significantly to organizational change because basic strategic distinctions and taken-for-granted knowledge are typically challenged and questioned. Information generated through weak ties may lead to the discovery of entirely new strategic responses that may evolve into organizational transformations and completely different conceptualizations of the organizational identity, as the relational identity orientation creates the context that permits corporate experimentation. Especially where the direction and form of strategic development cannot be defined a priori, cooperative experimentation may serve as a discovery process through which the variety in the company's knowledge may increase.

Hypothesis 3. For individuals with strong relational identity orientations, weak network ties will be strongly linked to learning through experimental integration.

Strong ties are likely to be formed among similar actors who tend to possess less diverse or novel information that may lead to the development of refinement networks and cooperations that are planned within a well-defined strategic domain. Furthermore the development of a relational orientation facilitates extensive and detailed communication which may help them employ validated knowledge from their partners to another strategic task. In this sense, refinement networks and cooperations remain in a well-known strategic domain based on existing distinctions, for instance the strategy of the companies. Lower-scaled distinctions may be refined, but basic strategic distinctions are assumed to be given. Decision-makers will typically converge around a prevailing archetype bounding strategic change to the industrial and institutional archetype (Fox-Wolfgramm et al., 1998). The underlying logic here is that the existence of strong ties together with a relational identity orientation may facilitate the exploitation and/or refinement of existing knowledge by extending the task system in a well-defined, clear line of development (Vicari et al., 1996).

Hypothesis 4. For individuals with strong relational identity orientations, strong network ties will be strongly linked to learning through refinement.

Methods

Context of the study
In June 2000, the first governmental intentions were announced in Greece regarding a big reform in the way of health-care provision and the man-agement of hospitals called 'Health for the Citizens'. The reform called for the development of regional regulatory and management bodies charged with overseeing and evaluating all hospital operations regarding provision of health service and cost-effectiveness. This indicates a change in the legal status underpinning their operations, since they lose most of their power in managing their operations and their staff, and they are competing with other hospitals at regional and even national level for resources. Moreover, new management teams are established whose members are selected according to qualifications rather than elected by the government, charged with the strategic management of the hospitals. This is the first time where

specific targets for each hospital are agreed between the management board and the regional boards and have to be achieved for further allocation of financial resources. The reform further suggests the merging and even the abolition of many clinics in order to be more profitable and provide better health-care quality. Finally, major plans for internal restructuring and re-engineering could be designed for the most effective operation of many departments and the hospital as a whole.

Given the market character of the governmental reform, with its attendant emphasis on service quality and competition, many hospitals had to try to adopt a more business-like orientation to accomplish intended changes. Thus, 'strategic' change in hospital management is a phrase that introduces its own ambiguity into hospitals not accustomed to thinking and acting strategically. Moreover, the formal reason stated by governmental leadership for implementation of the reform was to improve the quality of patient care by enhancing both the management of the hospitals and health professionalism. Thus improvement in care quality was the social account managers offered to justify the change. This conforms to what Sitkin and Bies (1998) referred to as an 'exonerating account' – legitimating the motives for the change by placing management's actions within a broader normative framework.

Implementation of change had been initiated in the hospitals six months after my first baseline surveys. After a year, where the second survey took place, implementation across hospitals varied widely, with some hospitals having fully developed plans for implementing intended changes and others having virtually not even started thinking about their new management boards. I studied response to the issue twice, exploring both strategic intent and strategic change: eight months after the publication of the governmental reform documents announcing the reform, and one year after, by which time most hospitals had been expected to implement strategic change. Moreover in order to avoid single-source bias, the type of implemented changes was evaluated by the employees in the hospitals and not only the decision-makers.

Sample and procedures
The survey was conducted in 35 hospitals in Greece as they prepared to undergo major administration and restructuring changes. The selection of the hospitals was based on the regional distribution of the population of public hospitals to ensure that all regions were well represented, and on their sizes to ensure that hospitals with different sizes were also represented. Of 800 questionnaires sent out at time 1, we received 607 usable questionnaires around the country and with different sizes, representing 35 hospitals out of the 40 initially contacted (organizational response rate = 90 percent; individual rate = 75 percent). Chi-square analysis revealed that in terms of region there was no significant difference between the respondents and

non-respondents. There was however a significant difference in size (number of staff) ($\chi^2 = 22.4$, $p < 0.0001$), for which I controlled in subsequent analyses. The number of respondents from each hospital at time 1 ranged from 10 to 20, with an average of 17. Sixty-two percent of the respondents were female and 31 percent were single. All of them were heads of clinics or departments and members of the existing hospital management board. All of them had postgraduate degrees and 12 percent had PhDs. Education was strongly correlated with region and had to be controlled in all analyses.

Baseline surveys were sent to staff after the governmental intent to re-engineer was announced, but several months before redesign planning began. The surveys were accompanied by a cover letter explaining that the surveys were part of a research project designed to 'better understand the process of change in the health-care industry.' The cover letter also assured respondents that their answers would be confidential. Included was a return envelope so that respondents could send completed surveys directly to the research officer situated in the country. After two weeks non-respondents were contacted via telephone, and after an additional two weeks non-respondents were sent replacement surveys. A total of 607 people responded, giving a response rate of 75 percent.

Following baseline surveys, extensive programs of hospital re-engineering began. Design teams worked for a year to achieve cost reductions and service improvements by introducing program management, designing evidence-based clinical pathways, redistributing tasks and introducing new and elected management teams. Moreover at regional level, control management teams were established charged with the role of overseeing the provision of service quality, negotiating and allocating budgets and overseeing the cost-effectiveness of hospital operations. At time 2, one year following the completion of the first survey, the same hospitals participated in a second survey and surveys were administered to members of staff of the participating hospitals. After preparatory short meetings to answer questions and ensure response confidentiality, research assistants provided self-administered surveys to each employee and sealed envelopes for their return to them. 1750 usable questionnaires were collected at time 2, representing a response rate of 48 percent. Sixty-seven percent of the respondents were female with average age of 35.3 years (s.d. = 17.6) and average organizational tenure of 15.7 years (s.d. = 13.2). By far the majority of the sample was non-supervisory employees (65.2 percent), indicating that different groups of people responded to the survey than at time 1.

Measures
All the measures used in this study were based on existing scales apart from the assimilation and identity orientation scales. I pre-tested the measures

to establish the clarity of instructions, the amount of time required to complete the instruments, the thoroughness and relevance of the items, and the psychometric properties of the scales. This pre-testing was conducted two months before the main survey but nevertheless after the announcement of governmental changes, with a sample of 20 members of staff from a local hospital. Immediately after the completion of the surveys, I conducted a focus group with them to obtain detailed feedback on their reactions to the survey instruments. Drawing on this feedback, I eliminated or replaced some items and changed the wording of items and instructions where needed. Scales developed for this study were subject to principal-axis factor analysis with varimax rotation. All scales were based on factors with eigenvalues greater than 1 and included those items meeting the requirements of simple structure.

For this study, I used each individual's unique set of social contacts, or 'egocentric networks' (Marsden, 1990) rather than focusing on the entire social structure of my population. Studies of egocentric networks are useful for understanding how a person's unique web of contacts (his or her egocentric 'universe') relates to variables at the individual level of analysis, such as social perceptions and attitudes (Walker et al., 1993). A focus on egocentric networks is ideal for studying decision-makers' perceptions since we are interested in the individual's unique web of contacts inside and outside the organization; and besides, taking a complete network approach would have meant a network that was too large to analyze.

Decision-makers' informational egocentric networks were assessed on the first survey at time 1, which was modeled after surveys used in prior studies (Burt, 1984; Ibarra, 1995; Podolny & Baron, 1997). Part 1 contained a chart for respondents to complete. Across the first row, they were instructed to write the initials of 'people inside and outside the organization who have been influential and valuable sources of information regarding your management strategy for implementing the required change'. The wording was based on similar measures used by Anderson (2002) studying managers' social networks. Ten columns were provided, and respondents were told to 'list as many or as few people as are relevant'. The decision to provide ten columns was based on interviews with ten members of staff at a local hospital who were not part of the sample. Interviews indicated that they had anywhere from three to eight sources of information, so I concluded that ten columns would be more than sufficient.

After writing initials across the first row, the decision-maker ('ego') responded to a set of questions for each of the listed persons ('alter'). In this way, a weak-ties network was operationalized as a function of frequency of interaction, duration and heterogeneity of status and hierarchical level (Krackhardt, 1992). The existence of unique and weak ties spanning boundaries within and surrounding the firm is consistent with Burt's (1997) concept of a network rich in structural holes. Here I used density as a structural holes measure. Decision-makers were asked to indicate each alter's organizational affiliation, the type of their organization, their job title, their functional unit, hierarchical position (1 = non-supervisory staff; 2 = experienced staff; 3 = manager; 4 = head of department; 5 = senior manager; 6 = senior executive), the average frequency with which they talked to or exchanged information with each other (1 = 'daily'; 2 = 'a few times a week'; 3 = '3–5 times a month'; 4 = 'once or twice a month'; 5 = 'less than once a month'), and the number of other persons in the network with whom each alter talked during any given week.

Using the data from this survey, I computed measures of size, density, tie strength, range and status for the decision-makers' informational and influential networks. I measured size as the number of alters listed (Podolny & Baron, 1997). Density is typically measured as the number of actual links between the members of a network (excluding ego) relative to the total number of possible links (Ibarra, 1995). In this case that was equal to ΣT_j $/n$ $(n-1)$, where T is the number of links from alter j and n is the total number of alters identified. Network size was also included since density is size-relative, thus size needs to be controlled for (Burt, 1997). Range was operationalized as the number of different industry groups represented within a network. Status was the average hierarchical level of the network members (Ibarra, 1995), and values could range from 1 (non-supervisory staff) to 6 (senior executive). Finally, I computed strength by averaging responses to the question about the frequency with which ego talked with each alter (rated on a five-point scale).

The survey then assessed the hypothesized outcomes of network structure: decision-makers' attitudes towards strategic change implementation. Decision-makers' responses and attitudes towards the specific announced change were measured with a short (21 items) form of the organizational learning modes questionnaire (Boydell & Leary, 1996; items were rejected or accepted on the basis of redundancy and relevance to the firm) in order to predict their responses and attitudes towards change. The questionnaire has achieved good reliability indices ranging from 0.79 to 0.85 (for example Boydell & Leary, 1996) and has been validated in a number of organizational contexts. The questionnaire measures three different attitudes towards change: integrating (measured with seven items, for example 'I encourage differences of opinion and use them in a creative and constructive way'), improving (measured with seven items, for example 'I try something new even if the outcomes are uncertain') and implementing, which refers to my conceptualization of refinement (measured by seven items, for example 'I stick to established routines and methods developed by my organization'). Assimilation was assessed with a four-item scale developed for this survey and operationalized as decision-makers' unwillingness to engage themselves to new organizational forms and transformations (for example 'There is no difference in the way we organize our operations in this industry'). All items were scored on a seven-point Likert-type response scale anchored by 'strongly disagree' to 'strongly agree'. Because all four sub-scales tapped attitudes towards change implementation, I factor-analyzed the entire set of 25 items to test for convergent and discriminant validity. Two items failed to 'load' clearly on a single factor (one assimilation item and one implementation item). I eliminated these items to ensure both discriminant validity and reliability. The remaining items formed four distinct factors. The alpha coefficients were 0.87 for learning experimentation, 0.91 for refinement, 0.88 for inertia and 0.77 for assimilation.

To develop the identity orientations measure, I examined literature on both organizational identification (Abrams, 1992; Breakwell, 1986; Dutton et al., 1994; Mael & Ashforth, 1992; Mael & Tetrick, 1992) and relational identity orientation (Brewer & Gardner, 1996; Brickson, 2000). Organizational identity orientation was operationalized as the cognitive link between the individual and the organization when the identity of the organization is perceived as enhancing members' self-esteem, continuity, distinctiveness and efficacy (Breakwell, 1986). Analogously, relational identification assumes that significant others rather than the organization are the focus of self-definition. The resulting (12-item) collective orientation scale (for example 'I am proud of being member of this organization') was rated on a seven-point scale anchored by 'strongly agree' to 'strongly disagree', as well as the 12-item relational orientation scale (for example 'When someone praises the people I know, it feels like a personal compliment'). A confirmatory factor analysis confirmed the predicted factor structure of the two scales. Both measures demonstrated good measures of reliability (collective, a = 0.91; relational, a = 0.89).

At time 2, after extensive interviews with the hospitals' management board, a list of changes (communicated to staff or implemented) was formulated and employees were asked to evaluate the listed changes according to the learning modes questionnaire (Boydell & Leary, 1996) with the developed three-item assimilation scale. Items were phrased accordingly to reflect the change in context and were scored on seven-point Likert scales anchored by 'strongly agree' to 'strongly disagree'. The items formed four distinct factors with alpha coefficients ranging from 0.77 for assimilation and 0.88 for refinement.

Data analysis

The moderating effects on the proposed relationships in the hypotheses were assessed by subgroup analysis (Arnold, 1982). A moderator has been defined as a variable 'which systematically modifies either the form and/or strength of the relationship between a predictor and criterion variable' (Sharma et al., 1981: 291). Using subgroup analysis I examined for differences in the form of the relationship between groups (for example groups with strong collective as opposed to strong relational identifications). Hence I do not investigate whether the moderator is a quasi or a pure moderator variable (see for example Sharma et al., 1981). If significant coefficients occur in the subgroups, it is assumed that the variable is a moderator.

Subsequently (linear) single and multiple regression analyses were applied on the outcome variables (decision-makers' attitudes towards strategic renewal and staff evaluations of the strategic implementation) with network variables as predictors. First, regression analyses were conducted for all observations not considering the subgroups (restricted run). Second, regression analyses were run for each subgroup, allowing the regression coefficient estimates to take on different values across subgroups (unrestricted run). Applying the Chow-test (Chow, 1960) I used the differences in the sums of squared residuals from the restricted and unrestricted runs. I examined the statistical significance of the difference in the regression coefficients in network variables across the different groups. I performed 32 single regression and 8 multiple regression analyses. The results of the single regression analyses were not dramatically different from the multiple regression analyses, hence providing some support for robustness. I report the findings based on multiple regression analyses as these results provide a more comprehensive knowledge. Further assessments indicate that multicollinearity was not a problem. Means, standard deviations and correlations for all variables are in Table 3.1.

Results
The results of the statistical analyses are presented in Table 3.2. As indicated, there is substantial support for the moderating effects of collective and relational identity orientation on the relationship between structural network elements and decision-makers' attitudes towards strategic renewal at time 1 as well as employee perceptions of implemented strategic renewal at time 2.

Hypothesis 1 predicts that decision-makers' collective identity orientations would moderate the relationship between the impact of weak structural relationships on their attitudes to innovate in implementing strategic change. More specifically, using inertia attitudes as the dependent variable, a significant difference is found in the regressions which consider the collective identity orientation moderator (Table 3.2; $F = 4.03$, $p < 0.01$). Since the strength of network relationships was also operationalized in terms of

Table 3.1   Correlations between all variables at time 1

Variable	Mean	s.d.	1	2	3	4	5	6	7	8	9	10	11
1. N. Size	5.49	3.32		-0.17*	0.21*	0.26**	0.31**	0.16*	0.10	0.04	0.09	0.11	0.15*
2. N. Density	0.49	0.32	-0.17*		0.07	-0.12	0.07	0.15*	0.09	0.06	0.11	0.10	0.14
3. N. Strength	4.36	1.01	0.21*	0.07		0.34**	0.31**	-0.35**	-0.27**	-0.18*	0.32**	0.36**	0.24**
4. N. Range	1.93	0.56	0.26**	-0.12	0.34**		-0.25**	0.41**	0.26**	0.12	0.07	0.08	0.26**
5. N. Status	2.21	0.69	0.31**	0.07	0.31**	-0.25**		0.43**	0.24**	0.10	0.05	0.12	0.32**
6. Integrative	5.07	1.83	0.16*	0.15*	-0.35**	0.41**	0.43**		0.21*	-0.23	-0.21*	-0.35**	0.42**
7. Improving	5.36	1.61	0.10	0.09	-0.27**	0.26**	0.24**	0.21*		-0.18*	-0.10	-0.16*	0.25**
8. Implementing	4.81	1.36	0.04	0.06	-0.18*	0.12	0.10	-0.23	-0.18*		0.27**	0.34**	-0.42**
9. Assimilation	4.35	2.03	0.09	0.11	0.32**	0.07	0.05	-0.21*	-0.10	0.27**		0.37**	-0.44**
10. Collective	5.25	1.22	0.11	0.10	0.36**	0.08	0.12	-0.35**	-0.16*	0.34**	0.37**		-0.23*
11. Relational	4.48	2.01	0.15*	0.14	0.24**	0.26**	0.32**	0.42**	0.25**	-0.42**	-0.44**	-0.23*	

Note: * $p < 0.05$; ** $p < 0.01$

45

Table 3.2 *Results of regression analyses for moderator variables*

Moderator Variable	Dependent	Independent				Adjusted R^2	Chow test
		Range	Density	Strength	Status		
Collective	Integrating	n.s.	n.s.	n.s.	n.s.	n.s.	F = 0.10
	Improving	n.s.	n.s.	n.s.	n.s.	n.s.	F = 0.11
	Implementing	0.32**	0.22**	0.26**	0.21**	0.21**	F = 4.03**
	Assimilating	0.36**	0.21**	−0.26**	−0.41**	0.29**	F = 3.13**
Relational	Integrating	0.37**	0.24**	0.47**	0.42**	0.29**	F = 5.62**
	Improving	−0.31**	0.19*	−0.31**	−0.38**	0.25**	F = 3.35**
	Implementing	n.s.	n.s.	n.s.	n.s.	n.s.	F = 0.10
	Assimilating	n.s.	n.s.	n.s.	n.s.	n.s.	F = 0.07

Note: * $p < 0.05$, ** $p < 0.01$

frequency, density, range and status, I tested whether collective identity orientation would moderate the relationship between each of these predictors and inertia. As shown in Table 3.2, for all constructs the regression coefficients are higher for the strong collective identity group ($\beta = 0.22, p < 0.01$, for density; $\beta = 0.26, p < 0.01$, for frequency; $\beta = 0.32, p < 0.01$, for range; and $\beta = 0.23, p < 0.01$, for hierarchical status). Relational identity orientation did not moderate the relationship between weak ties and inertia ($F = 0.10$, ns). Hence there is support for this hypothesis.

Hypothesis 2 predicts that a significant difference in the regressions occurs between subgroups of collective and relational orientation when assimilation is used as the dependent variable ($F = 3.13, p < 0.01$) with collective identity moderating the relationship between strong ties and assimilation. The coefficient of frequency is -0.26 ($p < 0.05$) compared to 0.21 ($p < 0.05$) for density. This relationship is negative as it indicates the existence of strong ties. In the case of range ($\beta = -0.36, p < 0.01$) and hierarchical status ($\beta = -0.41, p < 0.01$) significant relationships were found. Relational identity orientation did not moderate the relationship between strong ties and assimilation ($F = 0.07$, ns), providing support for hypothesis 2.

Hypothesis 3 predicted that a significant difference in the regressions would occur between subgroups of collective and relational orientation when integration is used as the dependent variable ($F = 5.62, p < 0.01$) with relational identity moderating the relationship between weak ties and integration. The coefficient of frequency is 0.47 ($p < 0.01$) compared to 0.24 ($p < 0.05$) for density. In the case of range ($\beta = 0.37, p < 0.01$) and hierarchical status ($\beta = 0.42, p < 0.01$) significant relationships were found. Collective identity orientation did not moderate the relationship between weak ties and integration ($F = 0.10$, ns) providing support for hypothesis 3.

Finally, hypothesis 4 predicted that a significant difference in the regressions would occur between subgroups of collective and relational orientation when improving is used as the dependent variable ($F = 3.35, p < 0.01$) with relational identity moderating the relationship between strong ties and improving. The coefficient of frequency is -0.31 ($p < 0.05$) compared to 0.19 ($p < 0.05$) for density. This relationship is negative as it indicates the existence of strong ties. In the case of range ($\beta = -0.31, p < 0.01$) and hierarchical status ($\beta = -0.38, p < 0.01$) significant relationships were found. Collective identity orientation did not moderate the relationship between strong ties and assimilation ($F = 0.11$, ns) providing support for hypothesis 2.

The same pattern of results emerged when employee interpretations of the implemented strategic changes served as the dependent variables at time 2. There were significant differences when inertia was the dependent variable with collective identities moderating the relationship between weak ties and inertia ($F = 3.62, p < 0.01$), and a significant difference in the regressions occurred for the relational identity moderator when integration was used as the dependent variable ($F = 4.27$, $p < 0.01$). Finally, there were significant differences when improving was the dependent variable with relational identities moderating the relationship between weak ties and improving ($F = 3.66$, $p < 0.01$), and a significant difference occurred for the collective moderated when assimilation was used as the dependent variable. Hence all hypotheses were supported at time 2.

Discussion
An important theme within the social network literature has been that interactions with and relationships to diverse organizational actors provide a valuable way for strategic renewal through knowledge exchange, experimental cooperation and learning. Yet the literature provides little insight into the socio-psychological processes, salient in any social organizational context and environment, that could facilitate or impede this process. An integration of structural and socio-psychological principles is potentially valuable because it enables a focus on the interactional effects of structures and identity principles on decision-makers' innovative ability to introduce strategic renewal. This study therefore, provides an insight into whether the number of relationships is important for innovative strategic renewal, whether a set of strong relationships is better than a set of weak ones, whether it is important for organizational actors to have a configuration of relationships that spans different areas and levels within and across organizational boundaries, and whether the answers to these questions differ depending on the type and strength of organizational actors' identity orientations.

The present study took into consideration the fact that the context of social relationships is not one-dimensional. Hence, it explored not only the extent of social relationships, but also the character of relationships in terms of their strength and the extent they span boundaries – organizational, functional and hierarchical. For the professional employees interested in navigating the organizational environments in which they reside, maintaining and cultivating weaker relationships both within and across organizational boundaries may be helpful. This should allow the individual to think in broader terms, to think outside the box, and to solve strategic issues in unique yet effective ways. As expected, structural characteristics of organizational actors' networks related in systematic ways to discrete attitudes and perceptions of organizational renewal outcomes. For example, decision-makers who reported having an information network characterized by weak ties were more likely to develop a learning attitude towards change, either innovating or refining strategies, rather than organizational actors with more strong-tied networks. However, the present study provided evidence that this relationship is not one-dimensional and simplistic but rather decision-makers' identity orientations play an important moderating role. People with strong collective identities were less likely to utilize the advantages generated from a weak-tied network due to the salience of impermeable organizational boundaries, and were less likely to perceive strong-tied networks as homogeneous due to pressures for assimilation and minimize innovative strategic renewal. On the other hand, people with strong relational identities were more likely to generate change, either innovative or refinement, exploiting the advantages of both weak and strong ties, since they can restrict the automatic cognitive processes accompanying collective identifications and develop enhanced and detailed understandings of the 'alter'.

Whereas most conceptualizations of the relationship between network structure and the generation of change are limited to an analysis of how the existence of strong and weak ties affects the generation of change, this chapter invited an analysis of how network structures interrelate with the self-definitions of organizational actors and affect the generation of change through knowledge and information transfer within the network.

Theoretical and practical implications
The concepts presented here extend existing theoretical models of social networks by incorporating a variety of social identity and self-categorization principles commensurate with the complexity of social relationships and the social environment. The present framework goes beyond the idea that communication and interaction in general facilitate attitudes towards strategic renewal, by describing the dynamic interplay between structural elements of social networks and socio-psychological principles. However, in presenting any new approach it is usually a mistake to suggest that its contribution and insights are entirely original. Accordingly in the present case it is important to note that there are significant points of contact between this framework and influential approaches to organizational practice. Indeed as I see it, much of the approach's appeal derives from its ability to incorporate and lend coherence to insights from research and practice across a range of areas.

A significant feature of the approach is that it attempts to counteract the negative consequences of strong collective identities in terms of strategic renewal by ensuring that organizational identities are explicitly premised upon relational and interpersonal memberships (which themselves provide an opportunity for the personal identities of employees to be expressed and affirmed). The approach of this chapter regarding four different attitudes towards strategic renewal is consistent with Hinings and Greenwood's (1988) suggestion about four potential 'tracks' through which organizations change their interpretative schemes in order to address a redesign in structures and processes. First is an 'aborted excursion' where there is limited departure but eventually returning to the initial shared archetype. Second is a 'reorientation', where an organization achieves second-order change. The third track is an 'unresolved excursion' where organizations often get locked into competing battles between different perspectives. Finally, 'inertia' involves the retention of existing strategies and perspectives.

This approach is also consistent with the insights of the dual concern model (Pruitt & Carnevale, 1993; Pruitt & Rubin, 1986) in which the success of any negotiation process is seen to depend on an ability to take the perspective of, and show concern for, both self and other. In relation to this work, the present findings suggest that a range of positive organizational outcomes flow from identity orientations that recognize, accommodate and encourage interpersonal and relational identities that reflect the shared self-determined interests and aspirations of organizational actors. Innovative and cooperative experimentation is encouraged because shared relational identifications motivate employees to find novel ways of translating different goals into common interpersonal and interactional activity. In this way, organic pluralism is intended to engender the sense and reality of authentic social, interpersonal and organizational choice (Kekes, 1993). Finally, it is worth noting that the current model is consistent with a number of contemporary models of leadership. In particular it accords with Deal and Kennedy's (1982) analysis of the role that symbolic management plays in creating cultures that recognize and celebrate the contribution that distinct subgroups and cultures make to an organization (Reynolds et al., 2000). Such arguments are clearly compatible with the general model outlined here and also with general recommendations that effective organizational leadership needs to center around the affirmation rather than the negation of the social and interpersonal identities in terms of which employees define themselves (Haslam & Platow, 2001). It is important for leaders to display commitment to a process that acknowledges and respects interpersonal and subgroup goals (together with the distinct identities that underpin them) and reconciles them with those of the organization.

Moreover the theme of this chapter meshes macro- and micro-oriented concepts in organizational behavior and provides another example of how the two areas are interrelated. As O'Reilly (1991) suggests, social network perspectives provide a viable approach to incorporating context into microorganizational behavior. The inclusion of socio-psychological moderators also advances this objective. This also supports the idea that organizations interested in developing decision-makers' ability for strategic renewal should consider facilitating interactions across workgroups, departments and other discrete subgroups, and the simultaneous development of relational identity orientations. Brickson (2000) argues that the immediate organizational context could affect which type of identity orientation becomes prominent and suggests structural interventions that promote a relational identity orientation. However we do need a thorough understanding of how contextual forces elicit identity orientations. Given the proposed enhancing role of a relational identity orientation, the contextual influences triggering this aspect of identity – organizational, cultural, societal – demand extensive future research.

Conclusion

This study provides a useful first look at the interaction between structural network elements and socio-psychological processes in the exploration of strategic renewal and suggests that further investigation will be fruitful. Research on decision-makers' identity orientations, and especially relational identification, will not only enrich our understanding of the strategic change process, but may also direct us toward more promising practical solutions to meet the challenge of managing networks for strategic renewal.

Note

1. The focus of this chapter is on understanding the intergroup and interorganizational dynamics rendering an exploration of a personal focus of self-definition outside the scope of this exploration.

References

Abrams, D. (1992), Processes of social identification, in Breakwell, G.M. (ed.), *Social Psychology of Identity and the Self Concept*, London: Surrey University Press and Academic Press, pp. 57–95.

Allport, G.W. (1954), *The Nature of Prejudice*, Cambridge, MA: Addison-Wesley.

Anderson M.H. (2002), How personality drives network benefits: need for cognition, social networks, and information amount, *Academy of Management Proceedings*.

Arnold, H.J. (1982), Moderator variables: a clarification of conceptual, analytic, and psychometric issues, *Organizational Behavior and Human Performance*, **29**, 143–74.

Ashforth, B.E. & Mael, F. (1989), Social identity theory and the organization, *Academy of Management Review*, **14**, 20–39.

Ashforth, B.E. & Mael, F.A. (1996), Organizational identity and strategy as a context for the individual, *Advances in Strategic Management*, **13**, 19–64.

Badaracco, J.L. (1991), *The Knowledge Link: How Firms Compete through Strategic Alliances*, Boston, MA: Harvard Business School Press.

Batson, C.D. (1998), Prosocial behaviour and altruism, in Gilbert, D.T., Fiske, S.T. & Lindzey G. (eds), *Handbook of Social Psychology* (4th edn): Boston, MA: McGraw-Hill, pp. 282–316.

Boydell, T. & Leary, R. (1996), Implications of learning in organizations, *Journal of European Industrial Training*, **19**, 31–42.

Breakwell, G.M. (1986), *Coping with Threatened Identities*, London: Methuen.

Brewer, M.B. & Gardner, W. (1996), Who is this 'we'? Levels of collective identity and self-representations, *Journal of Personality and Social Psychology*, **71**, 83–93.

Brickson, S. (2000), The impact of identity orientation on individual and organizational outcomes in demographically diverse settings, *Academy of Management Review*, **25** (1), 82–101.

Brown, A.D. & Starkey, K. (2000), Organizational identity and learning: a psychodynamic perspective, *Academy of Management Review*, **25**, 102–20.

Burt, R.S. (1982), *Toward a Structural Theory of Action*, New York: Academic Press.

Burt, R.S. (1984), Network items and the General Social Survey, *Social Networks*, **6**, 293–339.

Burt, R.S. (1991), STRUCTURE (Version 4.2), New York: Columbia University, Research Program in Structural Analysis, Center for the Social Sciences.

Burt, R.S. (1997), The contingent value of social capital, *Administrative Science Quarterly*, **42**, 339–65.

Chow, G.C. (1960), Tests of equality between sets of coefficients in two linear regressions, *Econometrica*, **28**, 591–605.

Deal, T.E. & Kennedy, A.A. (1982), *Corporate Cultures: The Rites and Rituals of Corporate Life*, Harmondsworth: Penguin.

Dixon, N. (1994), *The Organizational Learning Cycle*, Maidenhead: McGraw-Hill.

Dutton, J.E. & Dukerich, J.M. (1991), Keeping an eye on the mirror: image and identity in organizational adaptation, *Academy of Management Journal*, **34**, 517–54.

Dutton, J.E., Dukerich, J.M. & Harquail, C.V. (1994), Organizational images and member identification, *Administrative Science Quarterly*, **39**, 239–63.

Ellemers, N., de Gilder, D. & van den Heuvel, H. (1998), Career-oriented versus team-oriented commitment and behavior at work, *Journal of Applied Psychology*, **83**, 717–30.

Fiske, S.T. & Neuberg, S.L. (1990), A continuum of impression formation, from category-based to individuating processes: influences of information and motivation on attention and interpretation, *Advances in Experimental Social Psychology*, **23**, 1–74.

Fox-Wolfgramm, S.J., Boal, K.B. & Hunt, J.G. (1998), Organizational adaptation to institutional change: a comparative study of first-order change in prospector and defender banks, *Administrative Science Quarterly*, **43**, 87–126.

Gautam, A. (2000), Collaboration networks, structural holes, and innovation: a longitudinal study, *Administrative Science Quarterly*, **45**, 425–56.

Ginsberg, A. (1988), Measuring and modelling change in strategy: theoretical foundations and empirical directions, *Strategic Management Journal*, **9**, 559–75.

Gioia, D.A. & Thomas, J.B. (1996), Identity, image, and issue interpretation: sensemaking during strategic change in academia, *Administrative Science Quarterly*, **41**, 370–403.

Gioia, D.A., Thomas, J.B., Clark, S.M. & Chittipeddi, K. (1994), Symbolism and strategic change in academia: the dynamics of sensemaking and influence, *Organization Science*, **5**, 363–83.

Granovetter, M.S. (1973), The strength of weak ties, *American Journal of Sociology*, **78**, 1360–80.

Granovetter, M.S. (1982), The strength of weak ties: a network theory revisited, in Marsden, P.V. & Lin, N. (eds), *Social Structure and Network Analysis,* Beverly-Hills, CA: Sage, pp. 105–30.

Granovetter, M.S. (1985), Economic action and social structure: the problem of embeddedness, *American Journal of Sociology*, **91**, 1360–80.

Hamel, G. (1991), Competition for competence and interpartner learning within international alliances, *Strategic Management Journal*, **12**, 83–103.

Hansen, M.T. (1999), The search-transfer problem: the role of weak ties in sharing knowledge across organization subunits, *Administrative Science Quarterly*, **44**, 82–111.

Hansen, M.T., Podolny J., & Pfeffer, J. (1999), So many ties, so little time: a task contingency perspective on the value of corporate social capital in organizations, in Bacharach, S., Gabbay, S.M. & Leenders, R.T.A.J., *Social Capital of Organizations*, pp. 21–59.

Haslam, S.A. & Platow, M.J. (2001), The link between leadership and followership: how affirming a social identity translates vision into action, *Personality and Social Psychology Bulletin*, **27**, 1469–79.

Hinings, C.R. & Greenwood, R. (1988), *The Dynamics of Strategic Change*, New York: Blackwell.

Ibarra, H. (1992), Structural alignments, individual strategies, and managerial action: elements toward a network theory of getting things done, in Nohria, N. & Eccles, R.G. (eds),

Networks and Organizations: Structure, Form and Action, Boston, MA: Harvard Business School Press, pp. 165–88.

Ibarra, H. (1995), Race, opportunity, and diversity of social circles in managerial networks, *Academy of Management Journal*, **38**, 673–703.

Johnson, D.W., Johnson, R. & Maruyama, G. (1984), Goal interdependence and interpersonal attraction in heterogeneous classrooms: a meta-analysis, in Miller, N. & Brewer, M.B. (eds), *Groups in Contact: The Psychology of Desegregation*, Orlando, FL: Academic Press, pp. 187–212.

Keenan, P.A. & Carnevale, P.J.D. (1989), Positive effects of within-group cooperation on between-group negotiation, *Journal of Applied Psychology*, **19**, 977–92.

Kekes, J. (1993), *The Morality of Pluralism*, Princeton, NJ: Princeton University Press.

Krackhardt, D. (1992), The strength of strong ties: the importance of philos in organizations, in Nohria, N. & Eccles, R.G. (eds), *Networks and Organizations: Structure, Form, and Action*, Boston, MA: Harvard Business School Press, pp. 216–39.

Krackhardt, D. & Stern, R.N. (1988), Informal networks and organizational crisis: an experimental simulation, *Social Psychology Quarterly*, **51**, 123–40.

Kyriakidou, O. (2002), Identity orientation and networking, Academy of Management Conference, Colorado.

Lanzetta, J.T. & Englis, B.G. (1989), Expectations of cooperation and competition and their effects on observers' vicarious emotion responses, *Journal of Personality and Social Psychology*, **56**, 543–54.

Lau, D.C. & Murnighan, J.K. (1998), Demographic diversity and faultlines: the compositional dynamics of organizational groups, *Academy of Management Review*, **23**, 325–40.

Lin, N., Ensel, W.M. & Vaughn, J.C. (1981), Social resources and strength of ties: structural factors in occupational status attainment, *American Sociological Review*, **46**, 393–405.

Lincoln, J.R. & Miller, J. (1979), Work and friendship ties in organizations: a comparative analysis of relational networks, *Administrative Science Quarterly*, **24**, 181–99.

Lyles, M.A. (1994), The impact of organizational learning on joint venture formation, *International Business Review*, **3**, 37–45.

Mael, F. & Ashforth, B.E. (1992), Alumni and their alma mater: a partial test of the reformulated model of organizational identification, *Journal of Organizational Behavior*, **13**, 103–23.

Mael, F. & Tetrick, L.E. (1992), Identifying organizational identification, *Educational and Psychological Measurement*, **52**, 813–24.

Markus, H.R. & Kitayama, S. (1991), Culture and the self: implications for cognition, emotion, and motivation, *Psychological Review*, **98**, 224–53.

Marsden, P.V. (1990), Network data and measurement, in Scott, W.R. & Blake, J. (eds), *Annual Review of Sociology*, Vol. 16, Palo Alto, CA: Annual Reviews, pp. 435–63.

Miller, N. & Davidson-Podgorny, G. (1987), Theoretical models of intergroup relations and the use of cooperative teams as an intervention for desegregated settings, in Hendrick, C. (ed.), *Group and Intergroup Relations: Review of Personality and Social Psychology*, Vol 9, Beverly Hills, CA: Sage, pp. 41–67.

Nelson, R.E. (1989), The strength of strong ties: social networks and intergroup conflict in organizations, *Academy of Management Journal*, **32**, 377–401.

Nohria, N. & Eccles, R.G. (1992), *Networks and Organizations: Structure, Form, and Action*, Boston, MA: Harvard Business School Press.

Oakes, P.J., Haslam, S.A., Morrison, B. & Grace, D. (1995), Becoming an ingroup: re-examining the impact of familiarity on perceptions of group homogeneity, *Social Psychology Quarterly*, **58**, 52–61.

O'Reilly, C.A., III. (1991), Organizational behavior: where we've been, where we're going, *Annual Review of Psychology*, **42**, 427–58.

Perry-Smith, J.E. & Shalley, C.E. (2003), The social side of creativity: a static and dynamic social network perspective, *Academy of Management Review*, **28** (1), 89–106.

Podolny, J.M. & Baron, J.N. (1997), Resources and relationships: social networks and mobility in the workplace, *American Sociological Review*, **62**, 673–93.

Powell, W.W., Koput, K.W. & Smith-Doerr, L. (1996), Interorganizational collaboration and the locus of innovation: networks of learning in biotechnology, *Administrative Science Quarterly*, **41**, 116–45.

Prahalad, C.K. & Hamel, G. (1990), The core competence of the corporation, *Harvard Business Review*, **68**, 79–91.

Prahalad, C.K. & Hamel, G. (1994), Strategy as a field of study: why search for a new paradigm? *Strategic Management Journal*, **15**, 5–16.

Pruitt, D.G. & Carnevale, P.J. (1993), *Negotiation in Social Conflict*, Milton Keynes, Open University Press.

Pruitt, D.G. & Rubin, J.Z. (1986), *Social Conflict: Escalation, Stalemate and Settlement*, New York: McGraw-Hill.

Reger, R.K., Gustafson, L.T., DeMarie, S.M. & Mullane, J.V. (1994), Reframing the organization: why implementing total quality is easier said than done, *Academy of Management Review*, **19**, 565–84.

Reynolds, K.J., Turner, J.C. & Haslam, S.A. (2000), When are we better than them and they worse than us? *Journal of Personality and Social Psychology*, **78**, 64–80.

Sharma, S., Durand, R.M. & Gur-Arie, O. (1981), Identification and analysis of moderator variables, *Journal of Marketing Research*, **18**, 291–300.

Sitkin, S.B. & Bies, R.J. (1998), Social accounts in conflict situations: using explanations to manage conflict, *Human Relations*, **46**, 349–70.

Tajfel, H. (1969), Cognitive aspects of prejudice, *Journal of Social Issues*, **25**, 79–97.

Tajfel, H. (1970), Experiments in intergroup discrimination, *Social Issues*, **25** (4), 79–97.

Tajfel, H. & Turner, J.C. (1979), An integrative theory of intergroup conflict, in Austin, W.G. & Worchel, S. (eds), *The Social Psychology of Intergroup Relations*, Monterey, CA: Brooks/Cole, pp. 33–47.

Tesser, A. (1988), Toward a self-evaluation maintenance model of social behavior, in Berkowitz, L. (ed.), *Advances in Experimental Social Psychology*, Vol. 2, New York: Academic Press, pp. 181–227.

Tsai, W. (2001), Knowledge transfer in intraorganizational networks: effects of network position and absorptive capacity on business unit innovation and performance, *Academy of Management Journal*, **44**, 996–1015.

Tsai, W. & Ghoshal, S. (1998), Social capital and value creation: the role of intrafirm networks, *Academy of Management Journal*, **41**, 464–76.

Turner, J.C. (1982), Towards a cognitive redefinition of the social group, in Tajfel, H. (ed.), *Social Identity and Intergroup Relations*, Cambridge: Cambridge University Press, pp. 15–40.

Turner, J.C. (1985), Social categorization and the self-concept: a social cognitive theory of group behaviour, in Lawler, E.J. (ed.), *Advances in Group Processes*, Greenwich, CT: JAI Press, pp. 77–122.

Turner, J.C. (1991), *Social Influence*, Buckingham: Open University Press.

Turner, J.C., Hogg, M.A., Oakes, P.J., Reicher, S.D. & Wetherell, M.S. (1987), *Rediscovering the Social Group: A Self-categorization Theory*, Oxford: Blackwell.

Turner, J.C. & Oakes, P.J. (1989), Self-categorization theory and social influence, in Paulus, P.B. (ed.), *Psychology of Group Influence*, Hillsdale, NJ: Lawrence Erlbaum Associates, pp. 233–75.

Uzzi, B.D. (1996), The sources and consequences of embeddedness for the economic performance of organizations: the network effect, *American Sociological Review*, **61**, 674–98.

Uzzi, B.D. (1997), Social structure and competition in interfirm networks: the paradox of embeddedness, *Administrative Science Quarterly*, **42**, 35–67.

van Knippenberg, D. (2000), Work motivation and performance: a social identity perspective, *Applied Psychology: An International Review*, **49**, 357–71.

Veenstra, K. & Haslam, S.A. (2000), Willingness to participate in industrial protest: exploring social identification in context, *British Journal of Social Psychology*, **39**, 153–72.

Vicari, S., von Krogh, G., Roos, J. & Mahnke, V. (1996), Knowledge creation through cooperative experimentation, in von Krogh, G. & Roos, J. (eds), *Managing Knowledge: Perspectives on Cooperation and Competition*, Thousand Oaks, CA: Sage, pp. 184–202.

Walker, G., Kogut, B. & Shan, W. (1997), Social capital, structural holes and the formation of an industry network, *Organization Science*, **8**, 109–25.

Walker, M.E., Wasserman, S. & Wellman, B. (1993), Statistical models for social support networks, *Sociological Methods and Research*, **22**, 71–98.

Wegener, B. (1991), Job mobility and social ties: social resources, prior job, and status attainment, *American Sociological Review*, **56**, 60–71.

Wright, S.C., Aron, A. McLaughlin-Volpe, T. & Ropp, S.A. (1997), The extended contact effect: knowledge of cross-group friendships and prejudice, *Journal of Personality and Social Psychology*, **73**, 73–90.

4 Relational perspectives on collective learning and knowledge creation

David R. Schwandt, M. Turan Ayvaz and Margaret D. Gorman

Introduction

The idea that knowledge constitutes an economically important aspect of social existence has been a fundamental assumption since civilizations began to contemplate human interaction (Plato, 1941). For a while the notion of knowledge has been connected with economic survival of organizations (Hayek, 1945; Boulding, 1966; Lamberton, 1971).

Unfortunately, in an effort to better understand knowledge management, the literature has tended to treat knowledge as a commodity that can be exchanged between parties, much like money is exchanged for an automobile. In the process, knowledge has been disassociated from its dependence on a value context and its social relational origins. The differentiation of 'knowledge' from 'information' has been sacrificed so that terms such as 'management', 'transfer', and 'storage' might be applied in a traditional, pragmatic manner, not only to information, but also to knowledge. This leaves organizations open to the fallacies associated with over-relying on benchmarking and best practices designed to transfer knowledge from one organizational context to another, without consideration of the dynamic social relations that are required to value new information – so that new knowledge that is created is specific to their context, and only their context. If knowledge is only seen as passive – composed of facts that can be stored, retrieved and disseminated, with little concern for the context in which the facts were originally set – then there will be little concern for the new and often quite different contexts in which those facts will be used. Unfortunately from this perspective, knowledge management is nothing more than getting the right information to the right people at the right time.

Since the 1980s, much of the collective cognition literature, in conjunction with research methodology gains (Eden, 1997; Huff, 1990), have contributed to our ability to postulate collective learning processes, or the creation of knowledge. In addition, more recent work has provided an understanding of the role that sense-making plays in establishing meaning for managers and for the collective in general (Weick, 1995). One of the major implications for managers in organizations is the realization that their sense-making and judgements may be more dependent on social relations within the collective than on universal management perspectives (Johnson et al., 1998). Understanding the relationship between social actions and knowledge creation has implications not only for managers, but also for the management of knowledge.

To better understand the manager's role with respect to knowledge, one must consider the relational dynamics of the collective cognition processes. This requires an analytic framework that can include structuration (Giddens, 1979), institutionalization (Archer, 1988; Douglas, 1981) and their respective implications for interactions of actors (Bourdieu, 1977; Weick, 1995) in a highly complex environment. In a micro sense, these theories aid in understanding collective sense-making and knowledge creation. Interactions of agents and the relationship of agents to institutionalized values and structures become the ever-changing elements of a collective cognitive system. It is the integration of these concepts (both micro and macro, subjective and objective) into an analytical framework based on a functional action theory that will enable analysis of the actions of these agents (more specifically managers and executives) as they make judgements.

In this chapter we address human actions in the context of a social-cultural system as they pertain to knowledge creation and utilization. It is our premise that the creation and utilization of knowledge is dependent on the specific relations and values found within the collective itself. (For the purpose of this chapter, the terms 'collective' and 'organization' are used interchangeably.) We attempt to explain collective learning in the context of human relations and interactions, with a focus on collective knowledge. It is our premise that, to understand knowledge management, one must first understand the social and cultural nature of the collective relations. To make this argument, we first discuss the social nature of knowledge and its management by making a case for incorporating the relational aspects of the collective in understanding knowledge management. We then develop a sociological understanding of collective action as it relates to the creation of knowledge through organizational learning. We conclude with six analytical questions concerning the dynamic social relations in a collective and discuss three major implications for research and practice concerning these relational aspects of knowledge management and the collective.

The social nature of knowledge and its management
Few would argue that the concepts of management and organizational theory are not soundly based on the concepts of social systems (Hatch, 1993; Katz & Kahn, 1966, 1978). So when discussing 'knowledge management', it can be said that we are discussing the social relations and actions

of knowledge. The exact description of knowledge management depends on how the word 'knowledge' is defined, both implicitly and explicitly.

The inclusion of words such as 'meaning', 'beliefs', and 'value' to distinguish information from knowledge points to a 'valuing process' that is dependent on the dynamic collective relational nature of the social system. Because meaning and values vary across and sometimes within the collective, not all knowledge is the same. Knowledge can be explicit or tacit (Polanyi, 1966), declarative or procedural (Anderson, 1993); or, as Habermas (1987) contended, it can take three different forms based on communicative action: instrumental, communicative and emancipatory. Instrumental refers to technical knowledge oriented toward observable cause–effect relationships governed by rules of value or experiment; communicative knowledge is a practical understanding of each other and of the social norms associated with the culture; and emancipatory knowledge is derived from self-reflection of unquestioned assumptions that 'sustain inhibitions and patterns of interactions' (Mezirow, 1991: 87).

The emphasis on the technological aspects of information management often overshadows the social relationship between 'information' and 'knowledge' (Davenport et al., 1998; von Krogh, 1998; Snowden, 1997). Not all information is knowledge for the collective. For the purposes of this chapter, knowledge is defined as that information that is 'valued' by the collective. The valuing processes applied to information are driven by the cultural values, basic assumptions and social norms held by the specific collective (organization) and are manifested through actions, experiences and the collective's history. This definition encompasses all 'types' of knowledge, ranging from technical to procedural to emancipatory (Habermas, 1987). This definition also mandates that knowledge management processes be considered in the context of the social-cultural relations of the organization.

The literature is quite silent about how 'processing' or 'combining' transforms information into knowledge, or how information attains 'meaning' or develops into 'constituted' beliefs. The dominant perception of knowledge management is that it is very rational and organized – it is primarily considered a problem of capturing, organizing and retrieving information, suggesting notions of databases, documents, query languages and data mining. However this coherent picture of knowledge management is not satisfying when it is enacted. One of the reasons we are dissatisfied with the dominant picture of knowledge management is that it pays little attention to human and social relational factors associated with knowledge and information. Therefore we argue that knowledge management systems must take into account both human and social factors. That is, knowledge management and knowledge creation are relational processes by which information flows, is valued within the collective's social-cultural system, and becomes useful knowledge for the collective and its agents.

Collective relations and knowledge management
The construct of collectivity, although not new, has become important to scholars' understanding of human dynamics across the traditional levels of social analysis: individual, team, group, unit, organization, or industry. Its importance may emanate from the frustrations derived from a lack of cross-level theories that allow researchers more comprehensively to understand social systems and relate the individual's actions to those of the larger unit of analysis. Related efforts concerning organizational cognition (Schwandt & Marquardt, 2000), sense-making (Weick, 1995), structuration (Barley & Tolbert, 1997; Swanson, 1992), and complexity theory (Axelrod, 1997; Stacey et al., 2000) have rekindled the need to understand better the collective and the cross-level relationships.

Although the collectivity construct can refer to high levels of the social system such as societies or industries (Abrahamson & Fombrun, 1994; Astley, 1984; Astley & Van de Ven, 1983), the major focus of the present argument is limited to the organization and its members as the collective. This section of the chapter sets forth a definition of collectivity and delineates critical aspects that have implications for both research and practice in relational learning: emergence, dynamic action and interactions, and value-knowledge dependence.

Aspects of collectivity
In its most general form, collectivity represents a state or quality of the 'collective,' defined as being 'of, pertaining to, or derived from a number of individuals taken or acting together; common' (OED, 1991). The definition highlights the critical action aspects of collectivity. The phrase 'derived from' is a precursor to the concept of emergence, while 'number of individuals taken or acting together' indicates a dependence on social interaction and relationships. The last component of the definition is 'common,' which is an aspect of value-knowledge dependence that can be derived from a more specific sociological and anthropological definition of collectivity.

Sociologists have given the most consideration to the definition of collectivity, with anthropologists running a close second. Etzioni (1968) referred to the collective as a group of individuals who are bound together by a number of different relationships. Parsons and Shils (1952) added a more dynamic perspective when they defined the collective as the actions or integration of its members using a common value system. These authors imply that the members of the collective will under appropriate circumstances act in the 'defense' of their shared values.

For the purposes of this chapter, we operationalize collectivity as a continuously emergent social pattern of integrated individual and collective actions characterized by an accepted set of values (Pruzan, 2001) and common knowledge. This definition allows for the potential variance in the nature of collectives based on the extent of integration, the extent of the acceptance of collective values, and involvement in knowledge creation relationships.

The emergence aspect of collectivity has been supported by theoretical work concerning the social construction of reality (Berger & Luckmann, 1966), managerial sense-making (Weick, 1995), and the creation of meaning from *habitus* (Bourdieu, 1977). Of particular note is the work of Taylor and Van Every (2000) and their argument concerning the importance of communications in the emergence of organizational structure. They emphasized the temporal nature of the emergent organization as a function of conversation and language:

> If organization is emergent in communications, as we believe, then it is not a *being*, but a *becoming*. What we ought to be studying is not organization or ideology, because neither has any ontological status independent of communication, but the processes of communication by which we continue to construct both to become the world we live in. (Taylor & Van Every, 2000: x)

That social systems are always in the act of organizing, or becoming, only seems logical (Weick, 1979). As organizational situations change, so do the collective's actions and so might the nature of the collective's knowledge. The organization's knowledge is reflective of the nature of the specific collective relationships required to value the new information they are confronted with at that moment in time. Thus knowledge also emerges from these collective actions and is always 'becoming'.

We have made the case that the collective is constituted by the relationships between and among its members. These relationships define certain actions as required in the interest of the integrity of the system itself. These actions are governed by the collective's shared values and evolve to collective routines. However when the collective is confronted with novelty or ambiguous information, their actions (such as reflections, exploration or new uses of language) must either seek meaning in the context of their existing values, or augment or change their values to transform the information as knowledge. This process or series of relationships of social actions we define as collective cognition or learning.

Relational dependence of collective learning
Collective learning as an 'action system' cannot be represented as the simple sum of the learning actions of the individual actors involved. The

actions and interactions of individuals, whether knowingly or not, jointly produce and reproduce the operating relationships and knowledge for doing things together. There may be a preference for the individuals to make 'informed choices' concerning their actions; however they do so in situations that are heavily influenced by social structures that may encourage normative behaviors.

A basic frame of reference for understanding the collective is the theory of action (Parsons & Shils, 1952): 'a set of categories for the analysis of the relations of one or more actors to and in a situation' (p. 61).[1] The theory is primarily concerned with the structure and processes involved in the actor's relations to a situation, which includes other actors as persons and as members of the collective. Action is conceptualized as normatively expended energy in a situation that is goal-oriented (Parsons & Shils, 1952) and contextually linked to social structure.

In addition to Parsons, the duality of structure (Giddens, 1976) provides a theoretical platform to formulate and interpret the relationships between the structure provided by the collective and the interactions of the individuals involved in the work of the collective. Giddens (1984) affirmed the dynamic nature of this relationship: 'Structure is not "external" to individuals: as memory traces, and as instantiated in social practices, it is in a certain sense more "internal" than exterior to their activities in a Durkheimian sense' (p. 25). It is the dual nature of structure (constraining and enabling) that has provided an action–structure bridge for contemporary authors in their explanation of emerging qualities of the collective, such as identification (Scott et al., 1998), innovation (Coopey et al., 1998), identity (Gioia et al., 2000) and organizational transformations (Sarason, 1995). Such studies link action and structured relationships with the values and knowledge held by the collective.

It is in this sense that we define a collective learning system as 'a system of actions, actors, symbols and processes that enables an organization to transform information into valued knowledge which in turn increases its long-run adaptive capacity' (Schwandt, 1997; Schwandt & Marquardt, 2000). Figure 4.1 represents our extension of Parsons's (1937) concept of prerequisite functions from his theory of action (often referred to as AGIL) to collective learning and relational knowledge creation.[2] The four collective 'prerequisite' learning functions can be represented in terms of four subsystems of actions: Environmental Interface, Action and Reflection, Dissemination and Diffusion, and Memory and Meaning (Schwandt & Marquardt, 2000).

The Environmental Interface subsystem depicts those relationships of actions that allow and/or disallow information to enter the learning system. The Action and Reflection subsystem represents actions that are oriented

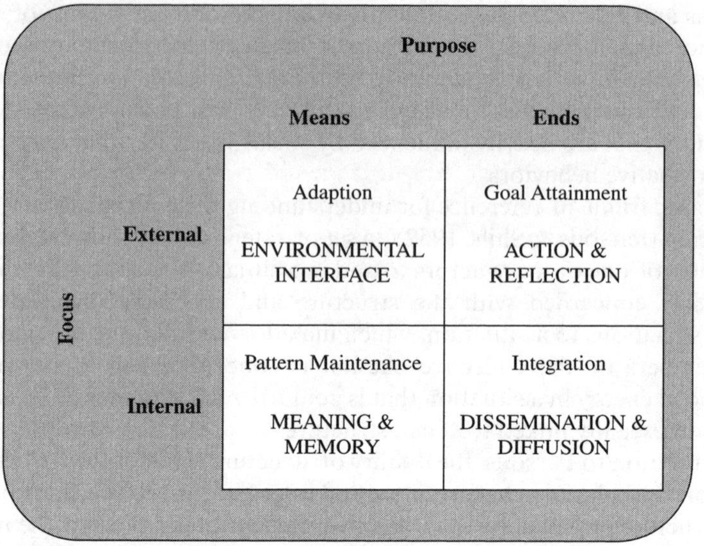

Source: Adapted from Schwandt et al. (1995).

*Figure 4.1   Learning subsystems and functional prerequisites: dynamic
social model of organizational learning subsystems*

towards inquiry and reflectivity that result in the creation of knowledge.
The Dissemination and Diffusion subsystem represents actions directed at
coordinating and controlling the collective's relationships necessary for
learning. Finally, the Meaning and Memory subsystem represents actions
of the collective that maintain patterns of values, meaning and sense-
making that allow the collective learning system to create knowledge
(Schwandt & Marquardt, 2000).

The actions of each learning subsystem carry out a prerequisite function
for collective learning and represent the relationships required for a knowledge management system. To increase the analytical nature of the collective learning model we pose two questions: (1) what is the nature of the
subsystems' mutual dependence? and (2) how do these subsystems operate?
The second question requires a more complex theory of human interaction
and the non-linear relationships between and among actions. At present,
the four subsystems' operations must be considered 'black boxes'. That is,
we can see what the antecedent conditions are and the subsequent consequences of the actions; however we do not have a sufficiently developed and
unified theory of behavioral science to understand the chaotic nature of the
simultaneous interaction of the multiple sets of human actions (although

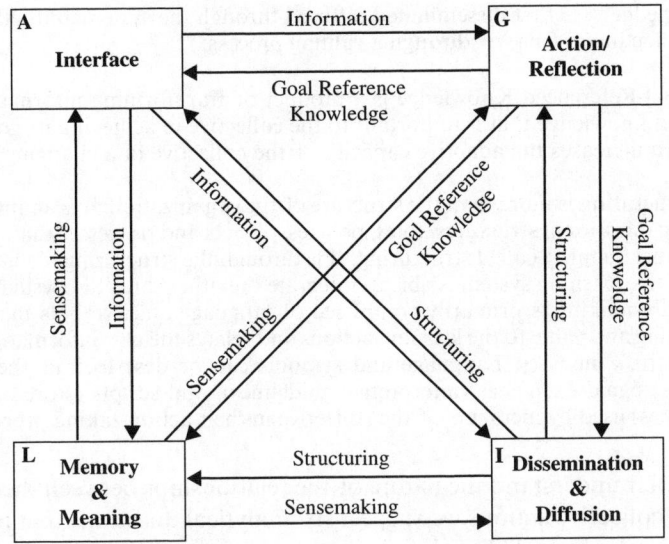

Source: Adapted from Schwandt et al. (1995).

Figure 4.2 Learning subsystems and exchange media

great strides are being made in this area: see Axelrod & Cohen, 2000; Calori et al., 1994; Hannerz, 1992).

Returning to answer the first question above, and to enhance the analytical nature of the collective learning model, the concept of 'exchange' (Blau, 2002) is used to understand better the dynamic relationship between the subsystems of actions and the relative contribution of each to knowledge creation. Each subsystem depends on the others for a critical 'input' that enables it to carry out its function with respect to the organizational learning system. In addition, each subsystem provides an 'output' that is critical for each of the other subsystems. These inputs and outputs constitute an exchange system of tangible and intangible media.

The collective learning media of exchange provide a more concrete level for understanding the relationship between subsystems. Each organizational learning subsystem generates a medium that symbolically represents its functional product. Figure 4.2 schematically represents the relationship between the four subsystems and the interchange media. The media of exchange are defined as (Schwandt & Marquardt, 2000):

New Information is constituted from the data obtained through the interactions with both the internal and external environments. This information is not yet knowledge; it is first disseminated/diffused through the system and reflected on and then made sense of through a valuing process.

Goal-Referenced Knowledge is a product of transforming information into valued knowledge that is important to the collective in achieving its goals. This in turn increases the adaptive capacity of the collective in a changing environment.

Structuring is more than the structure of the organization; it is an integration of organizational structures, roles, policies, objects and processes that provide a dynamic quantity called structuring. It is through the structuring media that the collective learning system is able to integrate the other three Subsystems.

Sense-making is primarily comprised of language and symbols that convey meaning and value to the learning actions and relates the new information to the collective's memory. Language and symbols can be described as the specific words, signals, schemes (interpretive guidelines), and scripts (stored response routines) used by members of the collective in their action-taking process.

To better understand the nature of the relationships between the subsystems of collective actions we suggest six analytical questions that incorporate the evaluation of the relationship between the media of exchange:

1. What is the relationship between the collective's actions of interfacing with their environments and their internal actions of collective reflection? This question is focused on determining the consistency of the goal-referenced knowledge derived from new information, and to evaluate the relationship of new information to the reflective actions of the collective.
2. What is the relationship between the collective's reflective actions and the structuring that influence these actions? In answering this question one must examine the relationship of the goal-referenced knowledge that is created and the norms and relational social structures that may inhibit or reinforce the reflective actions.
3. What is the relationship of the collective's reflective actions to their collective memory and the actions that they employ to assign meaning to their reflections on new information in the creation of goal-referenced knowledge? In answering this question we must turn to the evaluation of the collective's sense-making process and knowledge structures that relate their collective memory, values and basic assumptions of novel or ambiguous information.
4. What is the relationship of the collective's actions associated with memory retention and meaning assignment and its actions associated with its environmental interface? In answering this question one considers the relationship between the interchange media of sense-making and new information. Are the values of the collective reinforcing the

need for continuous search for new information in the external environment?

5. What is the relationship between the collective's actions associated with its interfacing with its environment and the actions of dissemination that structure the distribution of new information? Comparison must be made of the nature of new information and the internal networks that are supported by the collective to deliver the information to its members for reflection.

6. What is the relationship of the collective's structuring with the actions that maintain collective memory and patterns of values? To answer this question we must examine the congruency of the collective's sense-making values with its structuring mechanism such as norms and social structures.

Collectivity's dependence on the value-knowledge relationship
As one can see from the above analytical questions, the collective's values and the knowledge they create are related in several ways. The primary relationship is formed around the catalyst of new information. New information is the 'ordered data' that collectives are exposed to or purposefully seek. It plays an important role in sustaining the collective. However selection and use of information, or the creation of knowledge specific to the collective, are accomplished through a process of social valuing: the assignment of meaning to the information based on the collective's set of accepted values (Schwandt, 1997; Schwandt & Marquardt, 2000). The collective aspect of 'value-knowledge dependence' is meant to represent the dependence of the collective's patterns of actions on a close alignment of their accepted values set with the knowledge that they employ to sustain and/or change their situation.

Although we have been concentrating on the relationship between sub-systems of actions, it is important to understand collectivity in at least two respects. First, the relationship between the individual and the collective is also dependent on the informed actor's choosing of behaviors that continue to enhance or sustain the cognitive basis of the collective (Hendry, 1999). Being a member of a collective entails the transfer to the collective of large portions of control over the individual's actions. In many of these situations, each actor is attempting to maximize personal utility by making the unilateral transfer. For this to be effective for the individual, one must understand the values of the collective and how one is influential both in achieving the collective's goals and in directing one's own choice. It is only then that one can make informed choices concerning one's commitment to the collective, thereby avoiding becoming a mindless dupe of the culture (Coleman, 1990).

Douglas (1992) expanded on this micro–macro relationship of agent-motivated choice and collective cultural values as she described the coercion associated with a collective. Her premise was that the collective legitimates itself through three motivations: (1) the need for conformity and internal equity (sects); (2) the need for exchange (market) and preservation of the individual's freedom to negotiate; and (3) the need to coordinate and enhance mutual dependence (hierarchical) to alleviate the fear of failure to perform. Each of these legitimating forms can be seen as being related to the value–knowledge dependence of the collective.

Secondly, these questions allow us to assess the value–knowledge relationship and its impact on a collective's cognitive capacity. Hayek (1945) recognized that one of the major problems in designing economic systems was determining 'the best way of utilizing knowledge initially dispersed among all the people' (p. 520). Since the 1950s, determining the 'best way' of valuing and moving information in the collective has become the focus of organizational learning research and theorizing. This focus entails understanding not only cultural values but also the dynamics of individual and collective actions. For example Polanyi (1966) saw the growth of knowledge as depending on complex sets of social relations based on a largely institutionalized reciprocity of trust. Of course the reciprocal of the previous statement may also be true – social relations and trust can be institutionalized by the growth of knowledge.

The relational collective learning model discussed above offers researchers a framework from which to explore both the discrete and the interconnected elements that contribute to knowledge creation and management. Rather than assuming that cognition is an individual process, this approach sees cognition as a dynamic social process. This model reinforces the concept of distributed cognition.

Distributed cognition's main focus is on communicative structures (Wilson & Myers, 1999). In distributed cognition theory, knowledge is an emergent process (Salomon, 1993). For many, distributed cognition includes cognitive processes that are distributed across the members of a social group (Salomon, 1993). One can postulate that the emergence of collectivity as a social phenomenon is a dynamic and intricate function of the relationships among collective values, knowledge, actions and structures. In addition, the temporal nature of these aspects and their multiple linkages allow them to be considered to be highly complex and non-linear.

Relational learning: implications for research and practice
Collective relationships have always been present in most aspects of organizational science and managerial theory. Unfortunately it has not been a major focus of the field's research and practice (compared to the fields of

sociology and anthropology). If it has indeed been there all the time, one must ask why we haven't paid attention to it until now. The answer to this question is surely debatable; however it probably lies amongst issues of worldview, methodological means and a reluctance of humans (managers) to deal with 'soft issues' in the practice. This situation has begun to change with the advent of the knowledge society and an interest in network structures. Understanding the dynamic nature of the collective is becoming important to knowledge creation, organizational learning and the 'management' of knowledge.

Implications for theory, research and practice can be drawn from three lines of effort that appear to be progressing on parallel paths (with only minor crossover): agency–structure interactions, collective cognition and knowledge creation, and collectives as non-linear systems. Although at first glance these lines of effort may seem disjointed, each has the common purpose of understanding the dynamic nature of collectivity, and each has implications for how people relate to each other in those collectives.

Agency–structure interactions
Interest has been renewed in the relationship between action (agency) and social structure. These actions arise from both the individual and the collective. Barley and Tolbert (1997) fused institutional theory with structuration in a model of social behavior (agency actions) that composes institutions diachronically, while institutions (structure) constrain action synchronically. In a similar fashion, Seo and Creed (2002) developed a model that predicts institutional change through a dialectical relationship between praxis and institutional contradictions. They saw the praxis as being composed of reflective actions of the individuals and the collective.

Such research has implications for the interpretation of dualities and variations in the organizational structuration patterns (Giddens, 1984), as opposed to single, segregated variables in simple cause–effect relations. Linking structure to agency, especially in the context of collective learning (Hellgren & Lowstedt, 1998), has implications for how to view traditional constructs such as conflict, power, emotion and leadership – not in and of themselves, but regarding how they relate to patterns of collective actions and knowledge management.

Collective cognition and knowledge creation
Since the 1980s, much of the collective cognition literature has reflected descriptions of the phenomenon not the dynamics of the relationship. Theories have posed sets of variables that relate organizational learning and the environment (Hedberg, 1981), cognitive changes and behavioral changes (Fiol & Lyles, 1985), organizational transformation and learning

cycles (Lundberg, 1989), and organizational memory retrieval and storage (Walsh & Ungson, 1991). All of these works, in conjunction with research methodological gains (Eden, 1997; Huff, 1990), have contributed to the field's ability to postulate collective learning processes. However Weick's (1995) more recent work has provided a better understanding of the role that sense-making plays in establishing meaning for managers and the collective in general.

Sense-making is the conceptual bridge between collective action and the creation of knowledge. Although Weick's theorizing process used highly critical situations, such as aircraft carrier flight decks (Weick & Roberts, 1993), he made a strong case for the extension of his observations concerning sense-making to more 'normal or routine' organizational settings. These so-called normal settings can be characterized by high noise levels (poor communications), no clear reasons to change (lack of common knowledge), lack of trust (or the value of trust), high reliance on cause–effect relationships (linearity), lack of skills, fear of admitting failure, social dynamics such as pluralistic ignorance, and individual commitments to strong professional cultures (institutions) (Weick, 1993). It is in this normal context that organizations are expected to create new knowledge, be innovative, and at the same time be effective and efficient.

One of the major implications for managers in organizations is the realization that their sense-making and judgements may be more dependent on the social interrelation aspects of the collective than on a universal management perspective (Johnson et al., 1998). Thus if managers are to make sense in their environments and to 'manage knowledge', they must understand the dynamics of these relationships.

Understanding the relationship between social actions and knowledge creation has implications not only for managers but also for all members of a collective. As participants in the collective, all must search for new information, employ a social structure to reflect on that information and, finally, make critical judgements concerning the plausibility of its value as it may be applied to the organization. Because of its social nature, this process may also threaten the collective's ability to create new knowledge and may lead to conflicting actions taken by its members. Understanding the dynamics of collective cognition requires an analytic framework that takes into consideration structuration (Giddens, 1979), institutionalization (Archer, 1988; Douglas, 1981) and implications for interactions of actors (Bourdieu, 1977; Weick, 1995) in a highly complex environment.

Collectivity as a non-linear system
Collective cognition and behavior have sparked the interests of theorists in the science of complexity. This has sparked reciprocal interest in applying

complexity theory to collectives (Thietart & Forgues, 1995; Von Krogh & Roos, 1994; Wheatley, 1992). These efforts have urged organizational theorists to incorporate concepts of non-linearity, complexity and self-organizing systems into the formulation of the dynamics of collectives, especially if an assumption suggests that they are moving toward an 'unknowable' future. Stacey et al. (2000) justified this application of complexity theory to social systems:

> self-organization is an inevitable cooperative, participative dynamic, which is an intrinsic property of interaction and causes the emergence of pattern. Causality here is of interaction and that is very different to the neo-Darwinian version, because it is interaction, or relationship, that causes emergent form, rather than competition operating on chance. (p. 111)

Non-linear explanations of the collective may still be in the metaphoric stage of theory building; however the theory does provide interesting implications for understanding the unpredictability of the collective's actions, especially as they pertain to the debate concerning organizational planning and implementation (Eden & Ackermann, 1998; Mintzberg, 1994; Pressman & Wildavsky, 1984; Schwandt, 1997).

Although disciplines associated with the social sciences are moving slowly towards the theories of complex adaptive systems, the fields of information technology and complexity are proceeding with vigor towards social systems as potential applications of their theories. The 'knowledge management and distributed intelligence flags' are providing the rallying points for both complexity and information management theorists and practitioners. Advances in agent-based models (Axelrod, 1997; Carley, 1986) are enabling researchers to investigate issues of agent diversity, performance, networks and other micro–macro phenomena via computer simulations. Workshops such as those sponsored by the Santa Fe Institute are providing a forum for the discussion of collective cognition and theories of collectives that include understanding dialogue and the role of inter-agent communications and interactions. Complexity theory is at present a promising path for research and theory building. However it has implications for how we 'think' about the collective and our inherent needs to control actions as the only answer to ambiguous environments.

Conclusion
This chapter has scratched the surface of outlining the dynamic relationship between the actions in a collective, and the creation and use of knowledge. It has addressed what collectivity is, what aspects are important or interesting, and why the pursuit of understanding their complex nature might help us, as humans, to live in them. As Weick (1995) has explained, humans

assign meaning retrospectively (after the action). So we say unabashedly that 'we didn't know what we meant until we saw what we wrote'. In this context, the chapter represents a perspective on relational learning that relies on 'cultural collectivity' as it relates to the dynamics of a *negotiated* collectivity' Knowledge and values are grounded in the basic assumptions of the collective's culture. However the collective system of actions in the context of structuring constantly reflects a negotiated and dynamic emerging collectivity. This tension between existing knowledge and emerging knowledge is indicative of the non-linear nature of collectivity.

Notes

1. By using Parsons's (Parsons & Shils, 1952) theory, our work – like others (Alexander, 1983; Habermas, 1987; Luhmann, 1995) – starts with the critiques of functionalism (voluntarism, human choice, subjective interactions) and builds current sociological work into an action-theory approach to collective cognition. Mouzelis (1995) found that modern sociologists and scholars in general 'have failed to transcend functionalism in general, and Parsonian functionalism in particular' (p. 6). However this functional orientation allows for concrete analysis of abstract ideas and a starting point for praxis. As Douglas (1981) noted, 'without a functionalist form of argument, we cannot begin to explain how a thought world constructs the thought style that controls its experience' (p. 43). It is this 'thought world' that collectives in general, must probe via their actions to achieve foresight and knowledge.
2. In describing the social action system and extending Parsons' General Theory of Action (Parsons, 1937) to collective cognition, we pose questions concerning the processes used by the individuals and the collective to understand their external and internal environments. Incorporating the functional micro action framework enables the relating of concrete actions, individual and collective, to a learning system composed of subsystems of actions carrying out Parsons' functional prerequisites (1937). These actions are influenced by cultural patterns that are embedded in the social milieu. It is from this that both cognitive and emotional orientations impact managers' judgment.

References

Abrahamson, E. & Fombrun, C.J. (1994), Macrocultures: determinants and consequences, *Academy of Management Review*, **19** (4), 728–55.

Alexander, J.C. (1983), *The Modern Reconstruction of Classical Thought: Talcott Parsons*, Vol. 4, Berkeley, CA: University of California Press.

Anderson, J.R. (1993), *Rules of the Mind*, Hillsdale, NJ: Erlbaum.

Archer, M. (1988), *Culture and Agency: The Place of Culture in Social Theory*, New York: Cambridge University Press.

Astley, G.W. (1984), Toward an appreciation of collective strategy, *Academy of Management Review*, **9** (3), 526–35.

Astley, W.G. & Van de Ven, A.H. (1983), Central perspectives and debates in organization theory, *Administrative Science Quarterly*, **28**, 245–73.

Axelrod, R. (1997), *The Complexity of Cooperation*, Princeton, NJ: Princeton University Press.

Axelrod, R. & Cohen, M.D. (2000), *Harnessing Complexity: Organizational Implications of a Scientific Frontier*, New York: Basic Books.

Barley, S.R. & Tolbert, P.S. (1997), Institutionalization and structuration: studying the links between action and institution, *Organization Studies*, **18** (1), 93–117.

Berger, P.L. & Luckmann, T. (1966), *The Social Construction of Reality*, Garden City, NY: Doubleday & Company.

Blau, P.M. (2002), *Exchange and Power in Social Life*, London: Transaction Publishers.

Boulding, K. (1966), *The Impact of Social Sciences*, New Brunswick, NJ: Rutgers University Press.

Bourdieu, P. (1977), *Outline of a Theory of Practice*, trans R. Nice, Cambridge: Cambridge University Press.

Calori, R., Johnson, G. & Sarnin, P. (1994), CEOs' cognitive maps and the scope of the organization, *Strategic Management Journal*, **15**, 437–57.

Carley, K. (1986), An approach for relating social structure to cognitive structure, *Journal of Mathematical Sociology*, **12**, 137–189.

Coleman, J.S. (1990), *Foundations of Social Theory*, Cambridge, MA: Belknap Press of Harvard University Press.

Coopey, J., Keegan, O. & Emler, N. (1998), Managers' innovations and structuration of organizations, *Journal of Management Studies*, **35** (3), 263–84.

Davenport, T.H. & Prusak, L. (1998), *Working Knowledge*, Boston, MA: Harvard Business School Press.

Douglas, M. (1981), *How Institutions Think*, Syracuse, NY: Syracuse University Press.

Douglas, M. (1992), The normative debate and the origins of culture, in Douglas, M. (ed.), *Risk and Blame: Essays in Cultural Theory*, London: Routledge.

Eden, C. (1997), 'Cognitive mapping and scenarios in strategy making and risk management', paper presented at the 1997 European Managerial and Organizational Cognition Workshop, The Netherlands.

Eden, C. & Ackermann, F. (1998), *Making Strategy: The Journey of Strategic Management*, London: Sage.

Etzioni, A. (1968), *The Active Society*, New York: Free Press.

Fiol, C.M. & Lyles, M.A. (1985), Organizational learning, *Academy of Management Review*, **10** (4), 803–13.

Giddens, A. (1976), *New Rules of Sociological Method*, London: Hutchinson.

Giddens, A. (1979), *Central Problems in Social Theory: Action, Structure and Contradiction in Social Analysis*, Berkeley, CA: University of California Press.

Giddens, A. (1984), *The Constitution of Society*, Los Angeles, CA: University of California Press.

Gioia, D.A., Schultz, M. & Corley, K.G. (2000), Organizational identity, image, and adaptive instability, *Academy of Management Review*, **25** (1), 63–81.

Habermas, J. (1987), *Lifeworld and System: A Critique of Functionalist Reason*, Vol. 2, trans. T. McCarthy, Boston, MA: Beacon Press.

Hannerz, U. (1992), *Cultural Complexity: Studies in the Social Organization of Meaning*, New York: Columbia University Press.

Hatch, M.J. (1993), Dynamics of organizational culture, *Academy of Management Review*, **18** (4), 659–93.

Hayek, F.A. (1945), The use of knowledge in society, *American Economic Review*, **35** (4), 519–30.

Hedberg, B. (1981), How organizations learn and unlearn, in Nystrom, P.C. & Starbuck, W.H. (eds), *Handbook of Organization Design*, London: Oxford University Press, pp. 8–27.

Hellgren, B. & Lowstedt, J. (1998), Agency and organization: a social theory approach to cognition, in Eden, C. & Spender, J.C. (eds), *Managerial and Organizational Cognition*, London: Sage Publishing.

Hendry, J. (1999), Cultural theory and contemporary management organization, *Human Relations*, **52** (5), 557–77.

Huff, A.S. (1990), Mapping strategic thought, in Huff, A.S. (ed.), *Mapping Strategic Thought*, Chichester: John Wiley, pp. 11–49.

Johnson, P., Daniels, K. & Asch, R. (1998), Mental models of competition, in Eden, C. & Spender, J.C. (eds), *Managerial and Organizational Cognition*, London: Sage Publications, pp. 130–46.

Katz, D. & Kahn, R.L. (1966), *The Social Psychology of Organizations*, New York: John Wiley and Sons.

Katz, D. & Kahn, R.L. (1978), Organizations and the system concept, in Shafritz, J.M. & Whitbeck, P.H. (eds), *Classics of Organization Theory*, Oak Park, IL: Moore, pp. 161–73.

Lamberton, L.M. (ed.) (1971), *Economics of Information and Knowledge*, New York: Penguin Books.

Luhmann, N. (1995), *Social Systems*, trans. J.J. Bednarz & D. Baecker, Stanford, CA: Stanford University Press.

Lundberg, C.C. (1989), *On Organizational Learning: Implications and Opportunities for Expanding Organizational Development Research in Organizational Change and Development*, Vol. 3, Greenwich, CT: JAI Press.

Mezirow, J. (1991), *Transformative Dimensions of Adult Learning*, San Francisco, CA: Jossey-Bass.

Mintzberg, H. (1994), *The Rise and Fall of Strategic Planning*, New York: Free Press.

Mouzelis, N. (1995), *Sociological Theory: What went Wrong*, London: Routledge.

OED (1991), *The Compact Oxford English Dictionary*, 2nd edn, New York: Oxford University Press.

Parsons, T. (1937), *The Structure of Social Action*, New York: McGraw-Hill.

Parsons, T. & Shils, E.A. (1952), *Toward a General Theory of Action*, Cambridge, MA: Harvard University Press.

Plato (1941), *The Republic*, trans. R. Cornford, Oxford: Oxford University Press.

Polanyi, M. (1966), *The Tacit Dimension*, London: Routledge and Kegan Paul.

Pressman, J.L. & Wildavsky, A. (1984), *Implementation*, 3rd edn, Berkeley, CA: University of California Press.

Pruzan, P. (2001), The question of organizational consciousness: can organizations have values, virtues and visions? *Journal of Business Ethics*, **29**, 271–84.

Salomon, G. (1993), *Distributed Cognitions: Psychological and Educational Considerations*, New York: Cambridge University Press.

Sarason, Y. (1995), A model of organizational transformation: the incorporation of organizational identity into a structuration theory framework, *Academy of Management Journal, Best Papers Proceedings 1995*, Special Issue.

Schwandt, D.R. (1997), Integrating strategy and organizational learning: a theory of action perspective, in Walsh, J.P. & Huff, A.S. (eds), *Organizational Learning and Strategic Management* Vol. 14, Greenwich, CT: JAI Press Inc.

Schwandt, D.R., Johnson, C.G. & Gorman, M.D. (1995), 'Changing the dominant logic of strategic human resources planning through the development of deep structures social systems thinking: A three year case study', paper presented at the Strategic Management Conference, Mexico City.

Schwandt, D.R. & Marquardt, M.J. (2000), *Organizational Learning: From World-class Theories to Global Best Practices*, New York: St Lucie Press.

Scott, C.R., Corman, S.R. & Cheney, G. (1998), Development of a structurational model of identification in the organization, *Communication Theory*, **8** (3), 298–336.

Seo, M. & Creed, W.E.D. (2002), Institutional contradictions, praxis, and institutional change: a dialectical perspective, *Academy of Management Review*, **27** (2), 222–47.

Snowden, D.J. (1997), A framework for creating a sustainable programme in knowledge management, in Rock, S. (ed.) *Business Guide to Knowledge Management*, London: Caspian Publishing, pp. 150–75.

Stacey, R.D., Griffin, D. & Shaw, P. (2000), *Complexity and Management: Fad or Radical Challenge to Systems Thinking?* London: Routledge.

Swanson, G.E. (1992), Doing things together: some basic forms of agency and structure in collective action and some explanations, *Social Psychology Quarterly*, **55** (2), 94–117.

Taylor, J.R. & Van Every, E.J. (2000), *The Emergent Organization: Communication as its Site and Surface*, Mahwah, NJ: Lawerence Erlbaum Associates.

Thietart, R.A. & Forgues, B. (1995), Chaos theory and organization, *Organization Science*, **6** (1), 19–31.

von Krogh, G. (1998), 'Care in knowledge creation', *California Management Review*, **40** (3), 133–53.

Von Krogh, G. & Roos, J.G. (1994), An essay on corporate epistemology, *Strategic Management Journal*, **15**, 53–71.
Walsh, J.P. & Ungson, G.R. (1991), Organizational memory, *Academy of Management Review*, **16** (1), 57–91.
Weick, K. (1979), *The Social Psychology of Organizing*, 2nd edn, New York: McGraw-Hill.
Weick, K.E. (1993), Sensemaking in organizations: small structures with large consequences, in Murnighan, J.K. (ed.), *Social Psychology in Organizations: Advances in Theory and Research*, Englewood Cliffs, NJ: Prentice Hall.
Weick, K.E. (1995), *Sensemaking in Organizations*, Thousand Oaks, CA: Sage Publications.
Weick, K.E. & Roberts, K.H. (1993), Collective mind in organizations: heedful interrelating on flight decks, *Administrative Science Quarterly*, **38**, 357–81.
Wheatley, M.J. (1992), *Leadership and the New Science*, San Francisco, CA: Berrett-Koehler.
Wilson, B.G. & Myers, K.M. (1999), Situated cognition in theoretical and practical context, in Jonassen, D. & Lands, S. (eds), *Theoretical Foundations of Learning Environments*, Mahwah NJ: Erlbaum, pp. 57–88.

5 Relational coordination: coordinating work through relationships of shared goals, shared knowledge and mutual respect
Jody Hoffer Gittell

Introduction

In Thompson's (1967) seminal work on organizations, he argued that effective coordination in highly interdependent work settings is characterized by 'mutual adjustment' among participants, as outcomes from one task feed back and create new information for participants performing related tasks. However Thompson saw mutual adjustment as playing a limited role in organizations (Kogut & Zander, 1996). Because mutual adjustment is prohibitively costly, Thompson argued, coordination more commonly occurs through coordinating mechanisms such as supervision, routines, scheduling, pre-planning or standardization. These coordinating mechanisms enable organizations to achieve coordination while minimizing interaction among participants (Tushman & Nadler, 1978; Galbraith, 1977). Due to their limited bandwidth (Daft & Lengel, 1986), these mechanisms are typically argued to be most effective in settings with low levels of task interdependence and low levels of uncertainty (Thompson, 1967; Argote, 1982; Van de Ven et al., 1976).

Increasingly however work is characterized by high levels of task interdependence, uncertainty and time constraints, expanding the relevance of high bandwidth coordination beyond what Thompson had foreseen. But because it was expected to be the exception rather than the norm, the micro-dynamics of this form of coordination are seriously underdeveloped relative to our current need to understand them. Organizational scholars have begun to explore the micro-dynamics of coordination through theories of sense-making (Weick, 1993; Weick & Roberts, 1993; Crowston & Kammerer, 1998), expertise coordination (Faraj & Sproull, 2000; Faraj & Xiao, 2005), transactive memory (Liang et al., 1995) and social capital (Leana & Van Buren, 1999).

In this chapter, I explore the micro-dynamics of coordination in a work setting that is highly interdependent, uncertain and time-constrained. My qualitative analysis connects observations from the field with previous insights from the organizational literature, resulting in a more integrated theory of relational coordination. I propose that relationships provide the necessary bandwidth for coordinating work in settings with these characteristics, and specifically, that effective coordination in these settings is carried out through relationships of shared goals, shared knowledge and mutual respect. This relational theory of coordination goes beyond theories of mutual adjustment, sense-making, expertise coordination and transactive memory by expanding our understanding of the relational ties that underpin effective coordination. Consistent with contingency theory, relational forms of coordination are expected to be most useful under high levels of task interdependence, uncertainty and time constraints. However while many of the more recent theories emphasize the importance of shared knowledge or shared understandings, the theory of relational coordination argues that shared knowledge is necessary but not sufficient. If effective coordination is to occur, participants must also be connected by relationships of shared goals and mutual respect. These relationships matter, I suggest, because together they form the basis for collective identity and for coordinated collective action.

Methods
This relational theory of coordination emerged through a field study conducted in the context of the flight departure process. Repeated hundreds of times daily in dozens of locations, the success or failure of the flight departure process can make or break an airline's reputation for reliability. A highly interdependent set of tasks is performed under conditions of uncertainty and time constraints, between the arrival of the plane and its next departure, by representatives of 12 distinct functions: pilots, flight attendants, mechanics, gate agents, ticketing agents, ramp agents, baggage transfer agents, aircraft cleaners, caterers, fuelers, freight agents and operations agents. The wide array of functions involved in the flight departure process, and the differences in their functional perspectives create a significant challenge for coordination. The flight departure process is further complicated by rapid change in operational parameters like weather, connections and gate availability, such that information is often inaccurate, unavailable or obsolete. The executive vice-president of operations of a major US airline interviewed at the early stages of this study called the flight departure process one of the most complex work processes that an airline performs on a daily basis. A front-line employee explained: 'If everyone is trying to do their own thing, it's not going to work.'

Sample
The first site chosen for this study was a non-hub operation of American Airlines, selected based on researcher access and geographical convenience. The station manager there was working to improve performance of the airline departure process by improving communication and relationships across functional groups. It was common, she said, for employees at the ticket counter to be unaware of what baggage handlers and mechanics were doing, and vice versa. 'There has been, traditionally, an upstairs–downstairs split in the work process,' she said. In addition, members of the flight crews were remote from the airport-based work groups. Pilots just fly their flights then go out on their yachts, she said, rather than developing relationships with the other functional groups. 'By getting people to communicate and work together,' she argued, 'the efficiency of the operations could be greatly improved in a fairly short time.' She also believed that morale would increase as people understood how their work fitted into the overall process. Her efforts ended soon after however, when she left the company, perceiving a lack of support from the regional managers to whom she reported.

To develop the concept of relational coordination, I engaged in theoretical sampling based on maximizing differences (Glaser & Strauss, 1967; Eisenhardt, 1989). I chose as a second site a non-hub operation from another airline, Southwest Airlines, with a reputation for strong teamwork across functional boundaries. These two sites are identified hereafter as AMR and SWA.

Data collection and analysis
To develop valid theories of work and organization, it is useful and arguably necessary to observe directly how people work (Barley & Kunda, 2001). In order to understand the work that was being done, I shadowed employees as they carried out their tasks related to flight departures and observed their interactions with each other. To understand better what I was observing, I interviewed them while they worked, asking them to explain what they were doing and why. I also interviewed them in their break rooms, asking them to explain things I had observed while shadowing them. Interviews were unstructured and typically lasted from 15 to 30 minutes. I took notes recording my observations and their comments, and typed them up within a week of each visit. In typing up my notes, related observations were brought to mind and were recorded along with those captured in the original notes. I deliberately sought to understand the nature of interactions among employees in the flight departure process. I conducted 28 interviews and eight days of observations in AMR, and 20 interviews and five days of observations in SWA.

   To analyze the data collected at each site, I followed the guidelines suggested by Glaser and Strauss (1967) and Miles and Huberman (1984), developing empirically grounded sets of categories related to coordination of the flight departure process. I followed an iterative process, first developing hunches, then comparing those ideas to new data from the site, and further using the new data to decide whether to retain, revise or discard the inferences. My goal was not to impose a category scheme from the existing literature but rather to identify empirically the relevant dimensions of coordination. My criteria for identifying dimensions of coordination in this research setting were the following. First, that they described interactions among employees directly relevant to coordinating tasks in the flight departure process. This criterion resulted in a focus on interactions that occurred across functional boundaries, rather than within functional areas, because that is where the critical task interdependencies are expected to be. Second, that they had a plausible link to outcomes of the flight departure process.

   After the initial site visits, I compared my field notes across the two sites, looking in each site for evidence regarding the types of interactions that I had flagged in the other site. For some, I noted I had plentiful data from one site and little from the other. I had become sensitized to some issues in the second site that I had not noticed in the first. I then perused my notes from the first site, looking further for data that addressed that particular dimension. As I returned to each of the two sites for additional observations and interviews, I focused on the dimensions that had been overlooked. Again, I focused on these dimensions in the sense that when they arose in my observations or interviews, I asked follow-up questions and requested examples in order to develop a comparison with the other site.

Conceptualizing relational coordination

Communication
In the flight departure process, coordination occurred largely through communication. But the nature of that communication varied substantially between the two sites.

Frequency and timeliness   AMR employees expressed frustration with both the absence and the lateness of communication they needed from their colleagues to carry out their tasks. Reports of inadequate communication were common. According to a customer service supervisor at AMR: 'Here you don't communicate. And sometimes you end up not knowing things . . . Everyone says we need effective communication. But it's a low priority in action. On the gates I can't tell you the number of times you get the wrong information from ops. They tend to be optimistic. We call it the creeping delay. The hardest thing at the gates with off-schedule operations is to get information. They are leery to say the magnitude of the problem.' Similarly, an AMR gate agent reported: 'We have to rely on the maintenance group. If there's a delay, a problem with the operation, we have to be in touch with them. Through operations usually, but sometimes directly. It doesn't go especially well. Unfortunately those departments that don't deal directly with the public don't feel that sense of urgency. We get the brunt of it when other departments fail to load a bag, clean the cabin, tell us when there's going to be a mechanical delay . . . Timely communication is very, very important.'

At SWA, I observed more frequent and timely communication among employees. A SWA customer service supervisor reported: 'When there are irregular operations, bags have to be moved. There is constant communication between customer service and the ramp. Customer service will advise the ramp directly or through operations.' Similarly, a SWA customer service training coordinator explained: 'Ticketing calls the gate about late runners. If the flight is full, or you're running close to full, ticketing asks the gate if there's room before sending the customer up.' A SWA station manager reported: 'The pilot says the plane is broke when he calls in range to operations. The mechanic is usually here to meet the plane. If something is seriously wrong, we move to an off-terminal location and cancel the flight. If it's just two hours, we do an aircraft swap. Ops keeps everyone informed . . . It happens smoothly.' A SWA gate agent described the flow of communication. 'The ops agent is responsible for every bit of information going into the computer. We can tell the customer everything they need to know, because it's right there. Communication is ultimately the key.' Frequent and timely communication in turn enabled employees at SWA to respond quickly to changing circumstances.

Organizational theorists have long considered communication to be one of the primary ways that coordination is carried out (Benne & Sheats, 1948). Accordingly, many have explored the characteristics of communication that is carried out for the purpose of coordinating work processes (Van de Ven et al., 1976; Katz & Tushman, 1979; Argote, 1982; Allen, 1984; Ancona & Caldwell, 1992). In much of this work, the frequency of communication between various parties has played a central role. However communication around the flight departure process was also characterized in the data by its timeliness, a factor that has only recently begun to receive attention as a dimension of coordination (Orlikowski & Yates, 1991; Waller, 1999; Faraj & Xiao, 2005).

Problem-solving   The communication I observed in these two sites also differed in the degree to which it was focused on problem-solving rather than blaming when things went wrong. At AMR, employees involved in the flight departure process displayed a great deal of blaming and blame avoidance toward each other for late departures and other negative outcomes. There was a tendency to hide information to avoid blame for a delay, thus undermining the communication that was central to coordination. An AMR gate agent explained the tendency toward blaming: 'Around here when something goes wrong, everybody has to scramble. Unfortunately in this company when something goes wrong, they need to be able to pin it on someone. You should hear them fight over whose delay, which code. A lot of it has to do with which department gets charged.' The station manager at this site explained his philosophy: 'It helps a lot just to keep score. People are naturally competitive. They absolutely need to know the score. Once they know, they will do something about it. Every delay comes to my attention and gets a full investigation . . . The last thing most of them want is the spotlight on them. I just increased the amount they had to do to keep the spotlight off of themselves.'

By contrast, SWA employees were observed to communicate about the problem itself rather than assigning blame when difficulties occurred. When something went wrong, according to one representative description from a SWA pilot: 'We figure out the cause of the delay. We do not necessarily chastise, though sometimes that comes into play. It is a matter of working together. No finger-pointing, especially here and I'm sure that's the case elsewhere at Southwest.' A SWA station manager explained his philosophy: 'If there's a delay, we find out why it happened . . . Say there was a ten-minute delay because freight was excessive. If I'm screaming I won't know why it was late. They'll think, "He's an idiot, if only he knew." Then they'll start leaving stuff behind or they'll just shove it in and I won't know. If we ask, "Hey, what happened?", then the next day the problem is taken care of . . . You have to be in that mode every day. There's no one person who can do it. We all succeed together – and all fail together. You have to truly live it. I think we do here.'

Problem-solving communication enabled participants to adapt to unanticipated negative circumstances in a concerted way, thus playing a critical role in coordination. As Deming (1986) has argued, the resort to fault-finding rather than problem-solving is a common flaw in organizations that undermines the ability to engage in coordinated effort. Stevenson and Gilly (1993) explored emergent patterns of problem-solving communication, while Rubinstein (2000) identified problem-solving communication specifically as playing a central role in the coordination of work.

Relationships
But there seemed to be a deeper phenomenon at work, underlying these differences in communication patterns. In particular, the relationships of

shared goals, shared knowledge and mutual respect that I observed among SWA employees appeared to be substantially stronger than those I observed among AMR employees.

Shared goals   Relationships of shared goals appeared to be relatively weak at AMR. According to a customer service agent: 'If I sit back here for two hours [in the break room] I feel like nobody cares.' On the ramp, similar complaints were heard. According to a ramp manager: 'Ninety percent of the ramp employees don't care what happens. Even if the walls fall down, as long as they get their check.'

By contrast, shared goals at SWA appeared to be strong. According to a SWA customer service supervisor: 'The main thing is that everybody cares. We work in so many different areas but it doesn't matter. It's true from the top to the last one hired . . . Sometimes my friends ask me, why do you like to work at Southwest? I feel like a dork but it's because everybody cares.' At SWA, managers, supervisors and front-line employees in each functional area said their primary goals were safety, on-time performance and satisfying the customer. These goals seemed to be shared, in the sense that employees from each functional area referred to the same goals and could explain why they were important. When discussing the need for on-time performance, nearly everybody explained that 'our aircraft are valuable and they don't earn any money sitting on the ground'. A SWA flight attendant supervisor explained: 'Here it's one goal – one hundred percent customer service. Whatever it takes. You can see it just walking through the terminal. Rampers help board a flight. There's a desire to be part of the team.' According to a SWA pilot: 'From someone who drives the bus, as it were, if you don't mind my language, people work their asses off. I've never seen so many people work so hard to do one thing. You see people checking their watches to get the on-time departure. People work real hard. Then it's over and you're back on time.' From another pilot's perspective: 'When you come in [to the gate] and see everybody there ready to go to work, it makes you feel great.' Even outsiders emphasized SWA's uniqueness in this regard. A contract fueler for SWA explained: 'This airline is very different . . . Here, if there's something to do people want to do it right away. At USAir, it was "we still have 15 minutes".'

These observations suggest differences between AMR and SWA in the strength of shared goals. AMR employees did not seem to care so much about the outcomes of the overall process. Rather they were primarily concerned with avoiding blame for unsuccessful outcomes. Consistent with my observations at AMR, March and Simon (1958) described the potentially disintegrative effects of sub-goal optimization, when employees in an organization pursue their own task goals without reference to the over-arching goals of the work process in which they are engaged. Observations at SWA suggested that shared goals among participants in a work process can facilitate effective coordination. Consistent with these observations, other scholars have identified shared goals as playing an important role in enabling people to accomplish a set of interdependent tasks (Saavedra et al., 1993; Wageman, 1995).

Shared knowledge   Interviews with front-line employees at AMR revealed that they had little awareness of the overall process, and instead had a tendency to understand their own piece of the process to the exclusion of the rest. When asked what they were doing and why, AMR employees typically explained their own tasks without reference to the overall work process. 'When the bell rings, we know it's time to go out and unload the bags,' was a typical response when AMR employees were asked about how their jobs fit into the overall scheme of things.

By contrast, interviews with SWA front-line employees revealed relatively clear mental models of the overall work process – an understanding of the links between their own jobs and the jobs performed by their counterparts in other functions. When asked to explain what they were doing and why, the answers were typically couched in reference to the overall process. These descriptions by SWA employees typically took the form: 'The pilot has to do A, B and C before he can take off, so I need to be sure I get this to him right away.' After completing a flight departure, an operations agent explained to me that it was critical for her to accurately and quickly document information regarding bags, passengers and freight on the flight and send it along to the down-line station in order to facilitate the next turnaround. She explained how each piece of information she was entering into the computer would be used by colleagues at the down-line station to expedite the next turnaround. Rather than just knowing what to do, SWA employees knew why, based on shared knowledge of how the overall process worked. One pilot explained SWA's strength with regards to shared knowledge: 'Everyone knows exactly what to do . . . Each part has a great relationship with the rest . . . There are no great secrets . . . Everyone knows what everyone else is doing.'

In sum, employees at AMR appeared to have only a vague notion of the tasks their colleagues in other functional areas needed to accomplish during the flight departure process, and of the implications for their own tasks. SWA employees, by comparison, were linked by a shared understanding of the overall work process, and a shared understanding of the role that each of them played in that work process, despite their distinct roles and the distinct locations in which they worked.

Consistent with my observations at AMR, Dougherty (1992) showed in a study of new product development that employees from different functional backgrounds often reside in different 'thought worlds' due to differences in their training, socialization and expertise. She showed that these thought worlds were obstacles to effective communication and that they tended to undermine coordination of the new product development process. Consistent with my observations at SWA, sense-making theory suggests that collective mind, or shared understanding of the work process by those who are participants in it (Weick, 1993; Weick & Roberts, 1993; Crowston & Kammerer, 1998), can link distinct thought worlds and therefore enhance coordination. Transactive memory theory further supports the notion that when people understand each other's areas of expertise, they have a greater sum of knowledge upon which to draw (Liang et al., 1995). This shared understanding in turn facilitates the coordination of expertise (Faraj & Sproull, 2000; Faraj & Xiao, 2005).

Mutual respect   Status boundaries between employees in different functions appeared to pose a significant obstacle to coordination in the airline industry. Among station employee groups, there has been a tradition of name-calling like 'agent trash' and 'ramp rats.' As one gate agent explained to me, 'They call them ramp rats for a reason – they're pigs.' There is a hierarchy on the ramp that starts with the highly paid mechanics and ends with cabin cleaners. Some of these barriers are due to the very different work that each group does, and to the geographic distance that divides these groups, even though their work is highly interdependent. The pilots are at the top of the status hierarchy and tend to consider themselves to be first among equals. As one pilot explained: 'Pilots are great at being self-righteous. It's something about the job. The major airlines treat you well. People do what you say. It brings out a certain decisiveness that becomes arrogance.'

At AMR, status boundaries were perceived to be very real and to pose an obstacle to coordination. The relationships between the pilots and other groups were particularly problematic. According to a vice-president of AMR: 'Pilots are fundamentally unsupervised workers but we rarely have discipline problems within the cockpit. It is in the interface with other groups . . . He may be able to tell the copilot what to do, but he can't tell other people what to do. Yet he will try.' According to a station manager at AMR, ramp workers in particular 'have a tremendous inferiority complex. They think everyone is looking down on them. The pilots don't respect them.' This status barrier between the two groups had clear consequences for delays, according to the AMR station manager: 'We had a problem . . . with parking airplanes when they arrived. Captains would have to wait for the crews to come out and direct them in. The crews wouldn't necessarily be in any hurry to get out there.' Status barriers were also apparent between flight attendants and ramp workers at AMR. A cabin cleaner at AMR explained: 'It all comes down to respect. As long as the flight attendants think they're better than [us] when they're sleeping five to an apartment and they're just waitresses in the sky.'

Status boundaries not only divided flight and ground crews at AMR, but were rampant among AMR ground employees as well. According to a ramp supervisor at AMR: 'There are employees working here who think they're better than other employees. Gate and ticket agents think they're better than the ramp. The ramp think they're better than cabin services, think it's a sissy, woman's job. Then the cabin cleaners look down on the building cleaners. The mechanics think the ramp are a bunch of luggage handlers . . . I don't know how you break down that barrier, so that everyone says I am an employee of American, period.' An AMR ramp crew chief confirmed these status divisions: 'Cabin cleaning is like a stepchild. All of us have that attitude. "Get out of here and do your job." It's a macho thing – we call them pillow fluffers.' A customer service supervisor at AMR reported the apparent lack of respect she and her colleagues received from maintenance: 'Maintenance, they are highly specialized and won't talk. They don't have a sense of urgency. You ask them what's wrong with the plane and they look at you like you're female and wouldn't understand if they told you.' She reported that maintenance communicates with the ops center and the pilots 'but they just don't seem to take seriously the "little girl' at the gate."'

At SWA, by contrast, employees appeared to treat each other with a great deal of respect. A SWA manager of ramp and operations explained: 'There's a code, a way you respond to every individual who works for Southwest. The easiest way to get in trouble here is to offend another employee. We need people to respond favorably. It promotes good working relationships.' SWA employees were observed to speak respectfully of their colleagues in other functions and to interact comfortably with them, whether that person's job was to empty the toilets or fly the plane. According to a SWA customer service agent: 'No one takes the job of another person for granted. The skycap is just as critical as the pilot. You can always count on the next guy standing there. No one department is any more important than another.'

An operations agent compared SWA to other airlines: 'I would never go work at American Airlines. The animosity there is tremendous. Here it's so cool. Whether you have a college degree or a GED it doesn't matter. There's no status here, just a good work ethic.' Another SWA operations agent had a similar comment when asked about the relationship between operations and ramp agents: 'Some of us have degrees and some of us don't. But it doesn't matter. We need all of these positions.' One of SWA's chief pilots gave his perspective: 'It's this mutual respect that is not easily transported from one organization to another.' Another SWA pilot explained to me: 'We're predisposed to liking each other – I like the flight attendants and even that guy over there and I don't even know him. I guess it's mutual respect.'

Van Maanen and Barley's (1984) work on occupational communities suggests that members of distinct occupational communities are often divided by differences in status and that these communities may bolster their own status by actively cultivating disrespect for the work performed by others. As seen at AMR, when members of these distinct occupational communities are engaged in a common work process, the potential for these divisive relationships to undermine collective identity and effective coordination is apparent. Consistent with the patterns I observed at SWA, some have argued that respect for the competence of other employees in a work process may be fundamental to the coordination of interdependent work processes, whether in the context of research and development (Rubenstein, et al., 1971) or jazz improvisation (Eisenberg, 1990).

Relational coordination
The data presented above suggest that coordination does not occur in a relational vacuum. Relationships of shared goals, shared knowledge and mutual respect appear to play a critical role.

When positive, these relationships enabled employees to coordinate effectively the work process in which they were engaged by supporting frequent, timely, problem-solving communication. When negative, these same relationships served as obstacles. Employees who felt disrespected by members of another function avoided communication (and even eye contact) with members of that function. The absence of frequent dialogue in turn solidified the existence of distinct 'thought worlds' for each functional area, undermining relationships of shared knowledge. Without relationships of shared knowledge, employees were less able to engage in timely communication when circumstances changed, not knowing with sufficient precision who needed to know what and with what urgency. The lack of timely communication undermined relationships of shared goals, reinforcing the belief that each function was looking out for itself. Without shared goals, the easiest response to problems was to blame others for having caused the problem rather than to engage in problem-solving communication. The focus of communication around blaming rather than problem-solving further undermined mutual respect. This negative cycle decreased the potential for effective coordination to occur.

Figure 5.1 illustrates the mutually reinforcing ties between these dimensions that comprise relational coordination, and shows how relationships and communication ties can reinforce one another in a positive direction as at SWA or in a negative direction as at AMR.

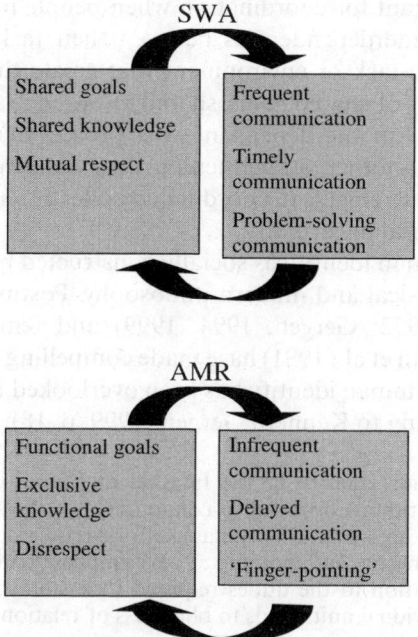

Figure 5.1 Mutually reinforcing dynamics among the dimensions of relational coordination

Discussion

In this chapter I am seeking to develop a relational theory of coordination through qualitative analysis of field data gathered in the context of the flight departure process, a work setting that is highly interdependent, uncertain and time-constrained. I have combined observations from the field with insights from organizational theory to develop a more integrated theory of relational coordination, and have concluded that relational coordination is coordination carried out through frequent, timely, problem-solving communication, supported by relationships of shared goals, shared knowledge and mutual respect.

At a deeper level, why do relationships matter for coordination? I suggest these relationships matter because they are the means through which our identities are constructed. Through relationships, others influence the development of our identities, just as we influence the development of theirs. Relationships of shared goals, shared knowledge and mutual respect help to build collective identity, a sense of 'we', which in turn facilitates the effective coordination of work. These relationships are expected to be particularly important for coordination when people must adjust to each other due to the interdependencies between their tasks, and due to the uncertainties in the task or environment that create the need for adjustment. Relationships of shared goals, shared knowledge and mutual respect enable employees in an interdependent work process to embrace their connections with one another, strengthening their collective identity and in turn enabling them to engage in coordinated collective action in the face of task or environmental uncertainty.

This view of human identity as socially constructed represents a departure from both classical and modern philosophy. Postmodern (Habermas, 1971; Foucault, 1972; Gergen, 1994, 1999) and feminist philosophers (Miller, 1978; Jordan et al., 1991) have made compelling arguments that the relational basis of human identity has been overlooked in our individualistic society. According to Kenneth Gergen (1999, p. 18):

> If we hold the individual to be the fundamental atom of society, so do we emphasize separation as opposed to community . . . As a result we give little attention to relations – to the coordinated efforts required, for example, to generate knowledge, reason and morality . . . We emphasize individual rights while paying little attention to the duties required to sustain our communities . . . Attention to individual units leads to blindness of relationship.

Furthermore, Fletcher (1998, 1999) has argued that the way people work together cannot be fully understood without this relational perspective. Although the division of labor is a powerful source of efficiency and productivity (Smith, 1776), there is also a potential alienation and fragmentation of human identity that accompanies this division of labor (Marx, 1845; Freud, 1927; Durkheim, 1933). Relationships serve to overcome the alienation created by the division of labor by creating more holistic, social identities in place of the more partial and fragmented identities that lead people to reject their connections with others. Collective identity at work depends on the recognition by each participant that his or her role in the work setting is connected to and valued by other participants, and that this collective identity is developed through relationships of shared knowledge, shared goals and mutual respect. These relationships are integral to coordination because they enable the formation of collective identity, which in turn facilitates coordinated collective action.

In addition to social construction, relational coordination builds upon several other streams of theory to make a distinctive contribution to our understanding of the micro-dynamics of coordination. Social capital theory is built upon the insight that value is embedded not only in physical capital and human capital, but also in the communication and relationship ties that exist among people (Burt, 1997; Nahapiet & Ghoshal, 1998). To understand organizations as social communities, one must look at the network of communication and relationship ties that bind parties together. Leana and Van Buren (1999) take an additional step, arguing that communication and relationship ties are relevant to the achievement of coordination. The theory of relational coordination goes further however, identifying the specific relational dimensions that matter for coordination – shared knowledge, shared goals and mutual respect.

Theories of sense-making, expertise coordination and transactive memory have also contributed to our understanding of the micro-dynamics of coordination. Sense-making theory suggests that collective mind, or shared understanding of the work process by those who are participants in it, is needed for effective coordination (Weick and Roberts, 1993; Weick, 1993; Crowston & Kammerer, 1998). Expertise coordination theory elucidates the challenges of coordinating across differences in specialized knowledge, and suggests the importance of developing shared understandings in the face of uncertainty and time constraints (Faraj & Sproull, 2000; Faraj & Xiao, 2005). Transactive memory theory argues that knowing the areas of expertise of others enables people to draw upon a larger body of collective knowledge, in a sense creating a collective mind that is distributed across multiple individual minds (Wegner et al., 1985; Liang et al., 1995).

Clearly, other scholars have recognized the importance of shared knowledge for coordinated collective action. Shared knowledge informs employees how their tasks fit relative to other tasks in the work process, enabling them to act with regard for the overall work process. Shared knowledge thus forms the cognitive basis for coordination. But shared knowledge is not enough. If effective coordination is to occur, participants must also be connected by relationships of shared goals and mutual respect. Shared goals motivate employees to act with regard for the overall work process. Mutual respect encourages employees to value the contributions of the others who are involved in the work process and to consider the impact of their own actions on the ability of others to do their work. These high-quality relationships together encourage frequent, high-quality communication, which in turn reinforces high-quality relationships, while low-quality relationships have the opposite effect. While shared knowledge forms the cognitive basis for coordination, shared goals and mutual respect can be seen as providing the energy and emotion that others have argued are essential for the effective coordination of work (Quinn & Dutton, 2005).

The theory of relational coordination is not complete and will require further work for its development. In particular, it is beyond the scope of this chapter to ask how organizations foster high levels of relational coordination among their employees, or fail to do so. The AMR scenario described in this chapter is consistent with Emile Durkheim's (1933) theory regarding the alienating effects of the division of labor, in which he claims that the work we do results in the formation of partial, fragmented identities that prevent us from recognizing our connections with others. Alienation may not be a necessary outgrowth of the division of labor however, but rather may result from the way our organizations are designed. As Michael Piore (1992: 20) argued:

> The organizational principles involved in Taylorism and Fordism have pushed us to . . . restrict communication among the people responsible for the way in which the different parts are performed . . . They have led us to divide the internal structure of large organizations into a series of functionally distinct divisions as well . . . But from the cognitive perspective, the problem is that it limits the hermeneutic process, the cycle back and forth between parts and wholes, through which cognitive structures evolve.
>
> If one looks at innovations in business practice and the critique of existing organizational structures within the management literature, the thrust is in precisely the opposite direction. The attempt is to break down barriers . . . between divisions and departments, and encourage direct, rich and textured communication ... forcing people who previously operated at arms length to confront coordination problems directly and resolve them cooperatively.

Though these organizational structures are beyond the scope of this chapter, other work has begun to identify organizational structures that support relational coordination and those that undermine it (for example, Gittell, 2000a, 2000b, 2001, 2002, 2003a; Gittell & Weiss, 2004). We have found that some structures like supervision and standardized protocols that have traditionally been argued to reduce the need for relational forms of coordination, as explained at the start of this chapter, work instead by facilitating relational coordination when they are properly designed (Gittell, 2003b). However it remains to be explored why some organizations have established structures that support relational coordination, while others neglect to do so and still others try to do so and fail, as did the station manager at AMR. More work is needed in this arena therefore to specify the structures that support relational coordination, as well as the obstacles to their adoption.

Finally, relational coordination has the virtue of being readily measurable, thus making the theory of relational coordination readily amenable to empirical exploration. The survey instrument shown in Appendix 1 was developed to measure relational coordination in the context of the flight departure process, to test the impact of relational coordination on objective measures of quality and efficiency performance, and to test hypotheses regarding the impact of organizational factors on achieving relational coordination. The instrument is designed to be given to all participants in a particular cross-functional work process whose tasks appear to be interdependent and in need of coordination. This instrument was used to show the impact of relational coordination on flight departure performance (Gittell, 2001, 2003). In addition, it has already been adapted for use in hospitals (Gittell et al., 2000; Gittell, 2002), in nursing homes (Bishop et al., 2003), and in local criminal justice systems (Bond, 2004). The data gathered from this instrument enable the construction of network measures of relational coordination which can be combined across all survey respondents, or which can be broken down to examine specific ties between particular functional groups, say between pilots and flight attendants, or between doctors and nurses. This network approach to measuring relational coordination is therefore conducive to the original goal of exploring the micro-dynamics of coordination and understanding the precise relational underpinnings of the coordination process.

In sum, the challenges ahead for coordination theory are many. There has been a recent explosion of interest in the relational underpinnings of coordination. Much of this interest is inspired by the influential works of Karl Weick on sense-making (1993) and the shared understandings that underpin effective coordination or heedful interrelating (Weick and Roberts, 1993). A challenge for coordination theorists going forward will be to consider multiple relational dimensions of coordination and to avoid reducing coordination to a process of shared cognition. Rather, we should remain open to exploring other relational dimensions such as shared goals, mutual respect or even trust, so that together we can build a rich, multi-dimensional theory of coordination.

Appendix I: Sample Relational Coordination Instrument[*]
Who Do You Communicate With?

[AIRLINE NAME, AIRPORT NAME]

Please circle the best answer to each question.

THANK YOU FOR TAKING THE TIME TO COMPLETE THIS
SURVEY!

1. *How* frequently *do you communicate with people in each of these groups about flight departures?*

	Never	Rarely	Occasionally	Often	Constantly
Pilots	1	2	3	4	5
Flight attendants	1	2	3	4	5
Gate agents	1	2	3	4	5
Ticketing agents	1	2	3	4	5
Ramp agents	1	2	3	4	5
Baggage transfer agents	1	2	3	4	5
Freight agents	1	2	3	4	5
Mechanics	1	2	3	4	5
Operations agents	1	2	3	4	5
Cabin cleaning	1	2	3	4	5
Fueling	1	2	3	4	5
Catering	1	2	3	4	5

2. *Do people in these groups communicate with you in a* timely *way about flight departures?*

	Never	Rarely	Occasionally	Often	Always
Pilots	1	2	3	4	5
Flight attendants	1	2	3	4	5
Gate agents	1	2	3	4	5
Ticketing agents	1	2	3	4	5
Ramp agents	1	2	3	4	5
Baggage transfer agents	1	2	3	4	5
Freight agents	1	2	3	4	5
Mechanics	1	2	3	4	5
Operations agents	1	2	3	4	5
Cabin cleaning	1	2	3	4	5
Fueling	1	2	3	4	5
Catering	1	2	3	4	5

3. When problems occur with flight departures, do people in these groups blame others or work with you to solve the problem?

	Blame others		Neither		Solve the problem
Pilots	1	2	3	4	5
Flight attendants	1	2	3	4	5
Gate agents	1	2	3	4	5
Ticketing agents	1	2	3	4	5
Ramp agents	1	2	3	4	5
Baggage transfer agents	1	2	3	4	5
Freight agents	1	2	3	4	5
Mechanics	1	2	3	4	5
Operations agents	1	2	3	4	5
Cabin cleaning	1	2	3	4	5
Fueling	1	2	3	4	5
Catering	1	2	3	4	5

4. How much do people in each of these groups know about the work you do?

	Nothing	Little	Some	A lot	Everything
Pilots	1	2	3	4	5
Flight attendants	1	2	3	4	5
Gate agents	1	2	3	4	5
Ticketing agents	1	2	3	4	5
Ramp agents	1	2	3	4	5
Baggage transfer agents	1	2	3	4	5
Freight agents	1	2	3	4	5
Mechanics	1	2	3	4	5
Operations agents	1	2	3	4	5
Cabin cleaning	1	2	3	4	5
Fueling	1	2	3	4	5
Catering	1	2	3	4	5

5.   *How much do people in each of these groups* respect *the work you do?*

	Not at all	A little	Somewhat	A lot	Completely
Pilots	1	2	3	4	5
Flight attendants	1	2	3	4	5
Gate agents	1	2	3	4	5
Ticketing agents	1	2	3	4	5
Ramp agents	1	2	3	4	5
Baggage transfer agents	1	2	3	4	5
Freight agents	1	2	3	4	5
Mechanics	1	2	3	4	5
Operations agents	1	2	3	4	5
Cabin cleaning	1	2	3	4	5
Fueling	1	2	3	4	5
Catering	1	2	3	4	5

6.   *How much do people in each of these groups* share your goals *for flight departures?*

	Not at all	A little	Somewhat	A lot	Completely
Pilots	1	2	3	4	5
Flight attendants	1	2	3	4	5
Gate agents	1	2	3	4	5
Ticketing agents	1	2	3	4	5
Ramp agents	1	2	3	4	5
Baggage transfer agents	1	2	3	4	5
Freight agents	1	2	3	4	5
Mechanics	1	2	3	4	5
Operations agents	1	2	3	4	5
Cabin cleaning	1	2	3	4	5
Fueling	1	2	3	4	5
Catering	1	2	3	4	5

Note: *This instrument has been adapted for use in health-care settings (for example Gittell, 2002), and can be adapted for use in any cross-functional work process.

References

Allen, T. (1984), *Managing the Flow of Technology*, Cambridge, MA: MIT Press.
Ancona, D.G. & Caldwell D.F. (1992), Bridging the boundary: external activity and performance in organizational teams, *Administrative Science Quarterly*, 37, 634–65.
Argote, L. (1982), Input uncertainty and organizational coordination in hospital emergency units, *Administrative Science Quarterly*, 27 (3), 420–34.
Barley, S. & Kunda, G. (2001), Bringing work back in, *Organization Science*, 12 (1), 76–95.
Benne, K.D. & Sheats, P. (1948), Functional roles of group members, *Journal of Social Issues*, 4, 41–9.
Bishop, C., Eaton, S., Gittell, J.H. & Weinberg, D. (2003), Improving institutional long-term care for residents and workers: the effect of leadership, relationships and work design, research proposal to Robert Wood Johnson Foundation and Atlantic Philanthropies.
Bond, B. (2004), Organizational management of offender reentry: do effective strategic change

models exist?, dissertation proposal, Brandeis University, Heller School for Social Policy and Management.

Burt, R.S. (1997), The contingent value of social capital, *Administrative Science Quarterly*, **42**, 338–65.

Crowston, K. & Kammerer, E.E. (1998), Coordination and collective mind in software requirements development, *IBM Systems Journal*, **372**, 227–45.

Daft, R.L. & Lengel, R.H. (1986), Organizational information requirements, media richness and structural design, *Management Science*, **32** (5), 554–71.

Deming, W.E. (1986), *Out of the Crisis*, Cambridge, MA: Massachusetts Institute of Technology Press.

Dougherty, D. (1992), Interpretive barriers to successful product innovation in large firms, *Organization Science*, **3** (2), 179–202.

Durkheim, E. (1933), *The Division of Labor in Society*, New York: MacMillan.

Eisenberg, E. (1990), Jamming: transcendence through organizing, *Communication Research*, **17**, 139–64.

Eisenhardt, K.M. (1989), Building theories from case study research, *Academy of Management Review*, **14** (4), 532–50.

Faraj, S. & Sproull, L. (2000), Coordinating expertise in software development teams, *Management Science*, **46** (12), 1554–68.

Faraj, S. & Xiao, Y. (2006), Coordination in fast response organizations, *Management Science*.

Fletcher, J. (1999), *Disappearing Acts: Gender, Power and Relational Practice at Work*, Cambridge, MA: MIT Press.

Fletcher, J.K. (1998), Relational practice: a feminist reconstruction of work, *Journal of Management Inquiry*, **7** (2), 163–86.

Foucault, M. (1972), *The Archaeology of Knowledge*, New York: Harper Colophon.

Freud, S. (1927), *Civilization and its Discontents*, New York: W.W. Norton & Company, Inc. (this edition 1989).

Galbraith, J. (1977), *Organization Design*, Reading, MA: Addison-Wesley.

Gergen, K.J. (1999), *An Invitation to Social Construction*, Thousand Oak, CA: Sage Publications.

Gergen, K.J. (1994), *Realities and Relationships: Soundings in Social Construction*, Cambridge, MA: Harvard University Press.

Gittell, J.H. (2000a), Organizing work to support relational coordination, *International Journal of Human Resource Management*, **11** (3), 517–39.

Gittell, J.H. (2000b), Paradox of coordination and control, *California Management Review*, **42** (3), 177–83.

Gittell, J.H. (2001), Supervisory span, relational coordination and flight departure performance: a reassessment of post-bureaucracy theory, *Organization Science*, **12** (4), 467–82.

Gittell, J.H. (2002), Coordinating mechanisms in care provider groups: Relational coordination as a mediator and input uncertainty as a moderator of performance effects, *Management Science*, **48** (11), 1408–26.

Gittell, J.H. (2003a), *The Southwest Airlines Way: Using the Power of Relationships to Achieve High Performance*, New York: McGraw-Hill.

Gittell, J.H. (2003b), A theory of relational coordination, in Cameron, K., Dutton, J.E., Quinn, R. (eds), *Positive Organizational Scholarship: Foundations of a New Discipline*, San Francisco, CA: Berrett-Koehler Publishing.

Gittell, J.H., Fairfield, K., Bierbaum, B., Jackson, R., Kelly, M., Laskin, R., Lipson, S., Siliski, J., Thornhill, T. & Zuckerman, J. (2000), Impact of relational coordination on quality of care, post-operative pain and functioning, and length of stay: A nine-hospital study of surgical patients, *Medical Care*, **38** (8), 807–19.

Gittell, J.H. & Weiss, L. (2004), Coordination networks within and across organizations: A multi-level framework, *Journal of Management Studies*, **41** (1), 127–53.

Glaser, B. & Strauss, A. (1967), *The Discovery of Grounded Theory: Strategies of Qualitative Research*, London: Wiedenfield and Nicholson.

Habermas, J. (1971), *Knowledge and Human Interest*, Boston, MA: Beacon Press.

Jordan, J.V., Kaplan, A.G., Miller, J.B., Stiver, I.P. & Surry, J.L. (1991), *Women's Growth in Connection: Writings from the Stone Center*, New York: Guilford Press.

Katz, R. & Tushman, M. (1979), Communication patterns, project performance and task characteristics: an empirical evaluation and integration in an R&D setting, *Organizational Behavior and Human Performance*, **23**, 139–62.

Kogut, B. & Zander, U. (1996), What firms do? Coordination, identity and learning, *Organization Science*, **7** (5), 502–18.

Leana, C. & Van Buren, H.J., III (1999), Organizational social capital and employment practices, *Academy of Management Review*, **24**, 538–55.

Liang, D.W., Moreland, R. & Argote, L. (1995), Group versus individual training and group performance: the mediating role of group transactive memory, *Personality and Social Psychology Bulletin*, **21** (4), 384–93.

March, J.G. & Simon, H.A. (1958), *Organizations*, New York: Wiley.

Marx, K. (1845), The German ideology, in Feuer, L. (ed.), *Marx and Engels: Basic Writings on Politics and Philosophy*, New York: Anchor Books (this edition 1959).

Miles, M.B. & Huberman, A.M. (1984), *Qualitative Data Analysis: A Source Book of New Methods*, Beverly Hills, CA: Sage.

Miller, J.B. (1978), *Toward a New Psychology of Women*, Boston, MA: Beacon Press.

Nahapiet, J. & Ghoshal, S. (1998), Social capital, intellectual capital and the organizational advantage, *Academy of Management Review*, **23**, 242–66.

Orlikowski, W.J. & Yates, J. (1991), Genre repertoire: the structuring of communicative practices in organizations, *Administrative Science Quarterly*, **394**, 541–74.

Piore, M. (1992), The social embeddedness of labor markets and cognitive processes, presented to the European Association of Labor Economists, September.

Quinn, R.W. & Dutton, J.E. (2005), Coordination as energy-in-conversation, *Academy of Management Review*, **30** (1), 36–57.

Rubenstein, A., Barth, R. & Douds, C. (1971), Ways to improve communications between R&D groups, *Research Management*, **14**, 49.

Rubinstein, S. (2000), The impact of co-management on quality performance: the case of the Saturn Corporation, *Industrial and Labor Relations Review*, **53** (1), 197–220.

Saavedra, R., Earley, P.C. & Van Dyne, L. (1993), Complex interdependence in task-performing groups, *Journal of Applied Psychology*, **78** (1), 61–72.

Smith, A. (1776), *The Wealth of Nations*, Cannan, E. (ed.), New York: Modern Library (this edition 2000).

Stevenson, W.B. & Gilly, M.C. (1993), Problem-solving networks in organizations: intentional design and emergent structure, *Social Science Research*, **22**, 92–113.

Thompson, J. (1967), *Organizations in Action: Social Science Bases of Administrative Theory*, New York: McGraw-Hill.

Tushman, M. & Nadler, D. (1978), Information processing as an integrating concept in organizational design, *Academy of Management Review*, **3** (3), 613–24.

Van de Ven, A., Delbecq, A. & Koenig, R., Jr. (1976), Determinants of coordination modes within organizations, *American Sociological Review*, **41**, 322–38.

Van Maanen, J. & Barley, S.R. (1984), Occupational communities: culture and control in organizations, in Staw, B.M. & Cummings, L.L. (eds), *Research in Organizational Behavior*, **6**, Greenwich, CT: JAI Press, pp. 287–365.

Wageman, R. (1995), Interdependence and group effectiveness, *Administrative Science Quarterly*, **40**, 145–80.

Waller, M.J. (1999), The timing of adaptive group responses to non-routine events, *Academy of Management Journal*, **42** (2), 127–37.

Wegner, D.M., Giuliano, T. & Hertel, P.T. (1985), Cognitive interdependence in close relationships, in Ickes, W.J. (ed.), *Compatible and Incompatible Relationships*, New York: Springer-Verlag.

Weick, K. (1993), The collapse of sense-making in organizations: the Mann Gulch disaster, *Administrative Science Quarterly*, **38**, 628–52.

Weick, K. & Roberts, K. (1993), Collective mind in organizations: heedful interrelating on flight decks, *Administrative Science Quarterly*, **38**, 357–81.

6 Stress and burnout: a relational perspective
*Ayala Malach Pines**

In the last decade stress has become one of the hottest areas of psychological research (numbering close to 28 000 studies). While less so than stress, burnout has also been a frequent topic of research (with over 1000 studies in the last decade). Burnout is often conceptualized within the framework of stress research (for example Farber, 1983; Paine, 1982) and people tend to use 'burnout' and 'stress' interchangeably. Nevertheless the two are different concepts with different etiologies.

Stress was defined by pioneer stress researcher Hans Selye as 'the non-specific result of any demand upon the body, be the effect mental or somatic.' (Selye, 1956, 1993). The stress reaction is the same regardless of the type of stressor in both animals and people. Other stress researchers (for example Aldwin, 1994; Sarason & Spielberger, 1979; Spielberger, 1979; Lazarus, 1966, 1993, 2000) view it as a broader relational concept that describes outcomes of interactions between the environment and the individual. Lazarus's cognitive–motivational–relational stress formulation for example emphasizes the mediating effects of appraisal and coping in the stress process.

Burnout, on the other hand, is the end result of a process in which highly motivated and committed individuals lose their spirit (for example Freudenberger, 1980: 13; Maslach, 1982: 3; Pines & Aronson, 1988: 9). Burnout happens most often to people who entered their careers with high hopes, ideals and ego involvement. It is experienced as a state of physical, emotional and mental exhaustion (Pines & Aronson, 1988), and a lowered sense of accomplishment (Maslach, 1982).

Stress is rarely the primary reason for burnout. An example is provided by a nurse who said: 'The days I enjoy work most are the days in which I work the hardest' whereas the most burnout causing days are 'when there is a patient that can not be helped'. For this nurse, it is not strenuous physical work but the perceived inability to help patients in pain that is the cause of burnout (Pines, 2000a).

Different conceptualizations have been used to explain burnout: psychoanalytic theory (Fischer, 1983; Freudenberger, 1980), social comparison theory (Buunk et al., 1994), social exchange theory (Schaufeli et al., 1996;

van Yperen et al., 1992), equity theory (van Dierendonck et al., 1994), social competence (Harrison, 1983), and the job demands–controls model (de Rijk et al., 1998; Landsbergis, 1988). Yet burnout is still described as a phenomenon in search of a theory (for example Burisch, 1993).

The present chapter proposes an existential perspective as especially suitable to explain the etiology of burnout and thus help differentiate it from the more general concept of stress. The implications of the existential approach to burnout are discussed from a relational perspective, a perspective that does not treat individuals as functioning independently, but rather in terms of their interconnections and dynamic relationships with other individuals in their and other work teams, organizations and cultures. It is assumed that the way workers interact with each other and with their service recipients, and the kinds of relationships they form in and out of the organization, are critical to the way they experience and express burnout.

The existential perspective on burnout

According to the existential perspective, the root cause of burnout lies in people's need to believe that their lives are meaningful, that the things they do are useful, important, even 'heroic' (for example Pines, 1993). Victor Frankl (1976) wrote that 'the striving to find meaning in one's life is the primary motivational force in man' (p. 154). Ernest Becker (1973) argued, similarly, that people's need to believe that the things they do are meaningful is their way of coping with the angst caused by facing their mortality. In order to be able to deny death we need to feel heroic, to know that our lives are meaningful, that we matter in the larger 'cosmic' scheme of things. According to Becker, people choose to become 'heroes' according to their culturally prescribed 'hero system'. In previous eras, religion was most often the chosen system. Today, for many people, religion is no longer adequate. For people who have rejected the religious answer to the existential quest, one of the most frequently chosen alternatives is work. People who choose this alternative try to derive from their work a sense of meaning for their entire life.

People who expect to derive a sense of existential significance from their work enter their professions with high hopes, goals and expectations, are idealistic and motivated, and relate to their work as a calling. When these hopes, goals and expectations do not materialize, they feel that they have failed, that their work is insignificant, that they make no difference in the world. They start feeling helpless and hopeless and eventually burn out.

The present chapter attempts to differentiate between the general concept of stress and burnout based on the existential perspective, using a wide range of subjects and occupations including especially nursing, police, teaching and management.

The following hypotheses were tested:

1. *Burnout will be correlated with lack of a sense of significance at work.*

2. *Burnout will not always be correlated with stress at work, but will always be correlated with lack of significance at work.*

3. *The identified causes of burnout will be related to frustrated goals and expectations.*

Method

Subjects

Three sets of subjects were used to test the three hypotheses. The first set included four groups of professionals: 100 Israeli hospital nurses primarily women, 97 Israeli teachers primarily women, 66 Israeli managers primarily men and 267 American police officers primarily men. The first set also included a group of 17 Israeli blue-collar workers, a group of 50 Israeli retirees, 25 men and 25 women, and two national samples, one with 511 Israeli Jews (a representative sample of the Jewish population – 82 percent of the total Israeli population) the other with 505 Israeli Arabs (a representative sample of the Arab population – 18 percent of the total Israeli population). Sampling was random and was done using stratification based on demographics. Of the Jewish sample, 54 percent were women; of the Arab sample 62 percent were women. Total N in this set of subjects was 1613.

The second set included nine professional and two non-professional samples. The professional samples included two samples of Israeli nurses (100 hospital nurses and 216 dialysis nurses), two samples of teachers (97 Israeli high, secondary and elementary school teachers and 271 American elementary and high school teachers), two samples of Israeli managers (66 high-level managers and 40 low-level transportation managers) and three samples of police officers (267 American police officers and two Israeli samples, 20 each, of traffic officers and an elite crime detection unit). The non-professional samples included 40 subordinates of the low-level transportation managers and 17 blue-collar workers. Total N in this set was 1154.

Some of the studies were conducted expressly to test the hypothesis that stress is not correlated with burnout (for example the study of transportation managers and their subordinates, the study comparing traffic police officers to an elite crime unit and the study of blue-collar workers). Some of the studies tested various correlates of burnout and the aspects related to stress were a by-product (for example the studies of American police officers and teachers and the studies of Israeli nurses and managers).

The third set of subjects included Israeli and American managers, nurses, teachers and police officers who participated in burnout workshops.

Measures
The study included both quantitative and qualitative measures. The quantitative measures included the Burnout Measure, a question about the work's importance and significance, and questions about different aspects of work that seemed related to the distinction between stress and burnout. The qualitative data was gathered during burnout workshops. It involved a multi-step exercise that analysed the professionals' goals, expectations and burnout-causing stresses.

Quantitative measures   The Burnout Measure (BM) (Pines & Aronson, 1988) is the second most frequently used measure of burnout after the Maslach Burnout Inventory (MBI) (Enzmann et al., 1998; Schaufeli & Enzmann, 1998). While the MBI was originally designed to measure burnout in human service professions, the BM was designed for use with all occupational and non-occupational groups, and thus was more appropriate for the current investigation. The BM is a self-report measure. It includes 21 items that are evaluated on seven-point frequency scales. The items assess the person's level of physical, emotional and mental exhaustion. Factor analyses suggest that the BM is a unidimensional measure (for example Cochran, 1986; Justine et al., 1981) even though there is research suggesting that it may involve three dimensions (physical, emotional, cognitive) (Schaufeli & Van Dierendonck, 1996; Enzmann et al., 1998). The BM is considered a reliable and valid research instrument (for example Schaufeli & Enzmann, 1998; Schaufeli & Van Dierendonck, 1996) with internal consistency coefficients exceeding 90 and a relatively high stability as indicated by a test–retest coefficient (r) ranging from 0.89 to 0.66 across one- and four-month intervals respectively (Pines & Aronson, 1988). Construct validity of the BM was examined using correlational analyses with other theoretically relevant measures. Thus for example BM scores were found to be negatively related to one's satisfaction from work and from oneself and positively related to turnover rates, poor physical health and on-duty physical symptoms such as headaches, loss of appetite, nervousness, backaches and stomachaches (Pines & Aronson, 1988; Schaufeli & Enzmann, 1988). Translated versions of the BM were used in studies in France, Germany, Holland, Hungary, Japan, Mexico, Poland and Israel. In some of the studies, the short, ten-item version of the BM was used (Pines, 2005).

In addition to the BM, respondents were asked to what extent their work (in the case of the retirees, their hobby) was important and provided them with a sense of significance and meaning. Answers were given on seven-point scales from 1 = 'not at all' to 7 = 'very much so'.

Respondents in the different groups were also asked about different aspects of their work that were assumed to be stressful or related to burnout. Answers were given again on seven-point scales from 1 = 'not at all' to 7 = 'very much so'.

Qualitative measures The managers, nurses, teachers and police officers participated in burnout workshops that included several structured exercises (Pines, 2001). The workshop exercise that provided information about goals and expectations as well as burnout-causing stresses went as follows.

The professionals were asked to write the goals and expectations they had when they entered their career. After doing so they met in groups of four (with three other professionals they knew the least) and discussed what each had written. Next they had to decide on the items (if any) that all four had in common. These shared goals and expectations were then presented by a spokesperson from each of the foursomes to the entire group and written on the board. Items that were already mentioned by a previous foursome were noted. The professionals soon discovered that once the first three or four foursomes presented their shared items, the remaining items were pretty much repetitions. In the next stage of the exercise the professionals were asked to write the aspects of their work that were most responsible for their burnout. Once again they shared those burnout causes with their foursome and chose those that all of them had in common to present to the whole group. Once again the causes of burnout that were written on the board turned out to be rather similar for most of the foursomes. In the last stage of the exercise, participants were asked about a possible relationship between their goals and expectations on the one hand and the causes of their burnout on the other hand. To their great surprise and amazement, a relationship was always found, and was noted on the board by drawing lines from the particular goal or expectation to the relevant burnout cause or causes.

Results

As can be seen in Table 6.1, in all four professional groups, as well as the two non-professional groups and the two national samples, there was a significant correlation between lack of a sense of significance at work and burnout.

For each of the four occupations included in the investigation, an attempt was made to find aspects of work that are stressful yet not correlated with burnout.

For the managers, innovation pressure and negative consequences that may result from their actions were found to be negatively correlated with burnout ($r = -0.27$ and $r = -0.37$ respectively, both $ps < 0.05$). Feeling overextended was not correlated with burnout ($r = 0.05$). Burnout was positively correlated with administrative hassles ($r = 0.40$) bureaucratic interference (0.31) and conflicting demands ($r = 0.26$) and negatively correlated

Table 6.1   Correlations between burnout and sense of significance at work

Group	r	p
97 Teachers	−0.44	0.000
17 Blue-collar workers	−0.40	0.05
50 Retirees	−0.40	0.001
66 Managers	−0.27	0.05
267 Police officers	−0.27	0.05
505 Israeli Arabs	−0.25	0.000
511 Israeli Jews	−0.24	0.000
100 Nurses	−0.24	0.05

with policy influence ($r = -0.40$), reciprocity ($r = -0.36$), rewards (-0.35), self-expression (-0.34), personal relations (-0.34) and success ($r = -0.26$) (All $ps < 0.02$).

In the group of low-level transportation mangers and their subordinates, the level of stress among the managers was significantly higher than it was among their subordinates (mean levels of stress: 4.5 vs. 3.7). However the managers experienced their work as more significant (mean levels of significance: 4.5 vs. 3.7) and their level of burnout was significantly lower than that of their subordinates (2.4 vs. 2.7). There was also a significant negative correlation between the sense of significance at work and burnout ($r = -0.30$) (all $ps < 0.05$).

For the nurses, there was no correlation between the number of hours in the work week and burnout ($r = -0.08$) but there was a significant positive correlation between helplessness and burnout ($r = 0.46$ $p = 0.000$). There were also negative correlations between burnout and accomplishment on the job ($r = -0.43$), productivity ($r = -0.34$), challenge ($r = -0.33$) and control ($r = 0.24$) (all $ps < 0.02$). In the sample of 216 dialysis nurses, it was found that there was no correlation between burnout and length of work day or job security ($r = -0.04$) but there was correlation between burnout and control ($r = -0.19$ $p < 0.01$) as well as sense of significance at work ($r = -0.15$ $p < 0.05$).

For the police officers burnout was not related to physical danger (0.09) but it was negatively related to self-actualization (-0.26), sense of success on the job ($r = -0.25$) and the quality of personal relationships at work ($r = -0.27$). Burnout was positively related to difficult decisions ($r = 0.26$), overload ($r = 0.23$) and conflicting demands ($r = 0.20$) (all $ps < 0.001$). In the two additional samples, the elite crime unit which had far longer work days and higher job-related stress and tension relative to the traffic unit, had a significantly lower level of burnout (mean burnout 2.2 vs. 2.8 $p < 0.05$).

For teachers, burnout was not correlated with class size, salary ($r = 0.03$ in both cases) or security ($r = -0.02$), but it was correlated with the meaningfulness of the work ($r = -0.20$) with feedback from students ($r = -0.22$) and school agents (-0.19) and with autonomy ($r = -0.18$). Among the Israeli teachers, religious teachers were less burned out than non-religious teachers (mean burnout 2.3 vs. 2.7 respectively $p = 0.008$).

The blue-collar workers were asked to evaluate the level of stress in their work. A negative correlation was found between the reported levels of stress and burnout ($r = -0.40$ $p < 0.01$). The more stress, the less burnout.

The outcomes of the structured exercise were as follows.

Managers
In response to the question about goals and expectations they had when they entered a career in management most of the managers mentioned:

- Have a significant impact on the organization.
- Be able to do my own thing, express myself.
- Have the resources to do my work well.
- Be number one, be a success.
- Make the organization the best it can be.
- Prove myself to myself and to the organization.
- Be appreciated and recognized.
- Have power and status.
- Do something significant.

The burnout-causing stresses that were mentioned most often by the managers were:

- Not enough power to have a real impact.
- Inadequate monetary resources.
- Inadequate staffing resources.
- Political pressures, not enough information.
- Administrative and bureaucratic interference.
- Inadequate recognition and monetary rewards.
- Not enough opportunities for advancement.
- Inability to do things the way they should be done.

Nurses
In response to the question about goals and expectations when they entered nursing, most of the nurses mentioned:

- Help people in pain.
- Professional fulfillment and self-actualization.
- Make a significant contribution. Nursing is a calling.
- Help people who really need help.
- Be a skilled professional.
- Have control and influence.
- Have the support and recognition of physicians and administration.
- Have the resources and authority to do the work right.

The burnout-causing stresses that were mentioned most often by the nurses were:

- Witnessing human suffering, being unable to help.
- A big patient load that affects the quality of the work.
- The suffering of people there is no way to help.
- Daily confrontation with suffering, pain, old age and death.
- Helplessness when confronting lost cases.
- Not enough control over patient care.
- Physicians who don't know their work and don't let you do yours.
- Lack of administrative support, lack of resources to do the work right.

Teachers
In response to the question about goals and expectations when they entered teaching, most of the teachers mentioned:

- Educate students.
- Influence students and inspire them, be a role model.
- Provide students with knowledge and values I believe in.
- Shape the students' personality and influence their future.
- Get students excited about the subject I am teaching.
- Work with children and have significant achievements as an educator.
- Show initiative, creativity, actualize myself.

The burnout-causing stresses that were mentioned most often by the teachers were:

- Discipline problems.
- Students being unmotivated.
- Students being inattentive and indifferent.
- Students who are impertinent, disparaging.

- School administration, bureaucracy.
- The low status of teaching.
- Non-supportive parents.
- Not enough resources to do the job right.

Police officers
In response to the question about goals and expectations when they entered police work, most of the police officers mentioned:

- Be successful.
- Have an interesting job.
- Have a significant job.
- Have variety on the job.
- Have power and influence.
- Have control.
- Be appreciated.
- Improve myself.

The burnout-causing stresses that were mentioned most often by the officers were:

- Lack of influence.
- Helplessness.
- Meaningless tasks.
- Inability to do the job the way it should be done.
- Lack of appreciation.
- A big discrepancy between the investment and the rewards.
- Lack of professionalism.
- Long work hours.
- Guilt feelings towards the family.

Discussion
The results seem to offer tentative support for all three hypotheses. The first hypothesis, that burnout will be correlated with lack of a sense of significance at work, is supported by the findings that in all the groups in which it was investigated, there was a negative correlation between burnout and sense of significance at work: the less significant the work, the higher the burnout.

Obviously, a correlation does not imply causality. It is possible, as suggested by the existential perspective, that lack of a sense of significance at work causes burnout. It is also possible that one of the outcomes of burnout is the feeling that the work is insignificant. And it could be that both burnout and lack of significance are the results of a third, more general stress factor. I will return to this interpretation later.

The second hypothesis, that burnout will not always be correlated with high levels of stress at work, is supported by a wide range of findings from four different occupational groups. Even though only parts of the studies mentioned were conducted expressively to test the hypothesis that stress is not always correlated with burnout, and in other studies these findings were a by-product, still as a whole they point – cautiously – to the conclusion that there are aspects of work that are stressful yet not correlated with burnout. Furthermore the aspects of work that are correlated with burnout tend to be those that provide a sense of meaning. Let's examine the evidence.

Among the managers, 'negative consequences that may result from your actions', which is considered a source of stress but can be interpreted as showing that your work is important (that is why a mistake can be so costly) was found to be negatively correlated with burnout. Similarly, 'pressure to be innovative', which is considered stressful but can be interpreted as implying that you are considered a creative manager whose contribution is valuable, and 'feeling overextended', which is considered a source of stress but can be moderated by feeling important and needed, were not correlated with burnout. On the other hand, burnout was negatively correlated with the ability to influence policy-making in the organization and the sense of success at work – both probably related to the managers' perceived efficacy and significance. Burnout was positively correlated with administrative hassles, bureaucratic interference and conflicting demands that prevent managers from accomplishing the things they want to accomplish.

The observation that high levels of stress are not necessarily the cause of burnout is evident in the comparison between the low-level transportation managers and their subordinates. Here, while the work stress of the managers was significantly higher than that of their subordinates, their level of burnout was significantly lower. The apparent reason: the managers experienced their work as more significant.

Burnout of hospital nurses was not correlated to the number of hours in a working week – an obvious cause of stress. But it was negatively correlated to the nurses' sense of accomplishment, productivity and challenge, all suggesting that the nurses perceive themselves as effective and significant. Dialysis nurses' burnout was not correlated to job security, but it was negatively correlated to their sense of significance at work.

Among the police officers, burnout was not related to physical danger – the most obvious occupation-specific cause of stress. But it was negatively correlated with self-actualization and sense of success on the job, both suggesting that police officers who burnout feel that they have failed, that the work does not allow them to express themselves in a significant way. The comparison between the elite police crime unit and the low-status traffic police shows that the elite group, which had far longer work days and far higher job-related stress and tension, had a significantly lower level of burnout. The likely reason: the high-status elite unit felt appreciated and felt it was doing highly important and meaningful work.

Among the teachers, burnout was not correlated with class size, salary or job security – all three well-known causes of stress among teachers – but it was correlated with the meaningfulness of the work, as well as with feedback from students and from school administration.

The finding that religious Israeli teachers were significantly less burned out than non-religious teachers can be explained by the higher sense of significance and a calling that the religious teachers seem to have in their work.

The distinction between stress and burnout is especially poignant in the results of the blue-collar workers. These workers were asked to evaluate their levels of stress and burnout. The result: a significant negative correlation between the two. The more stress, the less burnout. The likely reason: since the factory they worked in was in trouble, having a high level of stress at work meant that their contribution was important, hence they were not likely to be fired.

The third hypothesis, that the identified causes for burnout will be related to frustrated goals and expectations, was tentatively supported by the results of the experiential exercises.

If you are a manager, and your most important goal is to have a significant impact on the organization and make it the best that it can be, then your burnout is likely to be caused by not having enough power, monitory resources and manpower to have real impact. If your goal is to be number one, a success, and to be appreciated and recognized, then you are likely to burn out because of inadequate recognition and not enough opportunities for advancement. If your expectation is to do your own thing and express yourself, it can be expected that political pressures and administrative interference that prevent you from doing things the way you think they should be done are likely to be very difficult and burnout-causing for you.

If you are a nurse, and your greatest aspiration is to make a significant contribution to the world by helping ease people's pain, your greatest cause of burnout is likely to be witnessing human pain and suffering without being able to help or make a difference.

If you are a teacher and your most important goal is to educate students, influence and inspire them, be a role model, shape their personalities and influence their future, it is likely that a major cause of your burnout will be discipline problems and students being unmotivated, disruptive and disparaging.

If you are a police officer and you want very much to be successful and appreciated in your interesting and significant job, a job in which you expect to have power, influence and control, you are likely to burn out when you feel that your work is meaningless and unappreciated and you are help-less, with no influence and no power to do the job right.

Combined, the findings of the structured exercises suggest that people who choose a certain career (be it in teaching, nursing, police or manage-ment) tend to have shared goals and expectations. These goals can predict the major cause of their burnout. Namely, those aspects of the work which make it impossible for them to achieve their goals and thus derive a sense of existential significance from their work.

The relationship between the goals and expectations professionals had when entering a career and the causes of their burnout (that is, frustrated goals and expectations) provides further support for the existential per-spective on burnout.

Having said all that, it has to be clearly acknowledged that each of the three sets of data presented has problems and limitations. The first data set (showing a correlation between burnout and lack of significance at work) can be criticized on the grounds that both the BM and the sense of signific-ance question are based on self-reporting and consequently are subject to all the limitations inherent in this methodology. Another more fundamen-tal issue has to do with the possibility that this outcome may also be con-sistent with a stress perspective.

The second set of data (showing that stressful work features are not nec-essarily correlated with burnout, but lack of significance in the work is) can be criticized on the grounds that it presents segments of studies that were chosen because they support the chapter's underlying hypothesis and that the studies from which the data were drawn are selectively and unsystem-atically described.

The third set of data (showing that people who choose a particular occupation tend to have shared goals and expectations and shared causes of burnout that represent frustrated goals and expectations) can be criti-cized on the grounds that it is based on a subjective interpretation of the results of the group discussions. Even if the groups discovered on their own the connection between the goals and expectations they had as they entered their career and their eventual burnout it still does not exclude the pos-sibility that they were influenced by the group leader who believed in the existence of such a connection. It can also be argued that the workshop design contributed to the obtained relationship between the reported goals and the causes of burnout. The causes of burnout were reported after the presentation and discussion of the goals, which probably contributed to the perceived connection between them.

While all of these criticisms may be valid, the fact that the data presented are based on so many subjects (total $n = 2180$) from such a wide range of subject populations (including two national samples, four professional groups and three non-professional groups), that they were collected using both quantitative and qualitative methodologies, and that the conclusions based on them appear rather consistent, permits a tentative confidence in them.

Does the existential perspective on burnout falsify a stress-related view? Not necessarily. It can be argued, based on Maslach and Schaufeli (1993) for example, that lack of significance is one of the demands at the work-place that tax or exceed the individual's resources. Based on Hobfoll and Freedy (1993) it can be suggested that sense of significance is one of the resources that need conservation, and when it is lost the result is burnout. Or else, following Schaufeli and Enzmann (1998), it can be argued that lack of significance reflects an imbalance between job demands and the response capability of the worker. Unfortunately it does not seem that any of these interpretations helps clarify the unique characteristics of burnout even within a stress-framework.

On the other hand, some aspects of stress theory and research seem very relevant to the proposed existential perspective on burnout. One example is the recent work by Folkman and Moskowitz (2000) on the role of positive affect in coping with stress. Referring to the work of Lazarus (1966), Folkman and Moskowitz note that 'meaning has long been implicated in the appraisal of stress', 'where it helps determine the personal significance of a stressful situation'. 'The appraised or *situational meaning* shapes the emotions the person experiences in the stressful encounter. Appraised situ-ational meaning contrasts with *global meaning*, which refers to more abstract, generalized meaning related to people's fundamental assump-tions, beliefs, and expectations about the world and the self in the world' (p. 651).

Where would the sense of significance and meaning that people look for in their work fit into the Folkman and Moskowitz formulation? Is it a lack of a situational meaning that causes burnout or the lack of global meaning? It seems that neither one is true. Burnout seems to be neither the result of a situational lack of meaning nor the result of people's general-ized sense of insignificance. This is evident in the fact that people can burn out in one sphere of their life (such as their job), but not burnout in another sphere (such as their marriage) (Pines, 1996). Rather, it seems that the sense of meaning people look for in their work is a special category that falls between the two categories discussed by Folkman and Moskowitz.

Thus an alternative interpretation of the results presented in this chapter is that burnout is the result of an appraisal process that suggests to individuals, whose general expectation is to have a significant impact on the world, that their contribution is meaningless and insignificant.

This interpretation regards burnout as a subcategory of stress with certain distinct characteristics. It does not imply that stress and burnout are entirely different concepts, but it seems to have an advantage over the suggestions to view burnout as just 'occupational stress' or within one of the general theories of stress. The latter options are highly uninformative since stress has become such a general and umbrella-like concept.

Even if the existential perspective presented in the present chapter does not falsify or undermine a stress-related view, it still offers a way to specify and clarify the nature of burnout, especially in relationship to the concept of stress and within a relational perspective.

Summary and implications for a relational perspective

Burnout is often conceptualized within the more general framework of stress research. The current chapter offers an existential perspective as a way to differentiate the two concepts and point to the distinct characteristics of burnout. According to the existential perspective, the root cause of burnout lies in people's need to find significance in their life, and their sense that their work does not provide it. Tentative evidence based on three data sets is presented in support of the existential perspective on burnout. The first data set (that includes eight groups with a total $n = 1613$) shows a consistent correlation between burnout and lack of significance at work. The second data set (that includes nine groups with a total $n = 1147$) shows that stressful work features are not necessarily correlated with burnout, but lack of significance at work is. The third data set (that includes the results of structured exercises conducted during burnout workshops with managers, nurses, teachers and police officers) shows that people who choose a particular occupation tend to have shared goals and expectations and shared causes of burnout. The major causes of burnout can almost always be seen as frustrated goals and expectations.

These findings have important theoretical as well as practical implications for a relational perspective, a perspective that does not treat individuals as functioning independently, but rather in terms of their interconnections and dynamic relationships with other individuals. 'No man is an island, entire of itself; every man is a piece of the continent', wrote John Donne, the sixteenth-century poet. Poets, as well as scientists, have recognized that human beings are social animals, that their interdependence on each other is a vital aspect of their being human.

The human infant could not survive without being cared for. Adults are also dependent on their membership in an elaborate social system, without which their survival as human beings would be extremely unlikely. In the case of career burnout, these social systems include – in growing circles – their work team, their organization, their culture and the global village. This chapter is based on the assumption that the way workers interact with each other and with their service recipients, and the kinds of relationships they form in and out of the organization, are critical to the way they experience, express and cope with burnout. This assumption was based in part on the results of a study (Pines et al., 2002) that revealed a high negative correlation between the availability of different forms of social support and burnout among Israelis, Arabs, Hungarians and Americans. These results demonstrate the universality of the need for support and its importance for coping with burnout. Coming from a relational perspective, coping with burnout has to be done in three levels, and best done simultaneously.

The first level is the level of the individual, where a psychoanalytic-existential perspective dictates the following three steps:

- Identifying the conscious and unconscious reasons for the individual's career choice and how the chosen career was expected to provide a sense of significance.
- Identifying the reasons for the individual's failure to derive a sense of significance from the work and how this sense of failure is related to burnout.
- Identifying the changes that will enable the individual to derive a sense of existential significance from work (Pines, 2000a).

The second level is the level of the work team, where a psychoanalytic-existential perspective assumes that people have similar psychological issues (that drew them to the profession) and similar goals and expectations. The recommended approach is burnout workshops (described earlier and in Pines, 2001). The workshop exercises help work teams identify their shared goals and expectations as well as burnout-causing stresses, and join forces in coping with them. The workshop is also the first step in turning the work team into a social support group.

The third level is the level of the organization, where the existential perspective suggests that it will be more beneficial to focus on enhancing workers' sense of their work's importance and significance, than it is to focus on reducing their work stress.

The best approach for coping with burnout involves all three levels simultaneously, within a particular cultural context as well as cross-culturally within a universal global village perspective.

Note

* The author wishes to thank her students Dina Alboer and Nili Hamami, nurses, who collected the data from the hospital nurses; Muhamad Haskia, dialysis nurse, who collected the data from the dialysis nurses; Gai Malishkevitz, manager, who collected the data from the transportation managers and their subordinates, Mordechai Aviad, police officer, who collected the data from the elite crime detection unit and the traffic police unit, and Uriel Aliyat, manager, who collected the data from the blue collar workers.

References

Aldwin, C. (1994), *Stress Coping and Development*, New York: Guilford Press.

Becker, E. (1973), *The Denial of Death*, New York: Free Press.

Burisch, M. (1993), In search of theory: some ruminations on the nature and etiology of burnout, in Schaufeli, W., Maslach, C. & Marek, T. (eds) *Professional Burnout: Developments in Theory and Research*, Washington, DC: Taylor & Francis, pp. 75–94.

Buunk, B.P., Schaufeli, W.B. & Ybema, J.F. (1994), Burnout, uncertainty, and the desire for social comparison among nurses, *Journal of Applied Social Psychology*, **24**, 1701–18.

Cochran, K.J. (1986), Measuring burnout: a reliability and convergent validity study, *Journal of Social Behavior and Personality*, **1**, 107–12.

De Rijk, A.E., Le Blanc, P.M, Schaufeli, W.B. & De Jong, J. (1998), Active coping and need for control as moderators of the job demand-control model: effects on burnout, *Journal of Occupational and Organizational Psychology*, **71**, 1–18.

Enzmann, D., Schaufeli, W.B., Janssen, P. & Rozenman, A. (1998), Dimensionality and validity of the Burnout Measure. *Journal of Occupational and Organizational Psychology*, **71**, 331–51.

Farber, B.A. (ed.) (1983), *Stress and Burnout in the Human Service Professions*, New York: Pergammon.

Fischer, H.A (1983), Psychoanalytic view of burnout, in Farber, B. (ed.), *Stress and Burnout in the Human Service Professions*, New York: Pergammon, pp. 40–45.

Folkman, S. & Moskowitz, J.T. (2000), Positive affect and the other side of coping, *American Psychologist*, **55**, 647–54.

Frankl, V.E. (1976), *Man's Search for Meaning*, New York: Pocket Book.

Freudenberger, H.J. (1980), *Burn-out: The High Cost of High Achievement*, Garden City, NY: Doubleday.

Harrison, D.W. (1983), A social competence model of burnout, in Farber, B. (ed.), *Stress and Burnout in the Human Service Professions*, New York: Pergammon, pp. 29–39.

Hobfoll, S.E. & Freedy, J. (1993), Conservation of resources: a general stress theory applied to burnout, in Schaufeli, W., Maslach, C. & Marek, T. (eds) *Professional Burnout: Developments in Theory and Research*, Washington, DC: Taylor & Francis, pp. 115–29.

Justine, B., Gold, R.S. & Klein, J.P. (1981), Life events and burnout, *Journal of Psychology*, **108**, 219–26.

Landsbergis, P.A. (1988), Occupational stress among health care workers: a test of the job demands-control model, *Journal of Organizational Behavior*, 217–39.

Lazarus, R.S. (1966), *Psychological Stress and the Coping Process*, New York: McGraw-Hill.

Lazarus, R.S. (1993), Why we should think of stress as a subset of emotion, in Goldberger, L. & Breznits, S. (eds) *Handbook of Stress*, New York: Free Press, pp. 21–39.

Lazarus, R.S. (2000), Toward better research on stress and coping, *American Psychologist*, **55**, 665–73.

Maslach, C. (1982), *Burnout – The Cost of Caring*, Englewood Cliffs, NJ: Prentice Hall.

Maslach, C. & Jackson, S.E. (1981), The measurement of experienced burnout, *Journal of Occupational Behavior*, **2**, 99–113.

Maslach, C. & Schaufeli, W.B. (1993), Historical and conceptual development of burnout, in Schaufeli, W., Maslach, C. & Marek, T. (eds) *Professional Burnout: Developments in Theory and Research*, Washington, DC: Taylor & Francis, pp. 1–16.

Paine, W.S. (ed.) (1982), *Job Stress in Burnout*, Beverly Hills, CA: Sage.

Pines, A.M. (1993), Burnout – An existential perspective, in Schaufeli, W., Maslach, C. & Marek, T. (eds) *Professional Burnout: Developments in Theory and Research*, Washington, DC: Taylor & Francis, pp. 33–52.

Pines, A.M. (1996), *Couple Burnout: Causes and Cures*, New York and London: Routledge.

Pines, A.M. (2000a), Nurses' burnout: an existential psychodynamic perspective, *Journal of Psychosocial Nursing*, **38** (2), 1–9.

Pines, A.M. (2000b), Treating career burnout: a psychodynamic existential perspective, *Journal of Clinical Psychology. In Session: Psychotherapy in Practice*, **56**, 1–10.

Pines, A.M. (2001), A burnout workshop: design and rationale, in Golembiewski, R. (ed.), *Handbook of Organizational Consultation*, 2nd edn, New York: Marcel Dekker, pp. 841–50.

Pines, A.M. (2005), The Burnout Measure short version, *International Journal of Stress Management*, **12** (1), 78–88.

Pines, A.M. & Aronson, E. (1988), *Career Burnout: Causes and Cures*, New York: Free Press.

Pines, A.M., Ben-Ari, A., Utasi, A. & Larson, D. (2002), A cross-cultural investigation of social support and burnout, *European Psychologist*, **7**, 256–64.

Sarason, I.G. & Spielberger, G.D. (eds) (1979), *Stress and Anxiety*, Washington, DC: Hemisphere Publishing Corp.

Schaufeli, W.B. & Enzmann, D. (1998), *The Burnout Companion to Study and Practice: A Critical Analysis*, London: Taylor & Francis.

Schaufeli, W.B. & Van Dierendonck, D. (1996), A cautionary note about the cross-national and clinical validity of cut-off points for the Maslach Burnout Inventory, *Psychological Reports*, **76**, 1083–90.

Schaufeli, W.B., Van Dierendonck, D. & Van Gorp, K. (2002), Burnout and reciprocity: toward a dual-level social exchange model, *Work and Stress*, **10**, 225–37.

Selye, H. (1956), *The Stress of Life*, New York: McGraw-Hill.

Selye, H. (1993), History and present status of the stress concept, in Goldberger, L. and Breznits, S. (eds) *Handbook of Stress*, New York: Free Press.

Spielberger, C. (1979), *Understanding Stress and Anxiety*, New York: Harper & Row.

Van Dierendonck, D., Schaufeli, W. & Sixma, H.J. (1994), Burnout among general practitioners: a perspective from equity theory. *Journal of Social and Clinical Psychology*, **13**, 86–100.

Van Yperen, N.W., Buunk, B.P., & Schaufeli, W.B. (1992), Communal orientation and the burnout syndrome among nurses, *Journal of Applied Social Psychology*, **22**, 173–89.

7 Venturing as a relational process
*Mine Karataş-Özkan and William D. Murphy**

Introduction

Steyaert and Hjorth (2003) view the field of entrepreneurship as a number of movements which change our perspectives and offer us new relations. Based on a longitudinal research project, which explores the business venturing process in the context of UK creative industries, this chapter should be considered as a part of these movements. The research focuses on the intrinsic processes of venturing which are entrepreneurial learning, managing and networking as experienced by a set of actors whom we identify as being members of a venture team. Building on Wenger's (1998) notion of 'communities of practice', these actors are active participants in entrepreneurial processes which occur in a historical and cultural context. We place a particular emphasis on the processual, relational and creative qualities of entrepreneurial practices undertaken by these actors as and when they are engaged together in developing the venture on an everyday basis. It is their very engagement in the day-to-day conduct of the venture, their interpersonal relations, their shared knowledge and their negotiation of enterprise, which makes them a community of practice.

The processes of sense-making and social construction are explored by examining the ways in which members of a venture team attempt to create understandings of organisational emergence, that is, building relationships with clients, competitors, regional support agencies and members of a sectoral network. Therefore we develop the notion of 'venture community' throughout the chapter in order to reflect on the relational characteristics of the venturing process.

The chapter is fashioned as follows. First, we review previous literature on the entrepreneurial process of venturing and the underlying processes of learning, managing and networking by identifying three strands of thinking: processual, relational and process-relational perspectives on entrepreneurship. We attempt to take a process-relational stance in this chapter. The process-relational description of venturing process is followed by research methodology. The research is shaped from a social constructionist standpoint. Conversational and observational material have been accumulated over for 20 months during which the venture community members have created opportunities and enacted by discussing issues, events and problems occurring to them in their daily practices of developing the venture.

We go on to examine the case study through interplay between the findings of the study and the literature. We conclude the chapter by drawing out the two interrelated themes: (1) venturing process as a generative conversing and collective enacting; and (2) becoming a venture community. These relational processes shape personal, social and economic identities of entrepreneurs involved.

Business venturing from a process-relational perspective

There has been a shift towards more dynamic and processual accounts of entrepreneurship since the mid-1980s (Bhave, 1994; Bruyart & Julien, 2000; Bygrave & Hofer, 1991; Allinson et al., 2000; Gartner, 1985, 1990; Jack & Anderson, 2000; Watson 1994a, 2002, 2003, Low & MacMillan, 1988; Olson, 1985; Shane & Venkataraman; Stevenson & Jarillo, 1990). Approaching entrepreneurial behaviour or process from a variety of perspectives, these studies centre around the functions and activities associated with perceiving opportunities and creating ventures to pursue them.

One popular conceptualisation of entrepreneurship is Stevenson and Jarillo's (1990) which takes an opportunity-centred perspective. Stevenson and Jarillo (1990: 23) define entrepreneurship as a process by which individuals – either on their own or inside organisations – pursue opportunities without regard to the resources they currently control. Similarly, Bygrave and Hofer's (1991) definition includes all functions, activities and actions associated with perceiving opportunities and creation of organisations to exploit them. Recounting the idea of emergence of a new venture creation as the essence of entrepreneurial process, Bygrave (1993: 257) suggests that it is the 'entrepreneurial event' which should be the focal point in researching entrepreneurship, and he acknowledges its humanly and emerging attributes: 'It is initiated by an act of human volition, it is on the level of the individual firm, it is a change of state, it is a discontinuity, it is a holistic and dynamic process.' However Chell (1997, 1998) takes the view that it is the identification and pursuit of opportunities for capital accumulation and growth which can occur at any point in the life cycle of the business. Therefore she focuses on the economic outcomes of an ongoing process, which is beyond 'business founding'. In a slightly different way, Cope and Watts (2000) argue that the rich and complex process by which entrepreneurs learn to negotiate the management of a growing small business is de-emphasised. Aligning with Merz et al.'s (1994) stance, they maintain that a firm's growth or expansion through constant recognition of business opportunities is a valid indicator of the continuing process of entrepreneurship within firms well beyond the initial founding event (Cope & Watts, 2000: 115).

Locating entrepreneurial processes in a contextual framework, some scholars (Gartner, 1985; Bird, 1989; Gartner, 1990; Gartner et al., 1992;

Bouchikhi, 1993) recognised that they occur within a larger context – a framework of events, circumstances, situations, settings and niches. Entrepreneurs interpret these situations and coordinate their actions. These coordinations are historically and socially located, reproduced in certain relational processes and not others. Hence the academic discourse starts to give voice to the relational qualities of the entrepreneurial process in addition to its processual characteristics.

The relational perspectives on entrepreneurship are mainly portrayed by studies on networking (Johannisson and Nilsson, 1989; Johannisson et al., 2002; Lechner and Dowling, 2003). Networking has been described as a social construction process that is characterised by the individuals' creation and use of relationships (Johannisson, 1995). According to Dubini and Aldrich (1991: 305), entrepreneurship is inherently a networking activity because a crucial part of the process is mobilising resources to pursue opportunities that require entrepreneurial contacts, knowledge and confidence. To expand on this, Chell and Baines (2000: 196) state that networking comprises social processes over and above the normal economic trading relationship. The central idea is that entrepreneurs try to set up an elaborate web of relationships (Jarillo, 1989) in a variety of forms.

Using the idea of 'embeddedness' to explain how networking contributes to economic and social activity, its organising and its outcomes, Johannisson et al. (2002: 298) argue that networks constitute forms of 'voluntary co-operation that involve information sharing and/or mutual learning and exchange between their members as well as social control'. The 'social control' dimension of networking has been taken up in Varamaki and Vesalainen's (2003) study where they underline the significance of planning, promoting or building up cooperative arrangements as a device of generating and controlling future arrangements. As will be presented later, our case study relates to this since the key members of the venture team are steering a sectoral networking activity in the region and it is seen as a reflection of the concern to take ownership of the newly created set of relationships and shaping and reshaping the future ones.

Elaborating on the notion of social embeddedness, Jack and Anderson's (2002) work can be cited as one of the distinguishing examples to relational perspectives on entrepreneurship. It uses Giddens's (1984) structuration theory to explore the link between the entrepreneur as agent and the social context as structure in the creation and operation of their businesses. The idea is that entrepreneurial actions do not occur in a vacuum but are conditioned by ongoing structures of social relations (Young, 1997). Aldrich and Zimmer (1986) join this view by suggesting that entrepreneurship is embedded in a social context, channelled and facilitated or constrained and inhibited by the people's position in a social network (Jack & Anderson, 2002: 469).

A processual way of looking at entrepreneurship entails the examination of emerging characteristics and features of the entrepreneurial process. From processual perspectives, the dynamic process through which business opportunities are realized becomes the central focus of entrepreneurship studies (Fletcher, 2003). Relational approaches highlight the human relationships involved in the process. Entrepreneurial activities are realized and constructed through social processes. It builds on the Schumpeterian (1934) notion of contributing to economic change through new combinations of products or processes, whereby entrepreneurs bring about new ideas, products and processes by working in relation to a team, small community or network of people (Johannisson, 1990; Fletcher, 1997; Fletcher, 2003). Yet process relational perspectives on entrepreneurship combine the processual view of 'emergence' with 'relational' dimension in order to generate deeper insights. The relational part is in essence about relating to each other through language, narrative, discourse as well as enactment.

Process-relational approaches are relatively established in organisation studies (Weick, 1979, 1995; Hosking & Morley, 1991; Weick & Roberts, 1993; Czarniawska, 1997, 1998; Bouwen & Hosking, 2000; Hosking & Ramsey, 2000; Shaw, 2002; Watson, 2003). Underpinned by the social constructionist assumptions (Gergen, 1985), Watson (2003: 1306) suggests that a process-relational approach to study organisations has been grounded in the belief that processes of social construction create 'the organisation' in which multiplicity of goals, interests and understandings exist within the 'quasi' or 'virtual' entity. This is linked to the strategic exchange perspective developed by Watson (1994a), drawing on an ethnographic work. Returning back to Jack and Anderson's (2002) work on the social embeddedness of entrepreneurship, here is the focus on the strategic and reflexive nature of social relationships. Building on Watson's (1994a, 1994b, 2001b) interpretation of Giddens, an entrepreneur's initiative (agency) is not simply constrained by the circumstances in which it occurs (structure); it may equally be enabled. Therefore the circumstances in which entrepreneurs find themselves shape their thinking and acting, and also entrepreneurs shape those circumstances. They engage with each other through a number of networking activities which they do shape and are shaped by. These activities are driven by economic motives of wealth creation which will be termed as 'economic becoming' throughout the chapter.

The translation of these ideas to entrepreneurship studies is very recent. At the 2003 European Academy of Management (EURAM) conference, Fletcher and Tansley (2003) presented a variety of social constructionist approaches permeating entrepreneurship literature over the last ten years and argued that researchers approaching their entrepreneurial research with a constructionist orientation should be receptive to concerns about the interrelationship between process, context, language, discourse and interaction in shaping entrepreneurial outcomes. Their process-relational stance enables them to conclude that individuals relationally enact entrepreneurial practices in different contexts in ways that facilitate entrepreneurial becoming. At the same conference, Fletcher and Watson (2003: 1) defined entrepreneurship as 'a distinctive approach to making a living in which people with ideas for a product or service create, develop and realise those ideas as part of their social becoming'. In order to emphasise its relational and processual qualities, they describe how they 'make and remake themselves' as they engage imaginatively and creatively through economic exchange with the people who are willing to make or remake themselves (Fletcher & Watson, 2003: 3). Aligning with Steyaert's (2003) recent definition of the entrepreneurial process as a creation of a living world with economic outcomes, Fletcher and Watson's (2003) perspective takes account of how people work together to bring about economic change through new combinations of technological products or processes. Hence the attention is drawn to how groups of people collectively organise themselves in venture communities and partnerships, and act together by coming to acknowledge and realise their creative ideas as a part of this process of creation of a living world during which they are constantly evaluating information, talking through different scenarios and bringing to their interaction previous understandings, experiences and history of relationships (Fletcher & Watson, 2003).

According with Cope and Watts (2000) as noted above, this understanding takes the discussion beyond the founding event as the centre of entrepreneurship and highlights that it is a continual process which is always in movement and coming ever afresh into existence (Steyaert, 1998). Therefore people may enact entrepreneurial practices at any stage of the lifespan of the venture, as they develop their identities and businesses relationally and identify new entrepreneurial possibilities by negotiating and conversing about the new business ideas.

Some entrepreneurship scholars (Steyaert, 1998; Hjorth, 2003a, 2003b; Steyaert & Hjorth, 2003) emphasise the 'creative' dimension of the relational process. Steyaert (1998: 22) reinforced the need to engage in studies that approach entrepreneurship as a creative process in which it is accepted that 'entrepreneurs are creators of new realities walking on the boundary between destabilising existing situations and actualising implicit possibilities into new contexts'. This accords with Johannisson (1993: 27) who argued that entrepreneurship is concerned with the 'creative envisioning of that which does not yet exist'.

In a parallel vein, the similarities and differences between entrepreneurs and managers have been well studied in entrepreneurship research (for example Kets de Vries, 1977; Bird, 1989; Czarniawska & Wolff, 1991; Chell et al., 1991; Watson, 1995; Chell & Haworth, 1988; Perren, 2001), and one major argument has been the creative side of entrepreneurial process. Managers and entrepreneurs were both described as enactors of archetypes on the organizational stage; management as the activity of introducing order by coordinating flows of things and people toward collective action; entrepreneurship as the making of new worlds (Czarniawska & Wolff, 1991). How our research participants are creating their new world while they are forming and reforming their own personal identities, business identity and collective identity as a 'venture community' is one of the concerns in this chapter. These identity formations are marked by entrepreneurial learning, managing and networking and therefore, these processes receive particular attention in this study.

Drawn from different epistemological perspectives, the studies on entrepreneurial learning (EL) largely examine learning at the individual entrepreneur level or at the firm level (for example Young & Sexton, 1997; Deakins & Freel, 1998; Cope & Watts, 2000; Rae & Carswell, 2000; Bishop et al., 2001; Honig, 2001; Minniti & Bygrave, 2001; Rae, 2002). The collective learning of a set of actors has received little attention as a cultural, social and political phenomenon despite the literature on entrepreneurial teams or venture teams (for example Stewart, 1989, Kamm et al., 1990, Birley & Stockley, 1999; Vyakarnam et al., 2000; Ucbasaran et al., 2001). It is not within the scope of this chapter to review the aforementioned studies on EL; however it is worth noting that until recently the focus of this literature has been mostly on cognitive processes concerned with an entrepreneur's way of gathering, processing and evaluating information (for example Young & Sexton, 1997; Bishop et al., 2001; Honig, 2001; Minniti & Bygrave, 2001).

Building on a doctoral research which explored the learning process of individual entrepreneurs and its impact on both their personal development and that of their firms, Cope and Watts's (2000) paper developed a dynamic learning perspective by applying critical incidents technique and showed how the entrepreneur learns from these incidents within the wider context of business and personal growth. The lesson we draw from their work includes the importance of the critical incidents for accelerating the process of learning and growing self-awareness and hence these are established as seminal moments within this process of change. They touch on the contextual nature of critical incidents and the need to understand and interpret them in relation to the circumstances in which they occur. However it is difficult to infer the significance of context on the learning process from their work. Similarly, drawing on an empirical study of individual entrepreneurs in a wide range of industries and at different stages of their entrepreneurial career, Rae's (2002) work developed three themes of personal and social emergence, contextual learning and negotiated enterprise. The notion of 'negotiated enterprise' is based on Watson's (2001: 10965) conceptualisation of 'negotiated order of an organisation' where he contends that it is 'the pattern of activities which has arisen or emerged over time as an outcome of the interplay of the variety of interests, understandings, reactions and initiatives of the individuals and groups involved in the organisation'. As regards entrepreneurial learning, Rae (2002) argues that the business emerges through a constant process of negotiations and exchanges, just as do the personal and social identity of entrepreneurs.

Concurring with Watson's (2002, 2003) argument, our intention is to address how each member of the venture community brings their own understandings, social backgrounds and knowledge to the venture, (that is, the negotiated order), and yet how these elements shape this negotiation of order and are shaped by negotiations. Using the term 'organisational emergence' to highlight the social, processual and constructive aspects of new business venturing, Fletcher (2003) encourages entrepreneurship researchers to generate further insights into the underlying processes of venturing to facilitate new movements in entrepreneurial understanding. In the UK creative industries context, the processes of sense-making and social construction are explored in this study by examining the ways in which members of a venture team attempt to create understanding of organisational emergence, that is, building relationships with clients, competitors, financial organisations, regional support agencies, financial organisations and members of an industrial network. Yet they become a part – a leading part – of a venture community. Their personal, social and economic identities do emerge as they make sense of the world through interactions with other members of the venture community and their 'active use of discursive resources' as Watson (2002: 100) puts it. How these sense-making and social construction processes have been explored is the concern of the next part which describes the research methodology.

Research methodology

Underpinned by a social constructionist philosophy, the research is seen as an ongoing relational process between the participants and the researchers as argued elsewhere (Karataş & Murphy, 2002; Karataş-Özkan et al., 2003). Guided by Watson's (1994a, 1994b, 2002, 2003) strategic exchange perspective and drawn to process-relational perspectives on entrepreneurship, we are concerned with understanding the intrinsic processes of business venturing as 'lived experiences' by respecting the views of those who go through such entrepreneurial practices.

Steyaert (1997: 25) encourages the entrepreneurship researchers to develop research practices that point to a process-oriented, multi-perspec-tivistic and contextual research approach. In contrast with the positivist or functionalist paradigm (Burrell & Morgan, 1979), this type of research should strive to understand the actions and interactions of participants and to grasp the culturally appropriate concepts through which they conduct their social life (Reason, 1994; Shotter, 1993, 1995; Watson, 1994a; Steyaert, 1997; Hosking & Ramsey, 2000; Fletcher & Watson, 2003). To this end, we have attended their business meetings, we have observed them as they engage in the activities of the venture, we have talked to them about their experience and we have read their documents, mainly business plans which demonstrate a documentary version of social reality which is histor-ically and locally produced (Atkinson & Coffey, 1997). The detailed and repeated examination of the accomplishment of actual activities coupled with the analytic orientations provided us with the resources through which we can begin to identify the entrepreneurial practices which are produced and rendered intelligible. Building on these examinations through partici-pant observation and talk, we have conducted in-depth qualitative inter-views with the members of this young creative venture, allowing a deeper exploration of the social construction processes of venturing. Table 7.1 summarises the research process.

Using Spradley's (1980) model of the process of observational research, we started with the descriptions of the context, actors and activities and then shifted to more focused observations. Paying particular attention to the interactions between the team members, we took extensive notes during the venture team meetings and the meetings that shaped the creation of the industrial network organisation named as INO in the chapter. Using the meeting talk, transcripts were then constructed drawing on the obser-vation records. The interviews were tape-recorded and transcribed and then analysed through an interplay between emerging findings and the per-tinent literature by using qualitative research coding techniques (Miles & Huberman, 1994). The main theoretical framework, which was applied in undertaking data analysis, is Watson's (1994a, 1994b, 2001b, 2002, 2003) strategic exchange perspective (SEP). It has enabled us to take a multi-layered approach in examining business venturing process whereby indi-vidual entrepreneurs (personal dimension: micro-level) relationally form their new enterprises as a part of broader venture community (social dimension: meso-relational level) which is embedded in the macro-field (economic and political dimensions) of enterprise culture with its institu-tions and education programmes.

Table 7.1   Research process and phases

Phase	Methods	Number
Orientation phase (Sep 2002 – May 2003)	Preliminary interviews	6 interviews
	Attendance at the venture team meetings for observation	5 meetings
	Documentary search	2 business plans 2 national and 2 local government documents regarding the CI
Focused fieldwork (May 2003 – Mar 2004)	In-depth interviews within Halikarnas and others who have informed the research	12 interviews
	Attendance at the Halikarnas team meetings for observation	18 meetings
	Attendance at the steering group meetings of the industrial network organisation (INO)	3 meetings
	Documentary search	1 consultancy report for the INO

Grounded in social constructionism, Watson's SEP recognises the human dynamics of organisational life. Organisational activities are thus outcomes of actions of individuals and groups. Engaging in personal, social, economic and political dimensions of organisational processes at an in-depth level, SEP has been developed in order to understand the patterns and implications of human actions in organisations. It deals with the fundamental quality of social life that is two-sidedness: 'the side in which individuals can be seen to initiate, choose and shape their world and the side in which they can be seen as being constrained and shaped by influences external to themselves – circumstances which involve a constant struggle to cope and survive' (Watson, 1994a: 25).

The SEP focuses more on the purposefulness of these activities in life. At the core of the perspective is the notion that processes of exchange are central to all human interactions which are not random but strategically shaped; that is, they are associated with identity, values, interests, purposes and life projects of those who are involved in them. Recognising more about the social becoming in recent years, Watson (2002, 2003) puts greater emphasis on the 'situationally-sensitive' nature of human relating, which incorporates past experiences, current concerns and future aspirations with regard to their specific context. When shaping themselves and their businesses, entrepreneurs construct their narratives and in effect narrative construction is a temporal, social and cultural process through which people's identities are formed and reformed in relation to others. It is the purpose of the next part to present the case account of the entrepreneurial process of venturing in the creative industries, as lived by a set of entrepreneurs who develop their self and social narratives by establishing connections between people, events and business opportunities. In narrating the case account, we endeavour to relate ourselves to academics and equally to practitioners. Steyaert and Bouwen (1997: 59) alert us to a significant question when studying entrepreneurship: 'The question is how we can relate to the entrepreneurial audience and through what forms of dialogue the audience can play its own active role.' As discussed elsewhere (Karataş-Özkan et al., 2003), we see our role as assisting the readers' construction of their own understandings and drawing their own lessons.

Halikarnas: a case study in the UK creative industries (CI)
Halikarnas is the pseudonym we use to represent our case venture. The case study is about the emergence and further development of a young creative venture in Derby by a team of five entrepreneurs which grew to six during the course of the fieldwork as they employed a 'brand manager' whom they met through networking. Halikarnas is explored early in its becoming process where the venture team members choose deliberately not to go down the route of starting in an incubator organisation – which is the common practice in the region, particularly in the CI – but decided to develop the venture independently. To put the case study in context, the national and regional characteristics of the CI follow.

Creative industries in the UK and in the East Midlands
The importance of CI to national wealth is now well recognised in the UK by two recent government documents (DCMS, 1998, 2001). This is reflected in the special needs of these industries in policy development at national and regional levels. The British government identifies CI as 'those industries which have their origin in individual creativity, skill and talent which have a potential for wealth and job creation through the generation and exploitation of intellectual property' (DCMS, 1998: 2). Under this definition, the following individual industries are incorporated: advertising, architecture, the arts and antique market, crafts, design, designer fashion, film and video, interactive leisure software, music, the performing arts, publishing, software and computer services, television and radio. In relation to the speed at which CI are expanding and the increasing importance of the

cultural sector to the government's aims and objectives (Brown et al., 2002), the second government document (DCMS, 2001) highlighted the need for CI strategies to integrate with other related strategies including Regional Development Agencies, Regional Cultural Consortiums, Learning and Skills Councils and the Small Business Service. Business support agencies need to improve their awareness of creative businesses, and provide appropriate support mechanisms, including the need to help creative businesses network more effectively, encouraging communication and exchange.

Since the first mapping work by the government in 1998, CI have become more prominent as the sector has moved into the mainstream. CI constitute 7.9 per cent of the UK's GDP in 2000 and creative employment in the UK totalled 1.95 million in December 2001. Employment in CI grew at a rate of 9 per cent per annum over the period 1997–2001, compared to 1.5 per cent for the whole of the UK economy. These figures are hard to ignore. CI show great potential growth in virtually every region of the UK, often in areas where other traditional sectors are in decline.

The East Midlands is an area of such decline. Recognising that a balanced economy is the key to all successful cities, a CI strategy has been formulated at the regional level in Derby for the growth of its CI alongside traditional industries. Having an engineering and transport heritage, there are a number of new industries growing in the City including information technology and arts and design. Embodied in the Creative Industries Strategy Draft (CISD) (2002) document, the strategy identified the key local issues and attempted to address these issues by supporting and fostering the growth of the local CI sector. As in the other regions across the UK, there are a number of key players in each region leading the way in terms of strategy formation and implementation. They include Regional Development Agencies (RDAs), Arts Council England and local government. Recent developments in the sector place greater emphasis on the growth of networks and various forms of support such as business incubation and investment-readiness programmes. There is a particular focus on reaching those parts of the industry that have been traditionally hard to identify and foster, that is, small and medium-sized enterprises (SMEs), micro-enterprises, freelancers and the self-employed. Through more targeted support delivered by CI specialists at Business Links, all initiatives seek to raise the profile of these groups and address their needs.

As one of the RDAs, the East Midlands Development Agency (EMDA) identified the CI as a key cluster in 2001. Since then there have been a few reports prepared which aimed to map out the activities in CI in the region (CISD, 2002; INO, 2004). According to one of these documents, which is one of our fieldwork texts (INO, 2004), there are 12 375 creative enterprises in the East Midlands employing 79 395 people with a combined turnover of £6.9 billion. This represents 4.5 per cent of all those employed in the region's enterprises. Alongside EMDA, Arts Council England is concerned with funding and supporting activities that develop and grow, particularly in the not-for-profit sector. Derby City Council (DCC) focuses on the possibilities for new business development and the way that the sector can help generate new employment opportunities. To this end, there are a number of collaborative initiatives between the DCC and the local university to run business incubation programmes to foster new venture development.

Venturing process: its relational qualities
Interpreting this national and regional context, the members of Halikarnas followed a different route compared with many others.
   Alison (the managing director of the venture team):

> As soon as we looked at the incubators such as NH and BM, we decided consciously not to go down that route. Even though you are creating your own venture through incubation, your client basis wants to see you as an individual. You need to be seen as an independent entity. You know, incubators have this 'cotton-wool type' of label . . . From an outside perspective, we consequently might have that stigma because we are graduates of the university and developed the company while we were in the university . . . So developing the team outside is probably messier than developing it inside an incubator. You have to go to the deep end. Most of the time it is a search of what is going on, what and how we should go about conducting this business. We had to deal with an awful lot of details when we left the university but it was a conscious decision. Probably it motivated us to target forward in terms of how we can develop the company, how we can organise it to a quicker start.

Shaping their own understanding of the CI context and relationally enacting, they chose to pursue the challenging route of starting a business. Certain decisions had to be taken and implemented quickly. Talking through their experience, Alison reflected on the complex and emerging nature of venture creation as follows:

> There were many issues we needed to discuss. Financial, technological and other commercial issues. So it was a lot of hard work. You are committing yourself to something wholeheartedly, you are talking about personal investment, networking and long nights to work things out . . . We needed to prioritise things. The question of what is urgent becomes fundamentally important.

Halikarnas has therefore been developed as an independent venture by five university students who share different experiences but similar ambitions in life. As they put it in the most recent business plan:

> We have been operating Halikarnas for twenty two months. The business developed from our experiences and our shared ambitions during our time together

as students at the University. Halikarnas was an extra-curricular activity that existed separately from the coursework that we were producing for our degrees . . .

Looking over the past, present and future of the business the passion has continued to grow for what Halikarnas is and what it is becoming. The dedication and hard work is transparent in both the work that Halikarnas produces and how the business has developed and grown . . . The sustainable development of the business has been primarily through its people, community and profits in order to take the business forward.

The business plan notes that the team won a national entrepreneur of the year award and was recognised for its team development. This background is then followed by their description of the business in this plan which was written in May 2003:

We offer a comprehensive multimedia design and production service to businesses and organisations that make it their business to communicate, such as marketing and promotional firms or departments, trainers and educators, and other creatives. Initially our client base was focused in the leisure and culture industries, working with a specialist clientele providing bespoke, creative imaging and presentation solutions. This base has opened up to include other markets, and we have now secured business in the corporate and local government sectors. In addition we service the multimedia and e-media industry as content providers, supplying photography, design, music, video, graphic design and illustration either on commission or as an agency for other creatives. We set our mission statement as follows: 'Halikarnas offer a unique combination of cutting edge creativity and vision, with a comprehensive multimedia audio/visual presentation and production service to the increasing design-conscious commercial world.'

This statement is interesting because it goes beyond a simple view of developing a multimedia business. They pride themselves on having a unique combination of skills, that is, creative artistic talents and marketing communications skills which enables them to provide a combination of creative multimedia production and marketing strategy business.

Defining and redefining their business is a very crucial part of their venturing process. The processes of sense-making and developing understandings engaged in by the team members concerned with refining the business idea were observed. The following narrative is an extract from the meeting talk transcriptions and it illustrates how a small group of people – a community of practice – a venture community in this case, construct, deconstruct and reconstruct meaning in relation to developing a venture through a generative dialogic process. As will be taken up later throughout the chapter, the 'generative dialogue' underlying venture creation and further development effort is one of the themes emerging in this research, and tunes into the notion of 'generative characteristics of conversations' developed by Steyaert et al. (1996), who studied organisational innovation as a joint conversational event where new configurations of meaning are constructed in two case organisations.

[Alison (A) opens the meeting by mentioning that Freddie (F) has some agenda regarding brand positioning. Freddie is the new addition to the team who has been brought in to help them frame the emerging business.]:

Freddie: [Introduces and explains the goal.] Well, I have some form of internal document which sets out how we should talk about ourselves. What we do. How we do. Just looking at the process, Halikarnas Production's proposition is much clearer and clearly based in production in video whereas Halikarnas Studios' is basically in media. I see a number of issues here that you need to clarify. It is challenging but we should decide . . . I started to say 'We' now . . . Going down that route, you should tell me 'hang on we are not confident' and we should find the way you feel most comfortable (talking to everybody).

Luke (L):   That's why you are here to push us.

F: Yeah. [Soft laugh.] First of all, I'm not sure what Halikarnas Studios does. Or Halikarnas generically. We are going out there and what do you stand for. We have got to be consistent in that respect. Consistency in how we present ourselves to the market offerings is a must. Then creating value strategically and creatively is the key issue in brand positioning. Production arm is very important and it is based in certain areas and it does underline your expertise. So, we can say we do these. All this brand communication stuff. But we have got the production arm as well.

[Alison gives an example from one of the projects with a client. She reinforces Freddie's view that the business should focus on the unique combination of creative marketing and production. She talks about how they can realise that by providing the technical side as well.]

[Freddie asks a question around the name 'Studios' to everybody.]

F: What about Studios? Are you all comfortable with the name Halikarnas Studios?

Bill (B):   Well, not really and we discussed this before but it is about the web site, isn't it?

A: You can still have the domain name.

F: I wouldn't be worried about the domain name. What we are, what we are offering through what is the key issue to clarify.

L: Halikarnas becomes the solution to the creative consultancy and productions is the technical side of it.

F: Where does the 'studios' fit then? I'm inclined to have Halikarnas and Halikarnas Productions.

B: Halikarnas does employ a range of activities.

A: But it doesn't cover the strategic studio.

B: It doesn't exclude it. At the moment, it doesn't imply it. When I am going to a meeting, I'm saying I'm from Halikarnas Studios because it is longer. Better than saying just Halikarnas. Then the implication is I'm from a media company or what?

A: The trouble for me, is Halikarnas clearer?

F: Anthony is right. The name 'Halikarnas Studios' poses problem in people's minds. Something more strategic I'm after. I'm just thinking if it could work against us.

A: The whole future is very much on the people who we have. I mean the clients . . . [She does not appear to be sure of what she is saying . . . looking at the piece of paper in front of her.]

F: Well, future seems to me lies in agency type of consultancy rather than studios. I don't think Studios implies that.

B: Lots of things happened in the Studios. So I don't want to ditch Studios but it might mean that it is mainly around the production. What about is the strategy production and creation underneath? [Bill directs his question to Freddie.]

F: That's one of the things that I am coming to. We are not going to solve it here and now.

A: I've got to think in my head about how it communicates better.

[She seems to be confused and worried. She turns to Bill and carries on talking.]

A: We should have 'Halikarnas' as the main name, Brands Communications Agency. Everything you produce is brand communications, a website or a video.

B: [Replies.] *Not exclusively. Everything we do is brand oriented.*

F: I think it is the issue of whether the name poses obstacles. Yes, everything we do is brand oriented but . . . [Interrupted by Paul.]

[Paul (P) joins in the conversation. He is usually quiet and does not talk much at the meetings unless he is spoken to or he feels his interjection is necessary.]

P: The question is should the name have to be explicit in that respect? [He is asking Freddie.]

F: OK! If you take the name issue away for the moment, the thing is how much equity it does have. Are we going to use anything? Can we inject something into it? Does the word 'Studios' pose obstacles to where we want to be seen. [Pause.] The next issue is it is all about brand communication.

L: Well. Let's stick to the issue. What is brand? [Asking Neil.]

N: [Replies.] There is a wide interpretation of what a brand is. So, I would describe us as a brand communication agency . . .

[Luke is not convinced and repeats his question.]

L: From what you're saying I don't get what your definition of brand is . . .

[Alison seems to be bored with all this 'conceptual talk' as she puts it at times when we have informal talks with her. She asks Luke.]

A: How do you define it then?

L: I don't know . . . Brand is about everything that touches the consumer . . .

[Talking to everybody but looking at Alison mostly, Bill argues.]

B: Your corporate identity in a way. Clients want us to produce campaigns of the highest creative standard to achieve their brand positioning or strengthening . . . whatever . . .

F: [Replying in a reaffirming way.] Yeah but the other thing is to deliver what you suggest. I mean the issue is to meld production side with the strategy side. So, rather than talking about disciplines like video, website, motion graphics or print design we need to also talk about marketing activities: advertising, PR, live events, digital marketing . . . Talking about those things supports the fact that you guys are actually delivering the strategy side. We need to start talking about those things. Because what people want to see you are competent in this area. Two elements here: first, how we describe ourselves is the main issue . . .[Interrupted by Alison.]

A: It is about selling a package that people can relate to.

[Alison reminds that they had this discussion a year ago but at that stage they weren't sure about what they were. Advertising agency or a brands agency or a creative production company? Freddie continues.]

F: Why we need to be talking about advertising and direct marketing as well is because we are moving to the brand communications side. We are more than a creative production firm . . .

L: Are we? [Asking everybody.] I am not quite sure.

A: [Responding to L.] We should be . . . When Freddie talked about the emphasis on the brands agency, I thought we might lose some of our advertising customers but we need to consider from whom we can get proper projects. Production side will continue . . .

F: Absolutely . . . It doesn't deny it at all.

As emphasised by Anderson (2003), entrepreneurship as a process of becoming is a transitive process and it may be recognised as enacting a future. Nascent enterpreneurs in this case study undertake entrepreneurial activities of refining the business concept and mobilising resources to actualise new possibilities that occur through their active engagement with each other and other stakeholders. Having different roles, complementary contributions or overlapping skills, the actors, who are involved in the entrepreneurial process of developing this creative business, sustain dense relations of mutual engagement.

What we observed through our engagement with the research participants during the fieldwork meetings is that when the members of the venture community discuss their active jobs or opportunities as the two subheadings of their meeting agenda, they are able to use their responses or the responsive instructions in the conversations to guide organising and assembling bits and pieces of information available to them. For example they come to certain understandings about their relationships with their customers or regional bodies and try to identify different business opportunities.

These understandings are attained by conversing and yet the venturing process is realised by relationally enacting the business ideas. When engaging in the daily matters of the business they are simultaneously shaped by and shape their conversations in ways that allow them to proceed with the venturing process. Gergen and Thatchenkery's (1996) conceptualisation of generative dialogue has the potential to be applied to this case study. They describe it as a meaningful interaction between parties as a part of a transformative process. The generative dialogue enables the participants, working collaboratively, 'to formulate models of understanding or action that incorporate multiple inputs' (Gergen & Thatchenkery, 1996: 368). Having the focus on the relational process, we centre on the continual strategic exchanges between the venture team members through conversations. This does not necessarily indicate that the members of the venture team, who take part in the conversations, have reached a shared understanding by the end of the meetings. However they seemed to manage to find ways to develop enough confidence to plan the next step and enact the business as a team. Therefore venturing process is characterised by 'generative conversing and collective enacting' through which practical meanings and actions occurred between the venture team members spontaneously in the living responses to each other. Shotter and Cunliffe (2003: 17) take this argument one step forward and suggest that 'it is the particular way in which we voice our utterances, shape and intone them in responsive accord with our circumstances that gives our utterances their unique, one-occurrent meanings . . . Put simply, meanings are created in the spontaneously coordinated interplay of people's responsive relations to each other'.

Such dialogical practices are used by the venture community members to coordinate everyday activities. As noted by Holman and Thorpe (2003), it is from within these ways of relating to each other that people can make sense of their surroundings and come to know the world around them. Hosking (1995) supports this argument by suggesting that the way in which we come to know and what we know is based within these wider relational activities.

The entrepreneurial process of venturing is characterised by learning as a process of becoming through constructing, reconstructing the meanings, situations, problems and actions by the venture community members in the course of everyday life. The 'managing' side of the argument is connected to finding ways to take the venture forward by enacting what they are learning by accomplishing everyday tasks, by creating entrepreneurial practices in interaction with each other, with customers and other stakeholders and therefore by adapting and modifying these practices. The activity of engaging in networking cannot be divorced from these experiences as explored in the next part of the chapter.

Becoming a venture community
Relational enactment of the business ideas can be best explained as networking efforts. The nascent entrepreneurs in the case are constantly on the quest of networking opportunities to enhance their business. As pointed out by Chell and Baines (2000), the strength of networking activity lies in the possibility of the individuals to reach actively and purposively outside their immediate close social circle and to draw upon information, advice and assistance from a large diverse pool. When the members of Halikarnas actively engage in such relational activities of networking through fellow entrepreneurs, friendship, regional and national business support agencies or customers, they see this as a fundamental part of both their personal change and that of their business. This is in tune with Johannisson et al.'s (2002) suggestion that collective innovativeness, flexibility and capacity is created by relationships between different agents in entrepreneurial settings. When reflecting on their involvement in initiating the industrial network named INO, we had the following conversation with Alison:

Alison: . . . there is a whole world outside. You have to seek out opportunities. Creating a business is about filling a gap in this industry. Creating INO is similar to creating Halikarnas. Filling a gap that exists because people do not know each other. So we have seen the need to have a network within the region which could bring people together. Sixty, seventy five per cent of businesses in the CI do not have office bases. That's a major thing in taking an active role in INO. If you are a copywriter or photographer or architect who works with your equipment and mobile phone, how do other people know about you? . . . The network is about who knows who, so that who can help who? [She starts drawing a figure on a piece of paper.] It is actually a big thing that you have got main figures, actors. Then you have other people around the central figure. In the network, it has got everybody tied into it. You have got to make

> sure that all these circles are connected and then building this person here and there who knows that person and that person . . .
>
> *Mine*:   A sort of a relationship building?
>
> *Alison*:   Yes, exactly. It is basically a process . . . a process of creating something new. It is learning to do as well. And learning from those people who are more experienced, who have been in this business for a lot longer than we have. Or learning from each other when you come together by sharing different ideas, knowledge simply through chatting.

INO is a good example of how Halikarnas team members are deliberately networked and trying to build to this process of forming INO as a part of their own venturing process. In this way, they open up new business opportunities and give a structure to the networking activity in the CI by taking ownership of the emerging nebulous organisation. They have undergone a series of networking activities. They formed the venture by growing into five people while they were at university. That was a networking activity. And there were looser connections to people outside that small group of fellow students. They learned quite quickly of the need for networking with these other skills and expertise.

For the purpose of this study it is important to understand networking activity beyond the process of becoming part of the network. It is also about leading a sectoral network with a strong sense of ownership in order to raise the profile of the new venture. The venture team members become participants in other communities of practice through their involvement in other tasks with relevant parties to improve themselves. It therefore appears that the term 'venture community' is plausible to describe such a group of actors. They perform their roles by joining wider communities at times and, as Anderson (2003) points out, stage their performances in ways that make sense to others.

Returning to the literature, Jack and Anderson (2002) put forward the notion of social capital in entrepreneurial networks. They studied entrepreneurial network formation as an activity which provides the opportunity to observe the creation and use of social capital. Applying qualitative research methods, they explain how individual entrepreneurs whom they studied used the networking process as a way of generating information sources and developing resources, and as a mechanism for acquiring business potentials. To sum up, they argue that networks are a series of bridges that link numerous individuals with different sets of resources. The experience of Halikarnas team members is in tune with their argument. However they are seen as the main participants rather than observers in the process which Anderson and Jack (2002) describe as the creation of social capital.

They also develop their own social identity in relation to others.

Relating the above ideas to the process-relational readings of entrepreneurship, it is possible to note the concurrence with Fletcher and Tansley's (2003: 4) view on 'entrepreneurial emergence' whereby it is defined as 'a relational process – always occurring in relation to something else' and with the theme that Rae (2002) has developed: 'personal and social emergence'. Rae illuminates the processes of the personal and social identity formations in entrepreneurial contexts through an exploration of the learning experiences of the founders of independently owned businesses in the cultural media industry. He concludes that the entrepreneurs construct their personal and social identities in their narratives through which they describe how their enterprise is acted out and shaped by social relationships.

To sum up, the Halikarnas case illustrates that the venturing process is marked by generative conversing and relational enacting of the venture team members who become a leading part of a venture community in the creative industries. These relational processes can be understood by examining the intrinsic processes, which are entrepreneurial learning, managing and networking. They shape personal, social and economic identities of entrepreneurs involved. Therefore economic becoming needs to be added to the above discussions. Encapsulating these themes, Figure 7.1 illustrates the intrinsic processes of venturing as conveyed in this chapter.

These behaviours are driven by the economic motives in such entrepreneurial settings. Revisiting the perspectives of Chell (1997, 1998) and Steyaert (1998, 2003) on the economic aspects of the venturing process, the personal and social becoming of the venture community members are steered by their intentions to generate wealth. Therefore they are very concerned with expanding their client portfolio and yet generating revenue streams. Fletcher and Watson's (2003) incorporation of 'making a living' to the definition of entrepreneurship gains an additional dimension in this study: the individual and collective becoming of entrepreneurs are intertwined with their economic becoming characterised by their intention to accumulate wealth and by their risk-taking to enact the emerging business.

Concluding remarks

The chapter was dedicated to exploring the relational qualities of the business venturing process in the UK creative industries as experienced by members of a venture team. Two interrelated themes have been drawn from the study: (1) venturing as a generative conversing and collective enacting process; and (2) becoming a venture community. The intrinsic processes of venturing, which are entrepreneurial learning, managing and networking, have been emphasised. It is concluded that personal, social and economic identities of entrepreneurs are shaped by these relational processes.

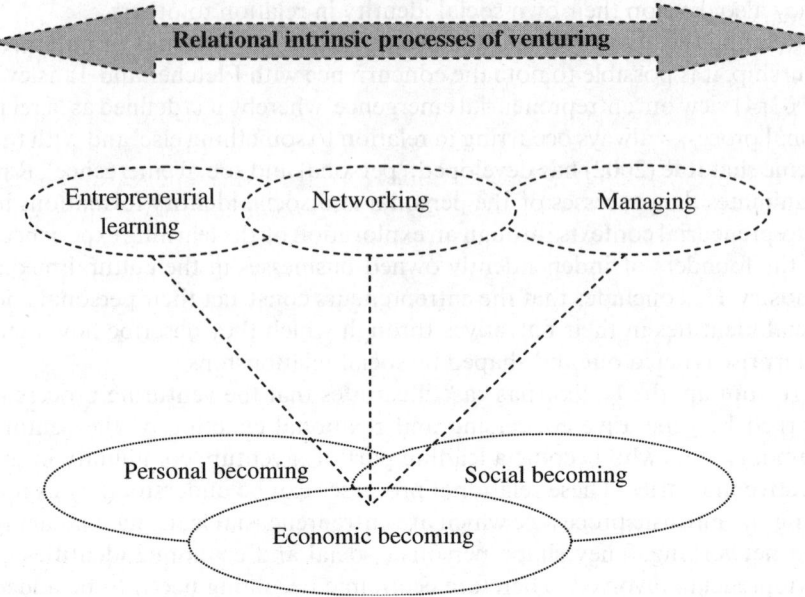

Figure 7.1   Venturing process

Briefly, the story of our research participants is as follows. The venturing process started with identifying a business opportunity and mobilising resources through networking to enact the opportunity. Observing them in the process of their everyday engagement with the pertinent parties, that is, clients, competitors, local government officials, financial organisations and officials of RDAs, we have identified that their venturing process is characterised by generative conversing and collective enacting.

Constructing and reconstructing the business ideas, the core venture team was formed. Operating within a creative industries community, there existed looser connections to people outside the small group of fellow entrepreneurs and their immediate social circle, that is, friends, family members, mentors and so on. Having formed a structure to bring them together outside an incubator – that is, the firm, Halikarnas, which could be described as their organisational emergence – they then developed the networks with other individuals with different skills, expertise, knowledge and resources.

The venture team members build the deliberate networking activity into their own venturing process. They lead a regional industrial networking group, which is tentatively emerging as an organisation, INO. They become a venture community in the creative industries which is dynamic. Venture community development can therefore be best understood through an understanding of its relational and discursive characteristics. In other words, the venture community becomes through discursive, relational, dynamic and generative resources.

Relying on these resources, we have attempted to establish the connections between personal, social and economic identities of the venture community members. In this way, we hope to understand some features of the relational changes in their social identities as members of a creative business community in the context of enduring personal identities. Their collective identity, Halikarnas first and then INO, is anchored in their individual and economic identities. Their personal entrepreneurial identity develops as each of them gains deeper understanding of her or his entrepreneurial skills, strengths and weaknesses and shapes the future aspirations. In this way, the venture community development process can be seen as the exploration of the personal, social and business identities through developing understandings about the world, sense-making and relationally enacting the business opportunities. Therefore entrepreneurial learning, managing and networking constitute the relational intrinsic processes.

We believe that the principal strength of a process-relational perspective on entrepreneurship lies in its ability to generate insights into such relational and discursive aspects of the entrepreneurial process of venturing. Grounded in a social constructionist approach, our everyday involvement with a set of entrepreneurs allowed us to investigate such intrinsic processes of venturing. Establishing the links between these processes, the future work entails a closer examination of the dimensions of relationships through which a venture community grows.

Note

*   We wish to thank two anonymous reviewers for their comments on the earlier version of this chapter, presented at the Relational Approaches to Organisations Track of the 2005 European Academy of Management (EURAM) Conference in Munich.

References

Aldrich, H.E. & Zimmer, C. (1986), Entrepreneurship through social networks, in Sexton, D.L. & Simlor, R.W. (eds), *The Art and Science of Entrepreneurship*, New York: Ballinger, pp. 3–23.

Allinson, C.W., Chell, E. & Hayes, J. (2000), Intuition and entrepreneurial behaviour, *European Journal of Work & Organisational Psychology*, **9** (1), 31–43.

Anderson, A.R. (2003), Enacted metaphor: the theatricality of the entrepreneurial process, Paper addressed at the Entrepreneurial Dramas Track of the European Academy of Management (EURAM) Conference, 3–5 April, University of Bocconi, Milan.

Anderson, A.R. & Jack, S.L. (2002), The articulation of social capital in entrepreneurial networks: a glue or a lubricant? *Entrepreneurship and Regional Development*, **14**, 193–210.

Atkinson, P. & Coffey, A. (1997), Analysing documentary realities, in Silverman, D. (ed.), *Qualitative Research: Theory, Method and Practice*, London: Sage Publications, pp. 45–62.

Bhave, M.P. (1994), A process model of entrepreneurial venture creation, *Journal of Business Venturing*, **9**, 223–42.

Bird, B.J. (1989), *Entrepreneurial Behaviour*, London: Scott, Foresman.

Birley, S. & Stockley, S. (1999), Entrepreneurial Teams and Venture Growth, in Sexron, D.L. and Landstrom, H. (eds), *Handbook of Entrepreneurship*, Oxford: Blackwell, pp. 287–307.

Bishop, K., Crown, D.F. & Weaver, K.M. (2001), Viewing entrepreneurs as learning individuals and related implications for entrepreneurial training, Working paper, University of Louisville, Kentucky.

Bouchikhi, H. (1993), A constructivist framework for understanding entrepreneurship performance, *Organization Studies*, **14** (4), 549–70.

Bouwen, R. & Hosking, D.M. (2000), Reflections on relational readings of organisational learning, *European Journal of Work and Organisational Psychology*, **9** (2), 267–74.

Brown, C., Creigh-Tyte, S. & Radin, C. (2002), UK creative industries: their growth during the 1990s and prospects for the 21st century, Paper addressed at ACEI 2002 Conference, Rotterdam, 13–15 June.

Bruyart, C. & Julien, P. (2000), Defining the field of research in entrepreneurship, *Journal of Business Venturing*, **16**, 165–80.

Burrell, G. & Morgan, G. (1979), *Sociological Paradigms and Organisational Analysis*, London: Heinemann.

Bygrave, W.D. (1993), Theory building in the entrepreneurship paradigm, *Journal of Business Venturing*, **8**, 255–80.

Bygrave, W.D. & Hofer, C.W. (1991), Theorizing about entrepreneurship, *Entrepreneurship Theory and Practice*, **16** (2), 13–22.

Chell, E. (1997), The social construction of the entrepreneurial personality, Paper addressed at the British Academy of Management Conference, London.

Chell, E. (1998), The critical incident technique, in Symon, G. and Cassell, C. (eds), *Qualitative Methods and Analysis in Organisational Research*, London: Sage Publications, pp. 51–72.

Chell, E. (2000), Towards researching 'the opportunistic entrepreneur': a social constructionist approach and research agenda, *European Journal of Work and Organisational Psychology*, **9** (1), 63–80.

Chell, E. & Baines, S. (2000), Networking, entrepreneurship and microbusiness behaviour, *Entrepreneurship and Regional Development*, **12**, 195–215.

Chell, E. & Haworth, J.M. (1988), Entrepreneurship and entrepreneurial management: the need for a paradigm, *Graduate Management Research*, **4** (1), 16–33.

Chell, E., Haworth, J.M. & Brearly, S.A. (1991), *The Entrepreneurial Personality: Concepts, Cases and Categories*, London: Routledge.

Cope, J. & Watts, G. (2000), Learning by doing – an exploration of experience, critical incidents and reflection in entrepreneurial learning, *International Journal of Entrepreneurial Behaviour and Research*, **6** (3), 104–24.

CISD (2002), Create@Derby: A creative industries strategy for Derby, Draft 2.5, May.

Czarniawska, B. (1997), *Narrating the Organisation: Dramas of Institutional Identity*, Chicago, IL: University of Chicago Press.

Czarniawska, B. (1998), *A Narrative Approach to Organisation Studies*, Thousand Oaks, CA: Sage Publications.

Czarniawska, B. & Wolff, R. (1991), Leaders, managers, entrepreneurs on and off the organizational stages, *Organization Studies*, **12** (4), 529–46.

DCMS (1998), Department for Culture, Media and Sport, *Creative Industries First Mapping Document*, London: DCMS.

DCMS (2001), Department for Culture, Media and Sport, *Creative Industries Second Mapping Document*, London: DCMS.

Deakins, D. & Freel, M. (1998), Entrepreneurial learning and the growth process in SMEs, *The Learning Organisation*, **5** (3), 144–55.

Dubini, P. & Aldrich, H. (1991), Personal and extended networks are central to the entrepreneurial process, *Journal of Business Venturing*, **6**, 305–13.

Fletcher, D. (1997), Organisational networking, strategic change and the family business, unpublished Doctoral Thesis, Nottingham Trent University.

Fletcher, D. (2003), Framing organizational emergence: discourse, identity and relationship, in Steyaert, C. and Hjorth, D. (eds), *New Movements in Entrepreneurship*, Cheltenham UK and Northampton, MA, USA: Edward Elgar, pp. 125–42.

Fletcher, D. & Tansley, C. (2003), A biographical account of entrepreneurial responsiveness, theatre management and performance, Paper addressed at the Entrepreneurial Dramas Track of the European Academy of Management (EURAM) Conference, 3–5 April, University of Bocconi, Milan.

Fletcher, D. & Watson, T. (2003), Making it otherwise for us – otherwise for them: drama, dialogue and enterprise creation, Paper addressed at Entrepreneurial Dramas track of the European Academy of Management (EURAM) Conference, 3–5 April, University of Bocconi, Milan.

Gartner, W.B. (1985), A framework for describing the phenomenon of new venture creation, *Academy of Management Review*, **10** (4), 696–706.

Gartner, W.B. (1990), What are we talking about when we talk about entrepreneurship, *Journal of Business Venturing*, **5** (1), 15–28.

Gartner, W.B., Bird, B.J. & Starr, J.A. (1992), Acting as if: differentiating entrepreneurial from organizational behaviour, *Entrepreneurship Theory and Practice*, **16** (13), 13–31.

Gergen, K.J. (1985), The social constructivist movement in modern psychology, *American Psychologist*, **40**, 266–75.

Gergen, K.J. & Thatchenkery, T. (1996), Organization science as social construction: postmodern potentials, *Journal of Applied Behavioural Science*, **32** (4), 356–77.

Giddens, A. (1984), *The Constitution of Society: Outline of the Theory of Structuration*, Cambridge: Polity Press.

Hjorth, D. (2003a), Transformative insinuations: an entrepreneurial drama of desiring and creating new worlds, Paper addressed at the Entrepreneurial Dramas Track of the European Academy of Management (EURAM) Conference, 3–5 April, University of Bocconi, Milan.

Hjorth, D. (2003b), *Rewriting Entrepreneurship*, Liber-Abstrakt: Copenhagen, Business School Press.

Holman, D. & Thorpe, R. (2003), Management and language: the manager as a practical author, in Holman, D. & Thorpe, R. (eds), *Management and Language: The Manager as a Practical Author*, London: Sage Publications, pp. 1–14.

Honig, B. (2001), Learning strategies and resources for entrepreneurs and intrapreneurs, *Entrepreneurship Theory and Practice*, **Fall**, 21–35.

Hosking, D.M. (1995), Constructing power: entitative and relational approaches, in Hosking, D.M., Dachler, H.P. & Gergen, K.J. (eds), *Management and Organization: Relational Alternatives to Individualism*, Aldershot: Avebury.

Hosking, D.M. & Morley, I.E. (1991), *A Social Psychology of Organising*, Chichester: Harvester Wheatsheaf.

Hosking, D.M. & Ramsey, C. (2000), Research, intervention and change: a constructionist contribution to process, Research paper, RP0004, Aston Business School, Aston University, Birmingham.

INO (2004), Consultancy document (fieldwork text), Industrial Networking Organization, Derby.

Jack, S.L. & Anderson, A.R. (2002), The effects of embeddedness on the entrepreneurial process, *Journal of Business Venturing*, **17** (5), 467–87.

Jarillo, J.C. (1989), Entrepreneurship and growth: the strategic use of external resources, *Journal of Business Venturing*, **4**, 133–47.

Johannisson, B. (1990), Community entrepreneurship – cases and conceptualization, *Entrepreneurship and Regional Development*, **2**, 71–88.

Johannisson, B. (1993), In search of a methodology for entrepreneurship research, paper presented at European Doctoral Programme, Copenhagen Business School, February–June.

Johannisson, B. (1995), Paradigms and entrepreneurial networks: some methodological challenges, *Entrepreneurship and Regional Development*, **7**, 215–32.

Johannisson, B. & Nilsson, A. (1989), Community entrepreneur: networking for local development, *Entrepreneurship and Regional Development*, **1**, 3–20.

Johannisson, B., Raminez-Pasillas, M. & Karlsson, G. (2002), The institutional embeddedness of local inter-firm networks: a leverage for business creation, *Entrepreneurship and Regional Development*, **14**, 297–315.

Josselson, R. & Lieblich, A. (1995), *Interpreting Experience: The Narrative Study of Lives,* Thousand Oaks, CA: Sage Publications.

Kamm, J.B., Shuman, J.C., Seeger, J.A. & Nurick, A.J. (1990), Entrepreneurial Teams in New Venture Creation, *Entrepreneurship Theory and Practice*, **14** (4), 7–24.

Katzenbach, J.R. (1997), The myth of the top management team, *Harvard Business Review*, **75** (6), 83–91.

Karataş, M. & Murphy, W.D. (2002), Emerging approaches to organisational analysis: a social constructionist proposal to entrepreneurial learning in organisations, Paper addressed at the 17th Annual ERU Conference, 9–11 September, Cardiff University.

Karataş-Özkan, M., Murphy, W.D. & Rae, D. (2003), A processual understanding of learning and managing during venturing: emerging issues, Paper addressed at the British Academy of Management Conference (BAM), Conference proceedings, Refereed paper no. 180, Leeds Metropolitan University, Harrogate, 15–17 September.

Kets de Vries, M.F.R. (1977), The entrepreneurial personality, *Journal of Management Studies*, **14** (1), 34–57.

Lechner, C. & Dowling. M. (2003), Firm networks: external relationships as sources for the growth and competitiveness of entrepreneurial firms, *Entrepreneurship and Regional Development*, **15**, 1–26.

Low, M.B. & MacMillan, I.C. (1988), Entrepreneurship: past research and future challenges, *Journal of Management Studies*, **14** (2), 139–61.

Merz, G.R., Weber, P.B. & Laetz, V.B. (1994), Linking small business management with entrepreneurial growth, *Journal of Small Business Management*, **32** (4), 48–60.

Miles, M.B. & Huberman, A.M. (1994), *Qualitative Data Analysis: An Expanded Sourcebook*, Thousand Oaks, CA: Sage Publications.

Minniti, M. & Bygrave, W. (2001), A dynamic model of entrepreneurial learning, *Entrepreneurship Theory and Practice*, **25** (3), 5–17.

Olson, P.D. (1985), Entrepreneurship: process and abilities, *Entrepreneurship Theory and Practice*, **10** (1), 25–32.

Perren, L. (2001), Comparing entrepreneurship and leadership: a textual analysis, Working paper, The Council for Excellence in Management and Leadership, London, available at: www.managementandleadershipcouncil.org/downloads/r 6.pdf

Rae, D. (2002), Entrepreneurial emergence: a narrative study of entrepreneurial learning in independently owned media businesses, *Entrepreneurship and Innovation*, **February**, 53–9.

Rae, D. & Carswell, M. (2000), Using a life-story approach in researching entrepreneurial learning: the development of a conceptual model and its implications in the design of learning experiences, *Education and Training*, **42** (4–5), 220–27.

Reason, P. (1994), *Participation in Human Inquiry*, London: Sage Publications.

Schumpeter, J.A. (1934), *The Theory of Economic Development*, Cambridge, MA: Harvard University Press.

Shane, S. & Venkataraman, S. (2000), The promise of entrepreneurship as a field of research, *Academy of Management Review*, **25** (1), 217–26.

Shaw, P. (2002), *Changing Conversations in Organizations: A Complexity Approach to Change,* London: Routledge.

Shotter, J. (1993), *Conversational Realities*, London: Sage Publications.

Shotter, J. (1995), The manager as a practical author: a rhetorical-responsive, social constructionist approach to social organisational problems, in Hosking, D.M., Dachler, H.P. and Gergen, K.J. (eds), *Management and Organisation: Relational Alternatives to Individualism*, Aldershot, UK and Brookfield, USA: Avebury.

Shotter, J. & Cunliffe, A.L. (2003), Managers as practical authors: everyday conversation for action, in Holman, D. and Thorpe, R. (eds), *Management and Language,* London: Sage Publications, pp. 15–37.

Spradley, J.P. (1980), *Participant Observation*, New York: Holt, Rinehart and Winston.

Stevenson, H. & Jarillo, J.C. (1990), A paradigm of entrepreneurship: entrepreneurial management, *Strategic Management Journal*, **11**, 17–27.

Stewart, A. (1989), *Team Entrepreneurship*, Newbury Park, CA: Sage Publications.

Steyaert, C. (1997), A qualitative methodology for process studies of entrepreneurship, *International Studies of Management and Organization*, **27** (3), 13–33.

Steyaert, C. (1998), A qualitative methodology for process studies of entrepreneurship: creating local knowledge through stories, *International Studies of Management and Organisation*, **27** (3), 13–33.

Steyaert, C. (2003), The prosaics of entrepreneurship: narration, drama and conversation, Paper addressed at the Entrepreneurial Dramas track of the European Academy of Management (EURAM) Conference, 3–5 April, University of Bocconi, Milan.

Steyaert, C. & Bouwen, R. (1992), Opening the domain of entrepreneurship: a social constructionist perspective, Paper presented at RENT, VI workshop, Barcelona, November.

Steyaert, C. & Bouwen, R. (1997), Telling stories of entrepreneurship – towards a narrative–contextual epistemology for entrepreneurial studies, in Donckels, R. & Miettinen, A. (eds), *Entrepreneurship and SME Research: On Its Way to the Next Millennium*, Aldershot: Ashgate Publishing Ltd, pp. 47–61.

Steyaert, C., Bouwen, R. & Looy, B.V. (1996), Conversational construction of new meaning configurations in organisational innovation: a generative approach, *European Journal of Work and Organizational Psychology*, **5** (1), 67–89.

Steyaert, C. & Hjorth, D. (2003), *New Movements in Entrepreneurship*, Cheltenham UK and Northampton, MA, USA: Edward Elgar.

Ucbasaran, D., Westhead, P. & Wright, M. (2001), The focus of entrepreneurial research: contextual and process issues, *Entrepreneurship Theory and Practice*, **25** (4), 57–82.

Varamaki, E. & Vesalainen, J. (2003), Modelling different types of multilateral co-operation between SMEs, *Entrepreneurship & Regional Development*, **15**, 27–47.

Vyakarnam, S., Jacobs, R.C. & Hadelberg, J. (2000), Formation and development of entrepreneurial teams in rapid growth businesses, Working paper, Nottingham Business School, Nottingham Trent University.

Watson, T. (1994a), *In Search of Management: Culture Chaos and Control in Managerial Work*, London: Routledge.

Watson, T. (1994b), Managing, crafting and researching: words, skills and imagination in shaping management research, *British Journal of Management*, **5**, 77–87.

Watson, T.J. (1995), Entrepreneurship and professional management: a fatal distinction, *International Small Business Journal*, **13** (2), 34–46.

Watson, T.J. (2001a), Negotiated orders in organisations, *International Encyclopaedia of Social and Behavioural Science*, Amsterdam, Elsevier: 10965–8.

Watson, T.J. (2001b), Speaking professionally: occupational anxiety and discursive ingenuity among human resourcing specialists, in Whitehead, S. and Dent, M. (eds), *Managing Professional Identities*, London: Routledge.

Watson, T.J. (2002), *Organising and Managing Work: Organisational, Managerial and Strategic Behaviour in Theory and Practice*, Harlow: FT Prentice Hall.

Watson, T.J. (2003), Strategists and strategy making: strategic exchange and the shaping of individual lives and organizational futures, *Journal of Management Studies*, **40** (5), 1305–23.

Weick, K.E. (1979), *The Social Psychology of Organising*, New York: Random House.

Weick, K.E. (1995), *Sensemaking in Organizations*, Thousand Oaks, CA: Sage Publications.

Weick, K.E. & Roberts, K.H. (1993), Collective mind in organizations: heedful interrelating on flight decks, *Administrative Science Quarterly*, **38**, 357–81.

Wenger, E. (1998), *Communities of Practice: Learning, Meaning and Identity*, Cambridge: Cambridge University Press.

Young, J.E. (1997), Entrepreneurship education and learning for university students and practicing entrepreneurs, in Sexton, D.L. & Smilor, R.W. (eds), *Entrepreneurship 2000*, Chicago, JL: Upstart Publishing.

Young, J.E. & Sexton, D.L. (1997), Entrepreneurial learning: a conceptual framework, *Journal of Enterprising Culture*, **5** (3), 223–48.

8 Relational cohesion model of organizational commitment*
Jeongkoo Yoon and Edward J. Lawler

Introduction

This chapter reviews the research program of relational cohesion theory (RCT) (Lawler & Yoon, 1993, 1996, 1998; Lawler et al., 2000; Thye et al., 2002) and uses it to develop a model of organizational commitment. Broadly, relational cohesion theory (RCT) has attempted to understand conditions and processes that promote an expressive relation in social exchange; an expressive relation is indicated by relational cohesion, that is, the degree to which exchange partners perceive their relationship as a unifying object having its own value. The research program argues that such relational cohesion is a proximal cause of various forms of behavioral commitment in a group setting, for example stay behavior, gift-giving and investment.

In this chapter, we develop a model of organizational commitment through the following three steps: First, we review the program of relational cohesion theory (RCT) and establish the key theoretical concepts and theorems through which it explains how instrumentally motivated actors in exchange relations develop an expressive relation. Second, we apply the concepts and theorems to derive a 'relational-cohesion model' of organizational commitment. Third, we examine the heuristic value of the new model by deriving predictions with respect to several organizational phenomena to which conventional organizational commitment theories may not have paid sufficient attention. The role of emotions is highlighted and our purpose is to theorize the interrelationships of instrumental, affective and normative forms of organizational commitment.

The original idea of commitment in RCT is inspired by Parsons's (1951) seminal distinction between person-to-collective attachment and interpersonal attachment (Lawler, 1992a). Building upon Parson's distinction, RCT defines commitment as an attachment of an individual to a collective entity such as a relationship, group, organization, community or society (see also Kanter, 1968). A leading social identity theorist, Hogg (1992), suggests a similar distinction by indicating that individuals' identification with social categories constitutes the minimal condition of a group, and this cannot be reduced to interpersonal attachments; psychological groups emerge through individuals' attachment to (or identification with) a group even in the absence of interpersonal relationships among its members (also see Hogg & Turner, 1985). On this view, an individual's attachment to a collective can be applied broadly to groups, organizations, communities or societies. To date, RCT has focused on relational and group attachments, and this chapter applies RCT to organizational commitment.

One of the key features that differentiate RCT from other exchange theories is its emphasis on emotions in organizing human activities and transactions. Most commitment models derived from exchange theories have neglected the potential significance of an expressive orientation. For instance one of the most well-developed commitment theories in the exchange theory literature, Rusbult's (1980, 1983; Rusbult & Buunk, 1993; Rusbult et al., 1998) investment model, defines commitment as a motivation to continue or remain in a relationship, a state that is in turn predicted by three instrumental indicators (investment, satisfaction and the quality of alternatives). Adopting exchange theory theorems (Homans, 1961; Thibaut & Kelley, 1959), the investment model indicates that satisfaction with a relationship is a function of rewards minus costs compared with a general expectation. Similar to sunk costs or side bets (Becker, 1960), an investment is the amount of resources put into a relationship that could not be retrieved even if the relationship ended; and the quality of alternatives is the totality of benefits of a current relationship relative to those obtainable from alternative relationships. Another exchange theory-based commitment model is provided by Cook and Emerson's (1978) study, which also adopts an instrumental orientation to commitment. They define commitment as stay behaviour that is fostered by a sense of predictability (uncertainty reduction) regarding one's partner. A series of successful transactions between partners in a network help them to know each other better, develop a common set of expectations, and thereby increase the costs of initiating new transactions with alternative partners. Reduced transaction costs and predictability in turn encourage the exchange partners to remain in the established relation. Extending this theory, Kollock (1994) theorizes commitment more explicitly as a behavioral strategy designed to reduce uncertainty when the quality of products is unknown.

In contrast to these instrumental approaches, RCT advocates viewing commitment as an expression of emotional attachment. Treating affective attachment as one of the key organizing principles of human behavior, RCT sheds light on a fundamental aspect of commitment behavior that has often been neglected in exchange theories. To understand the affective nature of a committed relationship, RCT highlights several structural conditions under which an instrumental exchange transforms into an expressive one, as well as emotional processes through which exchange partners perceive a relationship as valuable in itself, that is, as an expressive object.[1] In the sections that follow, we review relevant exchange theories that provide RCT with its theoretical background.

Theoretical background
Social exchange is a ubiquitous phenomenon. It occurs in neighbors' exchanges of favors, peers' exchanges of assistance, friends' exchanges of gifts, scholars' exchanges of research ideas, and even spouses or partners' exchanges of affection. A common principle underlying these exchanges is reciprocal obligation (Gouldner, 1960; Blau, 1964). If one asks a friend for a favor, this entails a general expectation of future return. Reciprocal obligations differentiate social exchange from economic transactions. Each economic transaction is discrete and independent, whereas the reciprocity principle in social exchange entails repetition and obligations for future interaction. If one buys a house from a seller, the transaction is consummated by paying the exact price for the house. The transaction does not require other obligations or interactions in the future. In contrast, commodities and services in social exchange do not have exact prices. Instead, consummating a social exchange necessarily builds up feelings of personal obligation, gratitude and trust among partners, all of which lay a foundation for social solidarity and micro social order even without binding contracts.

Social exchange theory emphasizes the structural context of transactions in which two or more actors seek to arrive at a satisfactory exchange of benefits. The context of a relationship is structured by repeated opportunities for social transactions among the same actors (Emerson, 1981). This structure constitutes the building block of a micro social order that is manifest in stable frequencies of interaction among a set of exchange partners (Cook & Emerson, 1978; Blau, 1977). Emerson's (1972, 1981) exchange theory analyzes enduring exchange relations in terms of power and dependence. From Emerson's power-dependence perspective (Emerson, 1972), A's power capability in exchange relation to B (Pab) is determined by B's dependence on A (Dba), and B's power capability in relation to A (Pba) is determined by A's dependence on B (Dab). The dependence of A on B ($Dab = Pba$) is, in turn, a joint function varying (1) directly with the value of the outcomes or rewards controlled by B (Vab) and (2) inversely with the availability and value of A's alternative sources.

Elaborating Emerson's power-dependence theory, Lawler and others advance a non-zero sum approach to power dependence (Bacharach & Lawler, 1981; Lawler, 1992b; Lawler & Ford, 1993). A zero-sum approach indicates an inverse relation between individuals' power capabilities; an increase in A's power by definition implies a decrease in B's power. As such, the focus in a zero-sum conception is on the differentiating, coercive and divisive effects of a power capability, ignoring the collaborative nature of power. A non-zero sum conception suggests an important, but neglected feature of power dynamics – namely, that the total or average power in a relation can change intentionally or unintentionally. For instance dependence on each other (total dependence) can increase or decrease simultaneously by mutually changing the value of the outcomes or the alternative outcome sources in the same direction. Emerson (1972) identifies this as a 'cohesion effect' of mutual power, and Thibaut and Kelley's (1959) notion of mutual-fate control also taps this aspect of power. Distinguishing total and relative power as two independent dimensions of power, Lawler and Yoon (1996) indicate that a structurally cohesive relationship occurs under higher total power and lower relative (unequal) power. In their research, they found that structural cohesion in exchange relations promotes relational cohesion and behavioral commitment to the relation as a social unit.

Among the standard exchange theory explanations for relationship development is that certain power-dependence conditions in exchange relations promote frequent exchange with the same actors (Emerson, 1972; Lawler et al., 2000). When actors repeatedly exchange resources, they learn more about one another, find each other more predictable, and infer that they have similar orientations to the exchange task. Predictability, expectation confirmation and reduced transaction costs are key benefits of staying with the same actor (Cook & Emerson, 1978; Emerson, 1981; Molm, 1994; Molm & Cook, 1995). Research in cognitive psychology explains this in terms of risk aversion, that is, the propensity for individuals to avoid unpredictable or uncertain decision contexts (Tversky & Kahneman, 1974). This same theme emerges in a variety of other commitment explanations, ranging from those centered on trust (Pruitt & Kimmel, 1977) or relation-specific assets (Williamson, 1981) to those dealing with embeddedness within larger social units (Granovetter, 1985). Taken as a whole, these theories generally agree that reduced uncertainty sets the focal relation or group apart from others and inclines actors to perceive greater instrumental value in focal relations or groups.

Relational cohesion theory (RCT) questions this instrumental explanation of commitment in exchange theories. First, the instrumental foundation assumed by exchange theorists explains only one class or form of commitment, that is, instrumental commitment in Kanter's (1968) terms. This instrumental explanation is analogous to an explanation of transactions in a grand spot market in which ties do form to realize instrumental incentives embedded in the relations. A problem is that it does not explain why actors remain in such relations in the face of better alternatives, competitive bidding and changing incentives in the environment (Frank, 1988,

1993; Lawler et al., 2000). Rational choice theories and network exchange theories have also attempted to resolve the same problem by embedding a variety of incentive configurations in social structures. They assume that once optimal incentive structures for multiple actors are configured and imposed exogenously on a given social relation or structure, actors would actualize them. The identities of those who carry the incentive structure do not matter because neither barriers nor coordination problems are assumed in realizing potential incentive structures (Hardin, 1968; Hechter, 1987; Macy, 1993; Yamagishi, 1995). In brief, the instrumental explanations proffered by both rational choice and network exchange theories treat human beings as cognitive calculators and their actions as reflections of the incentives embedded in structures.

RCT proposes that social structures or relations have both enabling and constraining effects on actors (see also Giddens, 1984); this aspect of social structure or relations provides actors with opportunities to experience certain emotions and cognitions; they actively construct and reconstruct reality based on these emotional and cognitive experiences. Like instrumental explanations, RCT treats social structures or relations as exogenous conditions. However RCT expands the instrumentally oriented approaches by emphasizing the process of emotional experience triggered by human action and social interaction. The theory assumes that human beings as voluntary agents interpret a given structure and use the experience of emotions in actively interpreting and reconstructing their own experience. This emphasis of RCT on emotions, cognition and agency in explaining commitment dovetails with Coleman's (1990) framework and Collins's (1981) interaction ritual chains. Coleman advocates the use of micro-order theories for explicating how human beings exploit or explore given structures and re-create new structures through rationally driven human agency. Collins (1981) also explains how actors experience emotional uplift through encounters and how these emotions help actors create solidarity. In sum, RCT focuses on emotional experiences and cognitive work and the role they play in transforming a purely instrumental relationship into an expressive one.

Relational cohesion theory
A core idea in RCT is that social exchange has emotional as well as instrumental effects on actors and, if these are attributed to social units, then social units take on expressive value or intrinsic worth. Persons develop stronger ties to groups that are perceived as sources of positive feeling or emotion and weaker ties to those perceived as sources of negative feeling or emotion (Lawler, 1992a). These ties are instrumental to the degree that they reflect the benefits of mutually satisfactory exchange; they are expressive to the degree that the social unit becomes a distinct object of affective

attachment. In this manner, RCT shows how emotions transform an instrumental relation into an affective object (Lawler & Yoon, 1996, 1998).

The theory contains three foundational ideas (Thye et al., 2002). First, exchange structures shape who is likely to interact and exchange with whom, by providing incentives for actors to exchange with some potential partners and not others (Skvoretz & Lovaglia, 1995). The same actors are likely to exchange with each other across time under fixed structural exchange conditions. Second, successful exchange efforts produce an emotional buzz, that is, mild, positive feelings; failure to accomplish exchange generates mild negative feelings (Lawler & Yoon, 1996, 1998). The emotions of concern here are involuntary and internal events that simply 'happen to people' (Hochschild, 1983). Parallel to this emotional process, successful exchanges also reduce uncertainties in the relation and strengthen the boundary between focal and alternative relations; this uncertainty reduction reduces transaction costs in the focal relation and builds a foundation of trust (Williamson, 1981; Kollock, 1994). Third, actors are motivated to understand the sources of these feelings because they want to reproduce good feelings and avoid bad feelings in the future. This stimulates cognitive work in which they are likely to identify social units – exchange relations or groups – in explaining their emotions. The emerging boundary between focal actors delineated by uncertainty reduction facilitates the actors' attributions by making the sources of positive emotions salient (Lawler, 1992a). Thus the relation to the group becomes an object of attachment by virtue of being perceived as a source of positive individual feelings. Cohesion and commitment are a result of this.

Based on the above discussion, Figure 8.1 shows the exogenous, endogenous and dependent variables in the theoretical model. The exogenous conditions are the structural relations of power dependence or interdependence among the actors (Emerson, 1981; Molm, 1994). Power is defined in terms of dependence, and as a structural capability distinct from both its use (tactics or strategies) and the actual or realized power resulting in the division of pay-offs (Emerson, 1972; Bacharach & Lawler, 1981; Lawler, 1992b; Molm, 1990). Given a group of multiple actors, each actor's dependence on the group is equal to the maximum benefit from the focal group compared with the maximum benefit from an alternative group. The total dependence in the group refers to the average of each member's individual dependence on the group. Dependence equality or inequality refers to relative differences in degrees of dependence on the group among its members.

RCT predicts that greater total dependence and equal dependence will produce more frequent and successful exchange in the focal group. Higher total dependence reduces the opportunity costs of opting for an alternative group; it also gives members greater adaptive flexibility in negotiations and more room for misperception or miscalculation. This is because under higher dependence there is a wider range of agreements that meet a 'sufficiency' criterion, that is, provide each actor with more than the expected value from the alternative group. Dependence inequality impacts negotiations negatively because inequalities of power raise issues of fairness and legitimacy that are unlikely to arise under dependence equality (Lawler & Yoon, 1993, 1996). The theory posits an interaction effect, predicting that the combination of high total and equal dependence on the group should produce an extra structural push toward repetitive exchange and the resulting group formation (that is, commitment) process. This structural cohesion effect is similar to Kollock's (1993) notion of running a 'loose accounting system' where partners do not keep exact tabs on each party's contributions and allow each other to remain unbalanced for long periods; a higher total dependence allows partners to reach agreement at a wider range of prices at an earlier stage and equal dependence allows them to rectify imbalances in pay-offs later, given repeated transactions.

The theory posits an indirect sequence by which structural power-dependence conditions promote group formation (see Figure 8.1). This sequence starts with the exchange frequencies produced by the structure of dependence. One endogenous path operates through the uncertainty reduction effects of exchange frequency, and the second endogenous path operates through emotional-affective effects. Uncertainty reduction is a 'boundary-defining' process in which actors come to see the group to which they belong as setting them off from other relations or groups, that is, as having distinctiveness in social identity terms (Brewer, 1993). The emotional effects of exchange are described in terms of a 'social bonding' process through which the group becomes an object of intrinsic or expressive value (Lawler & Yoon, 1996). Although the two endogenous processes are analytically and

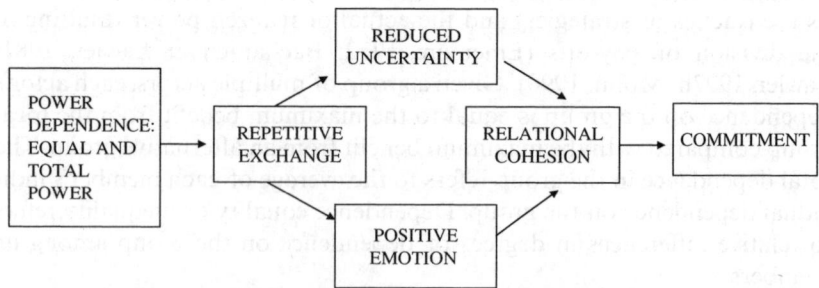

Source: Adapted from Lawler et al. (2000).

Figure 8.1   Relational cohesion theory (RCT)

empirically independent, they converge in that each enhances perceptions that the group is a unifying or cohesive unit (see also Bollen & Hoyle, 1990). This occurs because actors seek to interpret the source of positive emotions and the emerging group boundary prompts them to attribute the positive emotions to the group; the attribution, emotional buzz and salient boundary together induce actors to perceive their relationships to the group as having relational value.

RCT predicts that perceived relational cohesion among actors is the proximal cause of various forms of commitment behavior. RCT has tested this prediction by treating stay behavior, token gifts and contribution to a joint venture as forms of commitment behavior. Stay behavior is a standard indicator of commitment in the literature and measures the degree to which actors remain in the focal relation in face of better or at least equal alternatives (Lawler & Yoon, 1993, 1998). Token gifts are defined as the giving of resources to others in a unilateral way with no strings attached. Defined in this way, token gifts lack instrumental value and are symbolic of a shared group affiliation (Lawler et al., 1995). The theory treats the new joint venture as an N-person social dilemma where not contributing is the dominant strategy and the well-known disparity between individual and collective rationality is present (Axelrod, 1984; Platt, 1973). Among the three, stay behavior in the face of better alternatives can be construed as more instrumental than the others, gift-giving as more expressive, and contribution behavior as more normative. The conditions and the processes in RCT have been tested by setting up a series of experiments in which these commitment behaviors are observed after actors have had the opportunity to establish a sense of relational cohesion through frequent or repetitive exchange (See Lawler & Yoon, 1993, 1996, 1998; Lawler et al., 1995; Lawler et al., 2000).

Extrapolating Figure 8.1, RCT suggests further that given a group of multiple actors engaging in productive exchange,[2] members' greater total dependence or equality of dependence *on the group* promote member-to-group commitments, indirectly through the following steps: (1) High total dependence and equal dependencies generate more frequent, successful exchange among members. (2) More frequent exchange among these members increases (a) positive emotions or feelings and (b) the perceived predictability of the other members (uncertainty reduction). (3) Positive emotions and perceptions of predictability each make the relation more salient as a unifying, cohesive object in the situation. (4) Greater perceived cohesion produces a stronger commitment to a group, as reflected in stay behavior, gift-giving among members, and inclinations to undertake investments under risk or with the potential for malfeasance (Lawler & Yoon, 1996; Lawler et al., 2000).

The relational cohesion model of organizational commitment

The relational cohesion model of organizational commitment is a direct application of RCT to organizational contexts. Organizational commitment is defined as individual employees' attachments to their membership organization. Following Parsons's (1951) and Kanter's (1968) distinctions, the model stipulates that an individual attachment can be instrumental (utilitarian), affective (emotional) or normative (moral). Instrumental commitment (IC) is based on the perceived benefits of remaining with an organization, whereas affective commitment (AC) is based on an emotional or cathectic attachment to the organization. Normative commitment (NC) is the attachment to the moral values and norms of an organization (Kanter, 1968).

Meyer et al. (1990) explicate the three dimensions with reference to the motivation underlying stay behavior. In an employment relationship, employees with instrumental commitment stay with an organization 'because they need to'; those with affective commitment stay 'because they want to'; and those with normative commitment stay 'because they feel they ought to' (Meyer et al., 1990: 710). O'Reilly and Chatman (1986) also propose a similar typology of psychological attachment (that is, compliance, identification and internalization), equivalent, respectively, to instrumental, affective and normative commitment. Most scholars employing multiple dimensions of organizational commitment agree that high organizational performance can be attained through an organization's capacity to mobilize more than instrumental commitment from its members (O'Reilly & Chatman, 1986; Meyer et al., 1990; Mathieu & Zajac, 1990).

Studies of organizational commitment have tended to investigate these three dimensions of commitment synchronically (Mathieu, 1991; Williams & Hazer, 1986), focusing on differential causes of the three dimensions of commitment and differential consequences for organizations. In our model, we draw attention instead to the developmental aspect, that is, to how each dimension of commitment develops diachronically. Our model assumes that employees enter their membership organizations with instrumental motivations: there is an exchange with an organization, within which individual members invest their human resources in the organization in anticipation of salary, fringe benefits, social networks and reputation. Treating the instrumental motivation as one of the initial conditions however, our model pushes it further to understand how affective and normative commitments emerge from this instrumental base.

In the next sections, we elaborate the model. First, we review various forms of organizational capital that members depend on in exchange with organizations and the initial effects of these on instrumental commitment. Second, the two endogenous processes posited by RCT will be adapted to understand the development of affective commitment from an instrumental base. Third, the model will be expanded to explain how affective commitment generates normative commitment based on special forms of cultural capital in an organization.

Organizational capital, dependence, and instrumental commitment

The first part of the model (see Figure 8.2) indicates that instrumentally motivated members experience varying degrees of dependence, reflected in the benefits they enjoy from different forms of organizational capital (for example cultural capital, social capital and human capital). The different forms of capital are, in part, grounded in and fostered by the organizational membership. Human capital is defined as a combination of an individual employee's sets of knowledge, skills, expertise, experiences and abilities (Becker, 1964); human capital is applied to their jobs and projects to generate value for the membership organization. Social capital is the network of relations employees rely on to secure some other benefits (Portes, 1998). Employees use social capital for instrumental purposes, perhaps to do their jobs more effectively by acquiring information or skills from other experts in the network. Cultural capital is the system of cultural resources that help members derive shared understandings, justifications and interpretations of organizational events and routines (Bourdieu, 1984; Lamont & Lareau, 1988; Rentsch, 1990; Schein, 1985). Distinct from cultural forms such as rites and ceremonials, cultural capital consists of core assumptions, ideologies, missions, norms and values. Cultural capital works as a mental map, guiding appropriate ways of being and doing in organizational contexts (Argyris, 1993; Argyris & Schon, 1974, 1978; James & James, 1989; Schneider, 1975; Senge, 1990; Swidler, 1986). Cultural capital also encompasses an organization's reputation and its status in a given industry. As shown in Figure 8.2, the first prediction in our model is that as members perceive greater dependence on an organization for development and sustaining of human, social and cultural capital, they are likely to show greater instrumental commitment (IC) to that organization.

Our model assumes that employees use their human capital in the organization for instrumental purposes, that is, to achieve their personal and professional goals. Among the most prominent goals of individuals is to increase the value or marketability of their human capital in internal and external labor markets. Employees also expect their membership organizations to be instrumental in making their career paths resistant to threats posed by unstable economic conditions (Rousseau, 1995; Rousseau & Schalk, 2000). The acquisition and development of excellent human capital serves an instrumental purpose for the organizations as well. Organizations increasingly view and use human capital as a central strategic factor in

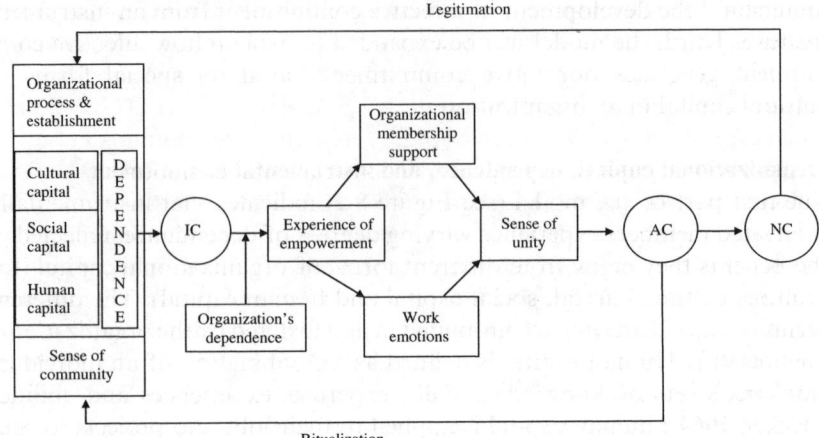

Figure 8.2   Relational cohesion model of organizational commitment

gaining competitive advantage (Delery & Doty, 1996; Huselid, 1995; Wright & Snell, 1998; Lepak & Snell, 1999; Pfeffer, 1994). An investment in human capital via education and training can generate a positive return on their investment (Becker, 1964).

Becker (1964) distinguishes between specific and general human capital investments. The former produces more dependence on the organization than the latter. Specific human capital investment refers to skills or knowledge that is useful only to one or a few employers, whereas general human capital investment is useful to virtually any employer. Organizations and their employees share the goal of increasing the return on such investments in human capital. On the other hand, employees want to increase the market value of their own human capital by investing more in general human capital, because such an investment reduces dependence on current employers; in contrast, employers want to invest in company-specific human capital, because such investment protects its return and makes employees dependent.[3] All in all, to the extent that employees perceive their current employer as adding more to their human capital potential than alternative employers, they will experience greater dependence on the employing organization.

Portes describes social capital as 'the ability of actors to secure benefits by virtue of membership in social networks or relationships in social structures' (Portes, 1998: 6). Social capital is not an individual actor's property; its value resides in the relational tie, which makes it more like a public good, especially when it is deployed within a collective boundary or a closed network (Coleman, 1988). Social capital requires a minimum level of mutual effort for the maintenance of commitment, trust, support and cooperation.

Members' social capital can be based on either internal or external ties (Adler & Kwon, 2002). Social capital in the form of external ties functions as a bridge that brings resources into an organization from other groups or networks outside the organization (Burt, 1992; Granovetter, 1973), whereas social capital in the form of internal ties functions as a communal bonding or sharing mechanism over individual resources within the boundary of a collectivity (Putnam, 2000; Coleman, 1988).

Despite this significant role, the dependence of individual members on this form of capital is largely implicit. Employees might not perceive its explicit value until they decide to leave an organization and search for a new organization. There is no common metric available to measure social relations as there is in the case of economic capital. Nevertheless when a member who has long benefited from a strong relationship with internal members seeks to move elsewhere, his or her dependence on social capital can emerge as an important factor. Similarly, when a member as a representative of an organization has also benefited from social networks with representatives of other organizations, such dependence also might come to the foreground. As with specific human capital, as the organization produces more non-transferable social capital, an employee becomes more dependent on the organization.

The model in Figure 8.2 also theorizes that employees' dependence on the organization is shaped by the degree that the organization produces access to cultural capital. We define cultural capital as a system of cultural resources (for example ideologies, missions, norms and values) which help members derive shared understanding, justifications and interpretations of organizational events and routines (Bourdieu, 1984; Lamont & Lareau, 1988; Rentsch, 1990; Schein, 1985). Much research indicates how cultural capital in the forms of ideologies, missions and values affects various organizational activities and behavior, such as organization–person fit (O'Reilly & Caldwell, 1981; O'Reilly & Chatman, 1986; Chatman, 1989), organizational learning (Senge, 1990; Nadkarni, 2003) and organizational transformation (Collins & Porras, 1996). However these forms of cultural capital do not foster members' instrumental dependence, because they mainly subsume members' normative orientations.

Instrumental dependence on cultural capital produced by organizations emerges instead from a special form of cultural capital: the status of an organization in its industry is an example of this. An organization's industry status is one of its cultural assets or resources, because organizational status is activated by cultural beliefs shared among organizations in a field of industry. Especially when evaluators in the labor market have no information on a given individual, they infer the status value and performance expectation of that individual from his or her membership organization's status and performance expectation. Organizational status is carried over in determining members' status in the market. Higher organizational status also becomes a source of pride for members that differs from the respect that results from an individual's status within an organization (Hogg, 1992; Hogg & Turner, 1985; Tyler, 2001). This organizational status argument predicts that, other things being equal, the higher the status and performance expectation of an organization within an industry, the greater is its members' dependence on this aspect of cultural capital. Most job candidates also have this status information in mind when they search prospective workplaces.

In brief, the first part of our model (see Figure 8.2) predicts that employees develop instrumental commitment (IC) due to the degree that organizations enhance their human capital (for example training and education), social capital (for example social support and relationships) and cultural capital (for example organizational reputation). The instrumental commitment in turn induces employees to stay with that organization. Stay behavior is a key behavioral indicator of instrumental commitment (O'Reilly & Chatman, 1986).

Endogenous processes and affective commitment
The relational cohesion model of organizational commitment extrapolates its key theoretical constructs from those in Relational Cohesion Theory (see Figure 8.2). Experiences of empowerment are, in RCT, equivalent to the accomplishment of repetitive exchange; organizational membership support is equivalent to predictability or reduced uncertainty; and positive work emotions are equivalent to positive emotions from exchange in RCT. As a part of these two endogenous processes, the relational cohesion model of organizational commitment proposes that a member's experience of empowerment triggers two pathways (emotional bonding and boundary defining) that lead to a sense of unity and affective commitment (AC).

Our model treats an organization's dependence on its member as a moderating factor for the impact of the member's perception of dependence on the experience of empowerment. Empowerment in our model refers to a state in which employees experience enhanced efficacy or sense of control in achieving personal and professional goals through their organization (Yoon, 2001; Bandura, 1982; Conger & Kanungo, 1988; Kanungo, 1979; Thomas & Velthouse, 1990). The organization's dependence, by offsetting the employee's own dependence, provides the employee with empowerment opportunities and experience. The more mutual the dependence, the more likely are employees to adjust their goals to achieve joint tasks and goals. Tsui and her associates (Tsui et al., 1997) confirm that mutual dependence (or investment) in the employment relationship enhances employees' commitments and organizational citizenship behavior as well as performance (see also Lawler, 1986).

In Figure 8.2, organizational membership support refers to individual members' beliefs that their organization will treat them as deserving members when the organization is under uncertainty, risk or financial difficulties. As employees perceive greater membership support in such situations, they are likely to experience greater certainty or predictability in the future of the relationship. Organizational membership support is adapted from Eisenberger and others' (Eisenberger et al., 1986; Rhoades & Eisenberger, 2002; Tyler, 2001) perceived organizational support (POS) by highlighting the aspect of membership in exchange for support (for example even if my organization found a person who could do my job better, they would not replace me; when my job is eliminated, my organization will transfer me to a new job rather than lay me off). We predict that empowered employees are likely to perform better and, given these contributions, be accepted as more deserving members by an organization. In a similar context, Hollander (1958) also indicates that members' repeated contributions can serve as credits that can be used to draw membership support from the organization, especially when they make unexpected mistakes, perform poorly, or fail at specific tasks.

Relational Cohesion Theory considers two facets of positive emotions: pleasure/satisfaction and interest/excitement (Izard, 1991; Watson & Tellegen, 1985; Larsen & Diener, 1992). Pleasure/satisfaction is 'feeling gratified', and interest/excitement is 'feeling energized'. Lawler and Yoon (1993, 1996) describe interest/excitement as a forward-looking emotion, one based on an awareness of potential satisfaction in anticipation of possible gains, and pleasure/satisfaction as a backward-looking emotion, which occurs after something has been gained. Assuming partners in an exchange relation simultaneously look forward and backward, RCT explores whether the corresponding emotions mediate commitment behavior. Following this lead, we construe positive work emotion as a positively gratified or energized state resulting from the appraisal of one's work experiences. Our model adopts both facets of positive emotions from RCT: pleasure/satisfaction and interest/excitement.

Rediscovering different types of affect in the workplace in the mid-1980s and 1990s, organizational researchers have argued that job satisfaction is limited in understanding various affective work experiences because its measurement captures mainly evaluative and cognitive states (Brief & Weiss, 2002). Our current conceptualization addresses this problem by incorporating interest/excitement as another key affective state and by treating pleasure/satisfaction as a global emotion beyond specific job evaluation. As a motivating state of curiosity and fascination (Izard, 1991), interest/excitement captures more active aspects of affective experiences and accounts for high levels of enthusiasm.

We argue that when employees experience more empowerment, they tend to be emotionally energized and gratified, and they attribute these feelings to the organization (Lawler, 1992a). RCT theory does not explain or theorize the conditions under which the emotions are attributed to the social unit. However the Affect Theory of Social Exchange (Lawler, 2001, 2002) takes up this issue. According to that theory, this attribution of feelings to the social unit occurs when the task engaged in by actors is high in jointness, and when it is likely to generate a sense of shared responsibility for results produced. Applied to our organizational commitment model, the greater the mutual dependence in the individual–organization relationship, the greater the degree that individuals will see their own individual efficacy as intertwined with the efficacy of the organization; in this sense, the individual experience of empowerment involves a sense of jointly accomplishing important tasks with the organization as such; this jointness and shared responsibility of empowerment make employees attribute their emotions in part to the relationship with the organization (Lawler, 2002). The emerging membership boundary along with organizational membership support also prompts members to interpret the sources of their positive emotions and attribute them to the member–organization relationship. As members begin to perceive such a relationship as an emotionally and cognitively binding force, the relationship becomes objectified as a valuable third force unifying them with the organization. The current model predicts that this sense of unity is the proximal cause of affective commitment (see Figure 8.2). That is, the model predicts that instrumental commitment (IC) develops into affective commitment (AC) when employees perceive a sense of unity with their membership organization.

Moral value and normative commitment
We conceptualized instrumental commitment as an attachment to the utilitarian value of an organization and affective commitment as an attachment to the relation with an organization. Similarly, we define normative commitment as an attachment to the moral-normative aspects of an organization. This definition of normative commitment is similar to Buchanan's (1974) definition. Buchanan construes commitment in terms of an attachment to the long-term goals (or visions) and values of an organization. Our definition is also suggested by Wiener's (1982) notion of normative commitment as personal convictions in support of the value system (for example missions and goals) of an organization. Weiner differentiates this form of normative commitment from the conventional normative commitment built upon generalized loyalty and duty. The standard definition of normative

commitment emphasizes the loyalty or obedience of members, whereas Weiner's defines normative commitment as a reflection of personal conviction; the latter approach assumes individual choices among distinctive value systems and individual initiatives to realize the chosen one (Wiener, 1982).

The moral value of an organization is determined primarily by the cultural capital the organization holds. To elaborate the role of cultural capital in normative commitment, we use the concepts of organizational mental model and organizational culture, as characterizations of 'espoused theory', based on Senge (1990) and Argyris and Schon (1974, 1978). Argyris and Schon's organizational theory differentiates theory in use from espoused theory. They state: 'When someone is asked how he would behave under certain circumstances, the answer he usually gives is his "espoused theory of action" for that situation. This is the theory of action to which he gives allegiance, and which, upon request, he communicates to others. However, the theory that actually governs his actions is this theory in use' (Argyris & Schon, 1974: 6–7).

Certain components of cultural capital act as either theory in use or espoused theory in an organization. Culure as theory in use is embedded in the cultural capital component as a tool kit or as a set of habitualized routines (Swidler, 1986). Without questionning its validity, members use it as a heuristic device to make sense of their environments (Argyris, 1993). In constrast, the culture as an espoused theory is the set of ideologies, values and purposes that constitutes the 'core mental model' of an organization (Argyris, 1993; Collins & Porras, 1996; Gentner & Stevens, 1983; Kieras & Bovair, 1984; Nadkarni, 2003). A mental model works as a cognitive filter or map through which people consciously make sense of significant problems; people utilize it explicitly when they need to justify the hows and whys of important issues in a problem situation (Senge, 1990; Nadkarni, 2003). Similarly, the 'organizational mental model' can be construed as a system of visions, values and purposes that provides moral justification or legitimacy for an organization. This notion of organizational mental model is also reflected in Argyris's (1993) Model II, Collins and Porras's (1996) corporate ideology, Swidler's (1986) cultural ideology and Weber's (1946) metaphor of switchmen. As implied by the nature of values, visions and purposes, mental models become the foundation of an organization's moral value.

Building upon these conceptualizations, we now define normative commitment formally as members' attachments to the moral values of their membership organization's mental model. With this definition in mind, our model proposes a mechanism through which affective attachment generates normative attachment. This mechanism requires a series of cognitive and evaluative steps (Fishbein & Ajzen, 1975; Wiener, 1988): First, members attempt to make broad sense of their affective attachment, that is, from the perspective of their organization's mental model (visions, purposes and values). Second, once the moral meaning of their relationship to an organization is primed by the organizational mental model, then members begin to perceive incipient moral values of the organizational mental model. Finally, members develop normative attachment to the organization, when they realize that the organizational mental model is also congruent with their personal values.

Once members develop normative commitment to their organization, they use the set of organizational mental models (that is, visions, purposes and values) more deliberatively in justifying and legitimating critical events in their organization. That is, they use the mental model purposively in explaining the hows and whys of significant issues in a problem situation (Nadkarni, 2003). In particular, decisions that members reach are justified or legitimized more explicitly by the core values an organization holds (Barrett, 2003). Members incorporate corporate visions, values and missions in articulating their own personal mental models (Levin, 2000). This infusion of a corporate mental model into members' moral orientations in turn drives members' greater engagement in realizing it by putting substantial effort and sacrifice into their action.

Despite such powerful explanatory potential, normative commitment has not drawn much research attention to date (see Wiener, 1982, 1988 for an exception). One reason is that normative commitment is conceptualized in terms of moral judgement and attitudes, making its scientific scrutiny difficult. Our model addresses this problem by defining normative commitment as an attachment to the organizational mental model that lays a moral legitimacy for the organization. Another reason is that some organizations may not yet have established their salient mental models as a foundation for normative commitment. Nonetheless scholars have begun to recognize the importance of normative commitment in understanding more dynamic aspects of organizational activities beyond performance and order (Collins & Porras, 1996; Kirkpatrick et al., 2002; Kotter, 1996; Larwood et al., 1995; Wiener, 1982; Lau & Woodman, 1995; Herscovitch & Meyer, 2002).[4] Our model opens an avenue for such research.

Along with this developmental focus, our model identifies various behaviors as reflections of these underlying dimensions of attachment. For example turnover and intention to stay are among the main behavioral indicators of instrumental commitment (Mathieu, 1991; Mathieu & Zajac, 1990; Williams & Hazer, 1986); as in gift-giving in RCT, organizational citizenship behavior can be construed as a behavioral indication of affective attachment (Organ, 1997; Podsakoff & MacKenzie, 1997; Podsakoff et al., 2000); extraordinary contributions and individual sacrifice are behavioral expressions of normative commitment (Wiener, 1982).

The reciprocal paths in Figure 8.2 suggest that if such affective and normative commitment behaviors are collectively expressed among members, these lay the foundation for ritualization of processes within an organization and legitimation for an organization as such. Specifically, the collective behavioral expression of affective commitment through extra role behavior or organizational citizenship behavior constitutes organizational rituals invoking a shared membership identity and its affective value for all members (Durkheim, 1915). Similarly, the collective behavioral expression of sacrifices and significant contributions among members becomes a strong source of validation for those members who seek affirmation of their personal beliefs about the value of the organizational membership (Fishbein & Ajzen, 1975; Scott, 1987; Walker et al., 1986). Furthermore the collectively validated organizational mental model works as a guiding framework legitimizing the current organizational structure and processes. Ritualization and legitimation offer ways of understanding why and how individual actions are organized and intertwined at the collective level.

Conclusions
This study applies Relational Cohesion Theory (Lawler & Yoon, 1993, 1996, 1998; Lawler et al., 2000; Thye et al., 2002) to the important task of understanding how employees within organizations develop affective and normative commitments from purely instrumental commitments. Instrumental commitment is the degree to which dependence leads individual members to believe that they can fulfill their personal and professional goals by remaining in their current organizations as opposed to joining alternative organizations. Affective commitment is the degree to which members perceive the relationship to the organization to be a salient force having significant value in itself; normative commitment is the degree that members ascribe moral value to their organization's core cultural system as reflected in the organizational mental model. From a developmental process, affective commitment develops when instrumental commitment generates a sense of unity, through boundary defining and emotional bonding processes. Normative commitment emerges and builds in strength when affectively committed relations acquire a larger moral meaning, with reference to a corporate mental model, such that members believe in the moral value of the organization. It adds a dimension to social identification processes (Meyer et al., 1990; O'Reilly & Chatman, 1986; Wiener, 1982). Instrumental commitment entails a utilitarian identification of an individual's goals with an organization's short-term operation and performance goals (Rusbult, 1980, 1983). Affective commitment entails an emotional bonding or identification of the self with the organizational identity (Porter et al., 1974; Meyer et al., 1990). Normative commitment involves a correspondence between an

individual's value orientation with that of an organization, that is, a moral identification with the organization (Buchanan, 1974; Wiener, 1982, 1988).

Parts of the relational cohesion model of organizational commitment have been tested in several field studies. Yoon and others (Yoon et al., 1994; Yoon & Lim, 1999; Yoon & Thye, 2000) have confirmed the role of social and human capital in promoting affective and instrumental commitment. Other studies (Yoon et al., 1996; Yoon, 2001) have investigated the path from social and human capital to experiences of empowerment, and demonstrated their significant roles for psychological empowerment. Yoon and Thye (2002) have documented the independent effects of the two endogenous processes (that is, boundary defining and emotional bonding) in organizational commitment. A comprehensive test of our model is a task for future research.

A key message of our model is the role of affective commitment in bridging instrumental and normative commitment. Affective attachment is important because it promotes sociability, that is, the capacity of an organization to facilitate workplaces in which open dialogue, voluntary cooperation and trustful interaction occur even among members who have not known each other (Onyx & Bullen, 2000; Kreijns et al., 2002; Leana & Van Buren, 1999). If individual members are committed affectively to an organization, this enhances the salience of organizational membership, thereby prompting members to initiate more interactions with fellow employees (see also Hogg, 1992; Tajfel & Turner, 1986). Such a common social identity also helps an organization overcome structural cleavages within itself by strengthening the overarching organizational identity. Low sociability for example inhibits individually-oriented members from sharing information with other members who need it. Social capital cannot be created and replenished without the generation of spontaneous collaboration among network members, and low sociability reduces this. Among the three forms of organizational commitment, the affective form is the primary determinant of sociability. Overall, we suspect that without affective commitment, organizations with substantial human resources and cultural capital would perform less well, due to insufficient sociability.

The roles of instrumental, normative and affective commitment can be likened to the functional system of a motor vehicle: instrumental commitment provides the fuel energizing members by helping them fulfill their individual goals within an organization; affective commitment is an engine transforming the fuel into collective power or efficacy through a healthy and trustful community of interaction; and normative commitment is a steering wheel directing the collective efficacy or power to whatever destination the organization desires to reach.

Notes

* This chapter was supported by the Korea Research Foundation (Grant #: 2001-042-C00135) awarded to the first author. The authors thank Shane Thye for constructive comments.
1. This part of the explanation is developed more explicitly by Lawler's affect theory of social exchange (Lawler, 2001, 2002). The theory indicates that different structural forms of exchange entail tasks with different degrees of jointness and shared responsibility. Shared responsibility and task jointness in turn lead actors to attribute distinct types of emotions to relevant social units as the context for actors' common focus and activity.
2. Lawler et al. (2000) conceptualize productive exchange in terms of the following properties: (1) productive exchange involves mutiple actors who combine resources to produce a joint outcome such as a paper authored by three actors or a department potluck dinner; (2) the joint production entails higher degrees of interdependence among members and considerable coordination problems; (3) unlike dyadic exchange in which inputs and benefits flow from person-to-person, inputs in a productive exchange flow from person-to-group and benefits flow from group-to-person.
3. Employees also make extra investments around their own human capital in a form known as side bets (Becker, 1964). These side bets also increase members' dependence on their membership organizations. For instance an employee might make a side bet in the form of buying a house near the company to save commuting hours or to transfer their kids into a particular school district. These side bets become sunk costs for members, in that their investment value is realized only insofar as they stay with a given organization.
4. Collins and Porras (1996) demonstrate that world class companies with records of long-term excellence have the communality in virtue of which their employees – including CEOs – are all normatively committed to their mental models and, moreover, that they cultivate such environments explicitly; Kirkpatrick et al. (2002) and Kotter (1996) show how salient visions and purposes commit employees to their organization's transformation efforts to adapt to pressures of competition. In a nutshell, Wiener (1982) concludes that only normatively committed people respond seriously to an organization's requests for substantial investment, effort and sacrifice.

References

Adler, P.S. & Kwon, S. (2002), Social capital: prospects for a new concept, *Academy of Management Review*, **27**, 17–40.

Argyris, C. (1993), *On organizational learning*, Cambridge, MA: Blackwell Publishers.

Argyris, C. & Schon, D. (1974), *Theory in Practice: Increasing Professional Effectiveness*, San Francisco, CA: Jossey-Bass.

Argyris, C. & Schon, D. (1978), *Organizational Learning: A Theory of Action Perspective*, Reading, MA: Addison Wesley.

Axelrod, R. (1984), *The Evolution of Cooperation*, New York: Basic Books.

Bacharach, S.B. & Lawler, E.J. (1981), *Bargaining: Power, Tactics, and Outcomes*, San Francisco, CA: Jossey-Bass.

Bandura, A. (1982), Self-efficacy mechanism in human agency, *American Psychologist*, **37**, 122–47.

Barrett, R. (2003), Improving your cultural capital, *Industrial Management*, **45**, 20–24.

Becker, G.S. (1964), *Human Capital*, New York: Columbia University Press.

Becker, H.S. (1960), Notes on the concept of commitment, *American Journal of Sociology*, **66**, 32–40.

Blau, P.M. (1964), *Exchange and Power in Social Life*, New York: Wiley.

Blau, P.M. (1977), A macrosociological theory of social structure, *American Journal of Sociology*, **83**, 26–54.

Bollen, K.A. & Hoyle, R.H. (1990), Perceived cohesion: a conceptual and empirical examination, *Social Forces*, **69**, 479–504.

Bourdieu, P. (1984), *Distinction: A Social Critique of the Judgment of Taste*, Cambridge, MA: Harvard University Press.

Brewer, M.B. (1993), Social identity, distinctiveness, and ingroup homogeneity, *Social Cognition*, **11**, 150–64.

Brief, A.P. & Weiss, H.M. (2002), Organizational behavior: affect in the work place, *Annual Review of Psychology*, **53**, 279–307.

Buchanan, B. (1974), Building organizational commitment: the socialization of managers in work organizations, *Administrative Science Quarterly*, **19**, 533–47.

Burt, R.S. (1992), *Structural Holes: The Social Structure of Competition*, Cambridge, MA: Harvard University Press.

Chatman, J.A. (1989), Improving interactional organizational research: a model of person-organization fit, *Academy of Management Review*, **14**, 333–49.

Coleman, J.S. (1988), Social capital in the creation of human capital, *American Journal of Sociology*, **94**, 95–120.

Coleman, J.S. (1990), *Foundations of Social Theory*, Cambridge, MA: Harvard University Press.

Collins, J. & Porras, J.I. (1996), Building your company's vision, *Harvard Business Review*, **74**, 65–77.

Collins, R. (1981), On the microfoundations of macrosociology, *American Journal of Sociology*, **86**, 984–1014.

Conger, J.A. & Kanungo, R.N. (1988), The empowerment process: integrating theory and practice, *Academy of Management Review*, **13**, 471–82.

Cook, K.S. & Emerson, R. (1978), Power, equity, and commitment in exchange networks, *American Sociological Review*, **27**, 40–41.

Delery, J.E. & Doty, D.H. (1996), Modes of theorizing in strategic human resource management: tests of universalistic, contingency, and configurational performance prediction, *Academy of Management Journal*, **39**, 802–35.

Durkheim, E. (1915), *The Elementary Forms of Religious Life*, New York: Free Press.

Eisenberger, R., Huntington, R., Hutchison, S. & Sowa, D. (1986), Perceived organizational support, *Journal of Applied Psychology*, **71**, 500–507.

Emerson, R.M. (1972), Exchange theory Part I: A psychological basis for social exchange, in Berger, J., Zelditch, M., Jr. & Anderson, B. (eds), *Sociological Theories in Progress*, vol. 2, Boston, MA: Houghton-Mifflin, pp. 38–57.

Emerson, R.M. (1981), Social exchange theory, in Rosenberg, M. and Turner, R.H. (eds), *Social Psychology: Sociological Perspectives*, New York: Basic Books, pp. 30–65.

Fishbein, M. & Ajzen, I. (1975), *Belief, Attitude, Intention, and Behavior*. Reading, MA: Addison-Wesley.

Frank, R.H. (1988), *Passions within Reasons: The Strategic Role of Emotions*, New York: W.W. Norton.

Frank, R.H. (1993), The strategic role of emotions: reconciling over and undersocialized accounts of behavior, *Rationality and Society*, **5**, 160–84.

Gentner, D. & Stevens, A. (1983), *Mental Models*, Hillsdale, NJ: Erlbaum.

Giddens, A. (1984), *The Constitution of Society*, Berkeley, CA: University of California Press.

Gouldner, A.W. (1960), The norm of reciprocity: a preliminary statement, *American Sociological Review*, **25**, 161–78.

Granovetter, M.S. (1973), The strength of weak ties, *American Journal of Sociology*, **78**, 1360–80.

Granovetter, M.S. (1985), Economic action and social structure: the problem of embeddedness, *American Journal of Sociology*, **91**, 481–510.

Hardin, G. (1968), Tragedy of the commons, *Science*, **162**, 1243–8.

Hechter, M. (1987), *Principles of Group Solidarity*. Berkeley, CA: University of California Press.

Herscovitch, L. & Meyer, J.P. (2002), Commitment to organizational change: extension of a three-component model, *Journal of Applied Psychology*, **87**, 474–87.

Hochschild, A.R. (1983), *The Managed Heart: Commercialization of Human Feeling*, Berkeley, CA: University of California Press.

Hogg, M.A. (1992), *The Social Psychology of Group Cohesiveness: From Attraction to Social Identity*, New York: New York University Press.

Hogg, M.A. & Turner, J.C. (1985), Interpersonal attraction, social identity, and psychological group formation, *European Journal of Social Psychology*, **15**, 51–66.

Hollander, E.P. (1958), Conformity, status, and idiosyncracy credit, *Psychological Review*, **65**, 117–27.

Homans, G.C. (1961), *Social Behavior*, New York: Harcourt, Brace & World.

Huselid, M.A. (1995), The impact of human resource management practices on turnover, productivity, and corporate financial performance. *Academy of Management Journal*, **38**, 635–72.

Izard, Carroll E. (1991), *The Psychology of Emotion*, New York: Plenum Press.

James, L.A. & James, L.R. (1989), Integrating work environment perceptions: explorations in the measurement of meaning, *Journal of Applied Psychology*, **74**, 739–51.

Kanter, R.M. (1968), Commitment and social organization: a study of commitment mechanisms in utopian communities, *American Sociological Review*, **33**, 499–517.

Kanungo, R. (1979), The concepts of alienation and involvement revisited, *Psychological Bulletin*, **86**, 119–38.

Kieras, D. & Bovair, S. (1984), The role of mental models in learning to operate a device. *Cognitive Science*, **8**, 255–73.

Kirkpatrick, S.A., Wofford, J.C. & Baum, J.R. (2002), Measuring motive imagery contained in the vision statement. *Leadership Quarterly*, **13**, 139–50.

Kollock, P. (1993), An eye for an eye leaves everyone blind: cooperation and accounting systems, *American Sociological Review*, **58**, 768–85.

Kollock, P. (1994), The emergence of exchange structures: an experimental study of uncertainty, commitment, and trust, *American Journal of Sociology*, **100**, 315–45.

Kotter, J.P. (1996), *Leading Change*, Boston, MA: Harvard Business Press.

Kreijns, K., Kirschner, P.A. & Jochems, W. (2002), The sociability of computer-supported collaborative learning environments, *Journal of Education Technology and Society*, **5**, 8–22.

Lamont, M. & Lareau, A. (1988), Cultural capital: allusions, gaps, and glissandos in recent theoretical developments, *Sociological Theory*, **6**, 153–68.

Larsen, R.J. & Diener, E. (1992), Promises and problems with the circumplex model of emotion, in Clark, M.S. (ed.), *Emotion*, Newbury Park, CA: Sage Publications, pp. 25–9.

Larwood, E.J., Fable, C.M., Kriger, M.P. & Miesing, P. (1995), Structure and meaning of organizational vision, *Academy of Management Journal*, **38**, 740–70.

Lau, C. & Woodman, R.W. (1995), Understanding organizational change: a schematic perspective, *Academy of Management Journal*, **38**, 537–54.

Lawler, E.E., III. (1986), *High-involvement Management*, San Francisco, CA: Jossey-Bass.

Lawler, E.J. (1992a), Choice processes and affective attachments to nested groups: a theoretical analysis, *American Sociological Review*, **57**, 327–39.

Lawler, E.J. (1992b), Power processes in bargaining, *Sociological Quarterly*, **33**, 17–34.

Lawler, E.J. (2001), An affect theory of social exchange, *American Journal of Sociology*, **107**, 321–52.

Lawler, E.J. (2002), Micro social orders, *Social Psychology Quarterly*, **65**, 4–17.

Lawler, E.J. & Ford, R. (1993), Metatheory and friendly competition in theory growth: the case of power processes in bargaining, in Berger, J. & Zelditch, M., Jr. (eds), *Theoretical Research Programs: Studies in Theory Growth*, Stanford, CA: Stanford University Press, pp. 172–210.

Lawler, E.J., Thye, S. & Yoon, J. (2000), Emotion and group cohesion in productive exchange, *American Journal of Sociology*, **106**, 616–57.

Lawler, E.J. & Yoon, J. (1993), Power and the emergence of commitment behavior in negotiated exchange, *American Sociological Review*, **58**, 465–81.

Lawler, E.J. & Yoon, J. (1996), Commitment in exchange relations: test of a theory of relational cohesion, *American Sociological Review*, **61**, 89–108.

Lawler, E.J. & Yoon, J. (1998), Network structure and emotion in exchange relations, *American Sociological Review*, **63**, 871–94.

Lawler, E.J., Yoon, J., Baker, M. & Large, M.D. (1995), Mutual dependence and gift giving in exchange relations, *Advances in Group Processes*, **12**, 271–98.

Leana, C.R. & Van Buren, H.J. (1999), Organizational social capital and employment practices, *Academy of Management Review*, **24**, 538–55.

Lepak, D.P. & Snell, S.A. (1999), The human resource architecture: toward a theory of human capital allocation and development, *Academy of Management Review*, **24**, 31–48.

Levin, I.M. (2000), Vision revisited: telling the story of the future, *Journal of Applied and Behavioral Science*, **36**, 91–107.

Macy, M.W. (1993), Backward looking social control, *American Sociological Review*, **58**, 819–36.

Mathieu, J.E. (1991), A cross-level nonrecursive model of the antecedents of organizational commitment and satisfaction, *Journal of Applied Psychology*, **76**, 607–18.

Mathieu, J.E. & Zajac, D. (1990), A review and meta-analysis of the antecedents, correlates, and consequences of organizational commitment, *Psychological Bulletin*, **108**, 171–94.

Meyer, J.P., Allen, N.J. & Gellatly, I.R. (1990), Affective and continuance commitment to the organization: Evaluation of measures and analysis of concurrent and time-lagged relations, *Journal of Applied Psychology*, **75**, 710–20.

Molm, L. (1990), Structure, action, and outcomes: the dynamics of power in social exchange, *American Sociological Review*, **55**, 427–47.

Molm, L. (1994), Dependence and risk: transforming the structure of social exchange. *Social Psychology Quarterly*, **57**, 163–89.

Molm, L. & Cook, K. (1995), Social exchange and exchange networks, in Cook, K.S., Fine, G.A. & House, J.S. (eds), *Sociological Perspectives on Social Psychology*, Boston, MA: Allyn and Bacon, pp. 209–35.

Nadkarni, S. (2003), Instructional methods and mental models of students: an empirical investigation, *Academy of Management Learning and Education*, **2**, 335–51.

Onyx, J. & Bullen, P. (2000), Measuring social capital in five communities, *Journal of Applied Behavioral Science*, **36**, 23–42.

O'Reilly, C.A. & Chatman, J. (1986), Organizational commitment and psychological attachment: the effects of compliance, identification, and internalization on prosocial behavior, *Journal of Applied Psychology*, **71**, 492–9.

O'Reilly, C.A. & Cadwell, D.F. (1981), The commitment and job tenure of new employees: some evidence of post-decisional justification, *Administrative Science Quarterly*, **26**, 597–616.

Organ, D.W. (1997), Organizational citizenship behavior: it's construct clean-up time, *Human Performance*, **10**, 85–97.

Parsons, T. (1951), *The Social System*, New York: Free Press.

Pfeffer, J. (1994), *Competitive Advantage through People: Unleashing the Power of the Work Force*, Boston, MA: Harvard Business School Press.

Platt, I. (1973), Social traps, *American Psychologist*, **28**, 641–51.

Podsakoff, P.M. & MacKenzie, S.B. (1997), The impact of organizational citizenship behavior on organizational performance: a review and suggestions for future research, *Human Performance*, **10**, 133–51.

Podsakoff, P.M., MacKenzie, S.B., Paine, J.B. & Bachrach, D.G. (2000), Organizational citizenship behaviors: a critical review of the theoretical and empirical literature and suggestions for future research, *Journal of Management*, **26**, 513–63.

Porter, K., Steers, R., Mowday, R. & Boulian, P. (1974), Organizational commitment, job satisfaction, and turnover among psychiatric technicians, *Journal of Applied Psychology*, **59**, 603–9.

Portes, A. (1998), Social capital: its origins and applications in modern sociology, *Annual Review of Sociology*, **24**, 1–24.

Pruitt, D. & Kimmel, M.J. (1977), Twenty years of experimental gaming: critique, synthesis, and suggestions for the future, *Annual Review of Psychology*, **28**, 363–92.

Putnam, R.D. (2000), *Bowling Alone: The Collapse and Revival of American Community*, New York: Simon & Schuster.

Rentsch, J.R. (1990), Climate and culture: interaction and qualitative differences in organizational meanings, *Journal of Applied Psychology*, **75**, 668–81.

Rhoades, L. & Eisenberger, R. (2002), Perceived organizational support: a review of the literature, *Journal of Applied Psychology*, **87**, 698–714.

Rousseau, D.M. (1995), *Psychological Contract in Organizations*, Thousand Oaks, CA: Sage Publications.

Rousseau, D.M. & Schalk, R. (2000), *Psychological Contracts in Employment: Cross-national Perspectives*, Thousand Oaks, CA: Sage Publications.

Rusbult, C.E. (1980), Commitment and satisfaction in romantic associations: a test of the investment model, *Journal of Experimental Social Psychology*, **16**, 172–86.

Rusbult, C.E. (1983), A longitudinal test of the investment model: the development (and deterioration) of satisfaction and commitment in heterosexual involvement, *Journal of Personality and Social Psychology*, **60**, 53–78.

Rusbult, C.E. & Buunk, B.P. (1993), Commitment processes in close relationships: an interdependence analysis, *Journal of Social and Personal Relationships*, **10**, 175–204.

Rusbult, C.E., Martz, J.M. & Agnew, C.R. (1998), The investment model scale: Measuring commitment level, satisfaction level, quality of alternatives, and investment size, *Personal Relationships*, **5**, 357–91.

Schein, E.H. (1985), *Organizational Culture and Leadership: A Dynamic View*, San Francisco, CA: Jossey-Bass.

Schneider, B. (1975), Organizational climates: an essay, *Personnel Psychology*, **28**, 447–79.

Scott, R.W. (1987), *Organizations: Rational, Natural, and Open Systems*, Englewood Cliffs, NJ: Prentice-Hall.

Senge, P. (1990), *The Fifth Discipline: The Art and Practice of the Learning*, New York: Doubleday.

Skvoretz, J. & Lovaglia, M.J. (1995), Who exchanges with whom: structural determinants of exchange frequency in negotiated exchange networks, *Social Psychology Quarterly*, **58**, 163–77.

Swidler, A. (1986), Culture in action: symbols and strategies, *American Sociological Review*, **51**, 273–86.

Tajfel, H. & Turner, J.C. (1986), The social identity theory of intergroup behavior, in Worchel, S. & Austin, W.G. (eds), *Psychology of Intergroup Relations*, Chicago, IL: Nelson-Hall, pp. 7–24.

Thibaut, J.W. & Kelley, H.H. (1959), *The Social Psychology of Groups*, New York: Wiley.

Thomas, K.W. & Velthouse, B.A. (1990), Cognitive elements of empowerment: an interpretive model of intrinsic task motivation, *Academy of Management Review*, **15**, 666–81.

Thye, S., Yoon, J. & Lawler, E.J. (2002), Relational cohesion theory: review of a research program, *Advances in Group Processes*, **19**, 89–102.

Tsui, A., Pearce, J.L., Porter L.W. & Tripoli, A.M. (1997), An alternative approaches to the employee-organization relationship: does investment in the employees pay off? *Academy of Management Journal*, **40**, 1089–121.

Tversky, A. & Kahneman, D. (1974), Prospect theory: an analysis of decision under risk, *Science*, **185**, 1124–31.

Tyler, T.R. (2001), Cooperative in organizations: a social identity perspective, in Hogg, M.A. & Terry, D.J. (eds), *Social Identity Processes in Organizational Contexts*, Philadelphia: Psychology Press, pp. 149–79.

Walker, H., Thomas, G.M. & Zeldidtch, M. (1986), Legitimation, endorsement, and stability, *Social Forces*, **64**, 620–43.

Watson, D. & Tellegen, A. (1985), Toward a consensual structure of mood, *Psychological Bulletin*, **98**, 219–35.

Weber, M. (1946), The social psychology of the world religion, in Gerth, H.H. & Mills, C.W. (eds), *From Max Weber*, New York: Oxford University Press, pp. 267–301.

Wiener, Y. (1982), Commitment in organizations: a normative view, *Academy of Management Review*, **7**, 418–28.

Wiener, Y. (1988), Forms of value systems: a focus on organizational effectiveness and cultural change maintenance, *Academy of Management Review*, **13**, 534–45.

Williams, L.J. & Hazer, J.T. (1986), Antecedents and consequences of satisfaction and commitment in turnover models: a reanalysis using latent variable structural equation models, *Journal of Applied Psychology*, **71**, 219–31.

Williamson, O.E. (1981), The economics of organization: the transaction cost approach, *American Journal of Sociology*, **87**, 549–77.

Wright, P.M. & Snell, S.A. (1988), Toward a unifying framework for exploring fit and flexibility in strategic human resource management, *Academy of Management Review*, **23**, 756–72.

Yamagishi, T. (1995), Social dilemmas, in Cook, K. and Fine, G. & House, J. (eds), *Sociological Perspectives on Social Psychology*, Boston, MA: Allyn & Bacon, pp. 311–34.

Yoon, J. (2001), The role of structure and motivation for workplace empowerment, *Social Psychology Quarterly*, **64**, 110–23.

Yoon, J., Baker, M. & Ko, J. (1994), Effects of interpersonal attachment on organizational commitment: subgroup hypothesis revisited, *Human Relations*, **47**, 329–51.

Yoon, J., Han, N. & Seo, Y. (1996), Sense of control among hospital employees: tests of choice process, empowerment, and buffering hypotheses, *Journal of Applied Social Psychology*, **26**, 686–716.

Yoon, J. & Lim, J. (1999), Organizational support in the workplace: the case of Korean hospital employees, *Human Relations*, **52**, 121–43.

Yoon, J. & Thye, S. (2000), Supervisor support in the workplace: an empirical test of legitimation and positive affectivity, *Journal of Social Psychology*, **140**, 295–316.

Yoon, J. & Thye, S. (2002), A dual process model of organizational commitment: job satisfaction and organizational commitment, *Work and Occupations*, **29**, 97–124.

9 Trust and commitment in the market

*Yoshimichi Sato**

Introduction: trust and commitment in an uncertain situation

How do people behave when they are in an uncertain situation? Purchasing chicken meat would be a good case for exploring for an answer to this question. The taste and the quality of chicken meat are difficult to judge by its appearance. Then how do consumers decide to buy certain chicken meat? They may decide by its brand name and/or price. It might be the case, however, that the brand name of chicken meat such as 'chicken meat produced in X village' is a false indication. A meat market may quote a high price to give consumers an impression that the meat is of high quality. Thus this case represents a situation in which all the information on the chicken meat is not reliable.

What would a consumer, say Mr A, do in this situation? He would buy chicken meat at a meat market if he trusts it. Here the target of trust by Mr A changes from the chicken meat to the meat market.[1] If the quality of the meat is lower than he expected, Mr A will buy chicken meat at another meat market next time. If the quality is as high as (or higher than) he expected, what does Mr A do? Will he buy chicken meat at the same meat market next time? He will probably do so because it is safer to buy at a meat market that once sold high-quality meat than another meat market at which Mr A has not bought meat.

Suppose the meat market sells chicken meat at the price of $10 per pound. Mr A is satisfied with the quality of its chicken meat, so he continues to buy at it. One day, however, he finds another meat market that sells chicken meat at the price of $5 per pound. The quality of chicken meat sold at the second meat market seems as high as that of chicken meat at the first meat market. Then what will Mr A do? Will he continue to purchase chicken meat at the first meat market? Or will he be attracted to the lower price offered by the second meat market and switch to it?

This chapter explores for an answer to this question. Mr A and the first meat market are in a commitment relationship. He has not continued to buy at it without any consideration. He has done that based on a sense of 'assurance' that it surely sells high-quality meat. Borrowing the terminology of Yamagishi (1998), we call a relationship based on such a sense of assurance a 'commitment relationship' in this chapter. If, on the other hand, he switches to the second meat market, it means that Mr A trusts it. The quality of chicken meat sold at the second meat market may be lower that that of chicken meat at the first one. Or it may not. If the latter is the case, Mr A can purchase high-quality chicken meat at a lower price. Mr A switches to the second meat market expecting this possibility and forms a trust relationship with it. Then the question I raised in the previous paragraph is converted into a question regarding under what conditions commitment relationships break down and trust relationships are formed.

Kollock (1994) places this question in a broader context. He studies with a series of experiments how uncertainty affects the emergence of different types of commodity exchange. In the beginning of his paper he introduces two types of commodity exchange in Thailand: rice and rubber. In the case of the exchange of rubber, merchants cannot discern its quality on the spot. They can do that only after it is processed. The quality of rice, in contrast, is immediately discerned after checking a sample of it on the spot. Then what effect does the difference in uncertainty about the quality of goods between rubber and rice have on types of commodity exchange? This is the question Kollock raises in his paper.

The crux of his argument is as follows. In such a quite uncertain situation as the market for rubber, the buyer has a tendency to maintain relationships with certain sellers. These long-term relationships are 'commitment relationships' as defined above. What is equally interesting to the topic of this chapter is that buyers in commitment relationships have a tendency to trust their partners. He does not state a causal relation between commitment and trust, however.

Yamagishi (1998) proposes a different relation between commitment and trust than Kollock's argument. According to his theory on trust, commitment relationships and trust relationships are in conflict with each other. He argues that assurance groups, which are substantially commitment relationships, destroy trust relationships. That is, if people are deeply involved in assurance groups, they do not have opportunities to develop skills to trust strangers.

Although they have different views on the relation between commitment and trust, Kollock and Yamagishi have one argument in common. They agree that whether people enter a commitment relationship or a trust relationship depends on transaction costs and opportunity costs. When uncertainty in the market is high, it is difficult to find a trustworthy partner in it. Thus once people have found a trustworthy partner, they tend to enter a commitment relationship with him or her in order to reduce the costs of finding a preferable partner in the market, that is, transactions costs. However it is often the case that there are better potential partners in the market. If this is the case, people in commitment relationships miss the opportunity to make a deal with them. Then people incur opportunity costs by staying in commitment relationships.

Based on Kollock's and Yamagishi's argument, this chapter studies the interactive mechanism of commitment and trust relationships by focusing on market attractiveness. As mentioned above, people incur opportunity costs when they stay in commitment relationships. As the market becomes more attractive, opportunity costs caused by staying in commitment relationships become higher. Thus more people who are in commitment relationships leave them to find better partners in the market and to form trust relationships with them. I explore this possibility with computer simulation based on an agent-based model.

Agent-based model of commitment and trust relationships
In general, agent-based models appropriately deal with temporal change in interaction among agents. (Actors are called 'agents' in the convention of agent-based modeling.) Thus this modeling method is well suited to analyze the process of creation and collapse of commitment and trust relationships that was described in the previous section.

The basic structure of the model used in this chapter is as follows.[2] There are N agents in a society. Each agent gets paired with another agent. Paired agents decide whether to make a deal with their partner. If and only if both of the paired agents decide to do so, they play an exchange game, which will be described below. Here the paired agents' decision to make a deal with each other means the establishment of a mutual trust relationship. Note, however, that this relationship is different from that described in the previous section. In the case of the purchase of chicken meat the trust relationship is unilateral in the sense that Mr A trusts the second meat market, not vice versa. The model proposed in this section, in contrast, analyzes mutual trust relationships. Paired agents, however, do not necessarily play the exchange game. If either of the paired agents does not trust his or her partner, the game is not played. In addition, even if the paired agents play the exchange game, it is possible that they betray their partner's trust.

Agent i ($i = 1, 2, \ldots, N$) has two alternatives in the exchange game. One alternative is to give one unit of the goods to his or her partner; the other is to give nothing to the partner. The former is to keep the partner's trust, while the latter is to betray it. Agent i's partner, agent j ($j \neq i$), has the same alternatives. If agent j gives agent i one unit of the goods, agent i receives the pay-off of v_j. The subscript j indicates that the goods come from agent j, and v_j is greater than 1 for every j.

Why does agent i receive the pay-off of v_j if agent j gives one unit of the goods to him or her? The model assumes that if agent j decides to give one unit of the goods to agent i, the experimenter adds $v_j - 1$ units of the goods to it and gives agent i v_j units of the goods as in a psychological experiment. In other words the model conducts a psychological experiment with a large number of subjects on computer. For the sake of simplicity however we use the expression 'agent j has v_j units of the goods'.

In the exchange game therefore, pay-offs of agent i depend on his or her choice and the choice of his or her partner; they are summarized in Table 9.1. If both of agent i and his or her partner, agent j, offer one unit of the goods to each other, agent i receives v_j units of the goods. However agent i gave one unit of the goods to agent j, so his or her net pay-off is $v_j - 1$. If agent i offers one unit of the goods but agent j does not, agent i cannot receive v_j units of the goods, which makes his or her pay-off -1. If agent i does not offer one unit of the goods but agent j does, agent i's pay-off is v_j. If both of them do not offer one unit of the goods to each other, their situation is the status quo, and thus their pay-offs are 0.

As is clear in Table 9.1, the pay-off order in this exchange game is the same as that of the Prisoner's Dilemma game. It is agent i's optimal choice not to give one unit of the goods to agent j, no matter what choice agent j makes. This is also the case for agent j. Thus the state in which both of the agents do not offer one unit of the goods is the Nash equilibrium in the game. Both of the agents receive nothing in the equilibrium, however. In contrast, if they offer one unit of the goods, pay-offs of agents i and j are $v_j - 1$ and $v_i - 1$, respectively. They are greater than 0, but this state is not a Nash equilibrium in the game because either of agents i or j has an incentive to switch their choice. Thus this state is not realized if the agents make rational choices.

In our model, however, agents are assumed to have 'backward-looking rationality' rather than 'forward-looking rationality'. That is, agents learn based on consequences and pay-offs of their choices in the exchange game and revise their choices in the game at the next round. Thus there is a possibility that the mutual exchange of the goods is realized if agents involved learn to offer one unit of the goods to their partner.

Table 9.1   Pay-off matrix of the exchange game

		Agent j	
		Offer one unit of the goods	Do not offer the goods
Agent i	Offer one unit of the goods	$v_j - 1, v_i - 1$	$-1, v_i$
	Do not offer the goods	$v_j, -1$	0, 0

Paired agents, however, do not necessarily play the exchange game. As pointed out above, if either of them does not trust the partner, the game is not played. In this case the paired agents are in status quo, and their pay-offs are 0.

Paired agents who played the exchange game form a commitment relationship if they exchanged the goods in the game. They are paired again at the next round and exchange the goods in the game. The reason for this maintenance of the commitment relationship is as follows. The model assumes an uncertain situation. An agent in a commitment relationship is not sure whether he or she can enter a trust relationship with a new partner if he or she leaves the commitment relationship. He or she is also not sure whether the partner is trustworthy and gives him or her one unit of the goods even if he or she and the partner form a trust relationship and play the exchange game. In this uncertain situation, as Kollock (1994) argues, the agent would play the game with the same partner at the next round once he or she made a deal with a trustworthy partner who gave him or her one unit of the goods in the game at the present round.

How should the market attractiveness be defined? There are two types of market attractiveness in the model. First, it is defined as the variance in value of the goods among agents. The market becomes more attractive as the variance becomes wider. This is because the possibility of getting better goods becomes higher as the variance becomes wider. However, the possibility of getting worse goods increases simultaneously. In this sense the wider variance makes the market riskier as well as more attractive. That is, it shifts the market from a low-risk and low-return one to a high-risk and high-return one. We manipulate the variance in value of the goods as the exogenous variable.

When the society is set in motion in the simulation, the difference between the average value of the goods in the market and the value of the goods of the partner becomes the second type of market attractiveness to an agent. The agent might compare the best goods and the goods his or her partner owns. However, there is no guarantee that he or she can make a deal with an agent who has the best goods and get the goods. Thus the model in this chapter assumes that the comparison is made between the average value of the goods in the market and the value of the goods of his or her partner. The average value, however, does not change over time in a trial of the simulation, so the market becomes more attractive as the value of the goods of the partner becomes lower. This type of market attractiveness is not manipulated exogenously but emerges from interactions among agents in the society.

The argument I made in the previous section leads to a prediction that commitment relationships become less likely to be formed as the market becomes more attractive. Thus as the variance in value of the goods among agents becomes wider in the simulation, commitment relationships are predicted to be difficult to form. We check the validity of this prediction in the next section.

Here I describe the details of the model. It consists of six stages. The temporal flow of the model is summarized in Figure 9.1. Details of each stage are explained in the remainder of this section.

Initialization

Initial values of three propensities, values of the goods, and accumulated pay-offs are assigned to agents. The propensities are a propensity to give one unit of the goods to the partner (or a propensity to cooperate), a propensity to check the partner's propensity to cooperate (or the partner's trustworthiness), and a propensity to maintain a commitment relationship with the partner. These propensities affect agents' behavior in a stochastic way, which will be described below. Initial values of the propensities are between 0 and 1, inclusive; they are randomly generated subject to uniform distribution. For example an agent's initial propensity to cooperate is 0.9, that to check his or her partner's propensity to cooperate is 0.2, and that to maintain a commitment relationship with his or her partner is 0.6. This agent is willing to give one unit of the goods to his or her partner in the exchange game, does not carefully check the partner's trustworthiness, and has a relatively high tendency to maintain a commitment relationship with the partner. The propensities agent i has at time t are expressed as $propcoop_{i,t}$, $propchk_{i,t}$ and $propcommit_{i,t}$. Thus at the initialization stage $propcoop_{i,0}$, $propchk_{i,0}$ and $propcommit_{i,0}$ are assigned to agent i.

Values of the goods held by agents are randomly assigned to them subject to normal distribution with the mean of 10. (The value of the goods agent i has is expressed as v_i.) Its standard deviation is exogenously manipulated ranging from 0.1 to 1.8. The results of the simulation show that the average minimum value of the goods is 9.66 and the average maximum value is 10.3 when the standard deviation is 0.1 and that the former is 4.06 and the latter is 16.0 when the standard deviation is 1.8. As these results show, we can manipulate the variance in value of the goods, which indicates the market attractiveness, by changing the standard deviation.

Agents accumulate their pay-offs over time in the simulation. At the initialization stage the accumulated pay-offs are set at 0. In other words there is no difference in endowments or wealth among agents at this stage.

No agents are in commitment relationships at this stage. The society in the simulation begins with all the isolated agents.

Pairing

Agents are paired at this stage. There are two types of agent at this stage: agents in commitment relationships formed in the previous round, and

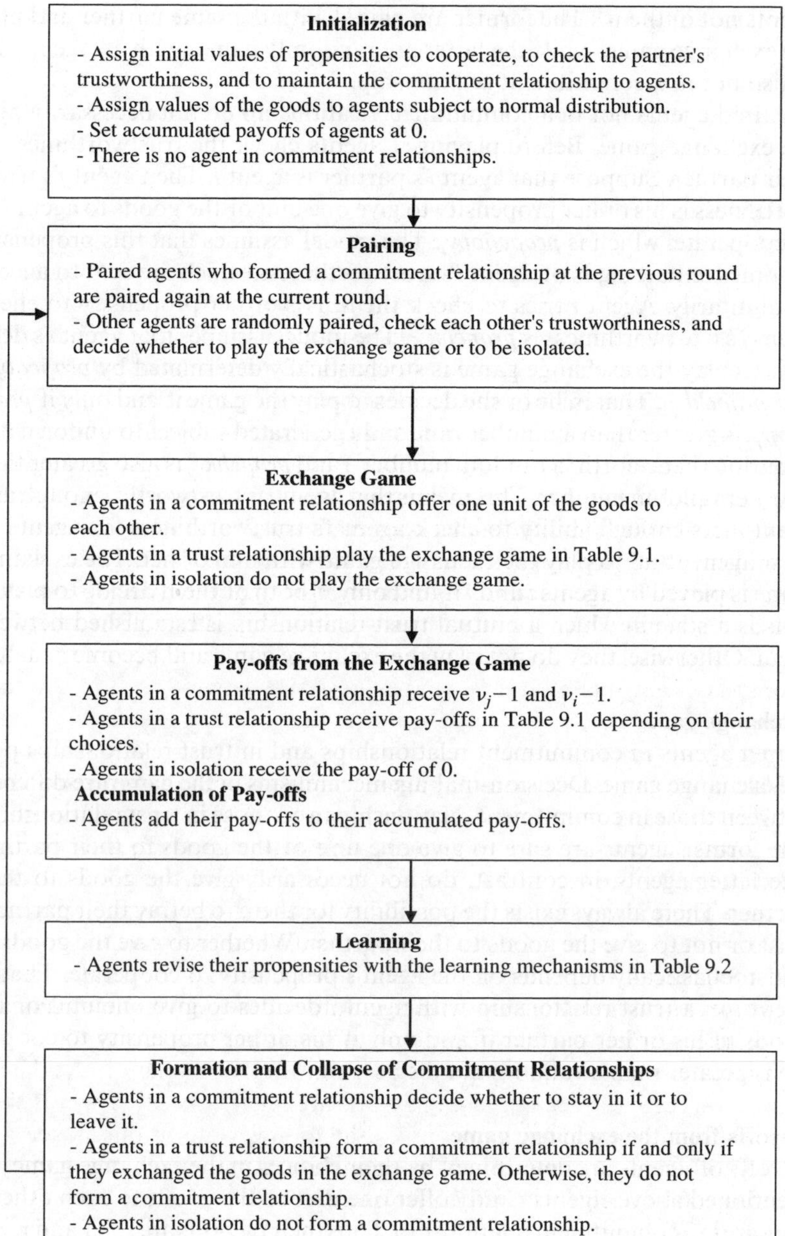

Initialization
- Assign initial values of propensities to cooperate, to check the partner's trustworthiness, and to maintain the commitment relationship to agents.
- Assign values of the goods to agents subject to normal distribution.
- Set accumulated payoffs of agents at 0.
- There is no agent in commitment relationships.

↓

Pairing
- Paired agents who formed a commitment relationship at the previous round are paired again at the current round.
- Other agents are randomly paired, check each other's trustworthiness, and decide whether to play the exchange game or to be isolated.

↓

Exchange Game
- Agents in a commitment relationship offer one unit of the goods to each other.
- Agents in a trust relationship play the exchange game in Table 9.1.
- Agents in isolation do not play the exchange game.

↓

Pay-offs from the Exchange Game
- Agents in a commitment relationship receive $v_j - 1$ and $v_i - 1$.
- Agents in a trust relationship receive pay-offs in Table 9.1 depending on their choices.
- Agents in isolation receive the pay-off of 0.

Accumulation of Pay-offs
- Agents add their pay-offs to their accumulated pay-offs.

↓

Learning
- Agents revise their propensities with the learning mechanisms in Table 9.2

↓

Formation and Collapse of Commitment Relationships
- Agents in a commitment relationship decide whether to stay in it or to leave it.
- Agents in a trust relationship form a commitment relationship if and only if they exchanged the goods in the exchange game. Otherwise, they do not form a commitment relationship.
- Agents in isolation do not form a commitment relationship.

Figure 9.1   The flow of the simulation

agents not in them.[3] The former are paired with the same partner and play the exchange game, while the latter are randomly paired with an agent who is also not in a commitment relationship.

Paired agents not in a commitment relationship do not necessarily play the exchange game. Before playing it agents check the trustworthiness of their partner. Suppose that agent i's partner is agent j. Then agent j's trustworthiness is his or her propensity to give one unit of the goods to agent i or to cooperate, which is $propcoop_{j,t}$. The model assumes that this propensity becomes telltale signs of agent j's trustworthiness, which are sent to agent i involuntarily. Agent i tries to check them. His or her propensity to check agent j's trustworthiness is $propchk_{i,t}$. The model assumes that agent i's decision to play the exchange game is stochastically determined by $propcoop_{j,t}$ and $propchk_{i,t}$. That is, he or she decides to play the game if and only if $propcoop_{j,t}$ is greater than a number randomly generated subject to uniform distribution (henceforth 'a random number') and $propchk_{i,t}$ is also greater than another random number. This means that agent j is trustworthy enough and agent i has enough ability to check agent j's trustworthiness for agent i to trust agent j and to play the exchange game with him or her. The exchange game is played by agents i and j if and only if both of them decide to play it. This is a state in which a mutual trust relationship is established between them. Otherwise, they do not play the exchange game and become isolated.

Exchange game
Paired agents in commitment relationships and in trust relationships play the exchange game. Decision-making mechanisms in the game are different between those in commitment relationships and those in trust relationships. The former agents are sure to give one unit of the goods to their partner. The latter agents, in contrast, do not necessarily give the goods to their partner. There always exists the possibility for them to betray their partner's trust or not to give the goods to their partner. Whether to give the goods or not stochastically depends on the agent's propensity to cooperate. That is, agent i in a trust relationship with agent j decides to give one unit of the goods to his or her partner if and only if his or her propensity to cooperate is greater than a random number.

Payoffs from the exchange game
Payoffs of agents are determined by their choices in the exchange game. As mentioned above, agents i and j offer one unit of the goods to each other if they are in a commitment relationship. Thus their pay-offs are $v_j - 1$ and $v_i - 1$, respectively. If they are in a trust relationship, they receive pay-offs in Table 9.1 depending on their choices. Isolated agents who do not play the exchange game receive 0. Then agents' pay-offs are added to their accumulated pay-offs.

Learning

Agents revise their propensities through learning after the exchange game. There are two types of learning: learning through their own experience and learning through vicarious experience. In the case of the former type of learning agent *i*'s propensities at the next round are determined by his or her propensities and pay-off at the present round. In the case of the latter type of learning, agent *i* copies propensities of a particular player and uses them at the next round. The learning mechanism varies depending on agent *i*'s location – in a commitment relationship, in a trust relationship or in isolation. Various types of learning mechanism are summarized in Table 9.2.

If he or she is in a commitment relationship, agent *i* does not revise his or her propensities to cooperate and to check his or her partner's trustworthiness. This is based on an assumption that he or she is not concerned about these propensities because the pay-off of $v_j - 1$ is automatically guaranteed to him or her if he or she is in a commitment relationship with agent *j*. He or she, however, revises his or her propensity to maintain the current commitment relationship. If his or her accumulated pay-off is greater than or equal to that of agent *j*, he or she revises it through the Bush-Mosteller learning algorithm. In this learning the difference between the value of the goods offered by agent *j* and the average value of the goods in the market is converted into the reinforcement ranging between -1 and 1, inclusive (henceforth R_1). If the reinforcement, R_1, is positive and large, the market is not attractive. Thus agent *i* wants to maintain the current commitment relationship with agent *j* and increases his or her propensity to maintain it. This learning process is described as follows:

$$propcommit_{i, t+1} = propcommit_{i, t} + R_1(1 - propcommit_{i, t}).$$

On the other hand, if the reinforcement is negative and its absolute value is large, the market is attractive to agent *i*. Thus he or she intends to leave the commitment relationship, and his or her propensity to maintain it becomes smaller. This process is expressed as follows:

$$propcommit_{i, t+1} = propcommit_{i, t} - |R_1|propcommit_{i, t}.$$

If his or her accumulated pay-off is smaller than agent *j*, agent *i* copies agent *j*'s propensity to maintain the commitment relationship. He or she, however, does not always copy it; he or she does so with the probability of 1 percent. In other words he or she does so once out of 100 times, while he or she does not 99 times.

If he or she is in a trust relationship, agent *i* revises his or her propensities to cooperate and to check his or her partner's trustworthiness. If his or her

Table 9.2 Agent i's learning mechanisms

	In a commitment relationship		In a trust relationship		In isolation	
	Agent i's accumulated pay-off		Agent i's accumulated pay-off		Agent i's accumulated pay-off	
	Greater than or equal to the partner's accumulated payoff	Smaller than the partner's accumulated pay-off	Greater than or equal to the partner's accumulated pay-off of	Smaller than the partner's accumulated pay-off	Greater than or equal to the accumulated pay-off of an agent with the highest accumulated pay-off	Smaller than the accumulated pay-off of an agent with the highest accumulated pay-off
Propensity to cooperate	No learning	No learning	Learning with the Bush-Mosteller learning algorithm	Imitation with the probability of 1 percent	Learning with the Bush-Mosteller learning algorithm	Imitation with the probability of 1 percent
Propensity to check the partner's trust-worthiness	No learning	No learning	Learning with the Bush-Mosteller learning algorithm	Imitation with the probability of 1 percent	Learning with the Bush-Mosteller learning algorithm	Imitation with the probability of 1 percent
Propensity to maintain a commitment relationship	Learning with the Bush-Mosteller learning algorithm	Imitation with the probability of 1 percent	No learning	No learning	No learning	No learning

accumulated pay-off is greater than or equal to that of his or her partner, he or she learns with the Bush-Mosteller learning algorithm. In this case his or her pay-off is converted into the reinforcement ranging between -1 and 1, inclusive (henceforth R_2).

Agent i revises his or her propensity to cooperate with R_2 in the following way. If he or she offered one unit of the goods in the exchange game and R_2 is positive, or if he or she did not offer the goods and R_2 is negative, agent i's propensity to cooperate increases. This learning process is described as follows:

$$propcoop_{i,\,t+1} = propcoop_{i,\,t} + |R_2|\,(1 - propcoop_{i,\,t}).$$

If he or she offered the goods and R_2 is negative, or if he or she did not offer the goods and R_2 is positive, agent i's propensity to cooperate decreases. This process is expressed in the following equation:

$$propcoop_{i,\,t+1} = propcoop_{i,\,t} - |R_2|\,propcoop_{i,\,t}.$$

Agent i revises his or her propensity to cooperate with the above learning processes if his or her accumulated pay-off is greater than or equal to that of his or her partner. If this is not the case, agent i copies his or her partner's propensity to cooperate with the probability of 1 per cent, as in the case of the learning of a propensity to maintain a commitment relationship.

Agents revise their propensity to check their partner's trustworthiness with R_2 as the reinforcement as they revise their propensity to cooperate.

If he or she is isolated, that is, not in a commitment or trust relationship, agent i revises his or her propensities to cooperate and to check his or her partner's trustworthiness as he or she would do in a trust relationship. He or she, however, does not have a partner for comparison. Thus the model assumes that agent i in isolation compares him or herself with an agent who has the highest accumulated pay-off in the society, who is called 'an agent with the highest accumulated pay-off' henceforth.[4] Thus if his or her accumulated pay-off is greater than or equal to that of an agent with the highest accumulated pay-off (in other words, if he or she is an agent with the highest accumulated pay-off), agent i revises his or her propensities with the Bush-Mosteller learning algorithm. This process is the same as that of agents in trust relationships. If he or she is not an agent with the highest accumulated pay-off, agent i copies propensities of an agent with the highest accumulated pay-off with the probability of 1 per cent.

Formation and collapse of commitment relationships

Commitment relationships are maintained, broken down, or formed at this stage. If paired agents are in a commitment relationship, they stay in it at the next round if and only if both of them decide to maintain it. This decision-making is done stochastically. An agent decides to maintain his or her commitment relationship if his or her propensity to maintain it is greater than or equal to a random number.

If paired agents are in a trust relationship, they form a commitment relationship if and only if they offered one unit of the goods to each other in the exchange game. Otherwise, that is, if mutual cooperation between them was not realized, they do not form a commitment relationship.

Agents in isolation do not form a commitment relationship.

After this stage the society returns to the pairing stage and enters the next round.

Analysis of results of the simulation
I conducted a simulation with the model described in the previous section. The design of the simulation is summarized in Table 9.3. Suppose there are 1000 agents in the society. We manipulate standard deviation of normal distribution of value of the goods to see the effect of the market attractiveness on commitment relationships. Twenty trials were implemented per value of standard deviation. As standard deviation was increased from 0.1 to 1.8 by 0.1, 360 trials were implemented in total. A trial consisted of 2000 rounds. Data was collected for the last quarter of the 2000 rounds to avoid start-up anomalies. Data collection was conducted in the following way. Take the rate of commitment relationships for example. If we denote the rate at the tth round (time t) by p_t, $p_t =$ (the number of agents in commitment relationships at the tth round)/1000, and the average rate of a trial is $\sum_{t=1501}^{2000} p_t/500$. If we calculate this number for 20 trials and take the average of the numbers, then the average is the average rate of commitment relationships at a value of standard deviation.

This average rate of commitment relationships should become smaller as the market becomes more attractive, if the argument in the first section

Table 9.3   The design of the simulation

The number of agents	1000
Manipulation of standard deviation	Increase from 0.1 to 1.8 by 0.1.
The number of trials per value of standard deviation	20
The number of rounds per trial	2000
Data collection for analysis	Collect data of the last 500 rounds.
Variables for analysis	Use averages for the last 500 rounds.

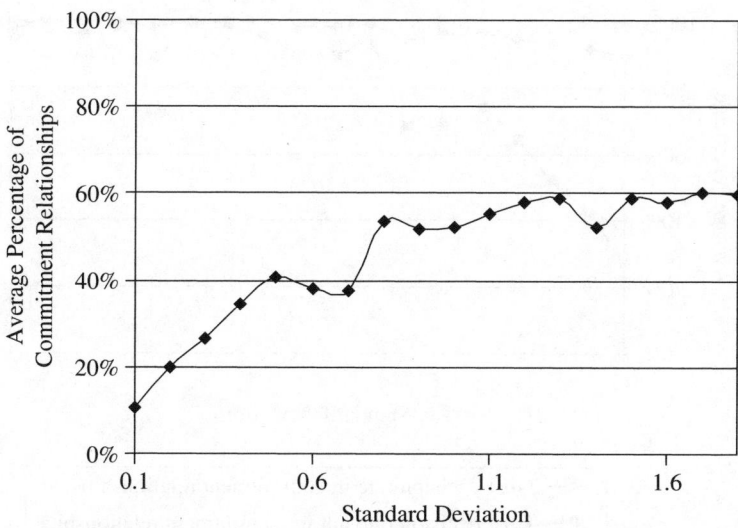

Figure 9.2   Commitment relationships and market attractiveness

is correct. To check this, I drew a graph of the relationship between commitment relationships and the market attractiveness (see Figure 9.2). The vertical axis of the graph is the average percentage of commitment relationships, which is the average rate of commitment relationships multiplied by 100. The horizontal axis is standard deviation, which expresses the market attractiveness. Obviously, the average percentage of commitment relationships increases as standard deviation becomes larger. This result is contradictory to the argument in the first section. According to the argument, the average percentage of commitment relationships should decrease as standard deviation becomes larger.

Why do we observe such a contradiction? To find reasons for it, I analyzed the relationship between agents' decisions about trust and cooperation and standard deviation of value of the goods (see Figures 9.3 and 9.4). The horizontal axis of the graphs is standard deviation as in Figure 9.2. The vertical axis of Figure 9.3 is the average percentage of agents who decide to trust their partner (henceforth 'the trust decision rate'). I calculated this rate for agents in commitment relationships and those not in them. The vertical axis of Figure 9.4 is the average percentage of agents who decide to cooperate (henceforth 'the cooperation decision rate'). I also calculated this rate for agents in commitment relations and those not in them.

The graphs show that when standard deviation is small, the trust decision and the cooperation decision rates of agents not in commitment relations are much lower than those of agents in them. Thus it is very unlikely

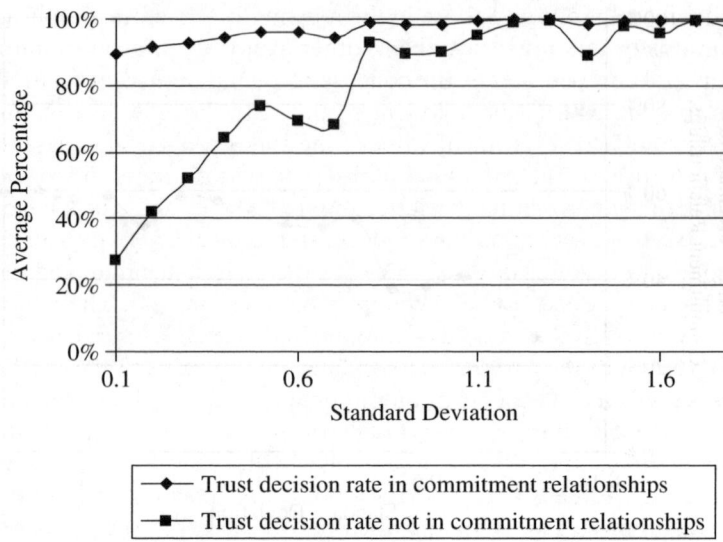

Figure 9.3 Trust decision rates and market attractiveness

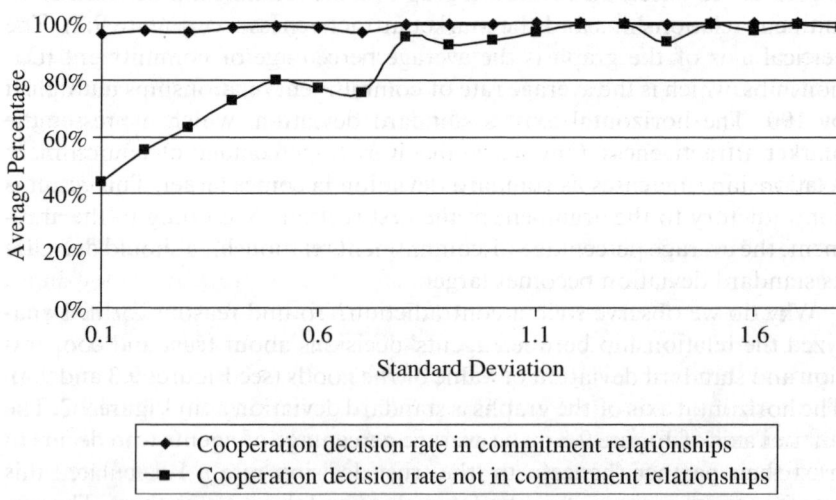

Figure 9.4 Cooperation decision rates and market attractiveness

that paired agents trust each other (play the exchange game), offer the goods to each other in the exchange game, and form a commitment relationship. In contrast, when standard deviation is large, the difference in the trust decision and the cooperation decision rates between agents not in commitment relations and those in them is small. Therefore even if agents in commitment relations leave them, other agents form new commitment relations and compensate for the collapse of old commitment relations.

This analysis leads to the following scenario. In the first place, no matter how large standard deviation of value of the goods is, agent *i* increases his or her propensities to check his or her partner's trustworthiness and to cooperate and forms a commitment relationship once he or she trusts his or her partner, exchanges the goods in the game, and receives a high pay-off. Then, if standard deviation is large, agents with the highest accumulated pay-off have a higher tendency to be in commitment relationships. The reason for this is as follows. If standard deviation is small, the difference between the value of the goods the partner offers and the average value of the good in the market is small. Thus being in a commitment relationship is not very attractive to the agent, so he or she does not necessarily stick to it. The situation is quite different if standard deviation is large. In the situation, if paired agents who have high values of the goods form a commitment relationship, they tend to maintain it. This is because the value of the goods the partner offers is higher than the average value of the goods in the market. Then the paired agents receive high pay-offs every round and, naturally, their accumulated pay-offs become high. The possibility therefore becomes higher that an agent with the highest accumulated pay-off is in a commitment relationship. This also increases the possibility that isolated agents copy his or her propensities. Note that agents should have relatively high propensities to check their partner's trustworthiness and to cooperate in order to form commitment relationships and that thus an agent with the highest accumulated pay-off in a commitment relationship also has such high propensities. Isolated agents copy these high propensities of the agent. Agents who copied the high propensities at the current round are much likely to trust their partner, offer one unit of the goods to the partner, and form a commitment relationship at the next round if they are paired with a partner who also has high propensities. Although their commitment relationship may dissolve at the next round, other isolated agents are likely to form new commitment relationships. As long as an agent with the highest accumulated pay-off is in a commitment relationship, there is a possibility that isolated agents copy his or her propensities to check his or her partner's trustworthiness and to cooperate, which in turn facilitates the creation of commitment relationships.[5] Because of this mechanism the average percentage of commitment relationships becomes larger as standard deviation of value of the goods becomes larger.

Conclusions
The results of the analysis in the previous section show the importance of imitation in society. An agent with the highest accumulated pay-off behaves

as a 'role model' to isolated agents and teaches them how to behave in order to get the highest accumulated pay-off. Then isolated agents learn from the 'model' to trust their partners and to cooperate with them. In this sense commitment relationships indirectly facilitate trust relationships. This is the most important lesson we learn from the results of the simulation.

This finding is complementary to Kollock's finding about the relation between commitment and trust (Kollock, 1994). As pointed out in the first section, he does not state a causal relation between them. The model in this chapter uncovers a mechanism that connects them. That is, some of the agents in commitment relationships 'teach' agents in isolation how to trust other agents, and the isolated agents learn to trust another isolated agent and form a commitment relationship with them. Thus the relation between commitment and trust is not a unilateral one. Subtle interactions among agents and between trust and commitment exist.

This finding, however, is different from Yamagishi's argument that commitment relationships destroy trust relationships (Yamagishi, 1998). The difference emerges from a subtle difference in assumptions used in his theory and our model. He maintains that people who stay in commitment relationships for a long time lose their skills to trust other people. Our finding that commitment relationships indirectly facilitate trust relationships means that agents in commitment relationships facilitate trust relationships between isolated agents. Although Yamagishi does not mention imitation in society, diffusion of behavioral traits through imitation is an important topic in the study of social change (Rogers, 1983; Coleman et al., 1966). Diffusion through imitation of behaviors of people with socially desirable characteristics has a possibility of fixing a certain behavioral pattern in society. Behaviors of excellent people are not necessarily 'desirable,' but our model shows the possibility that 'desirable behaviors' such as trust and cooperation diffuse in society through imitation of the propensities of an agent with the highest accumulated pay-off in a commitment relationship.

Notes

*   An earlier version of this chapter was published in Japanese as a chapter in *Network Dynamics: Social Networks and Rational Choice* edited by Yoshimichi Sato and Hiroshi Hiramatsu (Tokyo: Keiso Shobo, 2005). I thank Keiso Shobo for its permission for revising the earlier version and including the revised version as a chapter in this book. This research was supported by Grant-in-Aid for Scientific Research (B) (1) 14310084 (Principal Investigator: Kazuto Misumi). The academic support of the Center for the Study of Social Stratification and Inequality of Tohoku University is also gratefully appreciated.
1.   If the quality of a commodity is uncertain, trust in it is often converted into trust in an actor who sells it. See Sato (2000) for details of this mechanism.
2.   The model is a simplified version of the model proposed by Macy and Sato (2002).
3.   No agents are in commitment relationships at time 0, as explained above. Thus this sentence makes sense after that.

4. This assumption is strong in the sense that everybody in the society knows who agents with the highest accumulated payoff are. Weakening this assumption is our next task.
5. This logic is similar to Axelrod's argument on exclusive relationships among cooperators (Axelrod, 1984). However, this chapter focuses on diffusion of propensities by learning (imitation), while he assumes differential reproduction through natural selection.

References

Axelrod, Robert M. (1984), *The Evolution of Cooperation*, New York: Basic Books.

Coleman, James S., Katz, Elihu & Menzel, Herbert (1966), *Medical Innovation: A Diffusion Study*, Indianapolis,: The Bobbs-Merrill Co.

Kollock, Peter (1994), 'The emergence of exchange structures: an experimental study of uncertainty, commitment, and trust,' *American Journal of Sociology*, **100** (2), 313–45.

Macy, Michael W. & Sato, Yoshimichi (2002), 'Trust, cooperation, and market formation in the US and Japan,' *Proceedings of the National Academy of Sciences of the United States of America*, **99** (3): 7214–20.

Rogers, Everett M. (1983), *Diffusion of Innovations*, 3rd edn, New York: Free Press.

Sato, Yoshimichi (2000), 'Communication and choice of actions: an analysis of communication by rational choice theory', *Sociological Studies*, **67**, 47–58. (In Japanese)

Yamagishi, Toshio (1998), *The Structure of Trust: The Evolutionary Games of Mind and Society*, Tokyo: University of Tokyo Press. (In Japanese)

10 Social relational contexts and self-organizing inequality
Cecilia L. Ridgeway

Introduction

Everyday life is filled with social relational contexts in which people coordinate and shape their behavior in relation to others, be it in person, through the internet, on paper or with a cell phone. A great many of these contexts occur within organizations, although they occur almost everywhere else as well. In this chapter, I argue that the fundamental problem of these ubiquitous social relational contexts, which is to coordinate one's behavior with another, is in fact a driving source of self-organizing inequality in everyday life. Self-organizing inequalities are bottom-up processes of contingent, mutually reinforcing events that result in systematic structures of inequality between actors and/or social groups. Social relational contexts act, I will argue, as a taken-for-granted micro-engine of inequality that is missed by purely macro approaches to social inequality that focus entirely on processes at the institutional or socio-economic level. Missing this micro engine, I argue, limits the ability of such macro approaches to explain how some forms of inequality, such as gender or racial inequality, sustain themselves over major transformations in the macro-level socio-economic processes that sustain them.

The problem of coordinating behavior in social relational contexts gives rise to two processes that are key to the way such behavior leads to self-organizing inequality. First, as I shall describe, the problem of coordinating behavior fosters the development of what I call 'social difference codes' (Ridgeway, 2000b). Social difference codes are widely shared cultural beliefs that delineate the socially significant distinctions among people on the basis of which a society is structured and inequality is organized. Examples are occupation, race or gender. Social difference codes provide cultural schemas for enacting social relations on the basis of a given difference by indicating the attributes by which people may be categorized according to the distinction and the traits and behaviors that can be expected as a result.

Second, the problem of coordinating behavior to achieve a shared goal, which encompasses a large proportion of the contexts in which people coordinate, especially within organizations, gives rise to the development of influence or status hierarchies among the participants, as decades of research in expectation states theory has shown (Berger et al., 1977; Wagner & Berger, 2002). The development of social difference codes and the development of interpersonal status hierarchies, in turn, mutually reinforce one another and iteratively lead to the emergence of structures of inequality among people in a society. Because these mutually reinforcing processes develop implicitly, often without the conscious intention of the participants involved, they are appropriately termed 'self-organizing' processes of inequality.

To explain these processes more fully, I will first describe in greater detail the general argument about the coordination of interpersonal behavior in social relational contexts, and the emergence of social difference codes and status hierarchies. Since this is an argument about processes that are presumed to be inherent in the dynamics of social relational contexts themselves, I will focus initially on such contexts in the abstract. Then I will turn to a consideration of how such social relational processes are affected by the larger, organizational context in which they occur. After developing a general argument about how social relational contexts foster social difference codes and status hierarchies, I discuss a specific theory of how these two processes work together to create a particular form of inequality. This theory, called status construction theory, focuses on the emergence of inequalities based on status beliefs that rank some social groups in society as more respected and competent than others (Ridgeway, 1991, 2000a, 2004). Finally, I will discuss how these status beliefs conserve inequality based on social difference, such as gender or race inequality, over transformations in the institutional and socieo-economic structures that support that inequality.

The coordination problem and social difference codes

To decide how to act in a social relational context, an actor must first develop some means of anticipating how the other will behave, as symbolic interactionists and social identity theorists have long recognized (Hogg, 2003; Mead, 1934; Stryker & Vryan, 2003; Turner, 1987). Actors render people and other objects in their environment predictable and comprehensible by categorizing them, as an equally long tradition of social cognition research has shown (for example Fiske, 1992; Fiske et al., 1999; Fiske & Taylor, 1991; Howard & Renfrow, 2003). Cognitive category systems, in turn, proceed by contrast. A person or any other object is identified in contrast to something else. So a person is a woman rather than a man, or a person of color rather than white, and on that basis can be rendered 'known' and predictable. To anticipate how another will behave in a social relational context then, an actor must develop a way of categorizing the other on the basis of difference – that is, as different from or similar to known, socially predictable objects including the self. In this way, the problem of coordinating interpersonal behavior pushes people to form and use systems of social categorization based on difference.

I argue that this inherent coordination problem in social relational contexts is among the primary 'push' factors that lead cultures to develop social difference codes. Note that this 'push' factor does not emerge from individual psychology alone, but from the demands of relating to another. As Fiske (1992) argued in an influential review, the evidence of social cognition research is that 'thinking is for doing', and since relating to others is a form of doing that is central to human survival, much of everyday social cognition is in service of interpersonal interaction (Hardin & Conley, 2001).

To coordinate behavior effectively so that joint action is possible, actors not only need social categorization systems based on difference, but they also need systems that are roughly shared by others in the situation. Only shared categorization systems allow actors to accurately anticipate others' reactions to actors' own behavior, especially over multiple rounds of contingent behavior (Howard & Renfrow, 2003). Social relational contexts themselves facilitate the development of shared category systems because interactional processes transform them into cauldrons of mutual influence. Ethnographic analyses and experimental studies document that in interactional contexts, actors implicitly tune or align their behavior in relation to one another, creating an intense mutual influence process, in order to form a kind of 'working consensus' through which their interaction can proceed (Goffman, 1967; Hardin & Conely, 2001). This working consensus provides an implicit, shared definition of who each actor 'is' in the situation and what they are doing, that then guides participants' action (Goffman, 1967; Hardin & Higgins, 1996). As a result of the formation of a working consensus, the systems of social categorization that actors evolve to coordinate their behavior in a given relational context are roughly shared.

Studies show that the expectations for self and other that emerge in an implicit working consensus are generally more powerful determinants of an actor's behavior in the situation than are that actor's own separate, idiosyncratic assumptions (Hardin & Conley, 2001; Troyer & Younts, 1997). Consequently, interactional groups create shared local realities for their participants that powerfully shape their behavior. Fine (1979, 1987; Fine & Kleinman, 1979) has shown that within these shared local realities in interactional groups, participants not only draw on established cultural knowledge but also recombine it to develop novel elements of locally shared culture that none held before joining the group. Participants carry these novel cultural elements along their social networks and introduce them to other groups. Through this process, some novel cultural elements originally constructed in the micro contexts of interactional groups spread to become broadly shared in the society (Fine, 1987; Fine & Kleinman, 1979). New forms of music such as rap, or new forms of linguistic expression such as an argot or slang usage, often develop this way, but so might a wide variety of cultural elements.

Interactional contexts within a larger society then potentially become micro-factories for the construction and dissemination of elements of shared culture. Among a population of people in which individuals must regularly interact to achieve what they want or need, I argue that among the elements of shared culture that are likely to develop through such processes are widely shared systems for categorizing people on the basis of socially recognized differences – that is, social difference codes. In other words, the dynamics of social relational contexts not only push people to form social difference codes, but they also set in motion a set of processes that are sufficient to produce difference codes that are widely shared among people in a society or other collectivity. These processes are unlikely to be the only means by which differences codes emerge in a society, but the point here is that because the dynamics of social relational contexts are sufficient to create them, such contexts are a persistent social force acting to construct, spread and alter such codes.

Situating relational contexts within organizational structures

At this point, a pause may be useful to consider how the dynamics of relational contexts described thus far are affected by larger collectivities, such as organizations, in which many relational contexts occur. I have argued that the problem of coordinating joint behavior is inherent to social relational contexts and sets in motion processes that are sufficient to produce shared social difference codes among a population of people. Yet social relational contexts virtually always occur within larger social structures that provide the actors with substantial cultural tools, including institutionalized difference codes and established organizational practices, that the actors use to solve their coordination problem. Does this mean that organizational structures and procedures solve the coordination problem for actors, and thereby harness and contain the power of relational contexts to independently create, maintain and alter social difference codes? The answer is partly yes, but also no.

When social relational processes take place in well-ordered organizational contexts that clearly define actors' role identities and behavioral norms, these identities largely suffice to coordinate behavior. I say 'largely' because organizational scripts are almost never sufficiently detailed to fully specify behavior in any given context (Fiske & Taylor, 1991; Howard & Renfrow, 2003). As a result, even in well-ordered organizational contexts, social relational processes are likely to drive more detailed differentiation of identities and the development of locally shared codes for locally relevant distinctions among actors, such as shared ideas about types of bosses. In the main however, social relational processes in well-ordered organizational contexts become a means by which established social difference codes that are institutionalized within organizational structures and practices are enacted and reinforced.

Not all contexts are organizationally well ordered however. When actors come together at the interstices of an organization, as on a cross-divisional task force, or from across organizations, roles and identities are less clear and the coordination problem reasserts itself. This occurs even more strongly in newly forming organizations, such as start-up businesses or voluntary associations like neighborhood groups. The coordination problem increases as well in contexts in which organizational actors are faced with a substantial new problem or change in their environment that they must jointly manage, and for which established procedures provide little direction. In all these organizationally less well-ordered contexts, the independent effects of social relational processes come to the fore, potentially fostering new difference codes or acting further to perpetuate existing ones. As a result, although social relational processes rarely construct social difference codes or other elements of shared culture *de novo*, they act as a persistent, ubiquitous, sometimes latent, sometimes manifest social force that pushes the formation of such codes.

Social difference codes as rules for structure

As I noted at the onset, a social difference code is a cultural schema that describes a distinction on which people can be categorized, such as race or education, and the traits and behaviors that can be expected of those in one category of that distinction compared to another (Ridgeway, 2000b). As this description suggests, a society's social difference codes are, in effect, widely shared social stereotypes. They are more than that as well, however. They are rules for enacting a type of social structure.

Giddens (1984) and Sewell (1992) have argued that social structures can be thought of as having a dual nature. They are composed, on the one hand, of cultural schemas, or rules, for organizing social relations in a particular manner. On the other hand, they are also composed of the distributions of resources and material arrangements that result from people enacting those schemas or rules. As widely shared beliefs about socially significant differences among people, social difference codes are cultural schemas or rules in just this sense. They are cultural instructions for enacting relationships on the basis of a particular dimension of difference. Widely shared gender stereotypes for instance are cultural rules for behaving toward another and anticipating the other's behavior based on gender, actions which in turn result in a gendered structure to the relationship (Ridgeway & Correll, 2004). The problem of coordinating interaction drives people to develop social difference codes precisely for the purpose of organizing and structuring their social relations.

As rules for structure, social difference codes have additional effects as well. Difference codes take attributes like education or sex or skin color and disaggregate them from their inherently embedded source in complex, multi-attributed individual people. In so doing, social difference codes constitute new, abstract categories or groups of people, such as 'races'. It is only through the development of social difference codes that inequality can be based on such abstract, categorical distinctions among people, rather than on the specific, idiosyncratic differences among particular individuals.

This argument suggests that by driving the formation of shared difference codes, the problem of coordinating interpersonal behavior in social relational contexts becomes a proximate cause of the unfolding of what McPherson and colleagues label 'Blau space' (McPherson & Ranger-Moore, 1991; McPherson & Rotolo, 1996). Named after Peter Blau's (1977) foundational insights into heterogeneity and inequality in societies, 'Blau space' is the social grid of significant distinctions along which people in a given society locate themselves and around which social relations are organized. It provides the structural skeleton around which organizations and institutions in a society are developed. In the US for instance, sex, race, age, occupation and education are key dimensions of Blau space around which society is organized.

As one force that drives the formation of social difference codes and the unfolding of Blau space, the problem of coordinating interpersonal behavior lays a key foundation for the self-organization of inequality, since of course there can be no inequality without difference. The next step comes in the transformation of cultural codes of difference into cultural codes of inequality between the groups defined by the difference. Here too the dynamics of coordinating interpersonal behavior play an important role. Of particular consequence is the way the coordination of behavior in goal-oriented conditions gives rise to interpersonal status hierarchies.

The development of interpersonal status hierarchies
When people are dependent on one another to accomplish a shared, mutually valued goal, whether it be choosing a sofa for the living room or devising a national policy on Iraq, the usual problems of coordinating behavior take on a specific focus. In order to decide whether to speak up and forcefully assert their own suggestions or hesitate and wait for others to begin, in order to decide whether to change to agree with others or stick with their own views when disagreements develop, actors need to anticipate not simply how another will behave, but how valuable the other's contributions to the task are likely to be compared to the actor's own. In other words,

actors in goal-oriented situations are pushed to develop implicit expectations for their own performance in the situation compared to that of each other in the setting (Berger et al., 1974; Wagner & Berger, 2002).

As expectations often do (Miller & Turnbull, 1986), such performance expectations tend to have self-fulfilling effects on behavior. Expectation states theory argues, and research has shown, that the lower an actor's performance expectation for self compared to another, the more likely the actor is to (1) hesitate before offering an opinion; (2) ask for the other's views; (3) positively evaluate the other's views; and (4) change to agree with the other when disagreements emerge (see Ridgeway, 2001c; Correll & Ridgeway, 2003 for reviews). Out of this process, a behavioral status hierarchy of deference and influence emerges that is based on implicit presumptions about competence (Berger et al., 1974; Wagner & Berger, 2002).

In goal-oriented settings then, the coordination problem drives the formation of self–other performance expectations which in turn results in an interpersonal status hierarchy among the participants. Research has shown that such status hierarchies virtually always develop when actors are working on a shared, collective goal that none can solve by themselves, although the extent of the influence and status differences entailed by the hierarchy varies considerably by context (see Ridgeway, 2001c). Perhaps it is not surprising that these hierarchies develop in heterogeneous groups such as juries or research and development teams, in which members differ in socially established ways such as by occupational title, gender or age (Cohen & Zhou, 1991; Webster & Foschi, 1988). Yet research shows that such hierarchies also develop just as reliably in homogeneous groups, such as classroom discussion groups of Harvard sophomore males, in which members are highly similar in age, social background and organizational role (Bales, 1970; Correll & Ridgeway, 2003). The persistent tendency for status hierarchies to develop in both homogeneous and heterogeneous groups suggests that they are an inherent consequence of the distinctive coordination problems that actors face in goal-oriented social relational contexts.

Research in expectation states theory suggests that the need to form comparative performance expectations for one another in goal-oriented settings attunes actors to differences among them, such as in initial behaviors or social characteristics, that might provide clues to differences in performance capacity (Berger et al., 1977). In organizational settings, actors' formal roles and titles provide obvious frames for such inferences. However the demands of forming performance expectations also push actors to attend implicitly to other socially significant differences among them, such as race or gender, which the organization might prefer that the actors ignore. As they attend to these differences, the actors, often without realizing it, take the differences into account in forming implicit performance expectations for one another.

In this way, the tendency for social relational contexts to foster status hierarchies acts as a factor that implicitly writes inequalities based on race or gender into organizational practices and structures, even when such inequalities conflict with explicit organizational goals (Ridgeway, 1997; Ridgeway, 2001b).

Even among organizational actors who do not differ in race, gender or even organization role or title however, the need to form performance expectations in goal-oriented situations creates an implicit attention to difference. In this case however the salient differences are likely to be more subtle ones, such as behavioral style or more refined differences in background or expertise (Fisek et al., 1991).

The development of interpersonal status hierarchies in goal-oriented contexts then, also encourages the use of existing social difference codes and the formation of new ones. In particular it drives the salience for actors of characteristics that differentiate people within the population of actors that interact, rather than between that population and distant outgroups. Gender of course is a clear example of such a characteristic that differentiates within groups, but so are many other social distinctions such as race or education. Within an organization, social relational processes may drive the development of local codes of significant differences among organizational actors that for instance favor a particular type of training or experience over another (Troyer, 2003). These local codes become part of the organizational culture.

Status beliefs
While the development of status hierarchies in goal-oriented interaction reinforces the development of social difference codes, these hierarchies' most important impact on the self-organization of inequality is to provide a context in which difference may become associated with evaluative connotations of greater or lesser social esteem and competence. When a social difference code takes on such connotations for people in a society, it becomes a cultural 'status belief'. A status belief is a widely held belief that people in one category of a social difference, such as whites or men, are more respected and generally competent, particularly at the things that count most in the society, than are people in other categories of that difference such as non-whites or women (Berger et al., 1977; Ridgeway, 2001a). When status beliefs form about a particular categorical difference, they become part of the social stereotypes held for the categorical groups and add a distinctive content to those stereotypes (Fiske et al., 2002; Ridgeway, 2001a).

Since status beliefs are beliefs about which category of a difference is more respected, they are in effect beliefs about what 'most people' think about that difference. While people may personally endorse these beliefs to varying degrees, their assumption that 'most people' hold them is what gives those beliefs force in social relations (Ridgeway, 2004; Seachrist & Stangor, 2001). If people assume that most others respect one group over another and will behave accordingly, then they must take that status belief into account in their dealings with others, whether or not they personally endorse the belief.

Studies of social identity have repeatedly shown that the mere recognition of difference is enough to create an evaluative bias for one's own group (Brewer & Brown, 1998; Hogg, 2001). It is apparent then that difference codes inherently carry evaluative implications. The consequences of these inherent evaluative effects of difference for systematic inequalities between groups are unclear however, because the effects result in competing in-group biases in which each categorical group favors its own as 'best' (Tajfel & Turner, 1986). In contrast, when a difference code becomes a status belief, people in all categorical groups agree, or at least concede as a matter of social reality, that those in one group are more respected and held to be more competent than are those in other groups. Consequently, the implications of status beliefs for inequality are very clear (Jost & Burgess, 2000; Ridgeway, 2001a; Tajfel & Turner, 1986). If social difference codes are cultural instructions for organizing social relations around a given difference, status beliefs are instructions for organizing relations of inequality around that difference. Status beliefs act as the cultural 'DNA' by which systems of status inequality based on social difference are enacted and re-enacted over multiple contexts.

Decades of expectations states research has shown that when people encounter someone who differs from them on a characteristic about which they hold status beliefs, that belief becomes implicitly salient for them and shapes their performance expectations, and consequently their behavior towards one another (Berger et al., 1977; Webster & Foschi, 1988; Wagner & Berger, 2002). In this way, when status beliefs are widely held in society, they 'self-organize' inequalities of influence and esteem across multiple interpersonal contexts in a consistent manner. As a result, people in some social categories consistently emerge as more influential and apparently competent than those in other categories across a wide variety of organizational and other settings, creating systematic cleavages of inequality between categorical groups in society.

Status construction theory
How do social difference codes become transformed into status beliefs according to which both groups agree that one group is held to be socially 'better'? Although there are likely to be many ways that this occurs, status construction theory argues that one way status beliefs develop and become

widely held in a society is through the reccurring association of a social difference with people's positions in interpersonal status hierarchies (Ridgeway, 1991; Ridgeway et al., 1998; Ridgeway & Erickson, 2000).

The theory takes as a starting point a socially recognized but not yet consensually evaluated distinction that divides the population into at least two categorical groups. It assumes that people in these groups are to some degree interdependent in that they must regularly cooperate to achieve what they want or need. The theory focuses on these cooperatively interdependent encounters between people who differ on the categorical distinction. As in all goal-oriented encounters, hierarchies of influence and esteem are likely to develop in these intercategory encounters. Interpersonal status hierarchies usually develop implicitly, through multiple small behaviors that the participants rarely scrutinize. Since the actual orgins of their influence hierarchy are obscure to them, but their categorical difference is salient, the theory argues that there is some chance that the participants will associate their apparent difference in esteem and competence in the situation with their categorical difference. If this association is repeated for them in subsequent intercategory encounters, the theory argues that it will eventually induce them to form generalized status beliefs about the categorical distinction. Once people form such status beliefs, they carry them to their next encounters with those from the other group and act on them there. By treating those others according to the status beliefs, the theory argues, they induce at least some of the others to take on the belief as well. This in turn creates a diffusion process that could potentially spread the new status belief widely in the population.

Whether such a fledgling status belief does spread widely or dissipates in a cultural noise of conflicting beliefs, and which group it casts as higher status, all depends on the structural conditions that shape the terms on which people from each categorical group encounter one another. Do structural conditions give people from one categorical group a systematic advantage in some factor, such as material resources or technology, that is helpful in gaining influence in intercategory encounters? If such a biasing factor exists, the theory argues that status beliefs favoring the structurally advantaged group will emerge and spread to become widely shared in society (Ridgeway, 1991; Ridgeway, 2000a). And even if there is no such biasing factor, according to simulations by Noah Mark (1999), there is still some chance that widely held status beliefs will emerge through stochastic processes alone, although the group favored in the emergent beliefs will be a matter of chance.

Evidence for the theory
There is an accumulating body of evidence to support status construction theory's account of the emergence of widely held status beliefs. Simulations

of the diffusion processes described by the theory show that if people do form and spread status beliefs in intercategory encounters as the theory says, then the development of near consensual status beliefs is indeed a plausible result under many social structural conditions (Mark, 1999; Ridgeway & Balkwell, 1997). With this logical support for the theory in hand, research has turned to a series of experiments designed to examine whether people do indeed form and spread status beliefs in encounters with categorically different others as the theory suggests.

All of these experiments have some common aspects. First, a technique adapted from social identity studies was used to create a salient social distinction between participants about which no consensual evaluation yet existed (Tajfel et al., 1971). Participants chose between pictures by Klee and Kandinsky as a purported 'test' that distinguishes between two types of people with very different 'personal response styles'. Personal response style, they heard, is a stable trait of the self and there are about equal numbers of each response style in the population.

Second, the design of all the experiments provided participants with two repeated experiences of working on a shared task, each time with different partners, in which differences in 'personal response style' happened to be consistently associated with emergent differences among the participants in influence over their shared task decisions. Finally, at the end of these two goal-oriented encounters, participants rated how 'most people', and they personally, would rate the typical member of each response style group. This provided a measure of whether status beliefs had developed about the response style distinction.

One critical experiment examined whether this basic situation of two sequential, goal-oriented encounters in which emergent influence differences were consistently associated with participants' differences in response style was in fact sufficient to cause participants to form status beliefs about the response style distinction (Ridgeway & Erickson, 2000, study 1). In this study, participants worked with a partner of the opposite response style on a cooperative decision-making task and then worked with another partner, also of the opposite response style, on another round of the same task. Partners on both rounds were actually confederates who acted confidently and assertively or hesitantly and deferentially in the task discussion. These behaviors resulted in clear influence hierarchies that favored the participant when the confederate was deferential and favored the confederate when the confederate was non-deferential.

As predicted, at the end of these two encounters, participants formed beliefs that 'most people' would rate the typical member of the response style group that had been associated with greater influence in their encounters as higher status, more respected and more competent, but not as socially considerate as those in the other group. Importantly, participants whose own group was associated with lesser influence in the encounters agreed that most people would rate their group as lower status, less respected and less competent, although more considerate, than the other group. Thus in the classic sign of status beliefs, both those advantaged by the belief and those disadvantaged by it agreed that the advantaged group is seen as higher status and more competent.

Participants' personal ratings of the response style groups largely agreed with their estimates of 'most people's' evaluations. Again, even those whose own group had been associated with lesser influence agreed that the other group was more respected, higher status and more leaderlike than their own group. Even though they thought most people would see their own group as less competent than the other however, they personally rated it as of similar competence.

This study showed that people can indeed form status beliefs from repeated encounters with different others in which social difference is consistently associated with differences in influence in the encounters. However the theory also argues that whether beliefs formed by individuals in local encounters predictably spread to become socially significant status distinctions depends on the presence of a biasing factor that systematically advantages those from one group in gaining influence over those from another group in their goal-oriented encounters. For instance, at least since Weber (1968) it has been commonly noted that social groups often gain material advantages over others before the latter acquire status advantages over them as well. Status construction theory argues that social relational processes are one means by which structural advantages such as differences in material resources are transformed into status advantages that benefit even materially disadvantaged members of the higher status group.

To examine this part of the theory, two experiments investigated whether encounters between categorically different others in which material resources biased the emergent influence hierarchies would lead predictably to status beliefs favoring the resource-advantaged categorical group. In the first study, participants worked on two rounds of a task, each time with a different partner who differed from them in response style and who was also paid either less or more than them. Partners were again confederates who treated the participants deferentially when the participant was better paid, and confidently and assertively when the participant was lower in pay, mimicking the typical effects of pay on interaction (Harrod, 1980; Stewart & Moore, 1992). As expected, these behaviors resulted in influence hierarchies that corresponded to pay differences. After these two encounters in which pay consistently biased the emergent influence hierarchies, participants formed clear status beliefs favoring the response style group that had been better paid and more influential in the encounters. Once again participants, including those in the lower-paid group, agreed that most people would see the better-paid response group as higher status, more respected, competent and leaderlike, but not as considerate as the other group (Ridgeway et al., 1998, study 1).

A second study confirmed that these status beliefs were not simply inferred from a knowledge of pay differences alone but were a result of the corresponding influence hierarchies they experienced in the encounters (Ridgeway et al., 1998, study 2). In this study, participants learned of their response style and pay differences from their partner as before, but then completed the status belief measures without interacting with the partner. Clear status beliefs did not form in this situation because those participants whose group was lower paid refused to concede that most people would see them as lower status or less competent. These studies confirm that when the influence hierarchies in encounters between socially different participants are associated with a biasing factor such as material resources, status beliefs develop favoring the better-paid group. Thus social relational processes can indeed transform structural advantages between categorical groups in status advantages.

For status beliefs that individuals form in encounters to become widely shared in society however, encounters must not only induce some to form status beliefs, but also allow those who have acquired these beliefs to 'teach' them to others by treating those others according to the beliefs. The first study discussed above actually provides evidence that people can spread status beliefs to others by treating them according to that belief (Ridgeway & Erickson, 2000, study 1). In that study, after all, a confederate treated a socially different participant either deferentially or confidently and assertively, which is how people act when they presume the other is higher or lower status. Therefore the fact that participants formed status beliefs about the social difference that corresponded to how they were treated by the confederate also shows us that people can spread their status beliefs by acting on them in encounters, creating a diffusion process.

A final experiment in the series showed that goal-oriented encounters among socially different others have the potential to spread status beliefs not only to those who are directly treated according to these beliefs, but also to those participants who witness this belief (Ridgeway & Erickson, 2000, study 2). In this study, participants took part in two three-person decision-making teams in which they witnessed someone different from them (a confederate) either defer to or assert influence over someone similar to them in response style. After these experiences, participants formed status beliefs about the response-style distinction that corresponded to the treatment they witnessed. This study shows not only that a diffusion process would occur, but that it would spread beliefs rapidly and widely through the population. Taken together then these studies provide substantial support for status construction theory's account of how social relational contexts are sufficient to create and spread status beliefs about social differences.

Status beliefs and the conservation of inequality

Status construction theory shows how the micro-dynamics of coordinating interpersonal behavior not only foster social difference codes, but under many conditions also transform those difference codes into widely shared status beliefs that become cultural agents of self-organizing inequality. Once such status beliefs develop about a difference such as race or gender, I argue, their effects in interpersonal contexts give that inequality a resilience that allows it to persist over changes in the initial socio-economic or other structural conditions that initially fostered the status beliefs.

A system of gender hierarchy, in which men are seen as higher status, generally more competent and more appropriate for authority than women has persisted in Western society over massive transformations in its socio-economic base, such as industrialization or the movement of women into the paid labor force. Similarly, a racial hierarchy between blacks and whites has continued in the US despite the collapse of the economic system of slavery on which it originally rested. The self-organizing inequalities status beliefs based on gender and race created in interpersonal contexts play a role in this persistence (Ridgeway, 2006, in press).

When socio-economic arrangements change, the terms on which men and women or blacks and whites routinely encounter one another also change so that people have more and more experiences that are discrepant with their gender or racial status beliefs. These gender and racial status beliefs however are socially established for their holders in that they presume that most people take the beliefs to be the 'the way things are'. Given the presumption of social support for established status beliefs, people require extensive disconfirmation before they begin to change their status beliefs substantially (Fiske et al., 1999; Hewstone, 1994; Seachrist & Stangor, 2001). As a result, there is a time lag between people's changing circumstances and changes in their status beliefs. This time lag creates a window in which people implicitly organize their behavior according to the pre-established gender or racial status beliefs even as they deal with new socio-economic circumstances.

At the edge of social change, the contexts in which people take the first steps that lead to new ways of organizing economic relations are typically local, interpersonal contexts. An example is the famous garage in which an early computer company began. These local contexts in turn are shaped by the participants' established, taken-for-granted gender and racial status beliefs. Consequently, in these contexts, despite changing socio-economic conditions, people are likely to rewrite gender and racial inequality into the new social and economic forms that they create, conserving and translating gender and racial inequality into the new socio-economic system.

Conclusion

The problems of coordinating interpersonal behavior, then, cause social relational contexts to become micro-engines of inequality. These contexts foster the development of shared social difference codes that provide the social gridwork for inequality. They facilitate the transformation of many of these difference codes into status beliefs that act as cultural schemas that systematically and persistently organize unequal social relations between people from different social groups. Finally, precisely because of their implicit, self-organizing nature, these social relational contexts provide a forum for sustaining status inequalities based on difference over social structural change. For these reasons, I believe that we will never succeed in understanding, let alone dismantling, inequality in society if we do not take the micro-engines of social relational contexts into account.

Organizations ignore the micro-engines of social relations at their peril. The implicit, taken-for-granted processes of these contexts continually diversify the local difference codes that organizational actors use to work with one another, and not always in directions that enhance organizational goals. In addition, these processes implicitly enact and write into organizational structures establishing societal status inequalities, such as those based on gender or race, in ways that may undercut official organizational commitments to equal opportunity. Only by recognizing the self-organizing equalities that emerge through social relational processes can organizations hope to manage their effects.

References

Bales, R.F. (1970), *Personality and Interpersonal Behavior*, New York: Holt, Rinehart, and Winston.
Berger, J., Conner, T.L. & Fisek, M.H. (eds) (1974), *Expectations States Theory: A Theoretical Research Program*, Cambridge, MA: Winthrop.
Berger, J., Fisek, M.H., Norman, R. & Zelditch, M. (1977), *Status Characteristics and Social Interaction*, New York: Elsevier.
Blau, P.M. (1977), *Inequality and Heterogeneity: A Primitive Theory of Social Structure*, New York: Free Press.
Brewer, M. & Brown, R.J. (1998), Intergroup relations, in Gilbert, D.T., Fiske, S.T. & Lindzey, G. (eds), *Handbook of Social Psychology*, New York: McGraw-Hill, pp. 554–94.
Cohen, B.P. & Zhou, X. (1991), Status processes in enduring work groups, *American Sociological Review*, **56**, 179–88.
Correll, S.J. & Ridgeway, C.L. (2003), Expectation states theory, in Delamater, J. (ed.), *Handbook of Social Psychology*, New York: Kluwer/Plenum, pp. 29–52.
Fine, G.A. (1979), Small groups and culture creation, *American Sociological Review*, **44**, 733–45.
Fine, G.A. (1987), *With the Boys: Little League Baseball and Preadolescent Culture*, Chicago, IL: University of Chicago.

Fine, G.A. & Kleinman, S. (1979), Rethinking subculture: an interactionist approach, *American Journal of Sociology*, **85**, 1–20.

Fisek, M.H., Berger, J. & Norman, R.Z. (1991), Participation in heterogeneous and homogeneous groups: a theoretical integration, *American Journal of Sociology*, **97**, 114–42.

Fiske, S.T. (1992), Thinking is for doing: portraits of social cognition from daguerreotype to laserphoto, *Journal of Personality and Social Psychology*, **63**, 877–89.

Fiske, S.T., Cuddy, A.J.C., Glick, P. & Xu, J. (2002), A model of (often mixed) stereotype content: competence and warmth respectively follow from perceived status and competition, *Journal of Personality and Social Psychology*, **82**, 878–902.

Fiske, S.T., Lin, M. & Neuberg, S. (1999), 'The Continuum Model: ten years later, in Chaiken, S. and Trope, Y. (eds), *Dual Process Theories in Social Psychology*, New York: Guilford.

Fiske, S. & Taylor, S. (1991). *Social Cognition*, New York: McGraw-Hill.

Giddens, A. (1984), *The Constitution of Society: Outline of the Theory of Structuration*, Berkeley, CA: University of California Press.

Goffman, E. (1967), *Interaction Ritual*, Garden City, NY: Doubleday.

Hardin, C.D. & Conley, T.D. (2001), A relational approach to cognition: shared experience and relationship affirmation in social cognition, in Moskowitz, G.B. (ed.), *Cognitive Social Psychology: The Princeton Symposium on the Legacy and Future of Social Cognition*, Mahwah, NJ: Erlbaum, pp. 3–17.

Hardin, C.D. & Higgins, T.E. (1996), Shared reality: how social verification makes the subjective objective, in Sorrentino, R.M. & Higgins, T.E. (eds), *Handbook of Motivation and Cognition, Vol. 3, The Interpersonal Context*, New York: Guilford, pp. 28–84.

Harrod, W.J. (1980), Expectations from unequal rewards, *Social Psychology Quarterly*, **43**, 126–30.

Hewstone, M. (1994), Revision and change of stereotypic beliefs: in search of the elusive subtyping model, in Stroebe, W. & Hewstone, M. (eds), *European Review of Social Psychology* Vol. 5, Chichester: Wiley, pp. 69–109.

Hogg, M.A. (2001), Social categorization, depersonalization, and group behavior, in Hogg, M.A. & Tindale, S. (eds), *Blackwell Handbook of Social Psychology: Group Processes*, Maulden, MA: Blackwell, pp. 56–85.

Hogg, M.A. (2003), Intergroup relations, in Delamater, J. (ed.), *Handbook of Social Psychology*, New York: Kluwer/Plenum, pp. 479–502.

Howard, J. & Renfrow, D.G. (2003), Social cognition, in Delamater, J. (ed.), *Handbook of Social Psychology*, New York: Kluwer/Plenum, pp. 259–83.

Jost, J.T. & Burgess, D. (2000), Attitudinal ambivalence and the conflict between group and system justification in low status groups, *Personality and Social Psychology Bulletin*, **26**, 293–305.

Mark, N. (1999), The emergence of status inequality, Paper presented at the annual meeting of the American Sociological Association, Chicago, August.

McPherson, J.M. & Ranger-Moore, J. (1991), Evolution on a dancing landscape: organizational dynamics and networks in dynamic Blau space, *Social Forces*, **70**, 19–42.

McPherson, J.M. & Rotolo, T. (1996), Diversity and change: modelling the social composition of voluntary groups, *American Sociological Review*, **61**, 179–202.

Mead, G.H. (1934), *Mind, Self and Society*, Chicago, IL: University of Chicago Press.

Miller, D.T. & Turnbull, W. (1986), Expectancies and interpersonal processes, *Annual Review of Psychology*, **37**, 233–56.

Ridgeway, C.L. (1991), The social construction of status value: gender and other nominal characteristics, *Social Forces*, **70**, 367–86.

Ridgeway, C.L. (1997), Interaction and the conservation of gender inequality: considering employment, *American Sociological Review*, **62**, 218–235.

Ridgeway, C.L. (2000a), The formation of status beliefs: improving status construction theory, *Advances in Group Processes*, **17**, 77–102.

Ridgeway, C.L. (2000b), Social difference codes and social connections, *Sociological Perspectives* **43**, 1–11.

Ridgeway, C.L. (2001a), The emergence of status beliefs: from structural inequality to legit-imizing ideology, in Jost, J. and Major, B. (eds), *The Psychology of Legitimacy: Emerging Perspectives on Ideology, Justice, and Intergroup Relations*, New York: Cambridge, pp. 257–277.

Ridgeway, C.L. (2001b), Gender, status, and leadership, *Journal of Social Issues*, **57**, 627–55.

Ridgeway, C.L. (2001c), Social status and group structure, in Hogg, M.A. & Tindale, S. (eds), *Blackwell Handbook of Social Psychology: Group Processes*, Maulden, MA: Blackwell, pp. 352–75.

Ridgeway, C.L. (2004), Status construction theory, Unpublished manuscript, Department of Sociology, Stanford University, Stanford, CA.

Ridgeway, C.L. (in press), Gender as an organizing force in social relations: implications for the future of inequality, in Blau, F.D., Brinton, M.C. and Grusky, D.B. (eds), *The Declining Significance of Gender?* New York: Russell Sage.

Ridgeway, C.L. & Balkwell, J. (1997), Group processes and the diffusion of status beliefs, *Social Psychology Quarterly*, **60**, 14–31.

Ridgeway, C.L., Boyle, E.H., Kuipers, K. & Robinson, D. (1998), How do status beliefs, develop? The role of resources and interaction, *American Sociological Review*, **63**, 331–50.

Ridgeway, C.L. & Correll, S.J. (2004), Unpacking the gender system: a theoretical perspective on gender belief and social relations, *Gender and Society* **18**, 510–31.

Ridgeway, C.L. & Erickson, K.G. (2000), Creating and spreading status beliefs, *American Journal of Sociology*, **106**, 579–615.

Seachrist, G.B. and Stangor, C. (2001), Perceived consensus influences intergroup behavior and stereotype accessibility, *Journal of Personality and Social Psychology*, **80**, 645–54.

Sewell, W.H. (1992), A theory of structure: duality, agency, and transformation, *American Journal of Sociology*, **98**, 1–29.

Stewart, P.A. & Moore, J.C. (1992), Wage disparities and performance expectations, *Social Psychology Quarterly*, **55**, 78–85.

Stryker, S. and Vryan, K.D. (2003), The symbolic interactionist frame, in Delamater, J. (ed.), *Handbook of Social Psychology*, New York: Kluwer/Plenum, pp. 3–28.

Tajfel, H.M., Billig, G., Bundy, R.P. & Flament, C. (1971), Social categorization and inter-group behavior, *European Journal of Social Psychology*, **1**, 149–77.

Tajfel, H. & Turner, J.C. (1986), The social identity theory of group behavior, in Worchel, S. & Austin, W.G. (eds), *Psychology of Intergroup Relations*, Chicago: Nelson-Hall, pp. 7–24.

Troyer, Lisa. (2003), The role of social identity processes in status construction, *Advances in Group Processes*, **20**, 149–72.

Troyer, L. & Younts, C.W. (1997), Whose expectations matter? The relative power of first-order and second-order expectations in determining social influence, *American Journal of Sociology*, **103**, 692–732.

Turner, J. (1987), *Rediscovering the Social Group: A Self-Categorization Theory*, Oxford: Blackwell.

Wagner, D.G. and Berger, J. (2002), Expectation states theory: an evolving research program, in Berger, J. & Zelditch, M. (eds), *New Directions in Contemporary Sociological Theory*, New York: Rowman & Littlefield, pp. 41–76.

Weber, M. ([1918] 1968), *Economy and Society*, (eds), G. Roth & C. Wittich, Trans. E. Frischoff, New York: Bedminster.

Webster, M. & Foschi, M. (1988), Overview of status generalization, in Webster, M. & Foschi, M. (eds), *Status Generalization: New Theory and Research*, Stanford, CA: Stanford University, pp, 1–22.

11 Interorganizational cooperation between not-for-profit organizations: a relational analysis

Julie Battilana and Metin Sengul*

Recent years witnessed a notable increase in cooperative arrangements between not-for-profit organizations. Yet, despite the richness of the existing alliance literature in the for-profit sector, interorganizational cooperative arrangements between not-for-profit organizations are still understudied and undertheorized. This chapter addresses this gap and develops a theoretical background for further theoretical and empirical work on interorganizational cooperation between not-for-profits. We emphasize that for not-for-profits, unlike for-profits, neither inputs nor outputs are simple transactions, making both their needs and the boundaries they need to manage more complex. Importantly it is not the reasons of cooperation or the way they engage in those arrangements that differ; it is the mechanisms behind those arrangements. In explaining these mechanisms, we explore what a not-for-profit organization is and in which dimensions these organizations differ from their for-profit counterparts; why they might seek cooperative arrangements with other not-for-profits; with whom they are likely to engage in cooperative relationships; and how integrative these arrangements are likely to be. Overall, this study highlights the differences in motives and activities of not-for-profit organizations, and the need to develop additional theories to address those differences in explaining interorganizational arrangements between them.

Introduction

In 2003, La Bourguette,[1] a 7 million euro not-for-profit organization (NFPO) that takes care of autistic children and adults in Southern France, celebrated the thirtieth anniversary of its foundation. The year 2003 also marked the launching of an innovative partnership initiative by Georges Soleilhet, the manager of La Bourguette for these 30 years. The objective of this initiative was to promote cooperation between NFPOs taking care of autistic people in France and in other European countries. Most of these NFPOs were facing similar operational problems and financial pressures. However they were looking for solutions on their own and did not seem willing to cooperate. '[NFPOs] taking care of autistic people are often too reluctant to cooperate. They do not want to lose their autonomy. I do not want La Bourguette to lose its autonomy either. But I want organizations offering similar services for autistic people to share their know-how and to help each other whenever it is possible. We all have the same objective: helping autistic people. If we really want to do so, we should be able to cooperate', explained Mr Soleilhet. In November 2004, 15 French and European NFPOs taking care of autistic people had joined the partnership. In order to improve their services without losing their independence, they committed to sharing their resources and facilities, as well as information about donations and especially about public grants, whenever possible.

La Bourguette is not the only NFPO under pressure, nor is Mr Soleilhet the only manager in search of solutions. In fact most, if not all, NFPOs face similar financial and operational struggles. They largely depend on corporate or private donations and government grants, and as these sources of income are seldom guaranteed in the long run, they rarely have steady cash flows to ensure uninterrupted continuation of their activities.

In the last 20 years some significant changes in the not-for-profit landscape have made it even harder for NFPOs to raise funds. While the total amount of donations has increased (*The Economist*, 2004), the availability of some funds, for example corporate giving as a percentage of profits, has sharply decreased (Porter & Kramer, 2002), and the number of NFPOs has more than doubled (Wiesendanger, 1994; *The Nonprofit Almanac*, 2001) over the same period. As a result, competition for donations among NFPOs has significantly intensified. Government and regulatory agencies have become more demanding in terms of efficiency (Austin, 2000). Public policy shifts have taken place that have reduced funding or changed the way in which NFPOs receive grants (Harris et al., 2002). Donors also now put more pressure on the NFPOs to which they make donations: some put strict conditions on how and for which purposes their donations must be spent (Strom, 2004), whereas others, often dubbed venture philanthropists, demand a more efficient, business-like handling of operations (Byrne et al., 2002).

Interorganizational cooperative arrangements, like the one initiated by Mr Soleilhet of La Bourguette, have emerged as one of the potential responses to these mounting economic, regulatory and social pressures. Even though small-scale cooperative arrangements, like joint programming, have been pursued for a long time, both the quantity and quality of cooperation between NFPOs has dramatically changed over the last two decades. There have been more cooperative arrangements between NFPOs, especially in the late 1990s and early 2000s, than there were ever before. Today, not-for-profit executives regard these arrangements as an institutionalized practice that is likely to become even more widespread in the near future (Kohm & La

Piana, 2003). Moreover, and importantly, these arrangements are notably different in nature, as they are much more significant for the parties involved, in terms of resources and strategic centrality (Austin, 2000), and more integrative in nature (McLaughlin, 1998; Kohm & La Piana, 2003).

As such cooperative relationships have become more and more prevalent and significant in practice, a number of practitioner-oriented works have been published in recent years (see for example Arsenault, 1998; Bartling, 1998; McLaughlin, 1998). However scholarly attention to these interorganizational arrangements between NFPOs has been limited to a few noteworthy case-based studies (Kohm & La Piana, 2003; Yankey et al., 2001), and to our knowledge none of the existing work has yet explored the underlying mechanisms of interorganizational cooperation between NFPOs.

This lack of attention to interorganizational cooperation between NFPOs can be partially attributed to the scant attention paid to the not-for-profit sector in general in management research, despite the significant amount of assets controlled and contributions made by NFPOs.[2] Most of the few existing management studies that take NFPOs into account have focused on the impact of corporate philanthropy on for-profit organizations (FPOs) (for example Keim, 1978; Fry et al., 1982; Burt, 1983; Galaskiewicz & Burt, 1991), or on comparative aspects in industries where for-profit or not-for-profit organizations coexist (for example Rushing, 1974; Carper & Litschert, 1983; Nielsen et al., 1985; Baum & Oliver, 1996). Isolated examples exclusively focusing on NFPOs (for example Nutt, 1984; Golden-Biddle & Rao, 1997) are restricted in their focus, and ignore the network of relationships in which NFPOs are embedded. A notable exception is a prominent and very detailed empirical study of organizational change in the not-for-profit sector by Galaskiewicz and Bielefeld (1998).

The fact that interorganizational cooperation between NFPOs is a relatively recent phenomenon can also explain the lack of scholarly attention that it has received so far. In contrast, interorganizational cooperation among for-profit organizations has been extensively studied by management scholars (see for example Osborn & Hagedoorn, 1997). Notably, especially in the recent years since the mid-1990s, a complementary stream of research has emerged focusing on cooperative arrangements FPOs and NFPOs (Andreasen, 1996; Austin, 2000) and between FPOs and public actors, for example national governments, UN agencies (Rangan et al., forthcoming). Revived interest in corporate social responsibility has also contributed to the emergence of valuable research at the intersection of the for-profit and the not-for-profit sectors. Yet these studies do not tackle the issue of interorganizational cooperation between NFPOs, which requires different expectations, processes and techniques than those involving FPOs (McLaughlin, 1998). Hence we still know very little about this phenomenon.

In this study we develop a theoretical background for further theoretical and empirical work on interorganizational cooperation between NFPOs. We explore what an NFPO is and in which dimensions NFPOs differ from their for-profit counterparts; why they might seek cooperative arrangements with other NFPOs; with whom they are likely to engage in cooperative relationships; and how integrative these arrangements are likely to be. The answers we provide in the following pages emphasize some fundamental differences and similarities between FPOs and NFPOs. They are very different as they are characterized by different sources of income (donations versus revenue accrued following the sale of goods and/or services) and by different objectives (resources enhancement versus profit or shareholder value maximization). Yet they are quite similar in the way they engage in cooperative arrangements in terms of potential benefits, partner selection and mode of integration. An overarching conclusion of this study is the observation that for NFPOs, unlike FPOs, neither inputs nor outputs are simple transactions, making both the needs of NFPOs and the boundaries they need to manage more complex.

Not-for-profit organizations
Not-for-profit organizations (NFPOs) are privately controlled, tax-exempt organizations within which no one owns the right to share any profit or surplus (Weisbrod, 1988). These organizations thus have three defining characteristics. First, they are free from tax burdens, and frequently donations to them are tax deductible. Second, they are privately controlled such that donors, who fund these organizations, often do not have control rights over them at all (Glaeser, 2002). Even though frequently their boards are partially composed of donors, and boards naturally do have control rights, they are often not elected and are not ultimately accountable to shareholders and donors (Steinberg, 1987). Further, NFPOs are never subject to takeovers (Frech, 1980). As a result, managers of NFPOs have much greater autonomy than their for-profit counterparts (Glaeser, 2002: 3).

Third, and importantly, NFPOs are subject to a non-distribution constraint that prohibits the distribution of residual earnings to individuals who exercise control over the organization, such as officers, directors or members (Hansmann, 1980, 1987). All residual earnings must either be retained by the NFPO or given to other NFPOs (Hansmann, 1980; Simon, 1987). It is important to note that the non-distribution constraint prohibits NFPOs from distributing any profit to their stakeholders, but it does not prohibit them from earning profits. In the health-care industry for example, both for-profit and not-for-profit hospitals make profits (Davis, 1972). Hence the term 'non-profit' is a misnomer as NFPOs usually do make operating profits. For this reason, we prefer the term 'not-for-profit organization' to the term 'non-profit organization' that is usually used in the literature.

The members of the not-for-profit sector are not homogeneous in their interests as they can operate to serve private as well as public interests. Neither are they homogenous in their sources of income. Some NFPOs derive their income primarily or exclusively from sales of goods and services – either from mission-unrelated commercial or ancillary activities or from program service revenues – whereas others receive a substantial portion of their income in the form of donations (Weisbrod, 1998). In other words, the resources (inputs) they use to produce goods and services (outputs) come from either donations or sales.

This heterogeneity in interests and sources of income leads to the emergence of different kinds of NFPOs, which can be classified into three main categories: philanthropic organizations, private not-for-profit commercial enterprises and membership groups (Rudney, 1987). Philanthropic organizations are privately controlled, tax-exempt organizations to which donor contributions are tax deductible. Organizations helping victims of terrorist attacks (for example SOS Attentats in France), domestic violence (for example Refuge in the UK), or child abuse (for example PCA America in the US), and organizations helping people affected by leprosy (for example The Leprosy Mission International) are examples of philanthropic organizations. Although philanthropic organizations provide a wide range of services, they are most heavily concentrated in five sectors of activity: the health sector, the educational sector, the cultural and recreational sector, the social service sector and the religious sector (Rudney, 1987).

Private not-for-profit commercial enterprises differ from philanthropic organizations in their funding patterns and outputs. They provide goods and/or services directly to consumers who are required to pay some fees or dues for the output (Galaskiewicz & Bielefeld, 1998). Private not-for-profit hospitals are examples of not-for-profit commercial enterprises. Membership groups differ from both philanthropic organizations and private not-for-profit commercial enterprises in their overall objective. Whereas philanthropic organizations and private not-for-profit commercial enterprises provide services that benefit the people outside the organization (Weisbrod, 1988), membership groups are organized largely to confer mutual benefits on their members. Sport clubs and professional associations are examples of membership groups. In the frame of this chapter we only focus on philanthropic NFPOs, which constitute the great majority of all NFPOs.[3] Whenever we refer to NFPOs, we refer to this specific category.

NFPOs' behavioural drivers

While there is a consensus regarding what an NFPO is, NFPOs' behavioral drivers have been debated in the literature. Following the neoclassical tradition, many scholars use models that maximize different objectives to describe and predict the behavior of NFPOs. As summarized by Steinberg (1987), these models postulate different objectives for NFPOs, such as enrollment maximization, service maximization, maximization of the quality and/or quantity of the service produced, budget maximization, medical-demand maximization or expense-preference maximization. These models implicitly assume that the NFPOs minimize costs. Yet overall what NFPOs maximize is still a significant and difficult question (Glaeser, 2002).

Some researchers, on the other hand, argue that whatever objectives NFPOs may pursue with respect to quality or quantity of services (outputs), they are inherently subject to productive inefficiency (that is, failure to minimize costs) owing to the absence of ownership claims to residual earnings (Alchian & Demsetz, 1972; Hansmann, 1980, 1987). According to this stream of research, the absence of ownership claims to residual earnings in NFPOs, due to the non-distribution constraint, would reduce boards' and managers' incentives to ensure efficiency. Even though inherent inefficiency of NFPOs is a widely held belief, there is little empirical evidence supporting it (Kohm & La Piana, 2003).

These different approaches to NFPOs' behavior adapt conventional models of firms' behavior to the specific case of NFPOs. They assume that there is an objective function that describes the behavior of NFPOs. Such an assumption is oversimplistic because NFPOs do not pursue one single objective: they pursue heterogeneous objectives, such as service quality and quantity, budget maximization and growth, and survival (DiMaggio, 1987).

In addition, most of these approaches assume that NFPOs' behavior is driven by objectives related to the services (outputs) they offer. However donations constitute the primary source of income for many NFPOs, and they often compete with each other for donations (Rose-Ackerman, 1982; Feigenbaum, 1987). Thus competition for donations is frequently NFPOs' primary concern, as a recent study of 90 NFPOs in southeastern Michigan (Reisch & Sommerfeld, 2001) shows. Thus objectives related to resources (inputs) also drive NFPOs' behavior (Pfeffer & Leong, 1977; Provan et al., 1980). In this chapter, following this line of research, we consider that NFPOs' behavior is heavily driven by 'resource enhancement' (Galaskiewickz & Bielefeld, 1998). We assume that most NFPOs seek to maximize the resources they get (inputs) in order to better achieve their mission. We do not regard resource enhancement as the sole driver of NFPOs' behavior, but as being one of the most important ones.

Interorganizational cooperation between NFPOs
'Interorganizational cooperation' herein refers to voluntary arrangements between not-for-profit organizations for exchange, sharing and co-development of resources, services and programs, which may or may not require a change in these organizations' corporate structure. These arrangements differ from each other in at least two basic dimensions. First, they may differ in the number of NFPOs involved. It might be the case that only two NFPOs cooperate, whereas in other cases a larger number of NFPOs might be involved in a single cooperative arrangement. United fund-raising organizations, like United Ways, JustGive.org web portal or its French equivalent Aidez.org, are good examples of arrangements involving multiple organizations. They bring together many NFPOs, thereby enabling donors to donate to the united organization which then distributes funds among its members.

Second, these arrangements may also differ in the degree of structural change that they require from participating NFPOs. Some forms of interorganizational cooperation may need not-so-significant arrangements in the organizational structure of participating NFPOs (for example joint programming partnership), whereas other forms may require some level of structural integration (for example joint ventures). Yet these differences not withstanding, the incentives that lead NFPOs to cooperate and the mechanisms by which they select potential partners are fundamentally similar across different cooperative arrangements between NFPOs. In the following section we lay out the potential benefits of cooperation between NFPOs, which addresses the 'why' dimension of interorganizational cooperation. Then we turn to the relational factors affecting the likelihood of cooperation between NFPOs, thereby addressing the 'with whom' dimension of interorganizational cooperation.

Potential benefits of cooperation for NFPOs

Increasing efficiency Interorganizational cooperation may help participant NFPOs to increase their efficiency. Even though NFPOs have traditionally been portrayed as being less efficient than their for-profit counterparts (Hansmann, 1987), it does not imply that they should not aim at efficiency. In fact they take efficiency considerations into account especially when the scarcity of resources increases as a result of intensified competition among NFPOs (Steinberg, 1987). Inefficiencies may arise from the lack of managerial incentives to pursue efficiency, as mentioned earlier, or from high overhead expenses, which are particularly salient when fixed costs are very high. These inefficiencies can be – partially – eliminated by cooperative arrangements such as joint administration, joint fund-raising activities, joint programs or joint purchase of equipment and facilities (Kushner, 1996; McLaughlin, 1998). This type of arrangement frequently helps NFPOs to share managerial and operational resources, thereby enabling them to reduce their operating costs through elimination of duplicated services and/or through economies of scale in procurement and services (Austin, 2000; Kohm & La Piana, 2003).

Reducing resource competition   Interorganizational cooperation may serve to reduce overall competition by letting participants behave less aggressively in fund-raising. As mentioned before, NFPOs primarily compete for donations, as their survival crucially depends on the amount of donations they get from the limited pool of donors. When competition for donations is high, NFPOs are forced to devote more resources to fund-raising activities as those funds get scarcer (Rose-Ackerman, 1982). This is indeed a socially undesirable outcome, as a larger part of donations is then diverted to fund-raising instead of being used to provide services. Coordination between NFPOs may reduce resource competition, which ensures a better use of resources as NFPOs share the costs of fund-raising. It is for this reason for example, and due to concerns about an increase in the number of NFPOs involved in similar activities, that the Greater Milwaukee Committee, a group of major donors, issued a report in 1990 that suggested some local charities merge in order to provide more coordinated services, and reduce administrative and fund-raising costs (Millar, 1990). In the same vein, united fund-raising organizations too arise mainly to reduce resource competition and fund-raising costs (Rose-Ackerman, 1980). Therefore cooperation may increase survival chances of participant NFPOs by reducing resource cannibalization between them. For this reason, increased competition for resources is often associated with increased cooperative activity between NFPOs (Steinberg, 1987; La Piana, 1997; Bartling, 1998).

Enabling transfer of knowledge and skills   Interorganizational cooperation may enable organizations to transfer tacit knowledge and to learn skills from their partners (Doz et al., 1989; Khanna et al., 1998; Kogut, 1988). In the not-for-profit world, learning occurs at all levels of functioning, including administration, programming and fund-raising activities. NFPOs can learn from each other in at least two different areas. First, they may strengthen their competencies or develop new ones through cooperation. NFPOs' staff may lack some core competencies (Bartling, 1998), which they might be able to improve or acquire through cooperation by sharing staff, and engaging in joint training and joint operations. Cooperation may also enable participating NFPOs to benefit from the experience of skilled not-for-profit sector executives, who are in short supply (Kohm & La Piana, 2003).

Second, by engaging in partnership relationships NFPOs may get information and access to the set of donors that other NFPOs have. This information is crucial insofar as NFPOs' survival depends to a large extent on
the funding they receive. For this reason, NFPOs may not be willing to
share information regarding donors. They are more likely to do so in highly
integrative forms of cooperation (for example joint ventures and mergers)
than in less integrative ones (for example joint programming).

Improving strategic positioning   Interorganizational cooperation can help
organizations to improve their strategic positioning (Kogut, 1988). For
NFPOs, positioning is related to their status and visibility. The status of an
NFPO, as we discuss in detail later, is an indicator of its quality, impact and
trustworthiness, which derives from its prior performance, status of its
exchange partners and status of its donors. Insofar as the status of an NFPO
is influenced by the status of its exchange partners, cooperation with high-
status NFPOs is likely to have a positive impact on the focal NFPO's status
(Kohm & La Piana, 2003). Visibility of an NFPO, on the other hand, refers
to the extent to which it is known by potential donors. Cooperation may also
serve to increase their visibility by exposing them to a larger number of
potential donors, as they operate on a larger scale and perform a more diverse
set of activities (Austin, 2000; McLaughlin, 1998). Thus by performing joint
programs and fund-raising activities, NFPOs not only take advantage of the
scale economies and offer a wider range of activities, but they also have easier
access to potential donors due to their increased visibility. Taken together
these arguments imply that cooperation may help NFPOs to increase both
their status and their visibility, which in turn improves their strategic positioning and facilitates access to potential donors.

On the whole, it appears that successful implementation of interorganizational arrangements may result in increased efficiency, reduced resource
competition, enhanced knowledge and skills, and improved strategic positioning for NFPOs. Having addressed the 'why' dimension of interorganizational cooperation between NFPOs, in the following section we examine
'with whom' NFPOs are more likely to cooperate.

Relational factors affecting the likelihood of cooperation between NFPOs
There are multiple factors affecting the likelihood of cooperation between
NFPOs. One can make a distinction between relational and non-relational
factors. A relation is a collection of ties of a specific kind between pairs of
actors (Wasserman & Faust, 1994: 20). Thus relational factors refer to the
network characteristics of pairs of organizations. As stated by prior work
on for-profit organizations (for example Gulati, 1995; Gulati & Gargiulo,
1999), relational characteristics of any two organizations can be reliable

predictors of their propensity to engage in cooperative arrangements with each other. These relational characteristics are not the sole drivers of likely cooperation. There are also some non-relational factors affecting the likelihood of cooperation. These factors do not depend on the network characteristics of pairs of organizations, but are based on organization-specific characteristics, such as size, or on largely exogenous (that is, sector- or country-wide) forces, such as environmental changes, regulations and other institutional elements. However while these non-relational factors can help to explain why some organizations are more likely to cooperate, they do not explain why these organizations would more likely cooperate with certain organizations. Since we are primarily interested in addressing the 'with whom' question of interorganizational cooperation between NFPOs, in the next section we focus on relational factors, which are stronger predictors of such arrangements.

Interorganizational embeddedness　NFPOs, like any other type of organizations, are embedded in a variety of interorganizational networks. Embeddedness in various networks serves as a means of information which reduces the potential hazards associated with interorganizational cooperation (Gulati & Gargiulo, 1999). Gulati and Gargiulo (1999) distinguish three network mechanisms that shape the creation of new interorganizational ties. The first is relational embeddedness, which refers to the effects of prior direct ties between organizations on the likelihood of cooperation between those organizations. The existence of prior direct ties between two organizations helps them to learn about each other's competencies and reliability, and hence reduces uncertainty for future collaboration and increases the trust between them.

The second is structural embeddedness, which corresponds to the impact of the structure of relations among actors on the likelihood of cooperation between them (Granovetter, 1992). In particular, the existence of prior indirect ties between two organizations, which is an important structural characteristic of their relation, is likely to increase the likelihood of cooperation between them. These ties are important sources of information about the availability, capabilities and reliability of potential partners for any organization (Baker, 1990; Kogut et al., 1992; Gulati, 1995). Access to this information increases the likelihood of identifying new cooperation opportunities (Gulati & Gargiulo, 1999) and decreases the uncertainty an exchange partner faces (Podolny, 2001). For these reasons, past direct and indirect cooperative experiences are likely to increase the likelihood of cooperation between any pairs of organizations.

As for the third form of embeddedness, that is, positional embeddedness, it highlights the impact of the relative positions that a pair of organizations occupy in their network on the likelihood of cooperation between them. It has been shown that central actors have better information about a larger pool of potential partners (Krackhardt, 1990; Gulati 1999; Powell et al., 1996), and are relatively more visible (Podolny, 1993; Podolny & Stuart, 1995). Therefore as Gulati and Gargiulo (1999: 1449) argue, interorganizational ties are expected to be more common between organizations that occupy central positions. Taken together, the above arguments imply that:

Proposition 1. The more embedded two NFPOs are, the higher the likelihood of cooperation between them.

Functional similarity By functional similarity we refer to the extent to which NFPOs serve the same objective (for example reducing smoking). Organizations that are pursuing the same or highly similar objectives are very likely to offer similar services (for example counseling), perform similar activities (for example anti-smoking campaigns) and hence to use similar resources (for example advertisement services, experts' discourse). This parallel use of resources for the same objective implies additional costs and is considered to be wasteful (Harris et al., 2002). In such situations, cooperation enables NFPOs to decrease their operating costs by reducing or eliminating duplication of services, or by economies of scale (Austin, 2000). These benefits increase as the extent of duplication increases.[4]

In addition, the perceived similarity of the services offered by NFPOs increases the meaningfulness of cooperation. Donors are likely to evaluate cooperation between two NFPOs that offer similar services as a relevant managerial tactic. Donors often regard the use of managerial tactics, such as interorganizational cooperation, as indications of organizational accountability, reliability and trustworthiness (Galaskiewicz & Bielefeld, 1998). For this reason, cooperation between two NFPOs that offer similar services can lead to a more positive re-evaluation of these NFPOs by donors. Such a positive re-evaluation secures the relationship between these NFPOs and their donors. It is also likely to generate an increased amount of donations. In consequence, the more similar the services offered by two NFPOs are, the more likely they are to reduce operating costs and increase donations through cooperation. Thus we propose the following:

Proposition 2. The higher the degree of functional similarity of two NFPOs, the higher the likelihood of cooperation between them.

Note that up to now we did not make any claims regarding how embeddedness or functional similarity differ in the way they affect the likelihood of cooperation between for-profit organizations and between not-for-profit ones. Indeed one would expect to find differences between these two cases, as FPOs and NFPOs differ from each other in their sources of income and in their objectives. However, as we explained above, these two mechanisms operate in surprisingly similar ways. Below we introduce two additional relational factors that affect the likelihood of cooperation between NFPOs: status similarity and micro-niche overlaps. The former differs from the for-profit case not so much in the mechanisms leading to cooperation, but in the way it is defined. The latter, on the other hand, is, as we will see, entirely specific to NFPOs. Thus contrary to interorganizational embeddedness and functional similarity, these two factors are more specific to between-NFPO cooperation.

Status similarity   Firms' status is a signal of the underlying quality of firms' products and services, when such a quality is uncertain (Podolny, 1993). In the not-for-profit world, NFPOs' status plays a critical role, since both the quantity and the quality of services offered by NFPOs are most of the time uncertain. Frequently donors are in a poor position to determine whether the NFPOs they funded have actually performed the promised services and what the quality of the performed services is. The only guarantee donors have is the non-distribution constraint that is supposed to give them at least some insurance that their donations are being used to provide the services they wish to be provided (Hansmann, 1987). Yet, donors still do not know whether their donations are being devoted in their entirety to the purpose for which they were made and what the quality of the services offered by NFPOs is (Steinberg, 1987). In this context, donors use the NFPOs' status as a signal of the quality of the service they offer. Therefore, NFPOs' perceived status has an important impact on potential donors' evaluation of NFPOs, and hence on their decision to make a donation.

The status of an organization is derived, at least in part, from its prior performance, which serves as a signal of its capabilities and future actions (Wilson, 1985; Podolny & Phillips, 1996). For an NFPO prior performance refers to its longevity and the social impact of its prior activities, which is the NFPO's long-term influence on its environment (Kanter & Summers, 1987). Yet, as with their for-profit counterparts (Podolny, 1994; Podolny & Phillips, 1996), NFPOs' status derives not only from their past performance, but also from the status of the organizations with which they engage in exchange relations. In the case of NFPOs the set of exchange partners does not only include other NFPOs, but also includes their donors. Hence, the status of an NFPO derives not only from its prior performance and from the status of NFPOs it engages in cooperative relationships with, but also from the status of its donors. The status of donors may have tremendous effect on the amount of donations an NFPO might receive, since inclusion of high-status donors signals to other donors that it is a trustworthy organization which has already passed the evaluation of well-regarded donors (Useem, 1987; DiMaggio & Anheier, 1990).[5] Therefore an NFPO's status is a function of (1) its prior performance; (2) the status of its exchange partners; and (3) the status of its donors.

Whenever an NFPO engages in a cooperative relationship with another NFPO, its status is affected by the status of its partner. Since NFPOs' quality of services is uncertain by nature, the status of other NFPOs with which it interacts, as well as the other measures of status, that is prior performance (longevity and impact) and the status of donors, are used to gauge its quality (Podolny, 1993). When the status of potential partners is asymmetric, affiliation with a higher-status organization increases the focal organization's status, whereas affiliation with a lower-status one decreases it (Podolny & Phillips, 1996). As a result, high-status NFPOs usually prefer to avoid cooperating with low-status ones, since such cooperation may damage their own attractiveness. Therefore, as with their for-profit counterparts (Chung et al., 2000), the likelihood of cooperation between two NFPOs will increase with their similarity in status.[6]

Proposition 3. The more similar the statuses of two NFPOs are, the higher the likelihood of cooperation between them.

Micro-niche overlaps NFPOs, as it should be clear by now, are embedded in a network of relationships with other NFPOs that offer similar services, using similar resources. Importantly however, NFPOs are also embedded in a second network of indirect relationships with each other through the set of donors they have. This is a prominent set of relationships because, in contrast to the for-profit sector in which the output market determines the source of income through sales, in the not-for-profit sector the primary source of income is not the output market where organizations offer services, but rather the funding they receive from their donors. Therefore NFPOs primarily compete for donations, not for 'customers', even though the quality and usefulness of these services partially affect the level of donations they receive. Following the previous work on niches (Baum & Singh, 1994a, 1994b; Baum & Oliver, 1996; Podolny et al., 1996), we define a micro-niche as 'the area in the niche space where the organization feeds' (Galaskiewicz & Bielefeld, 1998), which mainly corresponds to the set of donors NFPOs have.

Note that there is no a priori expectation for these two networks of relationships (that is, the one between NFPOs that are functionally similar, and the one between NFPOs that are funded by the same set of donors) to overlap. For example any two firms may be serving the same objective (for example reducing smoking), but may have a very different set of donors, which locates them in different micro-niches. Conversely, any two NFPOs can be in the same micro-niche (that is, funded by the same donors), but may be providing totally different services (for example one may be helping AIDS patients while the other is helping the victims of terrorist attacks).

Micro-niche overlaps can be an important predictor of cooperation. At low levels of micro-niche overlaps, where two NFPOs have very few or no donors in common, the incentive to cooperate will be higher. The main reason is that their cooperation might provide information about and/or access to each other's donors. Similar to the brokerage role in structural holes (Burt, 1992), privileged access to different sets of donors is very beneficial for both parties. Their network of donors will be bigger following cooperation. This advantage will be more significant when participants have very few overlaps, hence a lot to learn from each other.[7]

At high levels of micro-niche overlaps, information advantages will be significantly diminished. At the same time, since NFPOs mainly compete for donations, the level of competition will be high. In this case, interorganizational cooperation may help to avoid cannibalization and to reduce fundraising costs (Steinberg, 1987), and hence is encouraged by donors since it enables them to more easily and more efficiently direct their donations to organizations they consider optimal (Rose-Ackerman, 1980). Further, at high level of micro-niche overlaps, boards' interlocks may also contribute to facilitate cooperation between NFPOs. NFPOs' boards are special boundary-spanning and control units that keep organizations connected to parts of their environment while also differentiating them from external elements (Middleton, 1987). At high levels of micro-niche overlaps, board interlocks are more likely, as major donors are usually represented on not-for-profit boards. Like their for-profit counterparts, boards' interlocks among NFPOs function as an important conduit of information between them (Useem, 1984; Davis & Powell, 1992; Haunschild, 1993), reducing the uncertainty they face about the quality of potential exchange partners, and thereby contributing to facilitating cooperation between NFPOs.

In contrast, at moderate levels of micro-niche overlaps the effect of the different motives cited above are less pronounced. When the extent of micro-niche overlap is only moderate, the level of resource cannibalization is less than in the case of high overlaps, and therefore there is less incentive to engage in cooperative arrangements in order to reduce it. In addition, at moderate levels of micro-niche overlaps, board interlocks are less likely. Last but not least, when the extent of micro-niche overlap is moderate, the need for cooperation for information sharing is less important than it is when there are few or no overlaps, because the number of distinct ties that the other party has goes down. Therefore, we predict a U-shaped relationship between micro-niche overlaps and the likelihood of cooperation among NFPOs, the likelihood being higher at low and high levels of micro-niche overlaps.

Proposition 4. The degree of micro-niche overlaps between two NFPOs has a U-shaped relationship with the likelihood of cooperation between them.

Since NFPOs are simultaneously embedded in both sets of relationships described above, their likelihood of cooperation will be jointly affected by them. Hence, combining our above-mentioned arguments, it is straightforward to deduce how embeddedness in these two sets of relationships will affect the likelihood of cooperation between any two NFPOs. As depicted in Figure 11.1, the likelihood of cooperation will be lowest when NFPOs serve different objectives and their micro-niches overlap moderately. The likelihood will be higher for those organizations that (1) serve more similar objectives; (2) feed from very different micro-niches; or (3) feed from very similar micro-niches.

Modes of collaboration
Interorganizational arrangements differ in the degree of structural change that they require from participating NFPOs. The degree of integration required in these arrangements ranges from punctual collaboration, which corresponds to the loosest type of integration, to merger, which of course

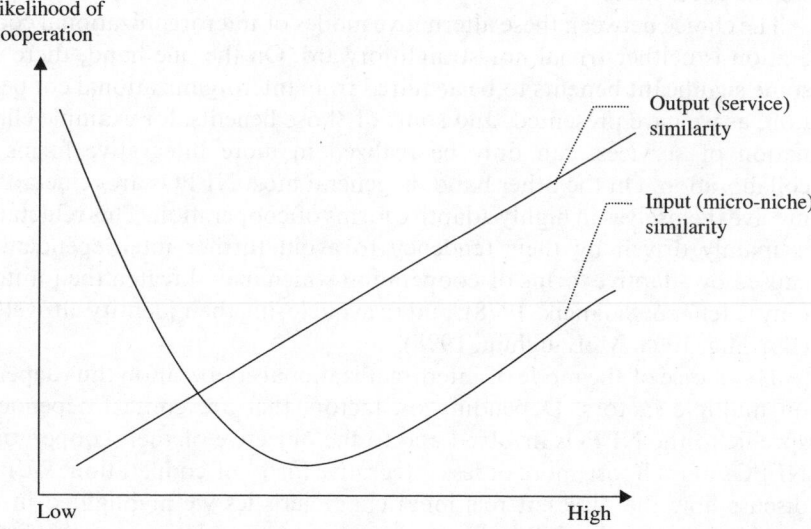

Figure 11.1   Similarity and likelihood of cooperation between NFPOs

corresponds to the tightest form of integration. Based on these criteria, Kohm and La Piana (2003: 4–8) distinguish seven types of interorganizational cooperation between NFPOs: collaboration, joint programming, administrative consolidation, management service organization, joint venture, parent–subsidiary and merger.

Collaboration refers to interorganizational arrangements that are about sharing information or coordinating efforts but do not include shared, transferred or combined services, resources or programs. In contrast, joint programming and administrative consolidation require NFPOs to commit, usually in writing, to an ongoing partnership. They both involve joint management of one or more organizational functions. While in the case of joint programming one or more programs are jointly managed, in the case of administrative consolidation one or more administrative functions are shared. The other forms of interorganizational cooperation, that is, management service organization, joint venture, parent–subsidiary and merger, are even more integrative. They involve changes to corporate control and/or structure, including the creation and/or dissolution of one or more organizations. Management service organizations are created by NFPOs in order to provide some or all of their back-office functions. Joint ventures are new organizations created by NFPOs in order to further a specific administrative or programmatic end. In a parent–subsidiary arrangement, one organization oversees others. Last but not least, merger enables previously separate NFPOs to combine programmatic and administrative functions as well as governance.

The choice between these alternative modes of interorganizational cooperation is neither trivial nor straightforward. On the one hand, there are some significant benefits to be acquired from interorganizational cooperation, as we have presented, and some of those benefits, for example elimination of services, can only be realized in more integrative forms of collaboration. On the other hand, in general most NFPOs are reluctant to involve themselves in highly adaptive forms of cooperation. This reluctance is mainly driven by their tendency to avoid further interdependencies caused by adaptive forms of cooperation which may threaten their autonomy (Pfeffer & Salancik, 1978), and to avoid losing their identity altogether (Bartling, 1998; McLaughlin, 1998).

The choice of the mode of interorganizational cooperation thus depends on multiple factors. Depending on factors that are context-dependent, specific to the NFPOs involved and to the objective of their cooperation, NFPOs may choose more or less integrative forms of cooperation. We now discuss how the different relational characteristics we highlighted in the previous section may influence the choice of more or less integrative forms of cooperation.

Both high interorganizational embeddedness and functional similarity lead to more integrated structural forms of cooperation, but for different reasons. Embeddedness, as we mentioned earlier, serves as a means of information about the availability, capabilities and reliability of potential partners, which reduces the potential hazards associated with interorganizational cooperation (Gulati & Gargiulo, 1999). Thus highly embedded organizations are more likely to engage in more integrative arrangements than loosely embedded ones, as such an arrangement bears relatively less uncertainty for them. Functional similarity, on the other hand – given the existence of cooperation – leads to more integrated structural forms of cooperation, because elimination of services is more efficient in integrated forms. Functionally similar organizations are more likely to use similar resources and perform similar activities. Further, elimination of duplication requires delegation, closure or even merger of some functional domains. Thus the efficiency of elimination of these services will be low whenever firms engage in very loosely integrated, autonomous structural arrangements.

Status similarity however will not be a significant predictor of the form of interorganizational cooperation between any two NFPOs. To be sure, high-status NFPOs may leverage the competitive pressures and thus may be able to engage in more autonomous forms of collaboration. Yet there is no a priori reason to expect the extent of similarity of two NFPOs' statuses to affect the form of cooperation between them.

High levels of micro-niche overlaps, on the other hand, are more likely to lead to more integrated structural forms of cooperation. At low and high levels of micro-niche overlaps the likelihood of interorganizational cooperation goes up, since there are significant information-sharing benefits at low levels, and cannibalization reduction benefits at high levels. Yet since both of these benefits take effect through interconnectedness over the indirect resource network, achievement of these benefits does not necessarily require any significant form of integration. Still, one might expect to observe more integrated forms of cooperation at high levels of micro-niche overlaps, for two reasons. First, more integrated forms may increase the credibility of cooperation, which is particularly important in the reduction of resource cannibalization. Second, one would expect, as we mentioned before, NFPOs to share information regarding their donors in highly integrative forms of cooperation (for example joint ventures or mergers) rather than in less integrative ones (for example joint programming), since the information regarding donors is crucial for NFPOs and they understandably are not willing to share this information with others.

Finally, the mode of cooperation between two NFPOs is not constant over time. As Austin (2000) explains in the case of FPO–NFPO alliances, cooperation between two organizations usually goes through various stages over time, from philanthropic to transactional to integrative. High integration is always more costly, harder to reverse, and hence overall more risky. For this reason, trust for the potential partner is especially important in highly integrative modes of cooperation. Prior experience, as we mentioned earlier, is important in building trust and providing information, and hence makes integration more likely. The same argument applies to between-NFPO cooperation as well.

Directions for future research
Interorganizational cooperation between NFPOs has received scant attention to date, and is still understudied and undertheorized. Clearly the rich alliance literature in the for-profit sector offers numerous valuable insights that can be directly applied to the not-for-profit case. At the same time, the differences in motives and activities of NFPOs, as it should be clear by now, require additional theories to address them. Of many fruitful research opportunities waiting to be addressed, we now mention a few.

First, empirical testing of the arguments presented in this chapter is necessary. Even though a few case studies (Kohm & La Piana, 2003; Yankey et al., 2001) provide some in-depth qualitative insight about interorganizational cooperation between NFPOs, they neither provide enough information to test all the arguments presented here nor have a sufficient number of observations to be used to justify and generalize our propositions. We believe that comprehensive empirical studies are likely to emerge in the near future, since the amount of available data on NFPOs' behavior is increasing as research centers on the not-for-profit sector flourishes both in the US and in the rest of the world.

A second intriguing area for research is to observe how diffusion of best practices, or more generally innovations, is affected by the existence of interorganizational ties between NFPOs. Research on for-profit organizations predicts that the existence of this type of relationships fosters the diffusion of practices (for example Haunschild, 1993), enabling more frequent and efficient knowledge transfer. We still expect to see a similar pattern. Yet it will be interesting to compare and contrast diffusion patterns in for-profit and not-for-profit organizations, since NFPOs are assumed to be slow responders to changes due to their lack of incentive to respond and limited resources (Kanter & Summers, 1987). However they may also be more flexible to change, if their donors force them to do so (Powell & Friedkin, 1987).

Third, it might be interesting to examine how interorganizational cooperation among NFPOs will affect donation patterns of corporations. Numerous studies have argued that corporate contributions are not completely altruistic, and are generally driven by self-interest (Keim, 1978;

Fry et al., 1982; Burt, 1983). Recently, Porter and Kramer (2002) have called companies to channel their donations in alignment with their strategic objectives to increase both their long-term profits and the social benefits. It would be interesting to see to what extent cooperative behavior patterns of NFPOs will be matched by the corporate world. It is for example possible that companies may refrain from channeling their donations to united funds, where their contributions, being one of the many contributors, will be noticed less publicly. But it is also possible they may be willing to donate to larger NFPOs, including united funds, since they simply attract more public attention than smaller ones.

Fourth, the role of geography in the context of interorganizational cooperation between NFPOs needs to be addressed. Even though there are numerous organizations serving multiple cities, regions or even countries, the great majority of NFPOs are geographically embedded both in terms of the services they offer and in terms of the potential donors they seek funds from. Still, it can be the case that an NFPO offers services locally in a certain area, but engages in cooperation globally, that is, with NFPOs from other cities, regions or countries. This is indeed what La Bourguette has been doing, as we mentioned at the very beginning of this chapter. Then the question is to know which constraints, if any, embeddedness in local networks put on an NFPO regarding its ability to engage in cooperative arrangements with others.

Additionally, it is necessary to analyze the dynamics of interorganizational cooperation between NFPOs over time, especially in response to macro-economic fluctuations. Evidently, recessions generally mark more difficult periods for NFPOs, during which the availability of donations is likely to decrease, whereas the need for them increases (Steinberg & Pearlman, 1982). In such situations, the imminence of financial problems ranges from immediate crisis to anticipated future challenges (Singer & Yankey, 1991). Thus one might expect to see more cooperative activity during economic slowdowns, and less during economic booms.

Conclusion

Our analysis highlights two observations, one empirical and one theoretical. First, in response to the economic, regulatory and social pressures that are reshaping the not-for-profit landscape, many more NFPOs have been engaging in interorganizational arrangements with other NFPOs in recent years than ever before. Yet scholarly work did not parallel the same trend and the phenomenon has received scant attention to date. It is still understudied and undertheorized.

Second, and importantly, we do need scholarly work on this area, not simply because it has not been studied much, but because what we know from the existing literature cannot address all the questions that emerge in the not-for-profit sector. It is true that many insights from the existing alliance literature can be directly applied to the not-for-profit sector. We have already highlighted some in this chapter. However there are also areas that require additional theories to address the differences of the not-for-profit world, mainly stemming from NFPOs' differing objectives, inputs, outputs, sources of income and activities. For interorganizational cooperation, these differences bring a heightened complexity in boundaries that need to be managed. Notably, it is not usually the reasons of cooperation or the way they engage in those arrangements that differ in the not-for-profit alliances; it is the mechanisms behind those arrangements. This chapter is an attempt at developing a theoretical background for further theoretical and empirical work. To us, interorganizational cooperation appears to be one of the great challenges of organizing for NFPOs, and also a fascinating opportunity for students of interorganizational cooperation, as well as those of the not-for-profit sector.

Notes

*   We would like to thank Gokhan Ertug, Martin Gargiulo, Julie Urda, and Tieying Yu for helpful comments and discussions. An earlier version of this chapter was presented at the 2003 Academy of Management conference in Seattle.
1.   More information about La Bourguette can be found on its website: www.bourguette-autisme.org
2.   In the United States, charitable foundations 'now hold over $330 billion in assets and contribute over $20 billion annually to educational, humanitarian, and cultural organizations of all kinds' (Porter & Kramer, 1999). Moreover, as of 1982, NFPOs employed over 8 percent of the total labor force (Rudney, 1987).
3.   In the US for example, philanthropic organizations constituted 92 percent of employment in the 1980s (Rudney, 1987). Today they still constitute the majority of the not-for-profit sector as 80 percent of all non-profit entities are philanthropic organizations, according to the Urban Institute (www.urban.org).
4.   However it is also true that learning benefits are usually higher in cooperation between organizations that are different (see Mowery et al., 1996).
5.   The total amount of donations received may also serve as a mechanism to affect the status of the NFPO, whenever donors are numerous and anonymous.
6.   As Ahuja (2000) mentions, important inventions can enable mismatched pairings, that is, cooperation between a high-status organization and a low-status one. While the same argument might apply to the not-for-profit world as well, it is necessary to keep in mind that important inventions, and subsequent cooperative arrangements, are very rare in this context.
7.   It is important to underline here that this information is crucial insofar as NFPOs' survival depends to a large extent on the funding they receive, and the existence of more NFPOs demanding donations from a given donor reduces the chances of any given NFPO to raise funds from that specific donor. For this reason, as we mentioned earlier, NFPOs usually may not be willing to share information regarding their donors. Hence, one would expect NFPOs to share information regarding their donors in highly integrative forms of cooperation (for example joint ventures or mergers) rather than in less integrative ones (for example joint programming).

References

Ahuja, G. (2000), The duality of collaboration: inducements and opportunities in the forma-tion of interfirm linkages, *Strategic Management Journal*, **21** (3), 317–43.

Alchian, A.A. & Demsetz, H. (1972), Production, information costs, and economic organiza-tion, *American Economic Review*, **62** (5), 777–95.

Andreasen, A.R. (1996), Profits for nonprofits: find a corporate partner, *Harvard Business Review* (Nov–Dec), 47–59.

Arsenault, J. (1998), *Forging Nonprofit Alliances*, San Francisco, CA: Jossey-Bass Publishers.

Austin, J.E. (2000), *The Collaboration Challenge: How Nonprofits and Businesses Succeed through Strategic Alliances*, San Francisco, CA: Jossey-Bass Publishers.

Baker, W.E. (1990), Market networks and corporate behavior, *American Journal of Sociology*, **96**, 589–625.

Bartling, C.E. (1998), *Strategic Alliances for Nonprofit Organizations*, Washington, DC: American Society of Association Executives.

Baum, J.A.C. & Oliver, C. (1996), Toward an institutional ecology of organizational found-ings, *Academy of Management Journal*, **39**, 1378–427.

Baum, J.A.C. & Singh, J.V. (1994a), Organizational niche overlap and the dynamics of organ-izational founding, *Organization Science*, **5**, 483–502.

Baum, J.A.C. & Singh, J.V. (1994b), Organizational niche overlap and the dynamics of orga-nizational mortality, *American Journal of Sociology*, **100**, 346–80.

Burt, R.S. (1983), Corporate philanthropy as a cooptive relation, *Social Forces*, **62** (2), 419–49.

Burt, R.S. (1992), *Structural Holes: The Social Structure of Competition*, Cambridge, MA: Harvard University Press.

Byrne, J.A., Cosgrove, J., Hindo, B. & Dayan, A. (2002), The new face of philanthropy: today's donors are more ambitious, get more involved, and demand results, *Business Week*, 2 December.

Carper, W.B. & Litschert, R.J. (1983), Strategic power relationships in contemporary profit and nonprofit hospitals, *Academy of Management Journal*, **26** (2), 311–20.

Chung, S., Singh, H. & Lee, K. (2000), Complementarity, status similarity and social capital as drivers of alliance formation, *Strategic Management Journal*, **21**, 1–22.

Davis, G.F. & Powell, W.W. (1992), Organization–environment relations, in Dunnette, M.D. & Hough, L.M. (eds), *Handbook of Industrial and Organizational Psychology*, 2nd edn, Vol. 3, Palo Alto, CA: Consulting Psychologists Press, pp. 315–75.

Davis, K.P. (1972), Economic theories of behavior in nonprofit, private hospitals, *Economic and Business Bulletin*, **24**, 1–13.

DiMaggio, P.J. (1987), Nonprofit organizations in the production and distribution of culture, in Powell, W.W. (ed.), *The Nonprofit Sector: A Research Handbook*, New Haven, CT: Yale University Press, pp. 195–220.

DiMaggio, P.J. & Anheier, H.K. (1990), The sociology of nonprofit organizations and sectors, *American Review of Sociology*, **16**, 137–59.

Doz, Y., Hamel, G. & Prahalad, C.K. (1989), Collaborate with your competitors and win, *Harvard Business Review*, **67**, 133–9.

The Economist (2004), Doing well and doing good, 29 July.

Feigenbaum, S. (1987), Competition and performance in the nonprofit sector: the case of US medical research charities, *Journal of Industrial Economics*, **35** (3), 241–53.

Frech, H.E. (1980), Health insurance: private, mutual, and government, in Greenberg, W. (ed.), *Competition in the Health Care Sector: Past, Present and Future*, Germantown, MD: Aspen Systems.

Fry, L.W., Keim, G.D. & Meiners, R.E. (1982), Corporate contributions: altruistic or for-profit? *Academy of Management Journal*, **25** (1), 94–106.

Galaskiewicz, J. & Bielefeld, W. (1998), *Nonprofit Organizations in an Age of Uncertainty*, New York, NY: Aldine de Gruyter.

Galaskiewicz, J. & Burt, R.S. (1991), Interorganization contagion in corporate philanthropy, *Administrative Science Quarterly*, **36** (1), 88–105.

Glaeser, E. (2002), The governance of not-for-profit firms, *Harvard Institute of Economic Research* Discussion Paper #1954.

Golden-Biddle, K. & Rao, H. (1997), Breaches in the boardroom: organizational identity and conflicts of commitment in a nonprofit organization, *Organization Science*, **8** (6), 593–611.

Granovetter, M. (1992), Problems of explanation in economic sociology, in Nohria, N. & Eccles, R. (eds), *Networks and Organizations: Structure, Form and Action*, Boston, MA: Harvard Business School Press.

Gulati, R. (1995), Social structure and alliance formation patterns: a longitudinal analysis, *Administrative Science Quarterly*, **40** (4), 619–52.

Gulati, R. (1999), Network location and learning: the influence of network resources and firm capabilities on alliance formation, *Strategic Management Journal*, **20** (5), 397–420.

Gulati, R. & Gargiulo, M. (1999), Where do interorganizational networks come from? *American Journal of Sociology*, **104** (5), 1439–93.

Hansmann, H. (1980), The role of nonprofit enterprise, *Yale Law Journal*, **89**, 835–901.

Hansmann, H. (1987), Economic theories of nonprofit organizations, in Powell, W.W. (ed.), *The Nonprofit Sector: A Research Handbook*, New Haven, CT: Yale University Press, pp. 27–42.

Harris, M., Harris, J., Hutchison, R. & Rochester, C. (2002), Mergers in the British voluntary sector: the example of HIV/AIDS agencies, *Social Policy & Administration*, **36** (3), 291–305.

Haunschild, P.R. (1993), Interorganizational imitation: the impact of interlocks on corporate acquisition activity, *Administrative Science Quarterly*, **38** (4), 564–92.

Kanter, R.M. & Summers, D.V. (1987), Doing well while doing good: dilemmas of performance measurement in nonprofit organizations and the need for a multiple-constituency approach, in Powell, W.W. (ed.), *The Nonprofit Sector: A Research Handbook*, New Haven, CT: Yale University Press, pp. 154–66.

Keim, G.D. (1978), Corporate social responsibility: an assessment of the enlightened self-interest model, *Academy of Management Review*, **3** (1), 32–9.

Khanna, T., Gulati, R. & Nohria, N. (1998), The dynamics of learning alliances: competition, cooperation, and relative scope, *Strategic Management Journal*, **19** (3), 193–210.

Kogut, B. (1988), Joint ventures: theoretical and empirical perspectives, *Strategic Management Journal*, **9** (4), 319–32.

Kogut, B., Shan, W. & Walker, G. (1992), Competitive cooperation in biotechnology: learning through networks, in Nohria, N. & Eccles, R. (eds), *Networks and Organizations: Structure, Form and Action*, Boston, MA: Harvard Business School Press, pp. 348–65.

Kohm, A. & La Piana, D. (2003), *Strategic Restructuring for Nonprofit Organizations: Mergers, Integrations, and Alliances*, Westport, CT: Praeger.

Krackhardt, D. (1990), Assessing the political landscape: structure, cognition and power in organizations, *Administrative Science Quarterly*, **35**, 342–69.

Kushner R.J. (1996), Contrasting theory and promise with practice and performance: network formation in nonprofit community groups, Presented to the Association for Research on Nonprofit Organizations and Voluntary Action, New York, November.

La Piana, D. (1997), *Beyond Collaboration: Strategic Restructuring of Nonprofit Organizations*, San Francisco, CA: James Irvine Foundation.

McLaughlin, T.A. (1998), *Nonprofit Mergers and Alliances: A Strategic Planning Guide*, New York, NY: John Wiley & Sons.

Middleton, M. (1987), Nonprofit boards of directors: beyond the governance function. In Powell, W.W. (ed.), *The Nonprofit Sector: A Research Handbook*, New Haven, CT: Yale University Press, pp. 141–53.

Millar, B. (1990), Too many charities? *Chronicle of Philanthropy*, **2** (July 10), 1, 18–19.

Mowery, D.C., Oxley, J.E. & Silverman, B.S. (1996), Strategic alliances and interfirm knowledge transfer, *Strategic Management Journal*, **17** (Winter), 77–91.

Nielsen, R.P., Peters, M.P. & Hisrich, R.D. (1985), Intrapreneurship strategy for internal markets: corporate, non-profit and government institution cases, *Strategic Management Journal*, **6** (2), 181–9.

The Nonprofit Almanac, (2001), Washington, DC: Independent Sector.

Nutt, P.C. (1984), A strategic planning network for nonprofit organizations, *Strategic Management Journal*, **5** (1), 57–75.

Osborn, R.N. & Hagedoorn, J. (1997), The institutionalization and evolutionary dynamics of interorganizational alliances and networks, *Academy of Management Journal*, **40** (2), 261–78.

Pfeffer, J. & Leong, A. (1977), Resource allocations in United funds: examination of power and dependence, *Social Forces*, **55**, 775–90.

Pfeffer, J. & Salancik, G.R. (1978), *The External Control of Organizations*, New York, NY: Harper & Row.

Podolny, J.M. (1993), A status-based model of market competition, *American Journal of Sociology*, **98** (4), 829–72.

Podolny, J.M. (1994), Market uncertainty and the social character of economic exchange, *Administrative Science Quarterly*, **39** (3), 458–83.

Podolny, J.M. (2001), Networks as the pipes and prisms of the market, *American Journal of Sociology*, **107** (1), 33–60.

Podolny, J.M. & Phillips, D.J. (1996), The dynamics of organizational status, *Industrial and Corporate Change*, 5 (2), 453–71.

Podolny, J.M. & Stuart, T.E. (1995), A role-based ecology of technological change, *American Journal of Sociology*, **100** (5), 1224–60.

Podolny, J.M., Stuart, T.E. & Hannan, M.T. (1996), Networks, knowledge, and niches: competition in the worldwide semiconductor industry, 1984–1991, *American Journal of Sociology*, **102** (3), 659–89.

Porter, M.E. & Kramer, M.R. (1999), Philanthropy's new agenda: creating value, *Harvard Business Review*, **77** (6), 121–30.

Porter, M.E. & Kramer, M.R. (2002), The competitive advantage of corporate philanthropy, *Harvard Business Review*, **80** (12), 5–16.

Powell, W.W. & Friedkin, R. (1987), Organizational change in nonprofit organizations, in Powell, W.W. (ed.), *The Nonprofit Sector: A Research Handbook*, New Haven, CT: Yale University Press, pp. 180–92.

Powell, W.W., Koput, K.W. & Smith-Doerr, L. (1996), Interorganizational collaboration and the locus of innovation: networks of learning in biotechnology, *Administrative Science Quarterly*, **41** (1), 116–45.

Provan, K.G., Beyer, J.M. & Kruytbosch, C. (1980), Environmental linkages and power in resource-dependence relations between organizations, *Administrative Science Quarterly*, 25, 200–25.

Rangan, S., Samii, R. & Van Wassenhove, L.N. (Forthcoming), Constructive partnerships: when alliances between private firms and public actors can enable creative strategies, *Academy of Management Review*.

Reisch, M. & Sommerfeld, D. (2001), *Assessing the Impact of Welfare Reform on Nonprofit Organizations in Southeast Michigan: Implications for Policy and Practice*, Washington, DC: Nonprofit Sector Research Fund, The Aspen Institute.

Rose-Ackerman, S. (1980), United charities: an economic analysis, *Public Policy*, **28**, 323–50.

Rose-Ackerman, S. (1982), Charitable giving and excessive fundraising, *Quarterly Journal of Economics*, **97**, 193–212.

Rudney, G. (1987), The scope and dimensions of nonprofit activity, in Powell, W.W. (ed.), *The Nonprofit Sector: A Research Handbook*, New Haven, CT: Yale University Press, pp. 55–64.

Rushing, W. (1974), Differences in profit and nonprofit organizations: a study of effectiveness and efficiency in general short-stay hospitals, *Administrative Science Quarterly*, **19** (4), 474–84.

Simon, J.G. (1987), The tax treatment of nonprofit organizations: a review of federal and state policies, in Powell, W.W. (ed.), *The Nonprofit Sector: A Research Handbook*, New Haven, CT: Yale University Press, pp. 67–98.

Singer, M.I. & Yankey, J.A. (1991), Organizational metamorphosis: a study of eighteen nonprofit mergers, acquisitions, and consolidations, *Nonprofit Management and Leadership*, **1** (Summer), 357–69.

Steinberg, R. (1987), Nonprofit organizations and the market, in Powell, W.W. (ed.), *The Nonprofit Sector: A Research Handbook*, New Haven, CT: Yale University Press, pp. 118–38.

Steinberg, R. & Perlman, S. (1982), A study of foundation behavior and a proposal for regulatory reform, University of Pennsylvania, Department of Regional Science, Metropolitan Philathropy Project Working Paper.

Strom, S. (2004), Big but not easy: as donors set terms, some charities resist, *New York Times*, 15 November.

Useem, M. (1984), *The Inner Circle: Large Corporations and the Rise of Business Political Activity in the US and UK*, New York, NY: Oxford University Press.

Useem, M. (1987), Corporate philanthropy. in Powell, W.W. (ed.), *The Nonprofit Sector: A Research Handbook*, New Haven, CT: Yale University Press, pp. 340–59.

Wasserman, S. & Faust, K. (1994), *Social Network Analysis: Methods and Applications*, Cambridge: Cambridge University Press.

Weisbrod, B.A. (1988), *The Nonprofit Economy*, Cambridge, MA: Harvard University Press.

Weisbrod, B.A. (1998), The nonprofit mission and its financing: growing links between nonprofits and the rest of the economy, in Weisbrod, B.A. (ed.), *To Profit or Not to Profit*, Cambridge: Cambridge University Press, pp. 47–64.

Wiesendanger, B. (1994), Profitable pointers from non-profits, *Journal of Business Strategy*, **15** (4), 32–7.

Wilson, R. (1985), Reputations in games and markets, in Roth, A. (ed.), *Game Theoretical Models of Bargaining*, Cambridge: Cambridge University Press, pp. 63–72.

Yankey, J.A., McClellan, A. & Jacobus, B.W. (2001), *Nonprofit Strategic Alliances Case Studies: Lessons from the Trenches*, Mandel Center for Nonprofit Organizations, Case Western Reserve University.

12 Knowledge integration in turbulent environments: a relational perspective
Laura A. Costanzo

Introduction

Considerable emphasis has been placed on the sources of competitive advantage in business contexts dominated by a fast pace of change. Computing, telecommunication, financial services and many others are examples of some of the industries characterized by hyper-competition (D'Aveni, 1994). In these contexts, in order to succeed, firms are compelled to adopt strategies of continuous change (Brown & Eisenhardt, 1997; Eisenhardt & Brown, 1999; Hamel & Välikagas, 2003). This has also required an increasing move towards greater internal flexibility and management focus on critical resources and capabilities. The critical role of knowledge (Grant, 1996) and dynamic capabilities (Teece et al., 1997), which are recognized as the most important firm's assets for competitive advantage, is well documented in the literature.

In the meantime, there has also been an increasing research focus on the type of organizational systems and management practices that enact firm's adaptation to external changes. Minimum structures, semi-structures, improvisation, modularity and networks are some of the organizational artefacts or solutions that many of today's companies implement so that they can cope with the challenges that frequent and rapid change poses to their organization. A considerable established body of literature on innovative forms of organization (Lewin & Volberda, 1999; Dijksterhuis et al., 1999; Ilinitch et al., 1996; Whittington et al., 1999) offers rich insights into the issues of organizational design and adaptation. Also, the social network theory (Granovetter, 1973) extensively elucidates on the relationship between forms of firms' collaboration and competitive advantage.

Although a large body of literature exists on the relationships between hyper-competition and organizational forms, there is a lack of a unified conceptualization of the core themes of the strategic management literature with particular regard to the resource-based theory, mobilization of critical firm's resources, that is, knowledge, and social network theory in the context of hypercompetitive environments.

Therefore the aim of this chapter is to develop a conceptual framework of how systems of social relationships contribute to the process of the firm's adaptation to changes in the external environment. Particularly, this conceptualization applies the social network theory to a macro-level context, the set of inter-firm relationships, drawing in the issue of speedy access to novel and diverse knowledge. Inter-firm relationships are conceptualized as both intangible resources and relational capabilities. Such capabilities develop and nurture, particularly in contexts characterized by rapid change in the external environment. Such conceptualisation is derived from the assumption that adaptation to changes is conceived as a co-evolutionary process where change is the ultimate outcome of managerial intentionality and environmental effects. Thus the process of adaptation is conceptualized as a recursive process derived from the set of interactions that exist among organizations. Finally, the social network theory is extended by considering the role of management in the process of resource mobilization. Particularly, the emphasis is placed on organizational actors, such as 'entrepreneurial managers' or 'network managers'. These organizational actors contribute to the mobilization of critical resources by bridging structural holes at both intra- and inter-firm levels. Furthermore the application of a social network theory to the issues of co-evolution, resource mobilization and entrepreneurial managers contributes to bridge different streams of strategy and organisation theory.

Given the proposed aim, the chapter is structured as follows. First, it will provide an overview of the meaning of hypercompetitive environments and their characteristics, with a focus on the challenges that they pose to organizations and the opportunities they present for strategic action. Then, by drawing in the concept of firm adaptation as a co-evolutionary process that alters the firm's resource base, the role of knowledge, dynamic capability and flexibility are explored into a context of hyper-competition. In particular, a relationship is established between firm reconfiguration and integration of specialized knowledge. Such integration is mediated by generalized knowledge and strategic flexibility. These aspects are then examined by considering the firm as embedded into a web of social relationships, whereby a bridge is established respectively between social network theory and resource mobilization, and social network theory and strategic flexibility. Later, the conceptualization brings in the effects of social networks attributes, primarily network centrality and density, on resource mobilization and flexibility. Finally, the developing theoretical conceptualization will elucidate on the role of network entrepreneurs with regard to resource mobilization.

Competing in high-speed environments: challenges and opportunities
Many industries are increasingly affected by hyper-competition, a process of 'continuously generating new competitive advantages' (D'Aveni, 1994: 218).

Hypercompetitive environments are also termed as 'high-velocity' or 'high-speed' environments to emphasize the features of 'frequent' and 'fast' change which regularly takes place in them (Brown & Eisenhardt, 1997). Computing, communications, biotechnology and financial services are some of the notorious high-speed industries where competition has been affected by the fast pace of technological change. In these industries firms compete on the basis of their capability to 'change continuously' (Brown & Eisenhardt, 1997; Costanzo, 2004). Continuous change is not just change concerned with the change of the firm's portfolio of products and services and related strategies, but also with the change of the firm's internal processes. By adopting such a holistic perspective, continuous change of the firm's portfolio of products and services and the firm's internal processes leads it onto a path of strategic renewal. For instance Hewlett-Packard's process of strategic renewal unfolded as a process of continuous change (Brown & Eisenhardt, 1997).

Similarly, 'continuous morphing' (Rindova & Kotha, 2001) featured the evolving nature of Yahoo!'s change in the range of products and services along the reconfiguration of the firm's resources, capitals and structures, which were determinant to Yahoo!'s strategic renewal and competitive advantage. Continuous morphing implies a process of continuous adaptation similar to 'patching', 'the strategic process by which corporate executives routinely remap businesses to changing market opportunities' (Eisenhardt & Brown, 1999: 73–4). Eisenhardt and Brown (1999) argue that when markets are turbulent, patching becomes crucial. It allows corporate managers to experiment with a number of different strategic initiatives, focus on the best opportunities and leave the less promising ones behind. Hewlett-Packard for example has made extensive use of patching, which sustained its long-term reinvention and growth (Eisenhardt & Brown, 1999). On a similar line of reasoning, Hamel and Välikagas (2003) argue that turbulent times increasingly require companies to be 'resilient'. Resilience refers to the capacity for continuous reconstruction. Hamel and Välikagas (2003) suggest that resilience requires new ideas and innovation not just with respect to products and services, but also with regard to 'those organizational values, processes, and behaviours that systematically favour perpetuation over innovation' (Hamel & Välikagas, 2003: 55).

Terms such as 'resilience', 'continuous reconstruction', 'continuous change', 'continuous morphing', 'continuous strategic renewal' are increasingly coupled with 'agility', which is one of today's imperatives for business success. Agility is 'the ability to detect and seize market opportunities with speed and surprise' (Sambamurthy et al., 2003: 238). In business contexts exposed to rapid and unexpected change caused by unpredictable events, such as SARS, September the 11th and so on, agility has become critical in any aspect of the firm's activities, including supply chains (Lee, 2004). As both demand and supply fluctuate more rapidly and widely than they used to, successful companies such as Nokia and Dell have developed agile supply chains that enable them to respond quickly and cost-efficiently (Lee, 2004). Similarly, successful brand apparels in Europe, such as H&M, Mango and Zara, have built agility into every aspect of their internal processes, including their own design processes tailored to the customers' needs and expectations (Lee, 2004).

Yet 'continuous change', 'patching', 'continuous morphing' or 'continuous reconstruction' are not the brutal or revolutionary type of change (Christensen, 1997) like the process described by the punctuated equilibrium model (Gersick, 1991). Instead, it is rather evolutionary and is better described by a process of co-evolution where 'change is not an outcome of managerial adaptation or environmental selection but rather the joint outcome of intentionality and environmental effects' (Lewin & Volberda, 1999: 523). Social science theorists have borrowed the term 'co-evolution' from biology where it is described as 'the successive changes among two or more ecologically interdependent but unique species such that their evolutionary trajectories become intertwined over time' (Eisenhardt & Galunic, 2000: 92). What does all this mean for the real world of business? Co-evolution means that businesses are adaptive entities that co-evolve via a web of links that exist among themselves. Thus the adoption of a co-evolutionary perspective leads us to consider the firm's process of strategic renewal as a recursive process, which occurs in a context of direct interactions with individuals, other firms and responses from the rest of the population (Lewin & Volberda, 1999). Competitive interdependencies may lead two or more business entities to evolve and succeed via a symbiotic relationship of collaboration, or to evolve into distinct non-competitive niches. Alternatively, competitive interdependencies may lead one or more business entities to drive out other businesses (Eisenhardt & Galunic, 2000). Put simply, any consideration of the firm's process of strategic renewal in high-speed environments cannot disregard the web of social relationships (Gulati, 1999) in which the firm is embedded.

Networks of social relationships have become important sources of competitive advantage for today's businesses (Van Laere & Heene, 2003), particularly with regard to the firm's access to specific types of resources (Van Laere & Heene, 2003) that otherwise would be difficult to obtain. In a non-linear world, one of the big challenges of managers and organizations is the capability to attract and channel the right resources (Hamel, 2003) towards experimental projects – the projects aimed at exploring opportunities for future competitive advantage (Hamel & Prahalad, 1996). These projects are very often regarded as a threat to the current core business that senior managers would tend to protect and defend under their own areas of control and influence. But, as argued by Hamel and Välikagas (2003), these projects might represent a portfolio of future opportunities, opening up new avenues for future success. Unlike revolutionary changes which, at one time, cause disruptions and cannibalization of the existing business and consequent redeployment of the existing assets to new business ventures (Christensen, 1997), continuous reconstruction is not a brutal event. It is an ongoing process, which still requires management support. This is aimed at ensuring organizational unity and the mobilization of critical resources to support a broad array of experiments within the existing core competences (Hamel & Välikagas, 2003). But how would such mobilization of resources take place? Which resources will have to be mobilized in particular? And by whom?

Also, being a co-evolving business means that in hypercompetitive contexts organizations will have to develop the capability to reconfigure themselves (Aupperle, 1996: 459) flexibly and rapidly (Hanssen-Bauer & Snow, 1996: 413). As Aupperle (1996: 459) argues, 'The ability of a firm to reconfigure itself . . . is a competitive asset truly essential in a hypercompetitive, dynamic, and global environment.' Moreover this capability of reconfiguration has to be coupled with the capability of being flexible and rapid enough in order to adapt. Change however has to be not only reactive, but also proactive so that in the co-evolutionary process a firm can shape the external environment or the web of relationships in which it is embedded. But how do firms reconfigure themselves? Which resources are essential to this end? As part of a web of relationships, which opportunities are out there that the firm can exploit for the attainment of its goals?

Given the above background and set of questions raised, the issues of resource mobilization, management role and the firm's reconfiguration in a hypercompetitive environment will be discussed by applying the main concepts that underpin social network theory (Granovetter, 1973).

Firm reconfiguration, resources and dynamic capabilities
The coevolving nature of the firm's adaptation process to external changes leads us to consider the firm's reconfiguration not as a simple outcome of the sole firm's strategic initiative, but as an outcome of the whole recursive process of interactions that occur among the actors, that is, other firms, that are part of the whole web of relationships in which the firm is embedded. The dynamics of the co-evolutionary process of adaptation alter the structure of the industry and the elements of the firm's resource-base (Barney, 1986a, 1986b, 1991; Peteraf, 1993; Wernerfelt, 1984).

Firms' resources normally include 'all assets, capabilities, organisational processes, information, knowledge controlled by a firm' (Barney, 1991).

Organizational relationships are also included in the notion of resources under the category of intangible assets (Barney, 1996). By offering the best protection against imitation, intangible assets such as relationships, systems, skills and knowledge are perceived to be sources of competitive advantage in the long run (Barney, 1996). However this condition may not be true in the presence of a dynamic business environment characterized by rapid and recursive discontinuities (Barney, 1997). Since the 1990s the external environment has experienced a fast pace of change, whereby established market- and resource-based theories cannot fully explain the sources of a firm's competitive advantage in turbulent environments. For this purpose, a more 'dynamic' perspective of the resource-based theory took shape during the 1990s. Such a perspective is more concerned with how firms develop capabilities that enable them to reconfigure themselves and adapt quickly to rapidly changing business environments.

Central to the dynamic perspective of the resource-based view of the firm is the concept of 'dynamic capabilities' developed by Teece et al. (1997). Dynamic capabilities are the 'firm's ability to integrate, build, and reconfigure internal and external assets and competencies to address rapidly changing environments' (Teece et al., 1997: 516). This perspective of dynamic capabilities indirectly emphasizes the key role of the management in the activities of 'adapting, integrating and reconfiguring internal and external organisational skills, resources and functional competencies within a changing environment' (Montealegre, 2002: 515). It also emphasizes the fact that some of the resources and competencies needed to respond to changing market conditions (Helfat, 1997) are not under the direct control of the firm's management as they are located outside the organizational boundaries. If these resources are crucial to the firm's reconfiguration, it is critical that appropriate structures of relationships are in place to facilitate the mobilization and transfer of such resources to the firm.

Firm reconfiguration through knowledge integration
It is extensively acknowledged that among all potential resources available to the firm, knowledge is the most important resource for the firm's competitive advantage (Grant, 1996). It is a resource that can be transferred, recombined, used or licensed to others in order to create value for the firm (Grant, 1996; Cohen et al., 2000). Also, new knowledge can simply be created from existing knowledge via the integration of different bodies of knowledge (Okhuysen & Eisenhardt, 2002). It is argued that the process of knowledge integration does not happen haphazardly; instead it is a process that has to be orchestrated by the management (Okhuysen & Eisenhardt, 2002). Precisely, the process of knowledge integration requires access to different levels of knowledge (Okhuysen & Eisenhardt, 2002) and the coordination of

different bodies of specialized knowledge (Grant & Baden-Fuller, 1995). To this end, it is important that the firm's actors – that is, managers – are aware of the different types of knowledge available to them and where such types of knowledge reside, so that they can be acquired, transferred and integrated for the pursuit of the organizational goals.

Firm reconfiguration through integration of specialized knowledge mediated by general knowledge

A distinction is normally made between two broad categories of knowledge, specialized knowledge and generalized knowledge. Specialized knowledge, which is originally individual knowledge, tends to reside in the expert or specialist (Alvarez & Busenitz, 2001), that is, the marketer, the technologist and so on. It is a type of knowledge that can be found at the low levels of management (Hamel & Prahalad, 1996). A typical example is represented by the sales and customer service representatives who are constantly in contact with the organisation's customers. The type of knowledge that these employees possess is specialized; that is, they know what the current customers' needs are. On the basis of the day-to-day interactions with customers – that is, customer service relationships – these employees can develop understanding (knowledge) about what is needed, in terms of the firm's final outputs, either products or services, for a better satisfaction of the customers' needs. Technologists within the firm also possess a specialized knowledge concerning the features of the technology being used within the firm. They are able to develop understanding and knowledge about the type of technical arrangements to be undertaken in order to satisfy the requirements of their IT functional area and other related organizational functional areas. By being closed to the 'voice' of the market (Hamel & Prahalad, 1996), these technologists, marketers, sales assistants and so on do not just possess specialized knowledge, but they are also able to develop awareness and understanding of the broad developments taking place in the market.

Clearly, the access to specialized knowledge is critical to the firm's competitive advantage in that it enables a firm to make sense of the current trends in the market and develop understanding of the potential market opportunities (Hamel & Prahalad, 1996). In this way, specialized knowledge via a process of integration and combination with other types of knowledge and information contributes to enact the firm's strategic foresight. In Hamel and Prahalad's (1996: 82) view, 'strategic foresight is more than a vision . . . Strategic foresight is about developing deep insights into the current trends in the industry'. Through this process of knowledge integration and developing strategic foresight, the management can envision and anticipate the next changes to take place in the market including customers' expectations (Hamel & Prahalad, 1996).

Put simply, according to this conceptualization, specialized knowledge is knowledge that resides in individual actors situated at the cross in relationships with other actors, either within or outside the organizational boundaries. In order that specialized knowledge can be used competitively, it must be mobilized into focused collective action. This is not an easy achievement in hypercompetitive environments (Hanssen-Bauer & Snow, 1996: 414). Firms must develop the capability to institutionalize various types of specialized knowledge into their operational routines. Integration of specialized knowledge is a process involving a number of different individuals, those who possess specialized knowledge and those who possess generalized knowledge. Generalized knowledge tends to reside in the entrepreneur, whose role is to coordinate the integration of different levels of specialized knowledge (Alvarez & Busenitz, 2001).

The process of integration takes place in groups (Okhuysen & Eisenhardt, 2002). It is argued that through integration, knowledge 'must spiral up to groups and even to organisations to further the goals of the organisation' (Okhuysen & Eisenhardt, 2002: 370). The process of knowledge integration develops as a hierarchy of organizational capabilities (Grant, 1996: 377). At the first level of integration, there are capabilities, which deal with tasks that require specialized knowledge. Moving up the hierarchy of capabilities, the span of specialized knowledge being integrated broadens. As argued by Grant (1996), task-specific capabilities are integrated into broader functional capabilities such as marketing, R&D, IT and so on. At the higher level of integration there are capabilities, which require wide-ranging cross-functional integration. An example is represented by new product development, which involves wide-ranging integration (Grant, 1996).

The evidence from many companies across many industries shows that there is no correspondence between the hierarchy of capabilities and the organizational structure of capabilities (Grant, 1996). Top managers for instance tend to deal with some individual tasks such as budgeting, lobbying and so on. These tasks do not require integration of knowledge within the firm; they can be very basic and therefore are closer to the base of the capabilities hierarchy rather than the apex of capabilities (Grant, 1996). Grant argues that effective knowledge integration requires a correspondence of the architecture of capabilities with the firm's organizational structures, as far as communication and decision-making are concerned. However the need of organizational capabilities to be supported by the organizational structure poses some problems to the creation of new capabilities. This is, according to Grant's argument, the reason for which new capabilities are created outside the existing structure.

The creation of new capabilities is a process that crosses organizational boundaries. Moreover some individual tasks, like those performed by the top management – that is, lobbying – or by the expert, although they do not require the span of specialized knowledge, might require access to lateral knowledge. This is the type of knowledge possessed by the top management and experts that reside in other organizations. For instance the top management of a firm can interact with the top management of another firm, not necessarily operating in the same industry, to share views about the firms' strategies. The technologist of a computing firm can exchange his views about the use of a technology with a friend who is a technologist operating in another firm. Therefore it is argued that the process of knowledge integration is a process that spirals up to groups forming within the same organization, whilst infiltrating across blurring organizational boundaries. It is a process that requires interactions among individuals and organizations. In this regard, managers should facilitate knowledge integration through improvisation and emergent processes unfolding within the organization from the low levels of the organization, where specialized knowledge resides, to the higher levels, as well as external network relationships (Lewin & Volberda, 1999: 522). Increasingly, the firm's competitive fitness is measured by the 'firm's ability to develop and apply knowledge, often in collaboration with other firms' (Hanssen-Bauer & Snow, 1996: 413). Also, firms need to learn how to influence the external environment. Without the ability to reshape internal and external relationships, companies in hypercompetitive environments will inevitably lose the ability to compete successfully (Hanssen-Bauer & Snow, 1996: 413).

Firm reconfiguration through strategic flexibility
Firms have increasingly responded to increasing environmental turbulence with moves toward greater flexibility (Djelic & Ainamo, 1999). The firm's renewal is not only achieved via reconfiguration of its pool of assets and the identification, development and nurturing of critical dynamic capabilities (Bartmess & Cerny, 1993), but also through increasing strategic flexibility (Brown & Eisenhardt, 1997) or 'flexible response capabilities' (Grant, 1996), which are crucial to the process of adaptation in chaotic environments (Brown & Eisenhardt, 1997; Chakravarty, 1997; Volberda, 1996, 1998; Dijksterhuis et al., 1999). Flexibility and adaptability are the two key ingredients for competing in turbulent environments. Volberda (1996) argues that firms must become flexible enough in order to adapt.

But what is strategic flexibility? There is no unified conceptualization of strategic flexibility. Sanchez (1995) contends that strategic flexibility enables a firm to achieve a dynamic equilibrium while managing technological and market change in a turbulent environment. In such an environment, there are two critical components of strategic flexibility: (1) resource flexibility; and (2) coordination flexibility. Resource flexibility 'illuminates the impact of new product creation technologies on resources for developing, producing, distributing, and marketing products' (Sanchez, 1995: 138). Coordination flexibility 'helps identify critical interdependencies between the flexibilities in a firm's product creation resources and the firm's ability to apply those resources effectively through new product strategies and organizational structures' (Sanchez, 1995: 138). In Grant's (1996) view, flexibility is gained through knowledge acquisition and integration (Ilinitch et al., 1996). Particularly, flexibility is achieved by acquiring specific knowledge efficiently and applying many areas of specialized knowledge integratively (Ilinitch et al., 1996). In these conceptualizations of strategic flexibility there is an inward focus on the firm's internal environment, particularly an emphasis on resources and coordination mechanisms that are crucial to the execution and implementation of strategy (Montealegre, 2002) in dynamic environments.

Hanssen-Bauer and Snow (1996: 415) argue that response to hypercompetition 'requires great organizational flexibility and adaptability, which are generated by the ability to develop and apply new knowledge quickly and consistently'. In Hanssen-Bauer and Snow's (1996: 415) perspective, there is also an emphasis on the external environment. The two authors contend that increasing flexibility would mean 'the ability to anticipate changes in the environment, becoming more proficient at learning from competitors and collaborators, integrating knowledge within and across organizations more efficiently, making greater use of the ideas of all managers and employees'.

On a similar line of reasoning, Javernpaa and Leidner (1998) suggest that strategic flexibility is not only the capability that enables a company to execute its strategy, but also the capability that enables a company to respond to surprises. Volberda (1996) extends this conceptualization by proposing the concept of 'control capacity management'. Volberda contends that strategic flexibility is a capability that enables a firm not only to respond to changes in the external environment, but also to control or shape changes in the external environment. In other words, strategic flexibility not only underlines the firm's capability of being a changeable organization (Eisenhardt & Martin, 2000), via a process of evolving internal deconstruction and reconfiguration, but also its capability to influence change in the external environment. This becomes a crucial capability to compete in hypercompetitive environments (Volberda, 1996) where change is the joint outcome of managerial adaptation (or intentionality) and environmental effects (Lewin & Volberda, 1999). In Volberda's (1996) words, flexibility is not only an organizational design task, but also a managerial task, which is to provide dynamic capabilities for organizational flexibility. In other words, the two concepts of dynamic capabilities and flexibility are interlinked.

The capability of strategic flexibility has an internal and external perspective. In the phase of executing the strategy, it is important to develop an internal flexible capability, which is intrinsic in resource flexibility and coordination flexibility. The internal flexible capability engenders the capability to integrate and engender trust. The capability to integrate resources and skills and diffuse knowledge across the organization depends on leadership, organizational culture and information technology (Montealegre, 2002). On the other hand, the capability to engender trust depends on path-dependence (Teece et al., 1997). The firm's action of strengthening external relationships is also critical to developing trust (Montealegre, 2002). Skills and functional competencies to reconfigure may reside outside the firm and the firm also needs to develop an external flexible capability that enables the firm to adapt to changes in the external environment. This capability also enables the firm to shape changes in the external environment by strengthening its relationships with other groups.

Mobilization of the firm's resources via social networks
As mentioned earlier in the chapter, by adopting a co-evolutionary perspective (Lewin & Volberda, 1999), the firm's strategic renewal is a recursive process, which occurs in a context of direct interactions with individuals, other firms and responses from the rest of the population. Consistent with the fact that in turbulent environments strategic action is increasingly taking place within social relationships (Granovetter, 1973), various forms of networks have developed among firms. The terminology of 'network, cluster, constellations, or virtual corporations' is increasingly used to indicate groups of companies joined together in a larger, overarching relationship (Gomes-Casseres, 1994). Firms' relationship or collaboration is no longer confined to the conventional two-company alliance, such as joint ventures or marketing agreements (Gomes-Casseres, 1994). Within global markets, competition does not just occur between one firm and the other, but between groups of firms that are connected together by the pursuit of a common purpose. This type of competition is called 'group versus group' competition and is spreading across global markets (Gomes-Casseres, 1994: 62). From a more general perspective, as argued by Hamel et al. (1989: 134), firm collaboration has become another dimension of competition in dynamic business environments.

Particularly, firms' relationships are seen as intangible resources (Barney, 1996) that generate new resources which are critical to the attainment of the firm's goals. Leenders and Gabbay (1999: 3) for instance refer to the notion of 'social capital' to indicate 'the set of resources, tangible or virtual, that accrue to an organization through social structure, facilitating the attainment of goals'. Different reasons may prompt a firm to establish a set of relationships with one or more partners, either because it is in a vulnerable strategic position or because it enjoys a strong social position within a social network (Eisenhardt & Schoohoven, 1996). In other words, strategic need and social opportunism are the two main reasons that lead to the formation of networks within contemporary firms. A strategic need to enter into a number of collaborative agreements may emerge when the firm is in an emerging industry, or competes in a highly dynamic environment, or when it wants to explore the strategic opportunities associated with a pioneering technology (Eisenhardt & Schoohoven, 1996). In situations of uncertainty, for example when exploring a pioneering technology, problems or challenges may arise. The existence of ongoing relationships between firms can represent useful mechanisms to cope with that particular problem or challenge (Mota and de Castro, 2004). Through inter-firm collaboration, a firm is seeking access to critical resources, that is, skills, competences or financial resources (Eisenhardt & Schoohoven, 1996). In this context, a relationship or relational resource (Cyert & March, 1992) is seen as an intangible asset able to generate a variety of other resources, even in a situation of high 'relational specificity' (Eisenhardt & Schoohoven, 1996).

Yet relational resources also refer to the way in which individuals and groups of individuals (organizations) interact with one another (Cyert & March, 1992) and with their environments (Lowendahl, 1997). Put simply, relationships are also coordination mechanisms (Mota and de Castro, 2004) that are crucial to mobilize resources, which the firm does not control, and to influence their use in such way that a firm can shape change in the external environment. By taking such an approach, a relationship is also a firm capability, a relational capability. This capability is concerned with how and when a firm is able to combine its existing competencies with the competences of others. Relational capabilities enrich the bundle of the firm's resources in an evolving manner. They emerge and deepen as the firm both develops existing capabilities and explores new ones (Powell, 1998: 229). In a highly uncertain situation, relational capabilities are nurtured as the firm interacts more with external parties in order to get access to the relevant knowledge and resources (Powell, 1998: 229).

Flexible and rapid adaptation via social networks
Being embedded in social networks also enhances the firm's strategic flexibility as it gives access to a wider set of knowledge linkages (Grant, 1996). Although firms' networks may lead to some inefficiency during the process of knowledge transfer and integration, in reality they are crucial to competitive advantage as they provide the firm with a speedy access to relevant resources, that is, knowledge (Grant, 1996), that cannot be freed up or mobilized within the firm. An example is given by those failing companies

that run the risk of being acquired by other companies because of a shortage of capital. Financial distress and bankruptcy can be overcome if the firm is embedded in a network of social strong groups. These relationships are established mainly for reasons of social opportunism. The firm's ongoing relationship with such strong social groups enhances its legitimacy and power, contributing to improve its market positioning. This is the case when the firm is led by large, experienced and well-connected top management teams. It is not unusual that banks are still willing to give money to failing companies because of the strong social position held by their senior managers (Eisenhardt & Schoohoven, 1996). Similarly, the rate of strategic alliances that a firm establishes with other firms tends to be very high when: (1) the top management team is larger; (2) the number of previous employers of the top managers is greater; (3) the number of previous jobs held by the management team is higher (Eisenhardt & Schoohoven, 1996).

Social networks are important for knowledge integration (Grant, 1996). Grant (1996) argues that while knowledge integration among a broad span of specialized knowledge is important to sustain competitive advantage, the attainment of superior competitive advantage in hypercompetitive environments requires the continual renewal of competitive advantage through innovation and the development of new capabilities. To this end, relationships that form among all groups involved in critical processes that are dynamic and responsive (Bartmess & Cerny, 1993: 84) are critical. Within a social network perspective, the firm is considered as a set of direct and indirect capabilities (Mota & de Castro, 2004). Each firm embedded in the social network builds an 'external organization' of capabilities that compliments its set of direct capabilities (Loasby, 1991; Mota & de Castro, 2004), such as dynamic capabilities and strategic flexibility.

Yet the coordination of inter-organizational relationships is also a part of the bundle of the firm's resources. It is difficult to imitate the combination of these resources (Griffith & Harvey, 2001: 598). In other words, such a coordination of relationships is a crucial dynamic capability in itself that enacts the integration of different bodies of knowledge either across different organizational levels within the same firm or among a group of firms. Many informal relationships emerge within the firm by cutting across many important strategic initiatives, such as new product development and many other core processes (Ross et al., 2002). In dynamic environments characterized by uncertainty, these informal relationships are crucial to the achievement of the firm's objectives as they promote innovation, flexibility and efficiency as well as quality of new products or services by simply pooling together unique expertise (Ross et al., 2002). The consideration of the firm's embeddedness within a network of internal and external relationships leads managers to a better allocation of resources within the firm (Ross et al., 2002).

Effects of network structure on resource mobilization and speed

In uncertain and dynamic environments, firms try to get access to relevant information and know-how in order to adapt quickly to evolving environments (Rowley & Baum, 2004). For this purpose, managers tend to pursue a 'network strategy perspective' where they try to access relevant information and seek opportunities across the network's structure (Rowley & Baum, 2002, 2004). For instance firms in rapidly emerging industries – that is, technologically intensive industries – have been heavily relying on collaborative relationships in order to access, survey and exploit emerging technological opportunities. In these industries, collaboration among different partners has substantially increased the rate of technological innovation. As argued by Powell (1998: 230), 'Firms with experienced partners competed more effectively in high-speed learning races.'

However the simple fact of entering into collaborative agreements with other companies is not sufficient to ensure that the firm can get access to relevant external resources and mobilize these for the pursuit of the organizational goals. Nevertheless, in high-velocity environments, mobilization of external resources has to be undertaken at a high rate of speed. Therefore any network strategy has to be pursued by ensuring that the salient features of the network structure support the achievement of the network strategy's objectives. In this regard, some types of structural arrangements might be preferable to others as far as access and speedy mobilization of resources are concerned.

Levels of centrality and density are the two common features against which configurations of network structures are assessed in order to determine whether some combinations of levels of centrality and density are more preferable to others with respect to access to the relevant knowledge and information. Centrality indicates the type of position occupied by a single actor in the network (Wasserman & Faust, 1994). Density refers to the 'extent of interconnection among the actors of the network' (Gnyawali & Madhavan, 2001: 438). Ideally, the type of network structure should give access to unique resources that other partners cannot access. In this way, enhancement of resource heterogeneity will represent a source of competitive advantage over competitors (Werneferlft, 1984).

However in hypercompetitive environments, competitive positions do not last forever, they are only temporary (Bartmess & Cerny, 1993). Indeed in these environments products are quickly obsolete (Bartmess & Cerny, 1993) and competitive advantage, due to specific market positioning or fit between the firm's resources and the industry's condition (Porter, 1980), is easily eroded (Bartness & Cerny, 1993). Also the excessive focus on the lowest cost, the highest quality, the most know-how, or the deepest pockets is not enough in order to sustain competitive advantage in hypercompetitive environments

(D'Aveni, 1994). In these circumstances, it is argued, 'The only source of competitive advantage [for the firm] is the ability to respond consistently to changing markets with new products and ever improved competitiveness' (Bartmess & Cerny, 1993: 81). To this end, the capability of continuous learning and applying knowledge rapidly to the ever-changing marketplace is critical to the firm's sustainable competitive advantage (Hanssen-Bauer & Snow, 1996: 414). Skills and competencies to envision the next technological changes and possible disruptions in the market are crucial (Hanssen-Bauer & Snow, 1996). Such skills hinge on the firm's ability to create new knowledge and/or redeploy the existing pool of knowledge in a proactive way. By recalling Nonaka (1994), Hanssen-Bauer and Snow (1996) argue that the passive view of the learning and knowledge-creating process is limiting in hypercompetitive environments. Instead the proactive view of knowledge creation where problems are first 'defined' or 'sought' and then knowledge is developed to solve them is crucial. In this way, co-evolving actors (firms) will not just adapt to changes, but they will also drive or shape change in the external environment.

Consistent with these theoretical arguments, any formalized cooperative agreement between one or more firms enables the quick mobilization of relevant resources, such as assets, information and status (Gnyawali & Madhavan, 2001: 433). Asset mobilization refers to the flow of physical assets such as money, equipment, technology and so on within the firms connected in a network. Information mobilization refers to the flows of information and knowledge about the pool of resources, strategies and strategic intent of the firms participating in the network. Status mobilization refers to the flow of intangible firm's attributes (values) such as legitimacy, power and recognition (Gnyawali & Madhavan, 2001).

A discussion of different attributes of network structures, with particular regard to the issues of network centrality and network density, is undertaken in the following sections. The aim is to determine the optimal form of network structure which facilitates fast resource mobilization in dynamic business environment.

Network centrality and resource mobilization
A high level of centrality occupied in the network is conducive to positive effects for the central firm. A high level of centrality, indeed, enables the mobilization of a higher volume of assets, information and status from the connected partners (Gnyawali & Madhavan, 2001; Galaskiewicz, 1979). Moreover it is expected that the speed of receiving information is higher than in less central positions. In other words, central actors receive information sooner than less central actors (Rogers, 1995). Having a high centrality is prestigious too (Brass & Burkhardt, 1992), whereby high centrality implies

that the central actor has more power and legitimacy than less central actors and can exploit the advantage of social opportunism. By recalling Gulati et al. (2000), Gnyawali and Madhavan (2001) propose that a central position gives actors easy access to better and more resources and opportunities. Hence a high central position is preferred to less central positions in hyper-competitive environments, where speedy access to information is crucial to envision the next market opportunities. Moreover as powerful central actors are able to get early access to a high volume of information and assets, they are able to initiate action first. As central companies position themselves at the centre of overlapping networks, they do not limit their relationships to a restricted number of partners. Instead they tend to undertake a number of multiple explorative projects at different stages of their development (Powell, 1998: 230). These projects will be carried out until the most promising ones are clearly identified, whilst the less promising ones are dropped.

Network density and resource mobilization
Density is another key dimension of network structure that impacts upon actors' behaviours. In particular, highly dense networks are characterized by greater interconnectedness among actors. Highly dense networks where everybody knows each other facilitate faster mobilization of information and other resources (Gnyawali & Madhavan, 2001; Coleman, 1990). Yet dense networks are like closed systems where actors share the same norms, values and trust, and consequently have similar behavioural patterns (Burt, 1998). Therefore as firms are exposed to the same type of information (Granovetter, 1973) and resources, they tend to follow the same patterns of strategic actions, with little variation, and no particular firm will have access to unique assets. Moreover when firms are part of a dense network of relationships, they see competition in a different way. For instance the exclusive ownership of an asset may not be necessary for competitive advantage, as a competitor on a project may become a partner in another project (Powell, 1998: 230). A firm may turn to outside parties to access a number of different resources and therefore develop a network profile, or a portfolio of ties to specific partners for certain activities.

In contrast with the perspective of the dense network positioning, it is claimed that the firm has to be embedded not within dense networks, but rather between them. If the survival of a firm depends on access to new and relevant information and a speedy identification of opportunities, it will prove more beneficial for the firm to bridge ties and sparse network positions (Burt, 2000, 2002). In other words, competitive advantage is sought across structural holes of the network. Strategies that seek partnerships that span across structural holes normally lead to superior performance. Rowley and Baum (2004) cite the example of investment banking, a sector where the access to relevant information and timely identification of opportunities is crucial to the competitive advantage of the firm. In their study of investment banking, Rowley and Baum (2004) found that investment banks that competed via collaboration in an unconnected and unconstrained network performed better than those banks that competed via collaboration in a dense structural network.

The mobilization of networked resources via network entrepreneurs
Network centrality and density are important features of network structure that impact on the location of important resources to be channelled to explorative projects for future competitive advantage. In particular, the structure of the network gives an 'indication of where the social capital is distributed in the industry and where opportunities are located' (Walker et al., 1997: 109). It is argued that such opportunities can be envisioned via exploitation of possible structural holes that might exist in the network (Burt, 1992). Indeed low density networks can provide partners with new non-redundant information, which lead partners to anticipate some useful strategic initiatives that, as time goes on, can impact on the structure of the industry. Partners that initiate such strategic actions are called network entrepreneurs or entrepreneurial managers (Walker et al., 1997; Burt, 1992). Through these strategic actions, the structure of the network will evolve as a result of the network entrepreneurs' attempt of establishing links with unconnected parties where structural holes and, therefore, windows of opportunities exist (Walker et al., 1997). These opportunities tend to stimulate entrepreneurial action to broker different segments of the industry.

However high-speed environments require organizations to be agile too, so that they can respond rapidly and flexibly to changes in the external environment. At the same time, organizations will need to retain their unity (Rindova & Kotha, 2001). Some firms might be at risk of losing such unity. This is particularly the case of multi-business companies that are split into small business units, and also high-growth single-business companies. Some important resources, which are crucial for the undertaking of new initiatives, can be available within the same organization and they need to be redeployed. However these resources may be difficult to capture. Reasons for this are to be seen in the protective attitudes of some managers towards their own areas (Hamel & Välikagas, 2003), their unwillingness to give up some resources to be redeployed in new promising ventures, and the exclusive focus of some individuals or functional areas on their immediate tasks to the exclusion of adjacent tasks (Burt et al., 2000). In this way, some functional groups can lose track of what other functions are trying to achieve and of the external environment. This is a case where structural holes exist within the same organizations. Burt et al. (2000: 123) argue that in such situations there might be 'a competitive advantage in building bridge relationships' between disconnected parts of the firm. Managers that provide links to disconnected groups are entrepreneurial managers (Burt et al., 2000) who are rich in social capital and therefore able to redirect flows of resources, including information and human talent, among different disconnected groups. Moreover these managers tend to be located between the top management of the firm and the dexterity of markets. By building bridges between disconnected parts of the organization, entrepreneurial managers ensure unity of vision and direction of all the organization units. Entrepreneurial managers can move information faster, and by possessing information and knowledge of the surroundings either inside or outside their organization are able to provide solutions to problems much earlier.

Through their links to both external and internal networks, entrepreneurial managers enact a co-evolving process of organizational change, so that change is the joint outcome of managerial intentionality and environmental effects (Lewin & Volberda, 1999). By occupying high centrality in low-density external networks, entrepreneurial managers capture flows of information and other resources, including tangible and intangible assets such as reputation effects, and the strategic intent shared by other managers in other firms. In co-evolving companies, entrepreneurial managers pay attention not only to the kind of relationships as far as types of mobilized resources are concerned, but also to the number of relationships (Eisenhardt & Galunic, 2000). In particular entrepreneurial managers try to reduce the number of links with external parties when the environment is too dynamic. Being involved with too many links is risky because it would restrict agility, and therefore the ability to adapt quickly (Eisenhardt & Galunic, 2000). Particularly in fast-paced markets, managers would prefer to have access to disconnected parties in order to have access to different information and identify the opportunities to pursue. However in a high-speed learning zone, managers do not have time to look after a high volume of strategic initiatives via collaboration. They will try to envision the best opportunities to pursue and drop the less rewarding initiatives (Eisenhardt & Galunic, 2000).

Conclusions

Increasing turbulence in the external environment requires companies to undertake strategies of continuous change in their process of renewal and adaptation to changes in the external environment. Moreover they need to respond to changes rapidly and flexibly. In this chapter the process of adaptation to changes in the external environment has been defined as a co-evolution process where change is the jointed result of managerial intentionality and environmental effects. In this context, the evolving process of strategic renewal is conceptualized as a recursive process, which occurs in a context of direct interactions with individuals, other firms and responses from the rest of the population. Moreover companies have responded to environmental turbulence with a move towards greater flexibility, which has prompted companies to adopt more agile forms of organizations, such as the 'networked organization'. This has offered opportunities for theoretical conceptualization with regard to the application of the social network perspective to the study of how systems of relationships at a macro level impact on or enhance the firm's capability to respond systematically to changes in the external environment. Emphasis is particularly placed on firm reconfiguration via resource mobilization, dynamic capabilities and strategic flexibility within the broad context of inter-firm relationships. In this context, the role of the organizational actors in the mobilization process of resources has also been considered. The application of the theory of social networks elucidates on how social relationships could help the development of a better understanding of the processes through which knowledge is integrated.

The embeddedness of the firm into a web of relationships offers strategic and social opportunism for access to crucial resources, primarily knowledge. Organizational actors would need to be aware of the different types of knowledge available to them and their location in order to attain the goals of the organization. Entrepreneurial managers are responsible for the process of integrating different types of specialized knowledge through mediation of the generalized knowledge that they possess. This is a process that takes place in groups. Specialized knowledge is the type of knowledge that resides in the specialist, normally located at the low levels of the organizational hierarchy. By being closed to the 'voice of the market', the knowledge specialists are able to develop understanding of the current trends taking place in the external environment. In this way they contribute to enact a process of developing strategic foresight. In order that specialized knowledge is used competitively, it has to be mobilized into focused collective action. Different levels of specialized knowledge are integrated via mediation of generalized knowledge. This is the type of knowledge located at the higher levels of the organizational hierarchy. Through integration, knowledge spirals up to groups to further the goals of the organization, whilst infiltrating across blurring organizational boundaries. Overall, it is a process that requires interactions among individuals and organizations. Managers should facilitate the process of knowledge integration via improvisation and emergent processes which unfold within both the set of intra-firm relationships and the set of inter-firm relationships.

As part of the resources, skills and functional competencies to reconfigure lie outside the firm, firms would need to develop external flexible capabilities which enable rapid adaptation to changes in the external environment. Organizational relationships are both resources and coordination mechanisms that are crucial to mobilize important resources, which the firm does not control, and to influence their use in such a way that the firm can shape change in the external environment. In this conceptualization, it emerges that a relationship is both a firm resource – an intangible resource that generates other resources – and a firm capability (a relational capability) which is concerned with how and when a firm combines its competences with the competences of other firms. It is argued that in contexts of high uncertainty and fast pace of change in the external environment, relational capabilities are developed and further nurtured, as in these contexts the firm is compelled to increase its interactions with external partners so that relevant knowledge and other critical resources can be mobilized.

Different levels of network centrality and density are relevant to the access of relevant resources. It is proposed that a high central position combined with low levels of density is normally preferred to less central positions with high levels of density. In turbulent environments, where speedy access to information and resources is critical to competitive advantage, firms should seek network strategies that span across structural holes. Such strategies normally lead to superior performance. Such partnerships give access to new and non-redundant information, leading to a speedy identification of opportunities. Moreover as powerful central actors are able to get early access to a high volume of information, assets and opportunities, they are in a privileged position to initiate some useful strategic actions which shape change in the external environment.

Finally, the chapter has addressed the issue of strategic unity in high-speed environments, where frequent and rapid change may lead organizations to lose their unity of direction. This might be the case for multi-businesses to split into a high number of business units or organizations where functional areas are disconnected from each other, as they are trapped into an excessive focus on their own functional tasks. The existence of organizational structural holes can prevent the organization from moving quickly and retaining its unity of direction. In this context, entrepreneurial managers who are rich in social capital, which has developed through their set of both intra- and inter-firm relationships, deploy an essential role in keeping the organization unified. As entrepreneurial managers possess the capability to move information faster and to access information and knowledge of the surroundings either inside or outside their organization, they are better suited to build bridges between disconnected parts of the organization, so that unity of vision and direction of the organization are retained.

References

Alvarez, S.A. & Busenitz, L.W. (2001), The entrepreneurship of resource-based theory, *Journal of Management*, **27**, 755–75.

Aupperle, K.E. (1996), Spontaneous organisational reconfiguration: a historical example based on Xenophon's anabasis, *Organisation Science*, **7** (4), 445–64.

Barney, J.B. (1986a), Organizational culture: can it be a source of sustained competitive advantage? *Academy of Management Review*, **11** (3), 656–65.

Barney, J.B. (1986b), Strategic factor markets: expectations, luck, and business strategy, *Management Science*, **32**, 1231–41.

Barney, J.B. (1991), Firm resources and sustained competitive advantage, *Journal of Management*, **17** (1), 99–120.

Barney, J.B. (1996), The resource-based theory of the firm, *Organization Science*, **7** (5), 469.

Barney, J.B. (1997), *Gaining and Sustaining Competitive Advantage*, Reading, MA: Addison-Wesley.

Bartmess, A. & Cerny, K. (1993), Building competitive advantage through a global network of capabilities, *California Management Review*, Winter, 78–103.

Brass, D.J. & Burkhardt, M.E. (1992), Centrality and power in organizations, in Nohria, N. and Eccles, E. (eds), *Networks and Organizations: Structures, Form and Action: 191–215*. Boston, MA: Harvard Business School Press.

Brown, S.L. & Eisenhardt, K.M. (1997), The art of continuous change: linking complexity theory and time-paced evolution in relentlessly shifting organisations, *Administrative Science Quarterly*, **42**, 1–34.

Burt, R.S. (1992), *Structures Holes*, Cambridge, MA: Harvard University Press.

Burt, R.S. (1998), The network structure of social capital, *Conference on Social Networks and Social Capital*, Durham, NC: Duke University.

Burt, R.S. (2000), Decay functions, *Social Network Analysis*, **22**, 1–24.

Burt, R.S. (2002), Bridge decay, *Social Network Analysis*, **24**, 333–63.

Burt, R.S., Hogarth, R.M. & Michaud, C. (2000), The social capital of French and American Managers, *Organization Science*, **11** (2), 123–47.

Chakravarthy, B. (1997), A new strategy framework for copying with turbulence, *Sloan Management Review*, **38** (2), 69–82.

Christensen, C.M. (1997), *The Innovator's Dilemma. When New Technologies Cause Great Firms to Fail*, Boston, MA: Harvard Business School Press.

Cohen, W.M., Nelson, R.R. & Walsh, J.P. (2000), Protecting their intellectual assets: Appropriability conditions and why US manufacturing firms patent (or not), National Bureau of Economic Research, (unpublished).

Coleman, J.S. (1990), *Foundations of Social Theory*, Cambridge, MA: Harvard University Press.

Costanzo, L.A. (2004), Strategic foresight in a high speed environment, *Futures*. **36** (2) (Special Issue), 219–35.

Cyert, R.M. & March, J.G. (1992), *A Behavioural Theory of the Firm*, Englewood Cliffs, NJ: Prentice-Hall.

D'Aveni, R.A. (1994), *Hypercompetition: Managing the Dynamics of Strategic Maneuvering*. New York: Free Press.

Dijksterhuis, M.S., Van den Bosch, F.A.J. & Volberda, H.W. (1999), Where do new organizational forms come from? Management logics as a source of coevolution, *Organization Science*, **10** (5), 569–82.

Djelic, M.L. & Ainamo, A. (1999), The coevolution of new organizational forms in the fashion industry: a historical and comparative study of France, Italy, and the United States, *Organization Science*, **10** (5), 622–37.

Eisenhardt, K.M. & Brown, S.L. (1999), Patching, *Harvard Business Review*, **77** (3), 72–82.

Eisenhardt, K.M. & Galunic, D.C. (2000), Coevolving, *Harvard Business Review*, **78** (1): 91–100.

Eisenhardt, K.M. & Martin, J.A. (2000), Dynamic capabilities: what are they? *Strategic Management Journal*, Special issue, **21** (10–11), 1105–22.

Eisenhardt, K.M. & Schoohoven, C.B. (1996), Resource-based view of strategic alliance formation: strategic and social effects in entrepreneurial firms, *Organisation Science*, **7** (2),
  136–50.
Galaskiewicz, J. (1979), *Exchange Networks and Community Politics*, Beverly Hills, CA: Sage.
Gersick, C.J.G. (1991), Revolutionary change theories: a multilevel exploration of the punc-
  tuated equilibrium paradigm, *Academy of Management Review* **32**, 274–309.
Gnyawali, D.R. & Madhavan, R. (2001), Cooperative networks and competitive dynamics: a
  structural embeddedness perspective, *Academy of Management Review*, **26** (3), 431–45.
Gomes-Casseres, B. (1994), Groups versus groups: how alliance networks compete, *Harvard
  Business Review*, **72**, 62–74.
Granovetter, M.S. (1973), The strength of weak ties, *American Journal of Sociology*, **78**,
  1360–80.
Grant, R.M. (1996), Prospering in dynamically competitive environments: organizational
  capability as knowledge integration, *Organization Science*, **7** (2), 375–87.
Grant, R. & Baden-Fuller, C. (1995), A knowledge-based theory of inter-firm collaboration,
  Academy of Management. Best Papers Proceedings, 17–21.
Griffith, D.A. & Harvey, M.G. (2001), Executive insights: an intercultural communication
  model for use in global interorganizational networks, *Journal of International Marketing*, **9**
  (3), 87–104.
Gulati, R. (1999), Network location and learning: the influence of network, resources and firm
  capabilities on alliance formation, *Strategic Management Journal*, **20**, 397–420.
Gulati, R., Nohria, R. & Zaheer, A. (2000), Strategic networks. *Strategic Management
  Journal*, **21**, 203–15.
Hamel, G. (2000), *Leading the Revolution*, Boston, MA: Harvard Business School Press.
Hamel, G. (2003), The radical fringe: an interview with Gary Hamel, *Business Strategy
  Review*, **14** (4), 35–7.
Hamel, G., Doz, Y.L. & Prahalad, C.K. (1989), Collaborate with your competitors – and win,
  Harvard Business Review, (January–February): 133–9.
Hamel, G. & Prahalad, C.K. (1994), *Competing for the Future*, Boston, MA: Harvard Business
  Review.
Hamel, G. & Prahalad, C.K. (1996), Competing in the New Economy: managing out of
  bounds, *Strategic Management Journal*, **17**, 237–42.
Hamel, G. & Välikagas, L. (2003), The quest for resilience, *Harvard Business Review*, **81** (9),
  52–64.
Hanssen-Bauer, J. & Snow, C.C. (1996), Responding to hypercompetition: the structure and
  processes of a regional learning network organization, *Organization Science*, **7** (4), 413–27.
Helfat, C. (1997), Know and asset complementarity and dynamic capability accumulation,
  Strategic Management Journal, **18** (5), 339–60.
Ilinitch, A.Y., D'Aveni, R.A. and Lewin, A.Y. (1996), New organizational forms and
  strategies for managing in hypercompetitive environments, *Organisation Science*, **7** (3),
  211–20.
Javernpaa, S. & Leidner, D. (1998), An information company in Mexico: extending the
  resource-based view of the firm to a developing country context, *Information Systems
  Research*, **9** (4), 342–61.
Lee, H.L. (2004), The Triple-A supply chain, *Harvard Business Review*, **82** (10), 102–12.
Leenders, R.Th.A.J. & Gabbay, S.M. (1999), *Corporate Social Capital and Liability*,
  Dordrecht: Kluwer.
Lewin, A.Y. & Volberda, H.W. (1999), Prolegomena on coevolution: a framework for research
  on strategy and new organizational forms, *Organization Science*, **10** (5), 519–34.
Loasby, B.J. (1991), *Equilibrium and Evolution: An Exploration of Connecting Principles in
  Economics*, Manchester: Manchester University Press.
Lowendahl, B.R. (1997), *Strategic Management of Professional Business Service Firms*,
  Copenhagen: Copenhagen Business School.
Montealegre, L. (2002), A process model of capability development: lessons from the electronic
  commerce strategy at Bolsa de Valores de Guayaquil, *Organization Science*, **13** (5): 514–31.

Mota, J. & L.M. de Castro (2004), A capabilities perspective on the evolution of firm boundaries: a comparative case example from the Portuguese moulds industry, *Journal of Management Studies*, **41** (2), 295–316.

Nonaka, I. (1994), A dynamic theory of organizational knowledge creation, *Organization Science*, **5**, 14–37.

Okhuysen, G.A. & Eisenhardt, K.M. (2002), Integrating knowledge in groups: how formal interventions enable flexibility, *Organization Science*, **13** (4), 370–86.

Peteraf, M.A. (1993), The cornerstones of competitive advantage: a resource-based view, *Strategic Management Journal*, **14** (3), 179–91.

Porter, M.E. (1980), *Competitive Strategy: Techniques for Analyzing Industries and Competitors*, New York: Free Press.

Powell, W.W. (1998), Learning from collaboration: knowledge and network in the biotechnology and pharmaceutical industries, *California Management Review*, **40** (3), 228–40.

Rindova, V.P. & Kotha, S. (2001), Continuous 'morphing': competing through dynamic capabilities, form, and function, *Academy of Management Journal*, **44** (6), 1263–80.

Rogers, E.M. (1995), *Diffusion of Innovations*, New York: Free Press.

Ross, R., Borgatti, S.P. & Parker, A. (2002), Making invisible working visible: using social network analysis to support strategic collaboration, *California Management Review* **44** (2), 25–46.

Rowley, J.T. & Baum, J.A.C. (2002), The dynamics of network strategies and positions, Paper presented at the Academy of Management Conference, Denver, CO.

Rowley, J.T. & Baum, J.A.C. (2004), Sophistication of interfirm network strategy in the Canadian investment banking industry, *Scandinavian Journal of Management*, **20**, 103–24.

Sambamurthy, V., Bharadwaj, A. & Grover, V. (2003), Shaping agility through digital options: reconceptualizing the role of information technology in contemporary firms, *MIS Quarterly*, **27** (2), 237–63.

Sanchez, R. (1995), Strategic flexibility in product competition, *Strategic Management Journal*, **16** (Summer Special Issue), 135–55.

Teece, D., Pisano, G. & Schuen, A. (1997), Dynamic capabilities and strategic management, *Strategic Management Journal* **18** (7), 509–33.

Van Laere, K. & Heene, A. (2003), Social networks as a source of competitive advantage for the firm, *Journal of Workplace Learning*, **15** (6): 248–58.

Volberda, H.W. (1996), Towards the flexible form: how to remain vital in hypercompetitive environments, *Organization Science*, **7** (4), 359–74.

Volberda, H.W. (1998), *Building the Flexible Firm: How to Remain Competitive*, New York: Oxford University Press.

Walker, G., Kogut, B. & Shan, W. (1997), Social capital, structural holes and the formation of an industry network, *Organization Science*, **8** (2), 109–25.

Wasserman, S. & Faust, K. (1994), *Social Network Analysis: Methods and Applications*, Cambridge: Cambridge University Press.

Werneferlft, B. (1984), A resource-based view of the firm, *Strategic Management Journal*, **5** (2), 171–80.

Whittington, R., Pettigrew, A., Peck, S., Fenton, E. & Conyon, M. (1999), Change and complementarities in the new competitive landscape: a European panel study, 1992–1996, *Organization Science*, **10** (5), 583–600.

13 Relational methods in organization studies: a review of the field
Mustafa F. Özbilgin

Introduction

Organizational studies host a diverse range of disciplinary influences and research in organization studies is underpinned by assumptions regarding the nature of reality (ontology) and of scientific practice (epistemology and methodology). In all areas of social science, and particularly in management and organization studies, the general tendency is towards leaving those assumptions unattended in research publications. However it is the ontological, epistemological and methodological assumptions, whether stated explicitly or remaining implicit, that shape the actual process of research and analysis (Özbilgin & Tatlı, 2005). Social reality, despite its layered, complex and interwoven fabric, and its irreducibly intersubjective meanings, relational properties and interdependent patterns and processes, is often treated in organization and management studies in a way which reduces its complexities to a set of definitions, patterns and linkages that are often acontextual, ahistorical or of homologous morphologies. This chapter seeks to review relational methods which, I argue, reflect social reality in a way that is true to its situated, interdependent, intersubjective and layered nature and form.

Historical review of social research methods reveals various turning points in approaches to social research methods and scientific practice. Denzin and Lincoln (2003) identify seven critical turns in the evolution of social research methods. The traditional period (1900s–1940) is characterized with attempts by social scientists to emulate 'objectivity' claims of the natural sciences. The research tradition of the period advocated an objective separation between the researcher, the research and the researched, which meant that the relationality between the three had to be eliminated or minimized if 'objectivity' was to be achieved. This tradition was underpinned by an assumption that organizational phenomena can be explored in terms of its own tenets in isolation from its situational context and relational properties.

The second phase in social research, according to Denzin and Lincoln (2003), is termed as the 'modernist phase' and it took place between 1940 and 1970, when the barriers between the researcher, the research and the researched had been corroded, in a way which prescribed greater involvement to the researcher with the research subjects and the object of research. However this did not mean that the barriers have been eliminated. Indeed the legacy of the modernist era has been the glorification of the researcher as a source of emancipatory knowledge, and capabilities and powers of social intervention. The authors note that the period between 1970 and 1986, the third phase, has witnessed blurred genres of method as traditional and modernist approaches were both evident.

With the influence of humanist, feminist and critical traditions in social research, research on social inequalities based on social group characteristics, such as gender, ethnicity and class, peaked in the 1980s, as the predominant research traditions proposed emancipatory roles to researchers to do research with, for and on communities that they are personally associated with. However the heterogeneity within these social groups has also brought about a challenge to these earlier claims of representation, between the researcher, the researched and the readers of research. The authors have therefore termed the period from 1986 to 1990 as the 'crisis of representation'. The period of postmodern, experimental and new ethnographic influences ensued between 1990 and 1995. The postexperimental inquiry of 1995 to 2000 has prepared the groundwork for the future of social research inquiry, which is today.

At the backdrop of these historical turns, relationality has emerged as a challenge to individualism and individualistic methodologies (for example Wheeler, 2000) of the traditional and modernist eras that are founded on the principles of separation of the researcher from the researched, and individuals from the organizational analysis. Relational methods, although studied often under different captions, have achieved mainstream recognition in organizational studies. It is possible to see relational methods being implemented in a wide spectrum of social science traditions in variable degrees.

Relationality in organization studies (the ontological position)
Tracing the trajectory that relational methods have taken in social sciences is difficult. It is possible to identify relationality in the philosophical works of Marx, Weber and Heidegger (see Weberman, 2001, for a discussion of Heidegger's relationalism). However it is well established that relational methods owe much to a scholar, Ferdinand de Saussure, a semiologist whose original work (1966) did not directly coin the term 'relational method' but nevertheless was recognized as a key contribution on the way: Saussure suggested that words and sounds do not have essential properties which give them their meanings, rather the meanings of sounds and words are relationally structured and constructed. In social sciences, Saussure's approach has paved the way for structuralism, which is underpinned by an

idea that social life and meanings are constructed and shaped by human thoughts, practices and relationships and that they do not have predetermined absolute meanings in themselves (Tyson, 1996). Bradbury and Lichtenstein (2000) provide another historical account of the relational ontology in social research. They trace the routes of their relational philosophy to Martin Buber (1970) and his work on dialogue and adopt the term 'the space between' from Buber to denote relationality as the space between, in which resides the interdependence between the self and the other. They argue that the self and the other in organizational studies should not be analysed in isolation from one another, as they co-evolve in a process of continuous interplay through which they give meaning to one another and the relationship in between.

Engaging with the structuralist tradition, with its foundations in Saussarean semiotics, Pierre Bourdieu, a late French sociologist and philosopher, has developed his relational method of social inquiry. Swartz (1997), in his book Culture and Power: the Sociology of Pierre Bourdieu, explains the significance of Bourdieu's relational method: 'The relational method is a cardinal principal of structural linguistics that locates meanings of signs not in themselves but in their contrastive relations' (p. 61). Criticizing the dualistic tradition of subjectivism and objectivism, which manifests itself as polarization of interpretivist and positivist approaches to the study of social phenomenon, in his book *Outline of Theory of Practice* (1977) Bourdieu offers an alternative methodological account of society and the individual that promises to bridge this superficial divide through an understanding of the relational properties of social phenomenon. In *Practical Reason: On the Theory of Action*. Bourdieu identifies a formula for a relational method which is conducive to the study of social reality relationally:

> At every moment of each society, one has to deal with a set of social positions which is bound by a relation of homology to a set of activities (the practice of golf or piano) or of goods (second home or an old master painting) that are themselves characterised relationally . . . (Bourdieu 1998: 5)

Then he explains how this formula is operationalised:

> This formula, which might seem abstract or obscure, states the first conditions for an adequate reading of the analysis of the relation between *social positions* (a relational concept), *dispositions* (or habitus), and *position-takings* (*prises de position*), that is, the 'choices' made by the social agents in the most diverse domains of practice . . . It is a reminder that comparison is possible only from *system* to *system*, and that the search for direct equivalences between features grasped in isolation, whether, appearing at first sight different, they provide to be 'functionally' or technically equivalent (like pernod and shochu or sake) or nominally identical (the practice of golf in France and Japan, for instance), risks

unduly identifying structurally different properties or wrongly distinguishing structurally identical properties . . . what is commonly called distinction, that is, a certain quality of bearing and manners, often considered innate . . . is nothing other than difference, a gap, a distinctive feature, in short, a relational property existing only in and through its relation with other properties. (1998: 6)

The relational method as envisaged by Bourdieu promises more comprehensive insights for the study of social phenomenon than other methods that attempt to explore 'difference' or 'diversity' in social settings, for example the comparative methods which merely expose the contrastive positions of two individual, cultural or structural phenomena against one another, failing to capture their rich relational interplay (see Everett, 2002, for a full discussion of how Bourdieu's contribution on relationality can relate to organization studies). In comparison to other earlier methodological perspectives, relational perspective promises three ontological benefits. Firstly, it allows for the socially and historically situated nature of social phenomena to be revealed, as social phenomena are examined in their situated context. Secondly, the relational perspective allows for a focus on 'the space between', where agency, action and structures have causal interdependence (Archer et al., 1998) and where they intertwine and co-generate social interdependencies and intersubjectivities. Finally, the layered nature of social reality can be revealed through relational methods as it permits objective structures, situated activity and subjective experience to be considered as relevant to understanding social reality.

Relational perspective, as envisaged by Bourdieu, is located in the middle of the ontological spectrum that ranges from essentialism to postmodern relativism, which were the isomorphic orthodoxies of the time. Mohr (2000) explains Bourdieu's relational approach in the context of mainstream developments such as the emergence of post-structuralism in social sciences of his time:

While post-structuralism as an intellectual movement swept across Europe and eventually, across the humanities in the United States as well, Bourdieu refused to make that turn. And indeed, it was here, probably more than anyplace else that Bourdieu has made what I think is probably his most important contribution to an empirical sociology of culture. It is through the development of practice theory that Bourdieu accomplishes this and provides something of a barrier against the infinite textuality of the world. He does this by asserting that meanings are always and invariably embedded within domains of practical activity. Thus to know something is to know it from the perspective of its locatedness within a material and sensual world. Meanings live in the world because they derive from the material experience of the world. (p. 3)

Potter (2000), in his assessment of Bourdieu's works and critiques, explains that through his relational and layered method of analysis

Bourdieu has demonstrated that cultural and material spheres of reality do exist and they cannot be reduced to either, although they are interrelated and operate in simultaneity. The relational analysis that Bourdieu uses, as outlined above, situates individuals in their respective social positions in terms of volume and composition of their capital. Mohr (2000) is critical of the way Bourdieu operationalizes his relational method on two accounts: the model ignores divergent dispositions that individuals may possess in choosing their respective social positions; the social field in which positions are taken is largely structured by macro-influences. This approach ignores other forms of competitions and contestations at micro and meso levels. In her very elaborate style, Somers (1998) proposes relational realism as a way forward for social science. She elaborates the ontological perspective of her proposal:

> A relational realist and pragmatist ontology is for those of us who accept, however unwillingly, the brutal fact that we and our social world are not angelic, existing out of time and space, but living breathing, changing, dying creatures and entities, embedded in time and constituted – not merely engaged – in relationships . . . A relational pragmatist ontology takes the basic units of social analysis to be neither individual entities (agent, actor, person, firm) nor structural wholes (society, order, social structure) but relational processes of interaction between and among identities. (pp. 766–7)

Besides the realist and relational ontology of Bourdieu in sociology, other disciplines such as anthropology (for example Storrie, 2003), psychology (for example Kwon, 2001), human geography (for example McDowell, 2004), and theology (for example Shultz, 2001), have also contributed to the development of the field. In the field of organizational studies, Bouwen (1998) explains the contribution of social constructionist perspective to the development of relational ontology by making a distinction between the two traditions in the field:

> The difference between a so-called entative concept of the organization and its associated entative concept of the person on one side, and a relational perspective on organising processes on the other side, is . . . [that] an entative perspective reflects the fundamental assumption that person and organization can be theorized as independent of each other. The organization is reified when it is conceived as a context that exists independently of the actions and sense-making activities of the actors . . . A lot of the literature in organizational behaviour and human resource management has this entative perspective as an implicit paradigm. Relational processes are considered to be instrumental to connect inputs to achieve outcomes. In contrast, when the relationship between person and context is seen as one of mutual creation, the concept of process is very different. This is because outputs cannot be reduced to the inputs of either actor or context, but rather are seen as the emergent product of their interrelation. (p. 302)

In organizational settings, Bouwen (1998: 305) summarizes the elements that make up the relational ontology of social reality: (1) he argues that there is a relationship of interdependence between the individual and the organization, through which they sustain their mutual existence; (2) through coordination of organizational activities, individuals and organizations constitute each other; (3) the language is a key component of this co-generative process; (4) communication makes it possible for language to gain meaning; (5) knowing from within has an influence on the self-determination of the individuals; (6) communities of practice negotiate and shape shared meanings; (7) interaction at the individual and group levels in organizational settings brings forth both innovation and continuity; and (8) interactions serve to generate and shape shared meanings.

These ontological developments, which clearly highlighted the relevance of relational thinking in organizational settings, have prepared the groundwork for methodological innovations that can record, assess, observe and analyse the reality of relationality in social settings.

Relational methods in organization studies (the epistemological position)
Owing to the above-mentioned critical turns in social research methods, four distinct traditions of method have remained in evidence in the organizational studies literature: The universalist tradition examines the organizational phenomenon in terms of its main tenets and often in isolation from its context or relationality, seeking to generate universal and generalizable explanations in its forms, patterns and processes. The methodological approaches in this tradition typically draw their inspiration from Humean positivism (Layder, 1990), which seeks to account for causation solely in terms of sequential occurrences in isolation from external context and other concerns of relationality. The second methodological approach includes research that examines organizational entities in their contextual settings at micro, meso and macro levels of analysis. This tradition is also termed the 'contextual' approach to organizational studies in that it does not prescribe one best way of organization, and allows for situated analysis. This tradition is characterized with methods that generate cultural descriptions, which are generated through a wide range of research techniques. The third tradition of method in organizational studies entails comparative evaluations of organizational phenomena, again at different levels of analysis and across different sites, such as sectors, industries or countries. The final tradition of method, which this chapter focuses on, sets out to examine the relational properties of organizational phenomena, using tools and techniques that are conducive to reveal such relationality between various constituencies of organizations including individuals, groups, structural conditions and the firm (see Table 13.1).

Table 13.1   Typologies of organizational method

	Typologies of organizational method			
	Universalist	Contextual	Comparative	Relational
Main properties	Examines individual *or* organizational phenomena	Situates individual *or* organizational phenomena	Compares individual *or* organizational phenomena	Compares, situates and examines individual *and* organizational phenomena in a state of interplay
Main assumptions	Individual and organizational phenomena can be examined in isolation from their context and relational properties	Individual and organizational phenomena are contingent upon situational variation	Individuals and organizations can be compared as independent phenomena	Assumes interdependence, intersubjectivity and relationality of individual and organizational phenomena

The relational method addresses some of the weaknesses of other traditions of method by combining their key strength. It involves contextual, contingent and comparative elements, setting two or more individual, structural and/or organizational phenomena against one another, whilst allowing for the phenomena to be situated in its social and historical context and the analysis of variance, that is, differences and similarities between various properties of phenomena. In addition, and more importantly, relationality of the individual, structural and organizational phenomena is revealed through relational methods.

There are many formulations and typologies of relational method in the literature. This diversity brings with it a richness of methodological choices, rather than constraints or closures to tools that are available for relational inquiry. In this chapter, I will review a number of these different methodological routes that are identified in the literature. It is possible to categorize relational methods in terms of their focus and emphasis on relationality and methods. Studies that incorporate relational issues can be examined under three headings in terms of their emphasis on relationality. Firstly, there are studies which emphasize 'relational' in 'relational method' and focus on relationality in their methodological approaches, incorporating methods that generate relational engagement, possibilities of observation and assessment of relational processes. For example Brewer's (2003) research on the civic attitudes and behaviour of public servants and their social capital does not use relational methods. However it uses multivariate analysis to demonstrate that public servants develop stronger social capital through relational practice, that is, civic activities. Although the study does not emphasize relational methods, it nevertheless tackles issues of relationality and chooses a method that can speak to the issue at hand.

Secondly, there are methodological approaches that are termed here as 'relationship method', which integrate human relationships rather than relationality between phenomena in their methodological considerations, emphasizing human relationships and interaction between individuals in dyadic and group settings in a way to inform their methods. Several concepts, including relational marketing (for example Schumacher, 1999), relational contract theory (for example Feinman, 2000), relational counselling (for example Garcia et al., 2003), relational trust (Politis, 2003) and relational assets (Mitchell, 2003) have been developed in recent years and these can be examined under this banner due to their explicit thematic focus on the issue of human relationships. For example Peetz (2000) refers to relational methods as methods that employers use as part of a three-pronged spectrum of decollectivist strategies. The other two strategies reside in employment practices and informational activities. In Peetz's study, 'relational' is about the relationships between workers and managers. Another example would be Cowan and Katchadourian's (2003) definition of relationality as a set of constructs: 'Relationality, implying sensitivity and responsiveness to the needs of others, can be expressed in terms of feelings (empathy), cognitions (connected knowing) and self-construals (relational self-construal)' (p. 301). The authors locate relationality at the level of relationships rather than using relationality in its broader sense or in order to inform their methodological design.

The final group of studies emphasize 'method' in 'relational method' and use the concept in its broader sense to capture the interrelatedness, intersubjectivity and interdependence of individual and organizational phenomena, adopting methods that are designed to capture relational aspects of the subject of their study. Tietel (2000) defines interview as a relational space, and engages with relationality in a way which informs the methodological choices. This presents an example of this perspective.

The relational method studies may consider individual relationships and relationality as significant in their methodological approaches in variable degrees, ranging from integrating relationality as a mere contingency factor impacting on various processes and outcomes of work (*relational* method), to exploring dyadic and group relationships amongst individuals in organizational settings (relationship method) and to considering relationality as a primary and orienting phenomenon which shapes the choice of methods that in turn would reveal relationality amongst individuals and organizations (relational *method*). The difference of the latter relational method is their use of relationality as the primary orienting tool for their research design, rather than a mere construct that serves as a factor of contingency as is the case in relationship and relational methods.

Relational perspectives to social research in organizational settings do not propose closure to the spectrum of methods that can be used in order to investigate relationality amongst individuals and organizational phenomena. Rather, they suggest that the way in which these methodological approaches are used should be informed by a relational orientation, which reflects an awareness of the interdependencies between individual, organizational and contextual phenomena. Bouwen (1998) for example attempts to explain how relational methods may be used in a field study. Although Bouwen (1998) does not propose specific techniques for a relational inquiry, he nevertheless argues that the choice of techniques should reflect a concern for relationality in organizational settings. The key considerations for the relational methods are that the data should not be disembodied but situated in context, and that the relational method does not only seek data on organizational phenomena but also on processes and relationships between and amongst individuals and organizations.

Relational methods research has taken a spectrum of routes at the level of empirical study, ranging from studies on the individual researcher and their reflexive practice to studies that explore the relationality between contextual or organizational phenomena. This chapter identifies seven strands within this spectrum of relational research in terms of focus of analysis: (1) relationality of the self: reflexivity in research and inner dialogue; (2) relationality between the self and the circumstances; (3) relationality between the self and the others; (4) relationality between the self, the others and the circumstances; (5) relationality between the other persons; (6) relationality between the other persons and circumstances; (7) relationality between organizational phenomena (that is, structures, conditions or circumstances). Figure 13.1 illustrates the possible permutations of these forms of relational methods in context.

1.   The self – reflexivity
Bradbury and Lichtenstein (2000) state that using relational methods entails the researcher in pursuing personal development on reflexive practice (see also Mauthner & Doucet, 2003, for a full description of reflexive methods in social sciences), engagement with the research context, and an ability to engage participants in the process of analysis and sense-making activities. Hall and Callery (2001) also advocate a similar approach which

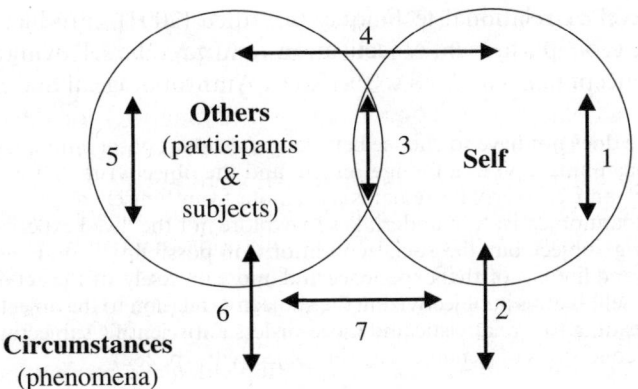

Note: Key to forms of relational methods:
1 Relational methods: the self – reflexivity
2 Relational methods: the self and the circumstances
3 Relational methods: the self and the others
4 Relational methods: the self, the others and the circumstances
5 Relational methods: the other persons
6 Relational methods: the other persons and circumstances
7 Relational methods: the organizational phenomena (i.e. structures, conditions or circumstances)

Figure 13.1   Relational methods in context

combines reflexivity and relationality in order to improve the rigour in grounded research. In the same vein, Luttrell (2000) describes her methodological approach in her ethnographic study, advocating a sensitizing process which involves recognition of the significance of reflexivity, and engagement with the research process and the subject of research. Her paper tackles some of the tensions in the process of research that emanate from such a reflexive practice. Luttrell elaborates further how a researcher can achieve such a relational reflexivity:

> It is possible to be a 'good enough' researcher – that is, a person who is aware that she or he has personal stakes and investments in research relationships; who dares not to shy away from frustrations, anxieties, and disappointments that are part of any relationship; and who seeks to understand (and is able to appreciate) the difference between one's self and another. The good enough researcher tries not to get mixed up between one's fantasies, projections, and theories of who the 'others' are and who they are in their own right. Good enough researchers accept rather than defend against healthy tensions in fieldwork. And they accept the mistakes they make – errors often made because of their blind spots and the intensity of their social, emotional, and intellectual involvement in and with the subject(s) of their research. The many times that they will do it right can compensate for these mistakes. (p. 515)

At the level of relational technique, Bourdieu (2003) introduces another elaborate tool, 'participant objectivation', and gave the following definition of the concept in his address to the Royal Anthropological Society:

> . . . one does not have to choose between participant observation, a necessarily fictitious immersion in a foreign milieu, and the objectivism of the 'gaze from afar' of an observer who remains as remote from himself as from his object. Participant objectivation undertakes to explore not the 'lived experience' of the knowing subject but the social conditions of possibility – and therefore the effects and limits – of that experience and, more precisely, of the act of objectivation itself. It aims at objectivizing the subjective relation to the object which, far from leading to a relativistic and more-or-less antiscientific subjectivism, is one of the conditions of genuine scientific objectivity. (p. 282)

He explains how this would work:

> What needs to be objectivized, then, is not the anthropologist performing the anthropological analysis of a foreign world but the social world that has made both the anthropologist and the conscious or unconscious anthropology that she (or he) engages in her anthropological practice – not only her social origins, her position and trajectory in social space, her social and religious memberships and beliefs, gender, age, nationality, etc., but also, and most importantly, her particular position within the microcosm of anthropologists. It is indeed scientifically attested that her most decisive scientific choices (of topic, method, theory, etc.) depend very closely on the location she (or he) occupies within her professional universe, what I call the 'anthropological field', with its national traditions and peculiarities, its habits of thought, its mandatory problematics, its shared beliefs and commonplaces, its rituals, values, and consecrations, its constraints in matters of publication of findings, its specific censorships, and, by the same token, the biases embedded in the organizational structure of the discipline, that is, in the collective history of the specialism, and all the unconscious presuppositions built into the (national) categories of scholarly understanding. (p. 283)

2.   The self and the circumstances

The relationality of the agency and structure, or the self and the circumstances, as termed here, has been one of the key concerns of contemporary social sciences, owing largely to its feminist and radical critiques. Weskott (1990) explains that the feminist approach to the dialectic relationship between self and circumstances is 'to approach social knowledge as open, contingent, and humanly compelling, as opposed to that which is closed, categorical and human controlling' (p. 65). Similarly Brewer et al. (2002) explore intersectionality in gender-, caste-, race- and class-based theorizing. They argue that the intersection of these categories as well as their relationality warrant adoption of different methods that allow for solidarity through recognition. Solidarity through recognition for social researchers is about understanding difference and heterogeneity in society with a view to seek the transformation and betterment of social life through solidarity. Their formulation highlights not only social divisions but also the issue of relationality or lack of it as pertinent considerations for social researchers. Furthermore by drawing on Crenshaw (1991) they explain that feminist attention to gender can avoid essentializing gendered difference, through revealing its interconnectedness and interdependence with race, class and sexuality. Hence the contribution of the feminist methods to the study of self and the circumstances seeks to reveal, bridge and connect social divisions, whilst allowing recognition of the construction of self in the context of structural circumstances.

Studying the lives of two Filipinas in situated context and in their network of relationships, Tyner (2002) concludes that individual identity is always in a process of becoming through encounters in different situations, space, geographies and relationships. Willmott (1999), in his study of structure and agency in a 'failing' school, provides a highly critical account of the Office for Standards in Education (OFSTED) in the UK, in which he locates the approach of OFSTED in the positivist framework and demonstrates its failure to capture the diverse range of structural conditions that underpin the effectiveness of a school. His choice of participant observation as a technique to reveal the interplay of agency and structure makes possible for him to evaluate the school effectiveness as is, from an open systems understanding with multiple stakeholders, interactions and influences at different levels. The research method also permits for dyadic and multiple forms of relationality between these different constituents to emerge, be recognized and be evaluated.

3. The self and the other

Relational methods between the self and the other have predominantly been considered in the context of the researcher and research participant or respondent relationship. Using a grounded theory framework, Bouty (2000) examines informal resource exchanges between research and development scientists at the interorganizational level. She concludes that 'there is no universal rule, no uniform line between individual and organizational interests. The economic interests of a firm and employees' social capital are intertwined' (p. 62). In a similar vein, she argues that organizations, through informal exchanges, make use of each other's resources, and the interdependency that this creates should lead to new understandings of organizational resources in the context of the research and development sector. In a different attempt at revealing relationality of the self and the other, with their aptly subtitled review paper 'Ties that split pies', Blyler and Coff (2003) examine how social capital and individual ties may lead to rent generation and appropriation in organizational settings. The article provides a set of proposals to set a research agenda, highlighting where the researchers may focus in order to locate hidden rent as an outcome of social capital.

Gergen and Gergen (2003) broaden the scope of relational method of the self and the others to the relationship between the researcher and the readers of research output, arguing that this relationship has historically served a wide range of purposes, including representation of the other. The authors argue that there are recent trends which seek to challenge the traditional modes of representation in writing, where the author assumed an authority of knowledge, in favour of writing and representation modes that are more egalitarian. They argue that this can happen if the metaphor of 'research' is replaced with the metaphor of 'representation', which is true to the nature of developments in social sciences. The authors explain what can be achieved in this way:

> Those formerly serving as the subjects of research and the readers of research outcomes become relational participants. And if we abandon the traditional goal of research as the accumulation of products – static or frozen findings – and replace it with the generation of communicative process, then a chief aim of research becomes that of establishing productive forms of relationship. [In this way] the researcher . . . becomes an active participant in forging generative, communicative relationships, in building ongoing dialogues and expanding the domain of civic deliberation. (p. 598)

4.   The self, the other and the circumstances

Bradbury and Lichtenstein (2000) explored relational methods in organizational research in their seminal paper, 'Relationality in organizational research: exploring the space between'. Exploring the intersubjective, interrelated and contextualized nature of relational methods in organization research, they surveyed a wide spectrum of methodological approaches that are informed by relational thinking. Bradbury and Lichtenstein (2000) note that although organizational research has engaged with the inter- and intra-play between individuals and organizational phenomena in a way which deems both to be inextricably intertwined, they set out to bring forward the relational qualities in these studies with a view to contribute to the development of relational methods. In social science research, a similar evolution happened even earlier, where social scientists particularly in the realist tradition have argued for a perspective of reality which captures the interdependence between the self and his or her structural circumstances (Bourdieu, 1977) and in the relational systems thinking. One of the most accessible methodological contributions in the realist tradition would be Layder's (1993) 'resource map'. The map is his attempt at understanding the interplay between layers of social reality at micro, meso and macro levels, as embedded in their social and historical contexts. The map

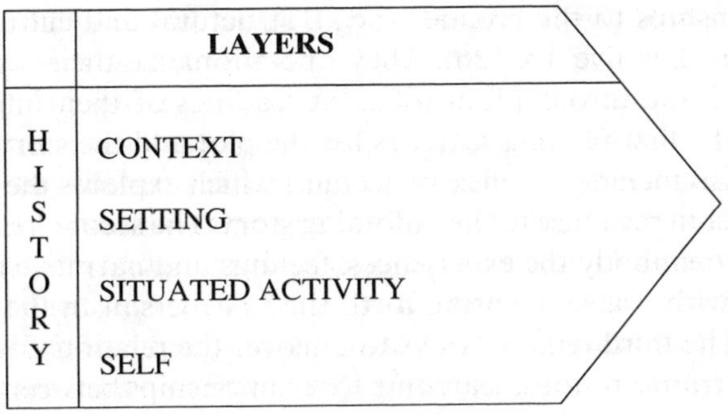

LAYERS	
H **I** **S** **T** **O** **R** **Y**	CONTEXT
	SETTING
	SITUATED ACTIVITY
	SELF

Source: Adapted from Layder (1993).

Figure 13.2   Resource map

contains four distinct layers: the self (includes identity and subjective individual experience), the situated activity (the dynamics of individual interaction), the setting (intermediate forms of social organization and immediate environment of social activity, for example work place or organization) and the context (wider macro forms of social and economic organization and structures). The interrelationships between these layers of activity are then located in their respective historical context. Macro, meso and micro layers are not independent of one another. Rather, they exist in a state of relational interdependence (see Figure 13.2).

Using a 'voice-centred relational method', Mauthner and Doucet (2000: 125) explored motherhood and domestic work, which they studied as part of their doctoral projects. Locating their relational method in the qualitative tradition of research, they used a specific relational method developed by the Harvard Project on Women's Psychology and Girl's Development at the Harvard Graduate School of Education. They allude to the kinship of their relational ontology to Giddens's sociological inquiries into the duality of structure and agency. Mauthner and Doucet explain the relational ontology that they adopted:

> The ontological image which has predominated in liberal political thought and the Western philosophical tradition is that of a separate, self-sufficient, independent and rational 'self' or 'individual'. In contrast, the 'relational' ontology posits the notion of 'selves-in-relation' . . . or 'relational-being' . . . a view of human beings as embedded in a complex web of intimate and larger social relations . . . and a different understanding of human nature and interaction so that people are viewed as interdependent rather than dependent. (2000: 125)

The authors achieve this in their study by 'exploring individual's narrative accounts in terms of their relationships to the people around them and their relationships to the broader social, structural and cultural contexts within which they live' (p. 126). They operationalize their version of the relational method through four different readings of their interview transcriptions. The first reading searches for the plot and the story of the narrative and also includes a reflexive account which explores the thoughts of the researcher in response to the unfolding story. The second reading entails an attempt to embody the experiences, feelings and narrative of the study participant with a view to bring forth the first person in the transcribed interviews. The third reading seeks to uncover the relationality in the narrative of the transcriptions, searching for relationships between the self and others in their situated context. The final reading aims to contextualize the accounts of the individuals, situating them in their respective social and cultural environments.

Following these purposeful readings, which examine, relate and situate the self, the second stage of the data analysis resumes a relatively conventional path where the rich descriptions that are generated through case studies and summaries in the earlier readings are thematically divided. The authors pay special homage to the issue of individual voice in narrative, the myth of shared female experience, and the imbalances of power between the researcher and the research, particularly in the process of translating and relating individual accounts to theoretical explanations. The authors conclude that feminist researchers should take note of the process in which individual 'voices' are transformed into theory and the outcomes. Their relational method engages with three different forms of voice, that of the participants, the researcher and the research community as reflected in the literature and theorization in a negotiated process in which these voices are reconciled. They also explain that their relational approach requires an understanding of social life with variable degrees, rather than as absolutes or linear and pure processes, outcomes or causal relationships. A parallel can be drawn with Zietlow's (2000) study of women and law, in which she argues that relational engagement and contextual reasoning are keys to what she terms the anti-subordinating method of process.

Bradbury and Lichtenstein (2000) argue that relationality is about examining rich interrelationships between organizations and their members as essentially interdependent and intersubjective. The authors portray relationality as a set of values and meanings that refer to organizations as richly interconnected relationships rather than as a discrete methodological tool. The value system that the relational methods proposes involves bridging the divide between subject and object of research, for example the superficial distinction between and separation of the researcher, the research and the researched (for example Özbilgin 1998), between knowledge and power, and between knowledge and action, revealing their interconnectedness. Seeking to operationalize some feminist theorizations through interviews with 38 nurses, focusing on their work lives in Canada, Keddy et al. (1999) demonstrate the strength of the interrelationship and interconnectedness between the nurses' work lives and conditions, their other life constituencies such as children, partners, friends and leisure, as well as the structural conditions pertaining to health-care reform.

Bradbury and Lichtenstein (2000) provide a framework for relational methods in organizational research. Their model includes two dimensions: (1) visibility of interactions: relational methods contains both tacit (interior) and explicit (exterior) forms of interaction; (2) position of relationality: the three layers of this dimension are multipersonal, research involving study of relationships between a group of participants; interpersonal, research which involves a researcher and research subjects; and intrapersonal, research involving research by oneself and on oneself. Juxtaposing these two dimensions along their three layers, respectively, against one another, the authors have generated six cells that characterize the matrix of relational methods: multipersonal exterior, multipersonal interior, intrapersonal exterior, intrapersonal interior, interpersonal exterior and interpersonal interior. They argue that most organizational studies research can be located in the multipersonal-exterior cell including network analysis and complex adaptive systems research. The multipersonal-interior cell is characterized by research that uses correspondence analysis linking tacit phenomenon with structural conditions. Richly ethnographic research with in-depth interviews has been common in this category of relational research. The interpersonal-exterior cell hosts a range of participative, involved research designs, which emphasize notions of insider–outsider and cooperative inquiry. Most feminist research would reside in and draw on this tradition of relational method. The interpersonal-interior cell involves case study research which situates the researcher in the context of research and makes the researcher and their understanding a significant part of the research inquiry. The intrapersonal-exterior cell expressly resides in the psychological domain. Studies of ego development would be an example. The intrapersonal-interior cell includes autobiographical writing which allows for a relational engagement between tacit and explicit selves. Table 13.2 below outlines the matrix with its associated methods and tools.

5.   The other persons
A strand of relational method examines relationality between a group of study subjects. Studies of social capital can be studied under this banner. For example in his study of social capital, Burt (1997) examines the value of managers' networks and reveals that the value of social capital is contingent upon the number of people doing the same job. The relational

Table 13.2   Relational methods based on locus and visibility

		Locus		
		Multipersonal	Interpersonal	Intrapersonal
Visibility	Exterior view	Network analysis Coevolutionary and complexity models	Participatory research Insider/outsider research	Investigation of self as research instrument
	Interior view	Correspondence analysis Structurational models	Case study methods Learning history Action science	Journalizing Action inquiry

Source: Adapted from Bradbury and Lichtenstein (2000: 560).

method of the study is in its use of network analysis to explore the social capital that managers accumulate through their networks.

In their theoretical paper which seeks to locate difference along class, race and gender dimensions in social relations, Bottero and Irwin (2003) argue that relationality in the context of locating difference along social cleavages should be informed by an understanding of the intertwined nature of the cultural and material bases of social relations. The authors argue that separating these two spheres of cultural and material social relations, as has been the case in earlier works, bodes ill to revealing the construction of symbolic and value-based as well as the material bases of social relations.

Pullman and Gross (2003) survey a hospitality organization and consider two different contextual elements, physical and relational, which moderate loyalty. The change in industrial composition, with the growth of the service sector in industrialized countries, has meant that the relational context became a primary concern in the service sector. Pullman and Gross's (2003) work reveals the impact of relational context on loyalty and emotional outcomes. Although their theoretical framework takes relational context as central, their methodological approach treats it only as a variable.

6.   The other persons and the social/organizational phenomena
Mohr (2000) argues that the relational method that Pierre Bourdieu proposes has many merits including its capacity to reveal the duality of culture and practice and its strong proposition that institutional life can be examined through relational methods. However Mohr (2000) also suggests that Bourdieu was more skilled in refining his version of relational methods

than operationalizing it. Bourdieu uses a two-dimensional mapping technique (correspondence analysis) with total volume and overall composition of capital in each dimension of the axis. The measure developed by Bourdieu and presented through correspondence analysis interrelates social phenomena with forms of capital possessed by different groups in society, and provides an example of this ideal type of research. Mohr (2000) explains how this works:

> This latter dimension runs from a measure (on the left) of a high proportion of cultural capital and a low proportion of economic capital to (on the right) the inverse measure reflecting a low proportion of cultural capital and a high proportion of economic capital. This space is then used to identify the social location of different groups (or what Bourdieu describes as class factions). Private sector executives are located toward the right side of the graph (because their capital is largely economic) and towards the top (because they possess a lot of capital). Artistic producers are located at about the same point on the vertical dimension (because they too have a lot of capital) but they are off to the far left because their capital is largely composed of cultural (rather than economic) resources.

In another exemplary study, Mahon et al. (2004: 171) use a network analytical method in order to explore the relationship between organizational phenomena that 'could have a negative impact on an organization's ability to reach its objectives if left unattended' and stakeholders simultaneously. Through this study, they identify that 'there is much insight to be gained from a structural analysis of the ties that bind social actors in the non-market context' (p. 185). The network analysis techniques at the group level also cross the group and context divide, revealing the relationality in between. In a similar piece of research, Buris (2004) employs network analysis to examine 'the academic caste system', and the interplay between postdoctorate job opportunities and the academic prestige of departments. The analysis reveals the material outcomes of academic hierarchies of group members and demonstrates that the higher the departmental prestige, the higher the graduate's employment chances.

7. Organizational phenomena (structures or circumstances)

In this methodological domain reside studies, which explore the relationality between structural circumstances, that is, the macro constructs of organizational studies. In her investigation of relationality at the firm level, Nelson (2004) introduces two approaches to relationality. These are ideal types of 'separative' versus 'soluble' relationship types. She describes separative relationality at the firm level as rejection of relationality with visible borders and divides between functional or strategic units of the firm. The soluble firm model is based on the recognition that firms are made up of interconnections at individual and group levels within and outside the firm.

Nelson explains that this distinction is reflected between neoliberal versus critical depictions of the firm.

Erickson (1996) also studied two structural phenomena – social networks and class structure – with a view to understanding their interdependence. The study was conducted in Toronto, Canada and drew comparative insights from Bourdieu, using a social network variety measure developed by the author. The paper suggests that social network variety is a better indicator of cultural variety than class, as proposed in Bourdieu's methodological approach in *Distinction* (1984). Massey's study allowed for two structural constructs to be explored in terms of their interplay. In human geography, Massey (2004) and McDowell (2004) argue that such interplay exists between space, time and structures.

Conclusions

Relational method is the new holy grail of social research. Much attention has been devoted to it in terms of its ontological, epistemological and methodological classification from a diverse range of disciplinary perspectives. The gold rush in search of relationality has engendered new methodological perspectives ranging from techniques which sought to situate the researcher in the research process through reflexivity, to methods which aimed to reveal the interplay between and amongst the self, the others and the circumstances in organizational settings. In this chapter, I have attempted to review this extensive body of literature with a view to explaining the ontological and epistemic position of relational methods and presenting a typology of relational methods that reflects its multidirectional and interdisciplinary development. Despite the possibilities of identifying further typologies of relational method in social sciences, I would like to conclude that what appears at first sight or otherwise to be autonomous, true to the nature of social reality, is imbued with relationalities that cross borders and build proverbial bridges.

References

Archer, M., Bhaskar, R., Collier, A., Lawson, T. and Norrie, A. (1998), *Critical Realism: Essential Readings*, London: Routledge.

Blyler, M. and Coff, R.W. (2003), Dynamic capabilities, social capital, and rent appropriation: ties that split pies, *Strategic Management Journal*, **24** (7), 677–86.

Bottero, W. and Irwin, S. (2003), Locating difference: class, 'race' and gender, and the shaping of social inequalities, *Sociological Review*, **51** (4), 463–83.

Bouty, I. (2000), Interpersonal and interaction influences on informal resource exchanges between R&D researchers across organizational boundaries, *Academy of Management Journal*, **43** (1), 50–65.

Bradbury, H. and Lichtenstein, B.M.B. (2000), Relationality in organizational research: exploring the space between, *Organizational Science*, **11** (5), 551–64.

Bourdieu, P. (1977), *Outline of Theory of Practice*, Cambridge: Cambridge University Press.

Bourdieu, P. (1984), *Distinction*, trans. R. Niche, London: Routledge.

Bourdieu, P. (1998), *Practical Reason: On the Theory of Action*, Cambridge: Polity Press.
Bourdieu, P. (2003), Participant objectivation, *Journal of Royal Anthropological Institute*, **9**, 282–94.
Bouwen, R. (1998), Relational construction of meaning in emerging organization contexts, *European Journal of Work and Organization Psychology*, **7** (3), 299–319.
Brewer, G.A. (2003), Building social capital: civil attitudes and behavior of public servants, *Journal of Public Administration Research and Theory*, **13** (1), 5–26.
Brewer, R.M., Conrad, C.A. and King, M.C. (2002), The complexities and potential of theorizing gender, caste, race and class, *Feminist Economics*, **8** (2), 3–18.
Buber, M. (1970), *I and Thou*, trans. W. Kaufmann, Edinburgh: Clark.
Buris, V. (2004), The academic caste system: prestige hierarchies in PhD exchange networks, *American Sociological Review*, **69** (2), 239–64.
Burt, R.S. (1997), The contingent value of social capital, *Administrative Science Quarterly*, **42** (2), 339–65.
Cowan, G. and Khatchadourian, D. (2003), Empathy, ways of knowing, and interdependence as mediators of gender differences in attitudes toward hate speech and freedom of speech, *Psychology of Women Quarterly*, **27**, 300–308.
Crenshaw, K. (1991), Women of color at the center: selections from the Third National Conference on Women of Color and the Law, Mapping the margins: intersectionality, identity politics, and violence against women of color, *Stanford Law Review*, **43**, 1241–79.
Denzin, N.K. and Lincoln Y.S. (2003), Introduction: the discipline and practice of qualitative research, in Denzin, N.K. and Lincoln, Y.S. (eds), *The Landscapes of Qualitative Research: Theories and Issues*, London: Sage, pp. 1–46.
Erickson, B.H. (1996), Culture, class and connections, *American Journal of Sociology*, **102** (1), 217–51.
Everett, J. (2002), Organizational research and the praxeology of Pierre Bourdieu, *Organizational Research Methods*, **5** (1): 56–80.
Feinman, J.M. (2000), Relational contract theory in context, *Northwestern University Law Review*, **94** (3), 737–48.
Garcia, J.G., Cartwright, B., Winston, S.M. and Borzuchowska, B. (2003), A transcultural integrative model for ethical decision making in counseling, *Journal of Counseling and Development*, **81** (3), 268–77.
Gergen, M.M. and Gergen, K.J. (2003), Qualitative inquiry: tensions and transformations, in N.K. Denzin and Y.S. Lincoln (eds), *The Landscapes of Qualitative Research: Theories and Issues*, London: Sage, pp. 575–610.
Hall, W.A. and Callery, P. (2001), Pearls, pith and provocation: enhancing the rigor of grounded theory: incorporating reflexivity and relationality, *Qualitative Health Research*, **11** (2), 257–72.
Keddy, B., Gregor, F., Foster, S. and Denney, D. (1999), Theorizing about nurses' work lives: the personal and professional aftermath of living with healthcare 'reform', *Nursing Inquiry*, **6**, 58–64.
Kwon, S-Y. (2001), Codependence and interdependence: cross-cultural reappraisal of boundaries and relationality, *Pastoral Psychology*, **50** (1), 39–52.
Layder, D. (1990), *The Realist Image in Social Science*, London: Macmillan.
Layder, D. (1993), *New Strategies in Social Research*, Cambridge: Polity Press.
Luttrell, W. (2000), 'Good enough' methods for ethnographic research, *Harvard Educational Review*, **70** (4), 499–523.
Mahon, J.F., Heugens, P.P.M.A. and Lamertz, K. (2004). Social networks and non-market strategy, *Journal of Public Affairs*, **4** (2), 170–89.
Massey, D. (2004), The political challenge of relational space: introduction to the Vega Symposium, *Geographiska Annaler*, **86** (1), 3.
Mauthner, N.S. and Doucet, A. (2003), Reflexive accounts and accounts of reflexivity in qualitative data analysis, *Sociology*, **37** (3), 413–31.
Mauthner, N. and Doucet, A. (2000), Reflections on a voice-centred relational method: analysing maternal and domestic voices, in Ribbens, J. and Edwards, R. (eds), *Feminist*

Dilemmas in Qualitative Research: Public Knowledge and Private Lives, London: Sage, pp. 119–46.

McDowell, L. (2004), Masculinity, identity and labour market change: some reflections on the implications of thinking relationally about difference and the politics of inclusion, *Geografiska Annaler*, **86** (1), 45–56.

Mitchell, W. (2003), Searching for theories of dynamic relationships in business strategy: comment on John Dunning's 'Relational assets, networks, and international business activity' paper, Managing multinationals in a knowledge economy: economics, culture and human resources, *Advances in International Management*, **15**, 57–66.

Mohr, J.W. (2000), Bourdieu's relational method in theory and practice, paper presented at the American Sociological Association Meetings, in a special session organized by David Swartz entitled 'Cultural producers and politics: the sociology of Pierre Bourdieu', Washington DC, August.

Nelson, J.A. (2004), Beyond small-is-beautiful: a Buddhist and feminist analysis of ethics and business, Global Development and Environment Institute Working Paper, No. 04–01.

Özbilgin, M.F. (1998), A cross-national study of sex equality in the financial services sector in Turkey and Britain, unpublished PhD thesis, University of Bristol.

Özbilgin, M.F. and Tatlı, A. (2005), Understanding Bourdieu's contribution to organization and management studies, *Academy of Management Review*, **30** (4), 855–69.

Peetz, D. (2002), Decollectivist strategies in Oceania, *Relations Industrielle*, **57** (2), 252–81.

Politis, J.D. (2003), The effects of managerial power and relational trust on the skills and traits of knowledge acquisition: evidence from the United Arab Emirates, *Electronic Journal of Knowledge Management*, **1** (2), 147–58.

Potter, G. (2000), For Bourdieu, against Alexander: reality and reduction, *Journal for the Theory of Social Behaviour*, **30** (2), 229–46.

Pullman, M.E. and Gross, M.A. (2003), Welcome to your experience: where you can check out any time you'd like, but you can never leave, *Journal of Business and Management*, **9** (3), 215–23.

de Saussure, F. (1966), Introduction, in Bally, C., Sechehaye, A. and Riedlinger, A., *Course in General Linguistics*, New York: McGraw-Hill, pp. 645–57.

Schumacher, R. (1999), Need for speed, *Intelligent Enterprise*, 9 March, **2** (4), 50–52.

Shultz, F.L. (2001), Theology, science, and relationality: interdisciplinary reciprocity in the work of Wolfhart Pannenberg, *Zygon*, **36** (4), 809–25.

Somers, M.R. (1998), Symposium on historical sociology and rational choice theory: 'We're No Angels': realism, rational choice and relationality in social science, *American Journal of Sociology*, **104** (3), 722–84.

Storrie, R. (2003), Equivalance, personhood and relationality: processes of relatedness among the Hoti of Venezuelan Guiana, *Journal of the Royal Anthropological Institute*, **9**, 407–28.

Swartz, D. (1997), *Culture and Power: The Sociology of Pierre Bourdieu*, Chicago, IL: University of Chicago Press.

Tietel, E. (2000), The interview as a relational space, *Forum: Qualitative Social Research: Theories, Methods, Applications*, **1** (3), 1–12.

Tyner, J.A. (2002), Geographics of identity: the migrant experiences of Filipinas in Northeast Ohio, *Asian Pacific Viewpoint*, **43** (3), 311–26.

Tyson, L. (1996), *Critical Theory Today: A User-Friendly Guide*, London: Garland Publishing.

Weskott, M. (1990), Feminist criticism of the social sciences, in McCarl Nielsen, J. (ed.), *Feminist Research Methods: Examplary Readings in the Social Sciences*, London: Westview Press, pp. 47–61.

Weberman, D. (2001), Heidegger's relationalism, *British Journal of History of Philosophy*, **9** (1), 109–22.

Wheeler, G. (2000), *Beyond Individualism: Toward a New Understanding of Self, Relationship and Experience*, Hillsdale, NJ: Analytic Press.

Willmott, R. (1999), Structure, agency and school effectiveness: researching a 'failing' school, *Educational Studies*, **25** (1), 5–18.

Zietlow, R.E. (2000), Beyond the pronoun: toward an anti-subordinating method of process, *Texas Journal of Women and the Law*, **10** (1), 1–44.

14 Discourses of relations and relational processes
Dian Marie Hosking

Introduction

This is a story of relations and relating. There is no wolf, no Little Red Riding Hood; there are no bears, nor little piggies. It is not a heroic tale of how one particular discourse proves its superiority by vanquishing other discourses; it is not a tale told from behind the wings, the modernist author's pen, or the realist painter's brush. This story, like all stories, is told from a particular point of view or standpoint – one that I shall try to make explicit – one that I shall call 'critical relational constructionism' (CRC). From this standpoint I shall provide a schematic overview of different discourses of relations by discussing three 'intelligibility nuclei' (Gergen, 1995) in terms of their interrelated 'lines of distinction' (Deetz, 2000). I shall call these discourses (1) 'this and that thinking'; (2) constructivism; and (3) critical relational constructionism. In each case I shall focus on how relations and/or relating are understood – given the wider network of distinctions. Illustrations from the literatures of organization studies and, in particular, Fred Fiedler's theory of leadership effectiveness, will be outlined – not to position a particular study or approach to say what it is, but rather to illustrate abstract conceptions. The third discourse, critical relational constructionism, will receive the most detailed exploration. CRC presents a radically different discourse of relations – one that opens up new possibilities for relational theorizing, inquiry, change work and other kinds of practice.

This and that thinking

Objects with characteristics

The discourse with which I am concerned here includes themes that have been variously referred to as 'objectivism' (Hermans et al., 1992) and 'the received view of science' (Woolgar, 1996). Others, speaking of competing 'paradigms' in qualitative research, have referred to some of these themes as 'positivist' (Guba & Lincoln, 1994) – a confusing simplification for those familiar with the philosophy of inquiry.

This and that thinking is reflected in narratives that for example distinguish between individuals and groups and more 'macro' units such as organizations and society in ways that are overly suggestive of concrete, separately existing objects with their own defining characteristics. For example from the 1960s onwards, management and organization studies were dominated by large-scale empirical studies and by what others have since seen as naive reifications of 'the' organization as the largely tacit and separate context for individual action, perceptions and satisfactions (for example Miner, 1980), and for groups, and inter-group relations (for example Child, 1977). Naive reifications treat someone or something as a unified, bounded and separate 'this or that' requiring its own explanatory theory. Speaking from within psychology, commentators reflected on what they saw as 'individualistic' and 'culturalist' fallacies (Allport, 1963). Other communities such as sociology and anthropology constructed the 'this and that' of individual action versus social structure, whilst the philosophy of social science distinguished 'individualism' and 'holism' (Hollis, 1994).

Language has a very particular role in this kind of thinking. In the words of Hermans and his colleagues, speaking of 'objectivism': 'language is needed to express concept mapped onto objects, properties and relations in a literal, unequivocal, context-independent fashion'. So the scientist, as a language user capable of correct reasoning (see below), is able to describe what she or he discovers about an already existing and independent reality. In other words, it is assumed that language can provide a 'naive reflection' of the world. In this discourse, ontology and epistemology are separate but related. In this discourse, the 'context of discovery' (for example the province of social scientists) and the 'context of justification' (the province of philosophers) are kept separate (see Gergen, 1995; Hosking & Morley, 2004) such that what science says about itself can be held apart from what it says about other.

This brings us to the related issue of methodology, often characterized as empiricism. Fiedler's work provides a helpful illustration. Fiedler presented his work in a manner suggestive of a classical, empiricist methodology. For example it was through observations of leaders, groups and their performance outcomes, and subsequent application of 'the traditional empiricist principle' of induction (Hollis, 1994: 45) that he arrived at his contingency hypothesis (see Fiedler, 1967). He then conducted a series of empirical validation studies designed to test his hypothesis – following the hypothetico-deductive process (see for example Kerlinger, 1964; Gergen, 1995). Truth was operationalized in terms of a probability coefficient (arrived at through sample statistics) applied to numbers produced from empirical measures (claimed to be reliable and valid). Statistically significant results were presented as evidence that the null hypothesis (of no significant difference) could safely be rejected. Fiedler claimed that many empirical studies had tested and validated his hypothesis such that the basis had been provided for the prediction and control of leadership effectiveness.

Relations between 'this' and 'that'

When things are represented as unified, bounded, and separate then relations are understood as being between independently existing entities. This
has been referred to as a 'subject–object' construction of relations (see for
example Dachler & Hosking, 1995; Fine, 1994; Harding, 1986; Hollis, 1994;
Jaynes, 1976; Reeves Sanday, 1988). So for example, writings in organisational behaviour often discourse people as behaving in or on groups and
organizations whilst writings in organisation studies often discourse the
organization as acting on, and influencing, individual motives, satisfactions
and actions. The discourse of subject–object (S–O) relations provides
the backdrop against which an alternative discourse of relations will be
identified when we come to explore relational constructionism. For this
reason, it is worth giving it some more detailed attention.

First, and by definition, S–O discourses construct an 'active–passive
binary' between an active and responsible agent (subject) and an acted upon
other – as a passive object. For example, the received view of science (RVS)
positions the scientist as the knowing subject (S) acting in relation to the
knowable objects (O) of his research. The scientist, mobilizing the discourses
of his scientific community, knows what he wants to find out (discover) and
knows how to do it in ways that produce objective knowledge about other.
Equally, many theories – claimed as scientific or not – do a similar job. For
example Fiedler theorized the leader as active and 'the leadership situation'
as passive, available to be known and acted upon by the leader.

Second, actions, relationships and outcomes are explained through reference to the assumed characteristics of entities. In 'this and that thinking'
these characteristics include the physicalist attributes of material objects, the
mentalistic characteristics of the mind, and a singular self. So we find the
RVS positioning the scientist as a cognizing agent (Woolgar, 1996) who can
know about self and other, and who can generate explanations in relation to
some sort of story of causes. Similarly, theories in organization studies offer
some sort of causal narrative about the characteristics of S and O and about
the relations between these characteristics. So for example contingency theories of organization and of leadership discoursed characteristics of entities
(organizations, leaders, leadership contexts) including goals, structures, cognitive capacities and leadership style and hypothesized causal relations
between these characteristics and contingent variables such as effectiveness.

Third, the S–O construction positions the subject as active in building his
individual knowledge. This is the Cartesian discourse of *cogito, ergo sum*
(I think, therefore I am). Knowledge is discoursed as an individual posses-
sion, a property of the rationalist mind; it is disembodied and divorced from
history and culture, knowledge is objective or subjective, about the world 'as
it really is' (accurate, true) or distorted and inaccurate. So in the RVS the

scientist (S) is considered to build his individual knowledge using 'scientific methods' to produce objective knowledge of what is real – including other people's subjective knowledge claims. These 'lines of distinction' are found in 'more micro' theories where for example organizational leaders are storied as people who can and must build their knowledge about other in order to act rationally.

Fourth, the knowing subject is assumed to exercise his knowing mind in order to influence, form, or structure other as object. So for example the meta-theory of the RVS positions the scientist as one who may use his knowledge rationally to design and manipulate the inquiry process ('methodology'), testing theory, producing knowledge that provides the basis for prediction and control of nature, organization design, leadership effectiveness and so on. Arguments and data (validated knowledge claims) should convince the rational actor of the truth of things. Similarly, Fiedler's leader–subject has to achieve 'power over' other (Gergen, 1995; Hosking, 1995) – in this case, the leadership situation – either by selection (moving from one situation to another) or by re-forming it (for example by restructuring the group's task).

Fifth, the S–O construction turns relations into instrumentalities for S. Other is an instrument for the subject in the pursuit of supposedly rational and value-free purposes. So the RVS produces value-free knowledge about the world 'in its so being', whilst Fiedler's theory positions the group as the leader's instrument for achieving 'leadership effectiveness'.

In sum, 'this and that' thinking assumes (and sometimes prescribes) S–O relations. These may be constructed in relations between the scientist and his research object and in 'scientific' or 'lay' theories about relations between people and the world. As we shall see, this subject–object construction of relations is revised in the second discourse we shall explore (constructivism and individual knowledge), and radically reconstructed in the third and last discourse of 'critical relational constructionism'.

Blurred images: post 'this and that'?

Post-positivism

The 'intelligibility nucleus' of the RVS embraces assumptions that have received much critical comment over the years. Criticisms include: the naive and simplistic assumption that linguistic categories represent 'innocent descriptions of segments of the natural world' (Danziger, 1997) – suggesting the need to reconceptualize the role of language; the assumption of causal relations: the relations between the independent variables caused the state of the dependent variable – inviting other ways of conceptualizing relations; the assumption of induction as a way to develop theory; the logic of verification; the assumed independence of theory and data; the assumed independence of the observing subject from the observed object and so on (see for example Gergen, 1995).

Some of these criticisms have been to some extent addressed in the 'post-positivist', meta-theoretical shift from the naive realism of 'this and that thinking' to a discourse of critical realism. The latter largely involves shifts in epistemology – for example accepting that we cannot know the world as it really is, accepting a changed view of truth (Guba & Lincoln, 1994), and shifting to talk of falsifying hypotheses rather than the language of 'brute facts' and proof. It is in this sense that all modern (and some would say 'modernist') Western psychology has long viewed its knowledge as constructed rather than straightforwardly representative (Hosking & Morley, 2004).

But the above shifts are accompanied by a continuing 'healthy respect for the "world as it is"' (Gergen, 1995: 67). The distinction between, and centring of, individual objective and subjective knowledge continues, even though it is recognized that objectivity is constrained. So too does the ontological construction of separate existences (this is independent of that). Equally, when it comes to the everyday practice of social science inquiry, the meta-theoretical shift to critical realism need not have major implications – particularly when the meta-theory keeps separate the contexts of justification and discovery. To do 'critical realist' science, the scientist must relate to other in ways that attempt to minimize contamination of the (outsider) knowledge he is able to build about other. The scientist must construct, as best he can, a methodology that will let him produce objective knowledge – knowledge that can be accepted[1] as justified true belief.

Constructivisms
In Western psychology, constructivist themes are found in (early twentieth-century) shifts: (1) from talk of sensation to talk of perception; and (2) from talk of sense-taking to that of sense-making. These shifts echoed themes in earlier philosophical work such as the writings of Vico and Kant (see for example Hosking & Morley, 2004; Watzlawick, 1984). Constructivist approaches assume that individual minds process sense data to construct knowledge about the world (for example von Foerster, 1984; von Glaserfeld, 1984; Kelly, 1955; Mead, 1934; Neisser, 1969; Piaget, 1954; Watzlawick, 1984). The constructivist orientation says that people do not know, and cannot know the world as it really is. Rather the mind 'combines what is in the head, with what is in the world' so to speak. Social constructivist approaches amend and supplement this 'cognitivist' story by paying particular attention to social influences and the effects they have on our knowledge claims.

(Social) constructivisms have developed differently in different human science communities in relation to their varied histories and varied practical and theoretical concerns (see for example Danziger, 1997). In recent years, the language of (social) constructivism has become increasingly prominent in business and management studies. The areas of business strategy and marketing, to name only two, increasingly put to work variants of constructivist thinking joined, for example, with more or less individualistic[2] versions of cybernetic systems theory[3] (see for example Stacey, 2003). At the same time, and as noted above (social) constructivist thinking is neither new nor radical in much of contemporary Western psychology[4] where behaviourism and the RVS have been replaced by the discourse of post-positivism, and where social influences on individual action and cognition are widely theorized.

Constructivist writings vary considerably in the particular S–O themes they blur. As far as meta-theoretical themes are concerned, the rationalist–empiricist construction remains part of the intelligibility nucleus but the dualist opposition is now collapsed.[5] Equally, even though reality cannot be known 'as it really is', 'external' reality usually remains the focus of scientific interest in objective knowledge.[6] These ontological and epistemological assumptions mean that talk of 'construction' is likely to be understood as talk about objective knowledge (now accepted as imperfect) or subjective knowledge. Should the constructivist writer seem immoderate for example in his critique of scientific practices, he will be supposed to be naive (of course we already know that knowledge is constructed). Equally, should the constructivist writer seem to go too far in his or her talk of construction, they will be thought foolish (daft enough to reject the assumption of an independently existing reality) – trapped in the relativist position that there are as many realities as there are knowing minds; trapped in the deeply problematic view that 'anything goes'.

Constructivist inquiries often continue to be oriented around an interest in 'aboutness knowledge' and its (in)accuracy as a representation of an independently existing world. So for example constructs such as mind maps, schema, narratives and discourses are treated as characteristics of mind operations and are awarded a central role in the processing of sense data and the production of knowledge. Language continues to be given the role of representing some non-discursive world. Last, and consistent with my earlier reflections, constructivist interests are often pursued through some empiricist methodology. One major consequence of this is that post-positivist science continues to discourse other as irrational and to discourse self as able to produce objective knowledge, thus providing the basis for rational action. Reflexivity remains an individual act in which scientists evaluate the reliability and validity of their findings but do not reflect on or revise their meta-theoretical assumptions, that is, 'the context of justification' (for example Steier, 1991).

In sum, post 'this and that' thinking succeeds in blurring, but not abandoning, some S–O assumptions about relations and continues to prescribe S–O relations in the conduct of scientific inquiry. The characteristics attributed to the human subject include a singular self (*I* think), with a knowing mind (I *think*)[7] and language ability, along with constructs such as motives and personality. The blurring of S–O is primarily epistemological and objective–subjective knowledge is about real objects, imperfectly knowable. A radical reconstruction of relations awaits our third discourse of relational constructionism.

Critical relational constructionism

Overview of premises
I want to use the term 'critical relational constructionism' to refer to an interrelated set of assumptions and interests that differ from post-positivism and constructivist thinking. Instead of centring mind and 'real' reality, CRC centres language and discursive practices – and these are seen as constructing relational realities – including what is thought to be a person. This is not talk of subjective interpretations; this is not adopting idealism in place of realism. This is another 'map' about another 'territory' (to borrow freely from Korzybski) – where the objective–subjective, real–relativist dualisms are no longer relevant. This discourse centres the construction of objects (self and other) and relations, construction not discovery. So for example the positioning of post-positivism as a special scientific way of knowing[8] can be treated as a particular language game with its related 'form of life' (Wittgenstein, 1953). The discourse of independently existing 'beings' can be set aside[9] in favour of a discourse that centres language-based relational processes. Language and 'real' reality may be discoursed as inseparable by seeing 'textuality' as a defining characteristic of all phenomena and not just of written and spoken 'texts' (for example Stenner & Eccleston, 1994; Dachler & Hosking, 1995; Gergen, 1995; Hosking et al., 1995).[10]

The 'lines of distinction' that contribute to CRC have very long histories and come from many different communities of practice (see for example Danziger, 1997; Gergen, 1995; Hosking & Morley, 2004). Turning to relatively recent times, contributing arguments come from literatures such as feminism and feminist critiques of science, literary criticism, cognitive and social psychology, interactionist, cognitive and phenomenological sociologies, radical family therapy, critical social anthropology and some expressions of 'postmodernism' and post-structuralism (for example Latour, 1987; Foucault, 1980). Some postmodern and poststructuralist lines of distinction are embraced for example in the construction of self–other as a relational unity that is ongoing in relational processes – rather than as separately existing entities, subjectively or objectively knowing and known. The assumption of separately existing individuals in a S–O relation is itself viewed as a historical-cultural construction that can be otherwise. This is consistent with for example Foucault's critique of the Cartesian separation of epistemology and ontology. According to Foucault, 'we should ask: under what conditions and through what forms can an entity like the subject appear in the order of discourse; what positions does it occupy; what functions does it exhibit; and what rules does it follow in each type of discourse?' (Foucault, 1977, pp. 137–8).

The following seem to me to represent some of the key features of a relational constructionist orientation:

● Talk of the individual self, mind operations, and individual knowledge gives way to discourses of relational processes, viewed as language based interactions.
● Relational processes are seen as processes that (re)construct self–other realities as local ontologies or 'forms of life' (person-world making); and (re)construct mind – metaphorized for example – as an imaginal space in which self–other relations are discoursed (for example Hermans et al., 1992; Jaynes, 1976).
● The unitary conception of self is replaced by a dialogical conception of self as multiple self–other relations such that other, including the body, is no longer discoursed as 'outside'.[11]
● Relational processes have a local cultural-historical quality such that discourses of the past and future are constructed and reconstructed in an ongoing present.[12]
● Relational realities are viewed as constructions such that subject–object relations may be constructed in particular relations (for example in 'scientific' inquiry) – but do not have to be.
● Power is (re)constructed in relational processes, for example by being linked to talk of crediting and discrediting knowledge or identity claims, closing down or 'opening up' possibilities, creating (more or less) local realities and relations between them.

Discoursing relational processes
A good deal of work emphasises the 'what' rather than the 'how' of relating (see Hosking, 1999; Pearce, 1992). I will finish by thickening some discourses of relational processes as multiple, simultaneous interactions and as local social-historical constructions of relational realities.

Multiple, simultaneous interactions   Language is centred as the primary medium of relating. In this discourse, language derives its significance from the ways it is used in human relationships and the forms of life it supports (Gergen, 1995). This is so whether the language game is called science or something else. Conceptual language is often given centred, although relating is also achieved non-verbal actions, and in coordinations of bodies, things and events (see for example Hodge & Kress, 1988; Latour, 1987). The literal–metaphoric distinction is no longer relevant, and all language is viewed as metaphorical.

A variety of linguistic tools are used for talking about relational processes including terms such as 'act-supplement' or 'text-con-text' (for example Gergen, 1995), or more everyday terms such as story-telling, conversation, performance, narrative or discourse. The most general point here is our focus on relating, regardless of what is being related with what. So for example relating goes on in the shaking of hands, in the telling of and listening to a story, in conversations about local markets and strategy, in playing and in listening to music.

Relational processes involve multiple, simultaneous, interrelated texts (con-texts). For example the process of relating to a painting such as Magritte's *Ceci n'est pas une pipe* simultaneously implicates multiple inter-related texts which could include relating: the visual symbol with the written text below it; the written text with the French language; the written text with the Dutch language (!); narratives of earlier viewings, of what others have said about the painting, of what is appropriately called a 'pipe' and so on. And of course multiple constructions of 'what it is' are also possible, depending on the particular interrelating of con-texts: it's a pipe, 'it's a painting of a pipe', 'it's a paradox', 'it is a work of art' and so on. The question 'what is it' is no longer meaningful; (il)legibility is a local-cultural-historical affair. In this discourse, action and language are joined, rather than separated through discourses of cognitive processes and representation. Relating (re)constructs the textuality of all phenomena.

Local-social-historical constructions   Relating produces and reproduces stabilized patterns as some performances are supplemented in ways that socially certify them as real, relevant, perhaps helpful and/or true (Hosking & Morley, 1991), (un)ethical, and/or aesthetically (dis)pleasing. Ethical and aesthetic aspects have been relatively underexplored by constructionists – perhaps because of continuing and unrecognized attachments to the post-positivist intelligibility nucleus and its related interest in propositional knowledge. Stabilized effects or patterns include particular self–other relationship constructions, social conventions, musical forms, organizational and societal structures, technology, and (what some may call) 'facts' and 'artefacts' (for example Latour, 1987), (un)ethical behaviour and so on. But not all texts will be supplemented; some will go unheard, unseen, unnoticed. Equally, some will be discredited, certified as not science (art, music . . .), claimed as heretical or irrational.

Supplementing may play with conventions and possibilities: the proffered hand may not be grasped and shaken but spat in; the improvising actor or jazz musician may take a process off in new directions. Whilst possible supplements might be infinite, not all are equally probable because there are (social-historical) limits to what is likely to be socially certified as relevant, true or good. Once a particular performance becomes 'stabilized' for example a greeting convention, 'how we do things around here', the sonata form, what counts as middle C, other possibilities have to be improvised. And, as Beethoven discovered at one of his premiers, it may be harder to have some new form socially validated when what is 'real and good' is already established! Such difficulties are especially likely to be encountered when subject–object relations (implicating discourses of 'right' and 'wrong') are already stabilized (see for example Deetz, 2000).

This reference to local social-historical processes should be understood in contrasting relation to narratives of general (trans-contextual, trans-historical) knowledge about reality (as ontology). CRC speaks of social practices – including what some might construct as 'knowledge' – and emphasizes that what is socially validated or discredited is local to the ongoing practices that (re)construct a particular culture or 'community of practice' (for example Lave & Wenger, 1991) and so, particular self–other relationship constructions. This said, local could be as broad as Western, or post-enlightenment. The 'natural attitude' may mean that particular ways of 'going on' are taken for granted as 'how things really are'. However the present line of argument emphasizes the essential artfulness of these 'stabilized effects' and draws attention to the relational processes that make and remake them (for example Chia, 1995; Latour, 1987).

This reference to the historical quality of relational processes should not be understood to imply a linear and unidirectional story in which the present is a moment between (the now finished) past and the (yet to come) future. Rather, relational processes are always ongoing, bringing past structurings into the present (for example the convention of shaking hands) and anticipating possible futures (for example that a greeting will be successfully performed). Another way of saying this is that all texts supplement other texts and are available for possible supplementation and possible crediting. Interactions, and particularly regularly repeated ones, 'make history' so to speak and history is constantly being remade (Vico, 1774; Hora, 1966).

Relational realities   Multiple, simultaneous, ongoing relatings (re)construct the textuality of people and worlds. The individual is not the agent of reality construction. In this view, identity and other assumed entity characteristics (such as personality, organizational goals and structures) are not singular and fixed and do not function as the necessary defining characteristic of someone or something. Rather identity, and other assumed characteristics become understood (1) as relational; and so (2) multiple and variable (for example different identities in different self–other relations); and (3) as performed, rather than possessed, in networks of ongoing relatings. In sum, relational processes are reality-constituting practice(s) that construct markets, management, science, self–other – all textualities. These relational realities are multiple and local rather than singular and transcendent; they may be explored with a greater or lesser emphasis on inquiry or transformation in relation to for example their local-cultural aesthetic, ethical and pragmatic qualities.

In my view, the critical relational constructionist orientation is best viewed as a discourse or 'intelligibility nucleus' that emphasizes the historical-cultural rather than the natural-scientific whilst differing from contextualism. Theory, method and data are seen as interwoven[13]. Inquiry is opened up to a different range of interests. These include for example not to 'tell it how it (probably) is' – but to 'tell how it might become' that is, to be 'world enlarging' (see Harding, 1986). Similarly, interest might be directed to particular discursive practices to see what forms of life or ways of 'going on' are invited, supported or suppressed. The critical interest is in dissensus – exploring how power-full processes construct dominance or facilitate openness and multiplicity – exploring how unitary constructions can be deconstructed and disrupted (for example Deetz, 2000). And last, inquiry can embrace its relational – constructive qualities by shifting emphasis – to 'opening' up new possible identities and (local) worlds – to transformation rather than simply 'finding out' (Hosking, 2004).

To conclude: I have attempted to distinguish different discourses of relational theory that are often confounded. In my view, it is only CRC that sets aside both *I* think (the individualistic self) and I *think* (the cognizing subject) (Hermans et al., 1992); only the CRC has room for useful fictions (Vaihinger, 1935) such as the three little piggies (I lied when I said there would be no piggies).

Notes

1. At least, by the scientific community.
2. And indeed, more or less realist or idealist, for example the radical constructivism of von Glaserfeld (1984) seems to adopt an idealist position by treating reality as an individual construction.
3. Wholistic developments such as for example in cybernetic systems theory, complexity and chaos theories – in danger of continuing to reproduce some crucial S–O themes, that is, science, systems, talk of processes, failing to get to grips with somatic life, emptiness and space, reflexivity and openness.

4. Although countries clearly vary in how much they are committed to strong versions of empiricism.
5. As it has been in the thought styles and practices of many who would now be called scientists including Galileo and Newton.
6. Although not of all, the radical constructivists shift their attention to the individual observer as one who participates in self-reflexive constructions of reality.
7. See Hermans et al. (1992) for an excellent discussion of this.
8. That is, one that can know about other ways of knowing and one that has the *unique* quality of self correction (see Kerlinger, 1964: 7).
9. Set aside, not rejected – as others have said – this discourse is 'ontologically mute' (Gergen, 1995).
10. Of course supporters of the RVS would regard many of these moves as constructing something that was 'not science' – but the definition of science is itself a contested terrain and its 'essence' undecidable.
11. 'Inside-outside' is now viewed as a discursive construction – and not one that CRC needs to make.
12. And so, contrary to analytic philosophy, the distinction between the contexts of discovery and justification is dropped (see Dachler & Hosking, 1995; Hosking & Morley, 2004).
13. For this reason, theorists will probably not use terms such as 'data' (it is too suggestive of a view of facts as independent of theory and methods) or 'method' (too suggestive of a technique that is theory-free).

References

Allport, G. (1963), *Pattern and Growth in Personality*, London: Holt, Rinehart & Winston.
Chia, R. (1995), From modern to postmodern organizational analysis, *Organization Studies*, **16** (4), 580–604.
Child, J. (1977), *Organization: A Guide To Problems and Practice*, London: Harper & Row.
Dachler, H.P. & Hosking, D.M. (1995), The primacy of relations in socially constructing organizational reality, in Hosking, D.M., Dachler, H.P. and Gergen, K.J. (eds), *Management and Organization: Relational Alternatives to Individualism*, Aldershot: Avebury, pp. 1–28.
Danziger, K. (1997), The varieties of social construction: essay review, *Theory and Psychology*, **7** (3), 399–416
Deetz, S. (2000), Describing differences in approaches to organisation science, in Frost, P., Lewin, R. & Daft, D. (eds), *Talking About Organisation Science*, Thousand Oaks, CA: Sage.
Fiedler, F.E. (1967), *A Theory of Leadership Effectiveness*, New York: McGraw Hill.
Fine, M. (1994), Working the hyphens: reinventing self and other in qualitative research, in Denzin, N.K. & Lincoln, Y.S. (eds), *Handbook of Qualitative Research*, London: Sage, pp. 70–82.
Foucault, M. (1977, 1980), *Power/knowledge: Selected Interviews and Other Writings*, New York: Pantheon Books.
Gergen, K.J. (1995), Relational theory and the discourses of power, in Hosking, D.M., Dachler, H.P. & Gergen, K.J. (eds), *Management and Organization: Relational Alternatives to Individualism*, Aldershot: Avebury, pp. 29–50.
Guba, E. & Lincoln, Y. (1994), Competing paradigms in qualitative research, in Denzin, N. & Lincoln, Y. (eds), *Handbook of Qualitative Research*, Milton Keynes: Oxford University Press.
Harding, S. (1986), *The Science Question In Feminism*, Milton Keynes: OUP.
Hermans, H., Kempen, H. & van Loon, R. (1992), The dialogical self: beyond individualism and rationalism, *American Psychologist*, **47** (1), 23–33.
Hodge, R. & Kress, G. (1988), *Social Semiotics*, Cambridge: Polity Press.
Hollis, M. (1994), *The Philosophy Of Social Science*, Cambridge: Cambridge University Press.
Hora, E. (1966), The dialogical self: beyond individualism and rationalism, in Hermans, H., Kempen, H. & van Loon, R., *American Psychologist*, **47** (1), 23–33.
Hosking, D.M. (1995), Constructing power: entitative and relational approaches, in Hosking, D.M., Dachler, H.P. and Gergen, K.J., *Management and Organization: Relational Alternatives to Individualism*, Aldershot: Avebury.

Hosking, D.M. (1999), Social constructions as process: some new possibilities for research and development, *Concepts and Transformation*, **4** (2), 117–32.

Hosking, D.M. (2000), Ecology in mind: mindful practices, *European Journal of Work and Organizational Psychology*, **9** (2), 147–58.

Hosking, D.M. (2004), Changeworks: a critical construction, in Boonstra, J. (ed.), *Dynamics of Organisational Change and Learning*, Chichester: Wiley.

Hosking, D.M., Dachler, H.P. & Gergen, K.J., (1995), *Management and Organization: Relational Alternatives To Individualism*, Aldershot: Avebury

Hosking, D.M. & Morley, I.E. (1991), *A Social Psychology Of Organising*, London: Harvester Wheatsheaf.

Hosking, D.M. & Morley, I.E. (2004), Social constructionism in community and applied social psychology, *Journal of Community and Applied Social Psychology*, **14**, 318–31.

Jaynes, J. (1976), *The Origin of Consciousness in the Breakdown of the Bicameral Mind*, London: Penguin Books.

Kelly, G. (1955), *The Psychology of Personal Constructs*, New York: Norton.

Kerlinger, F. (1964), *Foundations of Behavioural Research*, London: Holt, Rinehart & Winston.

Latour, B. (1987), *Science in Action*. Cambridge, MA: Harvard University Press.

Lave, J. & Wenger, E. (1991), *Situated Learning: Legitimate Peripheral Participation*, Cambridge: Cambridge University Press.

Maier, M. (1988), Psychology as storytelling, *International Journal of Personal Construct Psychology*, **1**, 125–37.

Mead, G.H. (1934), *Mind, Self, and Society*, Chicago, IL: University of Chicago Press.

Miner, J.B. (1980), *Theories of Organizational Behaviour*, Illinois: Dryden Press.

Neisser, U. (1969), *Cognition and Reality: Principles and Implications of Cognitive Psychology*, Englewood Cliffs: NJ: Prentice Hall.

Pearce, W.B. (1992), A 'Camper's guide to constructionisms', *Human Systems; The Journal of Systemic Consultation and Management*, **3**, 139–61.

Piaget, J. (1954), *The Construction of Reality In The Child*, New York: Basic Books.

Reeves Sanday, P. (1988), The reproduction of patriarchy in feminist anthropology, in McCanney Gergen, M. (ed.) *Feminist Thought and the Structure of Knowledge*, New York: New York University Press.

Rorty, R. (1991), *Objectivity, Relativism, and Truth*, Vol. 1, Cambridge: Cambridge University Press.

Stacey, R. (2003), *Strategic Management and Organisational Dynamics*, Harlow, Essex: Pearson Education.

Steier, F. (ed.) (1991), *Research and Reflexivity*, London: Sage.

Stenner, P. & Eccleston, C. (1994), On the textuality of being, *Theory and Psychology*, **4** (1), 85–103.

Vaihinger, H. (1935), in Hermans, H., Kempen, H. & van Loon, R. (1992), The dialogical self: beyond individualism and rationalism, *American Psychologist*, **47** (1), 23–33.

Vico, G. (1774), in Hermans, H., Kempen, H. & van Loon, R., The dialogical self: beyond individualism and rationalism, *American Psychologist*, **47** (1), 23–33.

von Foerster, H. (1984), On constructing a reality, in Watzlawick, P. (ed.), *The Invented Reality*, New York: W.W. Norton.

von Glaserfeld, E. (1984), An introduction to radical constructivism, in Watzlawick, P. (ed.) *The Invented Reality*, New York: W.W. Norton.

Watzlawick, P. (ed.) (1984), *The Invented Reality*, New York: W.W. Norton.

Wittgenstein, L. (1953), *Philosophical Investigations*, trans. G. Anscombe, New York, Macmillan.

Woolgar, S. (1996), Psychology, qualitative methods and the ideas of science, in Richardson, J.T.E. (ed.), *Handbook of Qualitative Research Methods for Psychology and the Social Sciences*, Leicester: BPS Publications.

15 Toward the development of a truly relational approach to the study of organizational behaviors: further consideration of the committed-to-participant research perspective
Thomas A. Wright

Introduction

According to many, our discipline has become one increasingly lacking in relevance and meaning. I have previously suggested that a primary reason for this lack of relevance and meaning is the failure of much organizational research to be responsive to all potential stakeholders. To help address these limitations, my father Vincent P. Wright and I proposed the committed-to-participant research (CPR) perspective (Wright & Wright, 1999; Wright & Wright, 2002). In this chapter I build upon previous discussions and expand the CPR framework to integrate a social modeling approach to human adaptation and learning (Bandura, 1977, 1991, 1997), along with recent work on character strengths and virtues (Peterson & Seligman, 2004). I close with suggestions for incorporating a more relational-based framework to the study of the wide range of organizational behaviors.

> The compass and square produce perfect circles and squares. By the sages, the human relations are perfectly exhibited.
>
> (Mencius, *Works*, bk. IV, 1:2.1)

Mencius (c. 372–289 BC) was obviously far ahead of his time with the highly astute observation that it takes the intercession of an outsider, in this case a sage, to help ensure that the patterns of relations among humans are carried out (perfected) in good order. In fact, while separated by over 2000 years of time, toil and various attempts at human relations, the introductory quote by Mencius well captures the theme of this book of chapters on further integrating a more relational-focused perspective to our organizational studies. The overriding book theme is to demonstrate tangibly that the people and the organizations in which they work are best considered as interdependent, not independent, entities. In the present chapter, building upon the committed-to-participant research (CPR) perspective (Wright & Wright, 1999), my particular intent is to bring an added relational focus

278

in the study of organizational behaviors to two groups of neglected stake-holders: the actual people who participate in applied scholars' research endeavors (aka: our subjects) and the actual students that we profess to teach.

To lead into my discussion of the CPR approach, consider the following example taken from Wright and Hobfoll (2004). Wright and Hobfoll's research examined the role of a number of predictor variables, including employee age, gender, ethnicity, organizational commitment and psycho-logical well-being (PWB) on employee burnout. In the course of their inves-tigation, the authors discovered that a number of the sample participants, stakeholders of the study, were deemed 'burnout-at-risk'. That is, their reported scores on the measured dimensions of job burnout – emotional exhaustion, depersonalization and diminished personal accomplishment – were found to be alarmingly high. Besides analyzing the results and writing up the findings for journal publication consideration, what we as academics typically do, what else did the authors do with this information? What should they have done with this information?

Or, what should the organizational researchers have done, when a female participant in their research study tied a rope in the form of a noose from the heating air vent in her work office, climbed up on her desk for balance, and committed suicide by jumping off and hanging herself. Conversely, as reported by Wright and Wright (1999), consistently high diastolic blood pressure readings taken on the job helped stimulate a high-ranking manager employed by a very large service-oriented organization to see his doctor and be immediately placed on blood pressure medication. His doctor emphati-cally told him that he had shown very good judgement in coming to see him before it was 'too late'. Similarly, a man in his mid-forties, with a wife and children to support, suffered a heart seizure on his way to work and literally crashed his car into his place of employment and died. Or, consider the example of a management student who, upon being caught 'red-handed' with a student cheat sheet in her hand during a class quiz, repeatedly con-tinued to deny that she was cheating. While never giving up her denial of guilt, she asked her professor why he is picking on her, questioned what she had to do in order to 'get on with her life' since the professor was obviously not being fair to her. As if that wasn't enough, the student told the professor that her tuition paid his salary, so how could she be possibly cheating on a service she paid for! Finally, consider the example of an upper division man-agement major who decided to turn himself in to his professor after he had successfully cheated (that is, was not caught) on the class final exam. He told the professor that one of the reasons for turning himself in was that he con-sidered the professor to be a positive role model and he (the student) wanted to do the 'right' thing.

What these six circumstances have in common was that each involved individuals who were either participants in one of the various field research projects conducted by me over the years, or one of my students. Of course, these types of occurrences do not just happen to me. In fact, Wright and Wright (2002) reported anecdotal evidence from a number of other organizational researchers and teachers indicating that they have experienced similar circumstances involving either their students or the participants in their research projects. After all, as Wright and Wright (2002: 174) noted, research participants not only spend their time 'filling out questionnaires, individuals also find the time to experience the various life passages (birth, first job, marriage, retirement, death) that go to make up our daily human existence'. Certainly, this observation also applies with equal vigor to the students we teach. We are all human, and each and every one of us interacts with and develops relationships of all kinds with our fellow life travelers.

Considered together, it would appear that the potential for meaningful involvement by organizational scholars in helping to better the lives of our stakeholders could be quite significant. Unfortunately my co-author Vincent P. Wright (my father) and I have presented telling evidence that this is not always the case (Wright & Wright, 2002). In fact, and apparently quite to the contrary, a number of applied scholars have noted that our (collective) research, and by direct association our teaching as well (Wright, 2004), are both quite often lacking in relevance and meaning (Beyer, 1997; Brief, 2000; Freeman, 1986; Slocum, 1999).

As my father and I have suggested (Wright & Wright, 1999; Wright & Wright, 2000; Wright & Wright, 2002), a primary reason for this perceived lack of relevance by many organizational scholars is the failure of much applied research to be responsive to the legitimate wants and needs of all our potential stakeholders or constituents. In particular, although there are at least four primary stakeholder groups for our research and teaching endeavors, the consequences of much of our effort appears to be primarily directed to satisfying the needs of only two of these stakeholder groups, the research scientists themselves and the actual study organization. Ironically, and especially so considering the overriding relational theme of this book, it appears that we have all too often neglected two of our most important stakeholder groups: the actual participants of our research endeavors and the students we teach.

In the present chapter, I expand upon previous discussions and introduce possible ways to consider the added relational stakeholder benefits of incorporating aspects of the CPR approach into how we both conduct our research and interact with our students in our classroom settings. Incorporating a social modeling approach to human adaptation and learning (Bandura, 1997) and recent work on character strengths and virtues

(Peterson & Seligman, 2004), I close with suggestions for incorporating a more relational-based framework to the study of organizational behaviors. But first, I provide brief overviews of the two most widespread approaches to conducting research, the committed-to-management research (CMR) and committed-to-science research (CSR) perspectives. Following this overview of the CMR and CSR perspectives, an expanded view of the CPR approach is provided, emphasizing its added relational stakeholder benefits to both our research and teaching responsibilities.

CMR perspective

The basic assumptions of the CMR approach are very familiar to students of organizational research.[1] Drawing heavily from the rational or 'intendedly rational' theoretical framework (see Cyert & March, 1963; March & Simon, 1958; Weber, 1947), according to the CMR perspective, the sole objective of research is to fulfill the goals as set forth by the management or ownership of the organization. The employees of the organization are basically a stakeholder afterthought, considered important only to the extent that they help fulfill the mission, goals and objectives of the organization. The CMR approach is consistent with the utilitarian values perspective typically taught in business schools (Wright & Wright, 2000; Wright & Wright, 2002). According to this utilitarian values approach, actions and policies should be primarily evaluated on the basis of the actual costs and benefits they impose on the organization (Boal & Peery, 1985; Velasquez, 2002; Wright & Wright, 2002). Highly consistent with the belief that the end justifies the means, utilitarianism focuses only on the anticipated consequences (invariably narrowly measured in financial terms) of the particular action. The emphasis is on organizational, not necessarily individual, efficiency. This perspective is epitomized by the classical economic viewpoint personified by the Chicago School of Economics (Friedman, 1968, 1970), proposing that an organization's stockholders should be the prime, if not sole, beneficiaries of corporate actions.

This utilitarian values perspective has been highly influential in determining the research focus for a wide range of organizational topics (Wright & Wright, 2002). For example such major theories of motivation as expectancy/valence (Kernan & Lord, 1990; Vroom, 1964) and operant conditioning (Luthans & Kreitner, 1985; Skinner, 1953, 1969) are predicated on utilitarian-based assumptions. In fact a number of writers, including myself, have suggested that the purpose of much organizational research has slowly (d)evolved into one too frequently concerned with developing various social charms, that is, collegiality and being a team player, to name but a few, designed to help 'facilitate' and 'lubricate' the process of human interaction (Covey, 1999; Wright & Wright, 2001).

As a prime example, consider the typical job ads and overall job search process for university professor positions in the fields of management and organizational behavior. Invariably these ads emphasize the need for candidates who are collegial, civil and good team players. As discussed by Wright and Wright (2001), most job applicants recognize these terms as 'code' words for being able to 'fit in' and not 'rock the boat' on the job. Unfortunately, a primary consequence of this awareness is that many job candidates feel the need to 'fake it' on their resume and during the job interview itself in order to be competitive in the hiring process (Rosse et al., 1998).

I propose that any situation where honest job candidates are at a disadvantage and the organization makes a potentially inferior hiring decision is a 'lose–lose' situation. Relatedly, a number of colleagues from a number of different schools have repeatedly told me that the most important component of teaching 'effectiveness' at their schools is to get evaluations high enough to guarantee that they get the benefit of a yearly raise or be promoted to the next academic rank. One of my colleagues at the University of Nevada, Reno put it most succinctly. We use a five-point scale in the College of Business to measure teaching effectiveness and this professor's philosophy is very simple: 'Do whatever it takes to get a 4 on the 5-point scale and the administration will leave you alone.' Naturally, from this approach, class rigor and course relevance take a back seat to the 'benefit' derived by the professor from receiving 'good' evaluations at a minimal 'cost.'

These are just a few examples of an increasingly distressing state of affairs, leading a number of social commentators to conclude that much of our applied research and teaching is lacking in relevance (see Beyer, 1997; J. Freeman, 1986; Slocum, 1997; Wright, 2004). As a consequence, it has been proposed that many of us have wholeheartedly adopted a purely utilitarian-based values perspective and, as a result, become merely high-priced pitchman for management (see Baritz, 1960; Brief, 2000; Perrow, 1972; Wright & Wright, 2001; Wright, 2005b). At the very least, this adherence to an organizational-focused, utilitarian, or cost–benefit values approach has led to a disconnect of our teaching and research with, if not two of our most important stakeholder constituencies, certainly a highly relevant component of our audience: the actual subjects we use in our research projects and the students we teach in our classes. Unfortunately this same disconnect pattern holds true for the second, or CSR, approach (Wright & Wright, 2002).

CSR perspective
Like the CMR approach, the CSR perspective has gained widespread acceptance and implementation (Wright & Wright, 2002). The CSR approach, and highly similar to the CMR perspective, is utilitarian or cost–benefit in its orientation. As a result, consideration of the stakeholder

needs of either our research participants or the students we teach does not appear to be a primary concern of those adhering to either the CMR or CSR perspectives. What does appear to be of primary interest for advocates of the CSR approach is a fascination with identifying organizational topics that are 'novel' and 'original' (Wright & Wright, 2002). Unfortunately the net result of this seemingly irresistible desire for the 'unique' is an increasingly widespread belief among both academics and practitioners alike that academics are 'writing to ourselves, and our prose has little impact' (Slocum, 1997).

As an example of just how little impact we are having, Mowday (1997) reported that on average an article in the prestigious *Academy of Management Journal*, the flagship journal of the Academy of Management, is only cited three times in a given year. The numbers are even more disturbing when considering other prominent management journals (Wright, 1999). Regarding our teaching, this emphasis on the novel or unique, to the extent that it distracts students from better learning the basics, appears to be a contributor to overall declines in student critical thinking capabilities as evidenced by declines in various achievement tests (see Wright & Larwood, 1998). These circumstances are disturbing because there is a pressing need for our research and teaching to have practical implication and relevance.

Mone and McKinley (1993) agreed with Slocum's assertion and suggested that this striving for the novel and original is related to the need to be unique, which they characterized by the term 'uniqueness value' (p. 284). Related to this overarching need to be unique, Davis (1971) noted that applied theory becomes more recognizable when it is counterintuitive in nature and appears to contradict widely accepted 'fact'. Composed of both descriptive and prescriptive elements, this need to be unique underscores the pressures placed on organizational scholars (that is, to obtain tenure, to be promoted and so on) to make a unique (translated: a showy and controversial) contribution to their specific field of inquiry (Wright & Wright, 2002). However herein lies the relational conundrum, as this apparent fascination to be, above all, unique is inherently contradictory to the primary needs of many of the major stakeholders of the organization(s) being studied (rank-and-file workers, families of the workers and so on), as well as our students interested in gaining a practical awareness of how organizations are really run. Summing up this dilemma, Wright (1999) noted that the pursuit of uniqueness has greatly impeded the generalizability of scholarly results across situations and organizations. As a consequence, while any number of our stakeholders want and need our research and teaching to be presented in a manner that is capable of generalizing across work situations and individuals, much of our work is becoming increasingly fragmented and situation-specific (Mone & McKinley, 1993; Wright, 2004).

John Freeman (1986: 298), in his role as editor of *Administrative Science Quarterly*, went so far as to propose that the limited degree to which much organizational research is able to generalize across endeavors has resulted in a 'pitiful state of affairs' in the field of organizational research. Likewise, a growing number of scholars have noted similar problems in management education (Wright, 2005b). In particular, the myriad range of problems resulting from the increased role of the market–consumer metaphor is gaining attention from a growing number of management scholars (Beatty, 2004; Ferris, 2002; Gross & Hogler, 2004; Kunkel, 2002; Zell, 2001). Simply stated, and similar to the utilitarian-based focus of the CMR and CSR perspectives, the consumer metaphor represents a pedagogical attempt to reduce the wide spectrum of organizational behaviors to the mere status of an economic good or commodity. As if that isn't problematic enough, Beatty (2004) suggested that this increased commodification of management education can be linked to the perceived ethical decline in society in general. Certainly this increased desire to place an economic value on the wide spectrum of human endeavor, including the pursuit of knowledge itself, has caused many, especially among our young, to reconsider the value of the education process itself. Fortunately, as my father and I have suggested elsewhere (Wright & Wright, 1999, 2000, 2001, 2002), all is not lost.

Following Wright and Wright (2002), I propose that expanding the domain of research stakeholders to include both the actual research participants themselves and our student audience will potentially lead to more relevant and meaningful research and teaching. Quite clearly, as a number of organizational scholars have noted, there is a pressing need for both our research and teaching efforts to have practical implications and relevance to all interested stakeholders, both practitioner and academic alike. To address the potential limitations of the CMR and CSR utilitarian-based values approaches, Wright and Wright (1999) proposed the CPR perspective. In this chapter, I expand upon Wright and Wright's earlier CPR model (Wright & Wright, 1999; Wright & Wright, 2000; Wright & Wright, 2002) to include the students that we teach.

CPR approach
Drawing on a number of sources, the CPR approach is most closely associated with the action research model in suggesting that the relationships among all stakeholders are important (Elsbach, 1999; Lewin, 1948; Wright & Wright, 2002).[2] Inherent in the framework of an action research model is the realization that 'good' theory must never be disconnected from its possible practical applications. According to Carl Rogers (as cited in Coghlan, 1994), social science researchers should actively develop feelings of empathy for the various work and life events experienced on a day-to-day basis by the

study clients or participants. Selznick (2000) expands upon traditional definitions of empathy and notes that a social science researcher should always consider the moral issues surrounding our research as fundamental guides. Relatedly, in an attempt to address the question of 'what matters most' regarding the development of more robust and meaningful theories of organizations, Frost (1999) forcefully proposed the need for our research endeavors to be more personal and compassionate in nature. Likewise Weick (1999) noted that our research becomes more relevant when it helps to narrow the gap between merely identifying organizational phenomena and actually addressing how our study participants live, work, play and eventually die. Finally, Schein (1987) proposed that researchers consider their role as that of 'expert' helpers.

Certainly in the CPR tradition, in addition to our research efforts, our teaching efforts as an 'expert' helper can also benefit from our being more empathetic, compassionate and relevant. Especially so when one realizes that an increasing number of today's students have come to reconsider their university learning experience from the perspective of what constitutes a just or fair exchange. Most assuredly, this collective reframing of what constitutes fair is significantly different from that of past generations (Gross & Hogler, 2004; Wright, 2005b). Looking at the issue of justice from a historical perspective, Cropanzano and his colleagues (Cropanzano et al., 2003; Cropanzano & Prehar, 2001; Cropanzano et al., 2001) contend that there are three bases for understanding how perceptions of fairness or justice can predict any number of valued outcomes. These bases include the previously discussed utilitarian framework, the basis for both the CMR and CSR perspectives, as well as the interpersonal and deontological approaches. In turn, each of these distinct perspectives for considering justice strongly influences how we view, as well as how we actually practice the relationally based, expert helper component of our job.

As with research, the most widely accepted and practiced approach to teaching (from the viewpoint of both student and professor alike) appears to be the utilitarian perspective. Highly consistent with the increased prevalence of the consumer metaphor in management education, I suggest that more and more of today's students are coming increasingly to view themselves as customers of their university. Thus they view themselves as purchasing a 'service' or commodity from a business that happens to be the university they attend (Gross & Hogler, 2004; Wright, 2005b). Under this reframed social contract, students are willing to pay their fees and attend (usually) class (Wright, 2005b). In return, the expectation is that they receive not just a passing grade, but in actual fact a good grade (preferably an 'A'). As a result, as many are well aware, grade inflation has reached epidemic proportions, with an 'A' increasingly often being the model grade

(Wright & Larwood, 1998). After all, since they paid market value for the service, one would be foolish not to demand the 'best' grade possible. As a consequence, the traditional mission of higher education to transfer knowledge to a new generation of students has been supplanted by an obsession on maximizing perceived, immediate individual gains (benefits) and minimizing immediate losses (costs).

In like fashion, I believe that more and more of today's academics have come to view their work as merely a Job (Pratt & Ashforth, 2003; Wrzesniewski, 2003). When work is considered as a Job, a professor focuses on the material benefits derived from working. In other words, being a professor simply provides the means necessary to a financial end: the paycheck. According to Wright and Cropanzano (2004), the fulfillment of personal happiness and contentment is sought during the time spent off the job. On the other hand, those with a Career orientation work for the rewards that accompany their advancement, whether it be organizational or professional in nature (Wrzesniewski, 2003; Wrzesniewski & Dutton, 2001). Professors with a Career orientation are driven by the strong desire to obtain power and prestige through the increased pay and promotional opportunities that becoming, say, a dean or university president brings.

Finally, professors with a Calling orientation do not work primarily for financial or promotional advancement opportunities. According to Wrzesniewski (2003), they primarily work for the fulfillment that doing their work affords. As noted by Wright and Cropanzano (2004), for these types of individuals, doing their work well is considered an end in and of itself. Considered together, academics with a Calling orientation should report a much more rewarding relation with the work itself, spend more time on teaching and research-related activities, and gain more enjoyment, fulfillment and satisfaction from these endeavors. Furthermore, those who look at their work as a Calling are more likely to report themselves as being more optimistic in their general outlook on life and are probably happier as well (see Wright, 2005a; Wright & Cropanzano, 2004). Whether we view our work as a Job, Career or Calling plays a significant role in how we perceive our students and participants in our research endeavors and, in like fashion, how they perceive us: the very core of the relational component to our work.

The second approach to a just or fair social exchange is an interpersonal one. The interpersonal approach emphasizes not only one's possible economic or instrumental benefits, but also the social nature of the relationships among stakeholders. Based upon the notion that issues of fairness or justice are among the most social of psychological processes, this stream of research treats these exchanges as types of relationships (Cropanzano et al., 2001). The interpersonal approach has been widely used in research on a number of organizational topics, including organizational citizenship behavior (Eisenberger et al., 2001), leadership (Mansour-Cole & Scott, 1998), organizational support (Wayne et al., 1997) and psychological contracts (Rousseau, 1995). This interpersonal orientation is likely to be manifested by those academics who have come to primarily view their work as a Career (see Wrzesniewski, 2003).

The final social exchange perspective is a moral or deontological principles approach, which focuses on the commitment to a set of ethical standards that are not solely predicated on only fulfilling one's vested self-interest, whether that is instrumental or interpersonal in nature. Strongly vested in the work of Kant (1964) and more modern justice proponents as Rawls (1971), the deontological approach suggests that individuals make 'fair' decisions through the application of universalistic standards (Cropanzano et al., 2001). While by no means rejecting the relevance of economic self-interest and interpersonal relations, Folger (2001) argues for the inclusion of a moral virtue or deontological consideration of what is fair or just. Thus from this perspective we make the results of our research available to each participant not only so we can benefit from collecting more data (utilitarian, Job-focused), or to continue and build upon a pleasant social exchange beneficial to our advancement (interpersonal, Career-focused), but because the participant has a right to know the results (moral, Calling-focused).

Similarly, we teach not only because we get paid for it (utilitarian, Job-focused), or because we enjoy engaging our students in intellectual exchanges and we see 'good' teaching as a way to advance our career (interpersonal, Career-focused), but because we truly believe that what we teach has relevance and will help our students discover what is ultimately important for understanding the meaning of life and their role in it (moral, Calling-focused). As should be evident, our earlier developmental work on the CPR approach was heavily influenced by moral or deontological principles (see Wright & Wright, 1999; Wright & Wright, 2002). In a nutshell, what distinguishes the deontological approach is the belief that people are fair and just, not only because it is in their best self-interest (either economically or interpersonally), but because it is the right thing to do (Folger, 1998). Naturally these varying justice perspectives affect how one views their role as expert helper.

CPR as helper
Wright and Wright (2002) noted that the key word regarding the relational component of our job is 'helper'. The idea of the helper is inexorably tied into the CPR framework for both our teacher and researcher roles. Along with discussing what constitutes the role of helper, it is important to note

also what helper does not encompass. For the most part, professors of organizational behavior and management are not medical doctors, licensed therapists or clinical psychiatrists. However as my introductory examples clearly demonstrate, the participants in our research endeavors, as well as our students, experience not only potentially life-threatening but also actual life-ending situations while undertaking their daily responsibilities.

Given the limitations to the scope of our professional expertise, it is unrealistic (and not legally prudent or morally acceptable) to believe that the typical management educator will be able to positively benefit each and every stakeholder – study participant and student alike – deemed at risk. For instance the woman who hung herself in her office told me just a day or two before her suicide that nothing of a stressful nature was bothering her and, as a result, she would not be able to fill out her coping question-naire for the research project (Wright & Wright, 2002: 175). Similarly, a good teacher cannot force students to learn, but by being dedicated, avail-able and truly interested in their betterment, we can certainly help in fos-tering the desire to learn in many of our students.

What the CPR perspective does propose is that organizational scholars act as critical observers, informational sources and referral agents for various stakeholders, especially those deemed to be at risk (Wright & Wright, 2002). Naturally, the level and depth of one's involvement regard-ing diagnosis and intervention will depend on a number of factors, includ-ing the nature of the risk behavior. For instance, regarding our role as researcher, conducting a study examining the relation of diastolic blood pressure to job stress involves a different dynamic from one considering employee retention rates, to one examining changes in an organization's performance appraisal system. Likewise we can and should challenge our students to examine why, for example, cheating is wrong and what it means to be kind to members of their organization. Alternatively, giving students advice on their marital or personal relationships is beyond the scope of the CPR approach and must be avoided.

Inherent in the CPR approach is the core value or belief that organiza-tional scholars have a sacred compact with all groups or stakeholders affected by either our research or our teaching. The opportunity we have been given to explore various aspects of the human experience brings with it the responsibility to help better and positively affect the human condition (see Boal & Peery, 1985; Brief & Cortina, 2000; Rosenthal & Rosnow, 1991). As a first step, as my father and I have previously noted (Wright & Wright, 1999; Wright & Wright, 2002), and similar to Selznick's (2000) viewpoint, I believe that we have a moral mandate (see Skitka, 2000) to expand our focus and actively consider the consequences of our efforts on all affected constituent groups and stakeholders. As teachers, we have an obligation to challenge our students to be able to think critically and reason for themselves, while being conscious not to influence them unduly regarding how to think about specific situational topics. We have similar obligations as researchers. To help in further demonstrating what the CPR approach might involve, consider the following research example from Wright and Sweeney (1990).

CPR example
Using a sample of seasoned employees from the highly stressful correctional field, Wright and Sweeney proposed that individuals experiencing higher diastolic blood pressure were more likely to cope using strategies characterized by wishful thinking, avoidance and minimization of threat, than were individuals exhibiting lower blood pressure. In addition, age, gender and whether the employee smoked were added to the model as control variables. The results were very supportive of the proposed relationships among diastolic blood pressure and the coping strategies. In particular, the three coping strategies explained a robust 27 percent of the change in diastolic blood pressure. Considered together, the entire model explained a whopping 35 percent of the variance in diastolic blood pressure.

According to the CPR perspective, and emphasizing the importance of the relational approach, each study participant was given a written summary of the results. Participants deemed to be at risk for high blood pressure were also advised to see their personal physician. In addition, follow-up procedures were incorporated to determine if the at-risk participants did in fact consult with their physicians or licensed professionals. A number of participants heeded the warnings that they were at risk and sought professional help. Unfortunately not every participant so advised took the advice. The individual who literally crashed his car into his office building was one who failed to heed the advice. This research participant consistently suffered from dangerously high diastolic blood pressure readings obtained at the job site (in the 120–130 range). He was also overweight and was a junk food junkie. He was repeatedly warned both by my medical assistant, a highly competent licensed RN, and myself, that he should seek immediate medical attention. Unfortunately he failed to heed these repeated warnings. As a result, within a relatively short time after the conclusion of the research project, the individual suffered his fatal heart attack, leaving behind a devastated wife, children, friends and co-workers.

I propose this as a prime example of how the CPR perspective, highly consistent with the action research format, shares a stated goal for demonstrating compassion, empathy and humanitarian concern toward the stakeholders of our research. Consistent with the theoretical framework for the multiple stakeholder approach (Donaldson & Preston, 1995; R.E. Freeman,

1984; Zammuto, 1984), all potential stakeholders or constituents are treated as 'granting agencies' from the CPR approach. Considered as granting agencies, each valued contribution of time, attention and cooperation of each stakeholder is acknowledged and rewarded in a just and equitable manner (Boal & Peery, 1985; Rosnow, 1997: 352; Wright & Wright, 2002). Not merely considered as a statistic, as in an American suffers a heart attack about every 20 seconds (Lee, 1998), my medical assistant and I were deeply concerned about the health of the heart attack victim because he was a human being, not merely a subject in my research endeavor. Unfortunately, to date, the CPR approach does not appear to have gained widespread acceptance and implementation in either the study or the teaching of organizational behaviors. As a very telling case in point, consider the Academy of Management's (AOM's) ethical credo as it pertains to the participants of our research endeavors.

The AOM's (1997) ethical credo, along with the ethical guidelines of the American Psychological Association (1992), requires informed consent from research participants, third-party review, ethical resolution of issues involving confidentiality and anonymity, and the minimization of deception. Interestingly these requirements all refer to either start-up issues before the project is undertaken, or to issues pertaining to the process of data collection (Wright & Wright, 1999; Wright & Wright, 2002). The credo devotes only the following sentence to the after-phase: 'To the extent that concealment or deception is necessary, the researcher must provide a full and accurate explanation to participants at the conclusion of the study, including counseling, if appropriate' (AOM, 1997: 1471).[3] One can reasonably conclude from the AOM ethics credo that if deception was not a part of the research design, then the ethical responsibility of the researcher to the study participants is fulfilled once the data are collected.

In contrast, researcher responsibility is not fulfilled once the data are obtained according to the CPR approach. As the example above well illustrates, researcher responsibility to participants extends beyond the data collection stage. Especially so if, as noted by Wright and Wright (1999: 1108), the primary stated goal of applied or organizational research is to provide improved theories of human behavior, theories designed to enhance the human condition. However even if one agrees with this stated research goal to enhance the human condition (Wright & Wright, 2002), the actual mechanism or means to enhanced theories of human behavior or development have long been subject to much debate (Davis, 1971).

Stanley Milgram and the CPR approach
The dynamics surrounding this debate are clearly evident when one examines Milgram's (1965) classic (and highly controversial) study on obedience.

Born to Eastern European Jews in the Bronx during the Great Depression, Stanley Milgram was understandably highly troubled by the reasons given by Nazi war criminals at the Nuremberg trials. Countless times, in answer to the question regarding why they were willing to inflict great mental and physical harm on millions of people, many of these criminals used as their sole defense that they were just following orders. To many Americans in the post-World War II era, Milgram included, one of the great unanswered philosophical questions was, could behavior such as this happen in America? (For a further discussion, see Adorno et al., 1950.) In his famous (some would claim infamous) experiments, Milgram (1963) provided the chilling answer that it probably could happen almost anywhere.

Providing a rigor not typically seen in social science research, Milgram began recruiting potential participants for his work with a display ad in the 18 June 1961 issue of the *New Haven Register* (Blass, 2004). Potential participants were told that they would be involved in a study on memory, and would be paid a total of $4.50 (50 cents of that amount was for transportation), a very reasonable sum for participating in a 1961-era experiment. Collectively, Milgram's research provided a very distressing view of human behavior. One can infer from Milgram's experiments that many Americans would be willing to blindly obey authority, even when their actions would lead to potentially painful and harmful consequences for others (Blass, 2004; Wright & Wright, 1999).

Of particular relevance to our discussion is the fact that a number of participants experienced a great deal of stress during and after participation in the experiment (Wright & Wright, 1999). Of course, experiments causing much stress to participants were not idiosyncratic only to Milgram. Zimbardo and his colleagues' simulated prison study using Stanford undergraduates (Haney et al., 1973) and Humphrey's (1970) investigation of illicit sexual behavior in public places – the 'tearoom trade' – are two rather notorious examples. Medical science endeavors have not been immune to legitimate criticism either, as witness the Tuskegee syphilis experiments in which southern, black males were not told they had syphilis and provided with adequate treatment. The reason for this shameful lack of treatment was that this provided medical researchers with the opportunity to study how the disease would progress if left unattended (Ho, 1997; Jones, 1981).

Baumrind (1964: 421) succinctly identified the core ethical dilemma common to researchers interested in organizational behaviors: researchers are continuously striving to 'balance [their] career and scientific interests against the interests of [their] prospective subjects'. In contrast, Milgram (1964) was confident that he had followed the 'right course' of action, proposing that the ultimate worth of a research endeavor rests not with issues of ethics or morality but with the level of intellectual contribution of the study (Milgram, 1965, 1977). In other words, for Milgram, the end justifies the means. Certainly providing support to Milgram's contention, as I noted earlier, the AOM credo is quite clear (and very brief) that if deception is not part of the study, the ethical responsibility of the researcher is fulfilled once the data are collected. Unfortunately, in agreement with a number of scholars, I suggest that this 'moral minimum' focus on minimizing harm neglects to examine adequately what is right or beneficial (Boal & Peery, 1985; Keeley, 1984; Simon et al., 1979). As a result, this focus on only a moral minimum fails to consider that research participants can and do experience a wide variety of life events, both good and bad, over the course of the design and implementation of a research study. As a counterpoint case to Milgram's apparent majority viewpoint, consider the Wright and Wright (2002: 176–7) example involving a study participant's self-inflicted gunshot suicide.

The AOM, CPR and suicide
Shortly before his tragic death, the individual in question, a bright, well-educated professional man, approximately 40 years old, was a participant in a research project of mine on job burnout. Employee burnout is widely studied, as it has been associated with a number of quality of work life and optimal organizational functioning issues (for reviews see Cherniss, 1993; Cordes & Dougherty, 1993; Kahill, 1988; Maslach, 1982; Wright & Cropanzano, 1998). The primary job burnout measure used in my research was Maslach and Jackson's (1986) Emotional Exhaustion Scale, one of their three dimensions of burnout. The scale measures how often one feels emotionally overextended and exhausted by one's work (anchored from 0 = never to 6 = every day). To emphasize the extent to which he was feeling emotionally exhausted, the participant added a 'how often' classification of 10, which he behaviorally anchored with an 'expletive deleted' phrase.

His responses were disturbingly similar on a second research instrument, the Positive and Negative Affectivity Scale (PANAS) developed by Watson and his colleagues (Watson, 1988; Watson et al., 1988). The PANAS is designed to measure both positive ('active, alert, enthusiastic, inspired, and interested') and negative ('afraid, hostile, irritable, jittery, and upset') affective descriptors. In this research application of the PANAS, the participants were asked to indicate the extent to which they experienced each descriptor of affect in general on a five-point scale ranging from 1 (very slightly or not at all) to 5 (extremely). This participant noted that he was 'dead!' alert as well as being 'extremely, extremely . . . angry'. Furthermore, in the margin of the questionnaire, he noted the need for various individual(s) to be killed (no specific names used). Finally, he used 'blood-red' pen ink to further emphasize his feelings. Tragedy struck within merely a matter of a few days after he completed this questionnaire. As noted by Wright and Wright (2002: 177), his suicide note focused on his great anger and despair. After learning of his suicide, I immediately pulled his question-naire and discovered his 'creative' work on recalibrating the items. Although he never formally threatened anyone at work, a number of co-workers noted his manifest anger and indicated what they thought was the real potential for him to 'go postal' either on or off the job. The mood of his department was quite somber for weeks after his death, with several co-workers commenting to me that they were having problems focusing on their job and family duties.

This death was disturbing for any number of reasons. More than once, I have ruminated what I might have been able to do 'if only I had discovered the writing on his questionnaire before he committed suicide'. However, based on the ethical credo of the AOM, my ethical responsibilities were fulfilled once the data were collected, as long as deception was not part of the study. Deception was not a part of the study. In fact all participants in this particular study were asked to participate by means of a direct contact procedure in which the study parameters were laid out in a simple and straightforward manner. According to the AOM credo, and consistent with the CMR and CSR values perspectives, my responsibility as a researcher was fulfilled once the data were collected. Furthermore the AOM's philos-ophy regarding participant rights is both consistent with Milgram's (1964) means-to-an-end philosophy and fully congruent with the utilitarian values perspective typically taught in our business schools (Wright & Wright, 2000). Similar to Milgram's (1977) belief that the end justifies the means in the pursuit of knowledge, utilitarianism focuses only on the anticipated consequences of the particular action, with the predominant emphasis on either organizational-based (from a CMR approach) or researcher-based (from a CSR approach) measures of efficiency (Wright & Wright, 2002). The possible relational benefits of the CPR approach are made further evident when one considers another typically neglected stakeholder group, the students we teach.

The CPR approach and our students
A number of scholars and laypersons have noted the fact that confidence levels in our largest multinational organizations are at an all-time low (Eisenberg, 2002; Wright, 2004). For example Andersen, BALCO, Dynergy, Enron, Global Crossing, Martha Stewart, Merck, Tyco and Worldcom, to name just a prominent few, are all very conspicuous, high-profile examples of an apparent public trust gone bad. In fact many see these dishonest and fraudulent 'cooking the books' actions as threatening not only the financial

well-being of our workforce, but also our societal moral fiber (Callahan, 2004; Fleming, 2004; Sobieraj, 2002; Wright, 2004).

Although the specifics may differ somewhat from case to case, they all have one thing in common. These violations of trust, apparently involving a total absence of such highly valued virtues as honesty and integrity, were all committed by real people, in many instances by the people we call friends, relatives, neighbors, classmates or even our students (Wright, 2005b). The fact that many of these unethical and illegal corporate actions are being committed by the very business students that we teach is a chilling and depressing thought. Asking publicly what, no doubt, many of us have asked ourselves privately at some time, Beatty (2004: 187) wrestled with, 'how we as professors may have contributed to it' (that is, the apparent increase in fraudulent corporate behavior).

Certainly, this is a question that needs to be discussed publicly. If left unattended, the cynic in us is wont to say that, sure, this apparent increase in fraudulent behavior is just one more manifestation of good losing out to bad. Without a doubt, cynicism appears to be a dominant way of perceiving life for many as we enter the twenty-first century (Dean et al., 1998; Reichers et al., 1997). I have previously noted that many students are quite candid in expressing almost a disdain for the supposed benefits of virtuous behavior as traditionally defined. As a vivid case in point, in Wright (2004), I reported a typical class discussion in one of my senior-level management classes in which all students present (N = 30) agreed that it solely depends on 'the situation' whether a person should lie or cheat. This troubling finding is highly consistent with a number of similar observations from previous classes of mine, and those of a number of colleagues. Before discussing possible CPR-friendly solutions to the problem of student cheating and our possible role in it as professors, it is worthwhile to examine briefly what the act of cheating encompasses, and to consider the scope of the problem.

Scope of student cheating behavior
However defined, academic dishonesty has long been recognized as a problem in education and research (Kibler, 1994; Maramark & Maline, 1993; Noah & Eckstein, 2001).[4] A major reason offered by many for why academic dishonesty is a serious concern is that it demonstrates a lack of personal integrity (Johnston, 1996; Wright, 2004). According to Pavela (1978: 72), cheating is 'intentionally using or attempting to use unauthorized material, information, or study aids in any academic exercise'. Without question, there is widespread evidence clearly demonstrating that more and more students appear to be engaging in cheating and other academically dishonest behaviors (Whitley & Keith-Spiegel, 2001; Wright, 2004). For instance in

research conducted around the start of World War II, Drake (1941) established a baseline of approximately 25 percent for student admitted cheating behavior. More recent studies consistently place the figures much, much higher, in some cases approaching 90 percent (cf., Noah & Eckstein, 2001; Whitley & Keith-Spiegel, 2001). As noted by a number of investigators, these figures appear to be consistent across any number of demographic and cultural variables. In fact, considered together, neither student age, marital status, level of financial independence, living arrangements, year in school, gender and country of origin appears to be related to propensity to cheat, although it does appear that business and economics students admit to cheating more frequently than other majors (see Baird, 1980; Brown, 1995; Meade, 1992; Moffatt, 1990; Wright, 2004).

Moffatt (1990) found that 87 percent of business majors reported engaging in unethical practices compared to 63 percent of humanities majors. Of further concern, this widespread increase in student cheating is being demonstrated in any number of ingenious ways by how-to-cheat books such as *The Cheater's Handbook* (Corbett, 1999) and the increase of such internet sites as www.cheathouse.com and www.schoolsucks.com. Wright (2004) sadly noted that these sites provide a virtual smorgasbord for huge numbers of term papers and examinations for students interested in cheating (for example Hickman, 1998; McCollum, 1996; Whitley & Keith-Spiegel, 2001). Unfortunately these figures mirror those reported to me by my students, with roughly 88 percent of junior- and senior-level undergraduate management major students sampled admitting to me that they cheat. Most disturbing, the model response for how often they cheat is 100+ times (Wright, 2005b). What many people in general, and college professors in particular, fail to realize is that student cheating has a number of serious consequences, both short- and long-term in nature (Callahan, 2004).

Students who engage in cheating behavior in grade school, high school and college not only frequently later cheat in graduate and professional school, but they also appear more likely to engage in unethical business practices (for example Baldwin et al., 1996; Sims, 1993; Whitley & Keith-Spiegel, 2001). Dalrymple (2004) reported that the number of Americans willing to cheat 'a little here and there' on their taxes has recently increased 50 percent. Additionally, academic dishonesty has been linked to such dysfunctional behaviors as petty theft and lying to friends and family (Blankenship & Whitley, 2000). In short, substantial evidence exists that students who cheat in college are also more likely to cheat in other aspects of their lives (Whitley & Keith-Spiegel, 2001). Alternatively, research also indicates that ethically acting undergraduates are less likely to engage in unethical behavior in the workplace (McCabe et al., 1996). Is it any wonder that we are facing a worldwide moral crisis at the corporate level? For whatever reason – cynicism, lack of integrity, too many temptations, lack of positive role models – a disturbingly high number of our students are reframing the social contract as it has been traditionally understood (Wright, 2005b). A recent personal example provides strong support for the potential benefit of adopting a deontologically-based CPR framework in the classroom.

Over the years, similar to many of my management colleagues, I have had all too numerous encounters with student cheating. As one of my earlier personal examples involving the female cheater personifies, a number of students are becoming increasingly bold in their willingness to both cheat and deny responsibility for their actions. The second cheating example was quite different from the first, as I will briefly describe. In this example, the student turned himself in to me after he had successfully cheated (that is, he was not caught) on the class final exam (for a further, more detailed discussion of this experience, see Wright, 2004). As is typical in many cases, the student cheated because he was not confident in his ability to perform on the final exam. While he knew that cheating was wrong (the deontological or moral approach), these doubts as to his ability ultimately led him to cheat. However, after the exam, he experienced another, different kind of doubt. He had a very difficult time emotionally after leaving the test. In fact, he reported to me that he was an 'emotional wreck'. Because of tightness in his chest, he had trouble eating later that day and even the next morning. His self-doubt was the result of his failure to do what, according to him, he knew to be the right thing: that is, not to cheat on the exam.

In addition, and consistent with the second or interpersonal approach to justice, the student considered me to be a positive role model (see Bandura, 1977). As a result, he did not want to disappoint and embarrass me. In the end, the student's moral mandate (Skitka, 2000) to do the right thing (the moral or deontological approach), coupled with his view of me a positive role model, led him to turn himself in to me. Similarly, this example is consistent with the findings from an increasing number of studies, taken from a number of research venues, providing increasing empirical support that people will often forsake self-interest and do the moral, right thing. For example Kahneman et al. (1986) and Turillo et al. (2002) demonstrated that people will forego economic gain in order to correct for past injustice. Consistent with the framework of the CPR approach, I offer Bandura's (1977, 1991, 1997) work on social modeling and learning to help in addressing such classroom-related problems as student cheating.

CPR and social learning theory
Early work by Bandura and his colleagues (Bandura, 1977; Bandura & Walters, 1963) provides consistent testimony to the important role of social

learning or modeling in human behavior. In a fascinating line of research, Bandura and Walters (1963) found that boys from intact, well-to-do homes modeled the hostile, aggressive attitudes of their parents. Later research extended the scope of social learning by demonstrating that learning could occur in the absence of immediate reinforcement (Bandura et al., 1963), leading Bandura (1977) to conclude that social modeling was a potentially powerful learning tool. Unfortunately it appears that positive social modeling is still an underdeveloped learning tool in secondary and higher education. Alas, my conversations with a number of students over the years confirm that too many suffer from a lack of positive role models (Wright, 2005b). Combining the CPR, moral justice and Bandura's human agentic approach to social learning theory, I propose several techniques for use by organizational scholars interested in fostering a more relational-based, collective approach to the meaning of their work.

Suggestions for research
Regarding our role as researchers, consider the following suggestions by Wright and Hobfoll (2004). Consistent with the CPR approach, I formally discuss research requirements with each prospective research study participant by means of a direct contact procedure. Each participant is treated as a research 'stakeholder' whose contributions of time and cooperation are highly valued and rewarded with respect (for example Donaldson & Preston, 1995; Rosnow, 1997). More specifically, at the conclusion of a study each participant is offered a written summary of the findings. Based upon these findings, participants deemed 'at-risk' are made aware of the problem and offered the opportunity to discuss potential solutions to the possible problem with me. In the Wright and Hobfoll (2004) study, this involved the topic of job burnout. As Wright and Hobfoll reported, a number of participants used the knowledge that they were 'burnout-at-risk' to investigate alternative employment opportunities. In particular, one participant told me that his job had become increasingly more stressful and the results of this study further convinced him that his overall health was being adversely affected. After weighing his options, he found another job in another state better suited to his interests, skills and abilities. Approximately one year after his move, he got in touch with me to tell me that he had indeed made the correct choice.

As was pointed out to me at a recent academic presentation by one of the members of the audience, 'Hey, Wright, this is all well and good, but this will involve a lot more work on the researcher's part.' I agreed with the individual that this approach does involves more work, but also noted that besides the obvious benefit of helping another individual, there are some additional benefits of a more utilitarian nature as well. For one thing, the participant response rate is much larger than typically obtained in research using a direct contact procedure. Wright and Hobfoll (2004) reported a participation rate of 67 percent. I have obtained participation rates as high as 91 percent in other research studies incorporating a CPR approach (for typical examples, see Wright & Cropanzano, 1998 and Wright & Cropanzano, 2000). Response rates that high make generalizing to the sample population much less problematic: the sample is the population.

In comparison, the two most common data collection methods involve the use of data banks and online experiments (Azar, 2000). Wright and Wright (2002) noted that the use of secondary data from a data bank all but guarantees that there will be minimal contact between the organizational researchers and study participants. After all, it is hard to establish any kind of positive relationship with someone that you never meet. Likewise, the use of online data collection methodologies, while fast and easy, has a number of problems for researchers interested in truly making a difference. For example how does an online researcher adequately monitor the degree to which their subjects become distressed or agitated as a result of participating in various forms of online research? As noted by Wright and Wright (2002: 181), at best, participants in online research endeavors are relegated to a reduced or minimal stakeholder role. At worst, it appears that they are no longer even considered as viable stakeholders. Taken together, these methods of conducting applied research do nothing to champion the interests of the research participants. Merging insights taken from Bandura's agentic approach to social learning and the CPR approach, I next discuss some possible steps that we can take in our classrooms to help stem the epidemic of student cheating.

Suggestions for teaching

Paradoxically, while professors overwhelmingly report that they consider cheating as very stressful (Keith-Spiegel et al., 1998), many are far from proactive in their approach to dealing with cheating behavior in their classes (Whitley & Keith-Spiegel, 2001; Wright, 2005b). In fact, far from being a positive role model (see Bandura, 1977), many do not formally address the topic in class, creating an 'If we don't talk about it, it doesn't exist' mentality. As I reported elsewhere (Wright, 2005b), almost 50 percent of the full-time faculty in my managerial sciences department made no reference to academic dishonesty in their Fall 2004 syllabi. In addition, a number of students have repeatedly told me that cheating is rarely, if ever, discussed in their classes. The first step must be to make all parties concerned both acutely aware of, and willing to take the initiative to change the problem of cheating.

As an initial step, an awareness of the evils of cheating must be fully comprehended by the students themselves. Emphasizing the relational component inherent in our role of professor, I have undertaken several methods to accomplish this in my classes (Wright, 2005b). First, I provide specific definitions of cheating in the class syllabus (roughly 75 percent of my department colleagues currently fail to provide specific definitions of cheating, a figure which from anecdotal evidence appears to be consistent with the percentages found at many departments of management across the country). Second, on the first day of class (and throughout the semester where appropriate), I engage the class in a discussion of what constitutes cheating and other forms of academic dishonesty. I note that I consider cheating to be wrong. Equally important, I then ask students if they agree with me that cheating is wrong. Interestingly, and consistent with the moral or deontological perspective, the vast majority will acknowledge that cheating is wrong, at least in the abstract. Therein lies our hope (Wright, 2005b).

I then ask why they believe that cheating is inappropriate. Once there is a class consensus that cheating is wrong, I briefly introduce the notion of character strengths and virtues (Park & Peterson, 2003; Peterson & Seligman, 2004), emphasizing that various forms of academic dishonesty, including cheating, are of serious concern because they demonstrate a lack of personal integrity (Johnston, 1996). Finally, using the framework of the interpersonal basis for justice, I engage the class in a discussion that if cheating is wrong, what should be the negative consequences, and why, for those who cheat. Each class has always concluded that punishment is in order for those caught cheating. Incorporating aspects of the psychological contract (Rousseau, 1995), all students are then asked to sign and turn in to me a signed 'psychological contract agreement' (which includes the pitfalls of academic dishonesty) stating that, 'By my signature, I confirm that I have read, understand and agree to abide by the terms and conditions of our class agreement.' When each student has turned in their signed agreement (required by the second week of class), I make this consensus agreement public to the class, further building student commitment to the actual terms of the class contract (Salancik, 1977).

In addition, once the class is under way, there are a number of other ways for faculty to further demonstrate positive model behavior. Wright (2004) noted that students consider the apparent reluctance of professors to proactively address instances of academic dishonesty as a form of professor ethical misconduct. One student outside the classroom setting told me that he felt this reluctance demonstrates a lack of courage, which coincidentally is listed by Peterson and Seligman (2004) as one of the six universal virtues (the others being wisdom and knowledge, humanity, justice, temperance and transcendence). Obviously this failure to tackle the tough issues, like student cheating, does not signal to students that the professor wants and is able to be a positive role model.

Concluding thoughts

I think most would agree that as organizational scholars, we have a moral obligation to treat all our stakeholders fairly and with respect (for example Keith-Spiegel et al., 1993; Wright, 2004; Wrzesniewski, 2003). In addition, and highly consistent with the CPR approach, the health and ethical betterment of all our stakeholders should be an integral part of the meaning of our work, whether that be consulting, conducting research or teaching our students (for example Dalton, 1985; Kibler, 1993; Wright, 2004).

The interested reader will note that the CPR approach is designed for us not only to be viewed as positive role models, but also to encourage our stakeholders to become more proactive and self-regulatory in monitoring their own behavior. By emphasizing this mutually beneficial relationship, the CPR approach is attempting to help interested stakeholders develop an agentic motivational perspective (Bandura, 1991). The basic premise of this agentic approach is that stakeholders come to view themselves as self-regulatory and self-reflective organisms, not just passive beings reacting to influences from various aspects of their work and life environments. In the true sense of the word, the CPR approach is a collective one. As I have stated elsewhere (Wright, 2004; Wright, 2005b), the overarching mission of the CPR approach is to afford us the opportunity to, in a small way, make a contribution to the betterment of others (including ourselves). I think Mencius would agree.

Notes

1. The sections on the CMR and CSR perspectives are based upon earlier discussions by the author; see especially Wright & Wright (2002).
2. As with the CMR and CSR approaches, the section on the CPR approach draws upon earlier discussions by the author; see especially Wright & Wright (1999) and Wright & Wright (2002).
3. Over the last few years, nothing has apparently changed for the AOM. In particular, exactly the same minimal consideration to the needs of participants at the conclusion of a study is all that is given on the AOM's website as of 21 January 2005.
4. A further discussion of the issue of academic dishonesty and cheating can be found in Wright (2004) and Wright (2005b).

References

Academy of Management (AOM) (1997), Academy of Management code of ethical conduct, *Academy of Management Journal*, **40**, 1469–74.
Adorno, T.W., Frenkel-Brunswik, E., Levinson, D.J. & Sanford, R.N. (1950), *The Authoritarian Personality*, New York: Harper.
American Psychological Association (1992), Ethical principles of psychologists and code of conduct, *American Psychologist*, **47**, 1597–611.
Azar, B. (2000), Online experiments: ethically fair or foul?, *APA Monitor*, April, 50–51.
Baird, J.S. (1980), Current trends in college teaching, *Psychology in the Schools*, **17**, 515–22.
Baldwin, D.C. Jr., Daugherty, S.R., Rowley, B.D. & Schwartz, M.R. (1996), Cheating in medical school: a survey of second-year students at 31 schools, *Academic Medicine*, **71**, 267–73.

Bandura, A. (1977), *Social Learning Theory*, Englewood Cliffs, NJ: Prentice Hall.
Bandura, A. (1991), Social cognitive theory of self-regulation, *Organizational Behavior and Human Decision Processes*, **50**, 248–87.
Bandura, A. (1997), *Self-efficacy: The Exercise of Control*, New York: W.H. Freeman.
Bandura, A., Ross, D. & Ross, S.A. (1963), A comparative test of the status envy, social power, and secondary reinforcement theories of identificatory learning, *Journal of Abnormal and Social Psychology*, **67**, 527–34.
Bandura, A. & Walters, R.H. (1963), *Social Learning and Personality Development*, New York: Holt.
Baritz, L. (1960), *The Servants of Power: A History of the Use of Social Science in American Industry*, New York: John Wiley.
Baumrind, D. (1964), Some thoughts on ethics of research: after reading Milgram's 'behavioral study on obedience', *American Psychologist*, **19**, 421–3.
Beatty, J.E. (2004), Grades as money and the role of the market metaphor in management education, *Academy of Management Learning and Education*, **3**, 187–96.
Beyer, J.M. (1997), Building on past strengths with incremental change, *Academy of Management*, **40**, 1436–42.
Blankenship, K.L. & Whitley, B.E. Jr. (2000), Relation of general deviance to academic dishonesty, *Ethics and Behavior*, **10**, 1–12.
Blass, T. (2004), *The Man who Shocked the World: The Life and Legacy of Stanley Milgram*, New York: Basic Books.
Boal, K.B. & Peery, N. (1985), The cognitive structure of corporate social responsibility, *Journal of Management*, **11**, 71–82.
Brief, A.P. (2000), Still servants of power, *Journal of Management Inquiry*, **9**, 342–51.
Brief, A.P. & Cortina, J. (2000), Research ethics: a place to begin, *Academy of Management: Research Methods Division Newsletter*, **15**, 1, 4, 11, 12.
Brown, B.S. (1995), The academic ethics of graduate business students: a survey, *Journal of Education for Business*, **70**, 151–6.
Callahan, D. (2004), *The Cheating Culture*, Orlando, FL: Harcourt.
Cherniss, C. (1993), The role of professional self-efficacy in the etiology and amelioration of burnout, in Schaufeli, W.B., Maslach, C. & Marek, T. (eds), *Professional Burnout: Recent Developments in Theory and Research*, Washington, DC: Taylor & Francis, pp. 135–49.
Coghlan, D.D. (1994), Research as a process of change: action science in organizations, *Irish Business and Administrative Research*, **15**, 119–30.
Corbett, B. (1999), *The Cheater's Handbook*, New York: Regan Books.
Cordes, C.L. & Dougherty, T.W. (1993), A review and integration of research on job burnout, *Academy of Management Review*, **18**, 621–6.
Covey, S.R. (1999), Why character counts, *Readers Digest*, pp. 132–5.
Cropanzano, R., Goldman, B. & Folger, R. (2003), Deontic justice: the role of moral principles in workplace justice, *Journal of Organizational Behavior*, **24**, 1019–24.
Cropanzano, R. & Prehar, C. (2001), Emerging justice concerns in an era of changing psychological contracts, in Cropanzano, R. (ed.), *Justice in the Workplace*, Vol. 2, *From Theory to Practice*, Mahweh, NJ: Erlbaum, pp. 245–69.
Cropanzano, R., Rupp, D.E., Mohler, C.J. & Schminke, M. (2001), Three roads to organizational justice, in Ferris, G.R. (ed.), *Research in Personnel and Human Resources Management*, Vol. 20, Kidlington, Oxford: Elsevier Science, pp. 1–113.
Cyert, R.M. & March, J.G. (1963), *A Behavioral Theory of the Firm*, Englewood Cliffs, NJ: Prentice Hall.
Dalrymple, M. (2004), More taxpayers say its OK to cheat, *San Francisco Chronicle*, B1, 31 October.
Dalton, J.C. (ed.), (1985), *Promoting Valued Development in College Students*, Washington, DC: National Association of Student Personnel Administrators.
Davis, M.S. (1971), That's interesting! *Philosophy of Science*, **1**, 309–44.
Dean, J., Brandes, P. & Dharwadker, R. (1998), Organizational cynicism, *Academy of Management Review*, **23**, 341–52.

Donaldson, T. & Preston, L.E. (1995), The stakeholder theory of the corporation: concepts, evidence, and implications, *Academy of Management Review*, **20**, 65–91.

Drake, C.A. (1941), Why students cheat, *Journal of Higher Education*, **12**, 418–20.

Eisenberg, D. (2002), Corporate greed, *Time*, 17 June, **159**, 47–9.

Eisenberger, R., Armeli, S., Rexwinkel, B., Lynch, P. & Rhoades, L. (2001), Reciprocation of perceived organizational support, *Journal of Applied Psychology*, **86**, 42–51.

Elsbach, K.D. (1999), Six stories of researcher experience in organizational studies: personal and professional insights, in Moch, S.D. & Gates, M.F. (eds), *The Researcher Experience in Qualitative Research*, Thousand Oaks, CA: Sage, pp. 54–74.

Ferris, W.P. (2002), Students as junior partners, professors as senior partners, the B-school as the firm: a new model of collegiate business education, *Academy of Management Learning and Education*, **1**, 185–93.

Fleming, J.E. (2004), The need for ethics in business, *Academy of Management News*, **35** (2), 5.

Folger, R. (1998), Fairness as a moral virtue, in Schminke, M. (ed.), *Managerial Ethics: Moral Management of People and Processes*, Mahweh, NJ: Erlbaum, pp. 13–34.

Folger, R. (2001), Fairness as deonance, in Gilliland, S.W., Steiner, D.D. & Skarlicki, D.P. (eds), *Research in Social Issues in Management*, New York: Information Age Publishers, 1: 3–33.

Freeman, J. (1986), Data quality and the development of organizational science: an editorial essay, *Administrative Science Quarterly*, **31**, 298–303.

Freeman, R.E. (1984), *Strategic Management: A Stakeholder Approach*, Boston, MA: Pitman.

Friedman, M. (1968), The role of monetary policy, *American Economic Review*, **58**, 1–17.

Friedman, M. (1970), A Friedman doctrine: the social responsibility of business is to increase its profits, *New York Times Magazine*, 13 September, 32.

Frost, P.J. (1999), Why compassion counts! *Journal of Management Inquiry*, **8**, 127–33.

Gross, M.A. & Hogler, R. (2005), What the shadow knows: exploring the hidden dimensions of the consumer metaphor in management education, *Journal of Management Education*, **29**, 3–16.

Haney, C., Banks, W.C. & Zimbardo, P.G. (1973), Interpersonal dynamics in a simulated prison, *International Journal of Criminology and Penology*, **1**, 69–97.

Hickman, J.N. (1998), Cybercheats, *The New Republic*, 23 March, **218**, 14–15.

Ho, D.D. (1997), It's AIDS, not Tuskegee: inflammatory comparisons won't save Africa, *TIME Magazine*, 29 September, 83.

Humphreys, L. (1970), *Tearoom Trade: Impersonal Sex in Public Places*, Chicago, IL: Aldine.

Johnston, D.K. (1996), Cheating: limits of individual integrity, *Journal of Moral Education*, **25**, 159–71.

Jones, J.J. (1981), *Bad Blood: The Tuskegee Syphilis Experiment*, New York: Free Press.

Kahill, S. (1988), Symptoms of professional burnout: a review of the empirical evidence, *Canadian Psychology*, **29**, 284–97.

Kahneman, D., Knetsch, J.L. & Thaler, R.H. (1986), Fairness and the assumptions of economics, *Journal of Business*, **59**, S285–S300.

Kant, I. (1964), *Groundwork of the Metaphysics of Morals*, trans. H.J. Paton, New York: Harper & Row.

Keeley, M. (1984), Impartiality and participant-interest theories of organizational effectiveness, *Administrative Science Quarterly*, **29**, 1–25.

Keith-Spiegel, P., Tabachnick, B.G., Whitley, B.E. Jr. & Washburn, J. (1998), Opinions of a national sample of psychology instructors, *Ethics and Behavior*, **8**, 215–27.

Keith-Spiegel, P., Wittig, A.F., Perkins, D.V., Balogh, D.W. & Whitley, B.E. Jr. (1993), *The Ethics of Teaching: A Casebook*, Muncie, IN: Ball State University Press.

Kernan, M.C. & Lord, R.G. (1990), Effects of valence, expectancies, and goal-performance discrepancies in single and multiple goal environments, *Journal of Applied Psychology*, **75**, 194–203.

Kibler, W.L. (1993), Academic dishonesty: a student development dilemma, *NASPA Journal*, **30**, 252–67.

Kibler, W.L. (1994), Addressing academic dishonesty: what are institutions of higher education doing and not doing?, *NASPA Journal*, **31**, 92–101.

Kunkel, S.W. (2002), Consultant learning: a model for student-directed learning in management education, *Journal of Management Education*, **26**, 121–38.

Lee, T. (1988), *Understanding Heart Attacks*, Boston, MA: Harvard Medical School Health Publications.

Lewin, K. (1948), Action research and minority problems, in Lewin, G.W. (ed.), *Resolving Social Conflicts: Selected Papers on Group Dynamics*, New York: Harper & Brothers, pp. 201–16.

Luthans, F. & Kreitner, R. (1985), *Organizational Behavior Modification and Beyond*, Glenview, IL: Scott, Foresman.

Mansour-Cole, D.M. & Scott, S.G. (1998), Hearing it through the grapevine: the influence of source, leader–member relations, and legitimacy on survivors' fairness perceptions, *Personnel Psychology*, **51**, 25–54.

Maramark, S. & Maline, M.M. (1993), *Academic Dishonesty among College Students*, Washington, DC: US Department of Education. (ERIC Document Reproduction Service No. ED 360 903).

March, J.G. & Simon, H.A. (1958), *Organizations*, New York: John Wiley.

Maslach, C. (1982), *Burnout: The Cost of Caring*, Englewood Cliffs, NJ: Prentice Hall.

Maslach, C. & Jackson, S.E. (1986), *Maslach Burnout Inventory*, 2nd edn, Palo Alto, CA: Consulting Psychologists Press.

McCabe, D.L., Trevino, L.K. & Butterfield, K.D. (1996), The influence of collegiate and corporate codes of conduct on ethics-related behavior in the workplace, *Business Ethics Quarterly*, **6**, 461–76.

McCollum, K. (1996), Web site where students share term papers has professors worried about plagiarism, *Chronicle of Higher Education*, 2 August, 28.

Meade, J. (1992), Cheating: is academic dishonesty par for the course?, *Prism*, **1**, 30–32.

Milgram, S. (1963), Behavioral study of obedience, *Journal of Abnormal Social Psychology*, **67**, 371–8.

Milgram, S. (1964), Issues in the study of obedience: a reply to Baumrind, *American Psychologist*, **19**, 848–52.

Milgram, S. (1965), Some conditions on obedience and disobedience to authority, *Human Relations*, **18**, 57–76.

Milgram, S. (1977), *The Individual in a Social World: Essays and Experiments*, Reading, MA: Addison-Wesley.

Moffatt, M. (1990), Undergraduate cheating, ERIC Document No. 334931.

Mone, M.A. & McKinley, W. (1993), The uniqueness value and its consequences for organization studies, *Journal of Management Inquiry*, **3**, 284–96.

Mowday, R.T. (1997), Celebrating 40 years of the Academy of Management Journal, *Academy of Management Journal*, **40**, 1400–1413.

Noah, H.L. & Eckstein, M.A. (2001), *Fraud and Education: The Worm in the Apple*, Lanham, MD: Rowman & Littlefield.

Park, N. & Peterson, C.M. (2003), Virtues and organizations, in Cameron, K.S., Dutton, J.E. & Quinn R.E. (eds), *Positive organizational scholarship: Foundations of a new discipline*, San Francisco, CA: Berrett-Koehler.

Pavela, G. (1978), Judicial review of academic decision-making after Horowitz, *School Law Journal*, **55**, 55–75.

Perrow, C. (1972), *Complex Organizations: A Critical Essay*, Glenview, IL: Scott, Foresman.

Peterson, C. & Seligman, M.E.P. (2004), *Character Strengths and Virtues: A Handbook and Classification*, New York: Oxford University Press.

Pratt, M.G. & Ashforth, B.E. (2003), Fostering meaningfulness in working and at work, in Cameron, K.S., Dutton, J.E. & Quinn, R.E. (eds), *Positive Organizational Scholarship: Foundations of a new discipline*, San Francisco, CA: Berrett-Koehler, pp. 309–27.

Rawls, J. (1971), *A Theory of Justice*, Cambridge, MA: Harvard University Press.

Reichers, A.E., Wanous, J.P. & Austin, J.T. (1997), Understanding and managing cynicism about organizational change, *Academy of Management Executive*, **11**, 48–59.

Rosenthal, R. & Rosnow, R.L. (1991), *Essential of Behavioral Research: Methods and Data Analysis*, New York: McGraw-Hill.

Rosnow, R.L. (1997), Hedgehogs, foxes, and the evolving social contract in psychological science: ethical challenges and methodological opportunities, *Psychological Methods*, **2**, 345–56.

Rosse, J.G., Stecher, M.D., Miller, J.L. & Lenin, R.A. (1998), The impact of response distortion on preemployment personality testing and hiring decisions, *Journal of Applied Psychology*, **83**, 634–44.

Rousseau, D.M. (1995), *Psychological Contracts in Organizations: Understanding Written and Unwritten Agreements*, Thousand Oaks, CA: Sage.

Salancik, G.R. (1977), Commitment and control of organizational behavior and belief, in Salancik, G.R. and Staw, B.M. (eds), *New Directions in Organizational Research*, Chicago, IL: St. Clair Press, pp. 1–54.

Schein, E.H. (1987), *The Clinical Perspective in Fieldwork*, Newbury Park, CA: Sage.

Selznick, P. (2000), On sustaining research agendas: their moral and scientific basis, *Journal of Management Inquiry*, **9**, 277–82.

Simon, J.G., Powers, C.W. & Gunnemann, J.P. (1979), The responsibilities of corporations and their owners. in Beauchamp, T.L. & Bowie, N.E. (eds), *Ethical Theory and Business*, Englewood Cliffs, NJ: Prentice Hall, pp. 160–68.

Sims, R.L. (1993), The relationship between academic dishonesty and unethical business practices, *Journal of Education for Business*, **68**, 207–11.

Skinner, B.F. (1953), *Science and Human Behavior*, New York: Free Press.

Skinner, B.F. (1969), *Contingencies of reinforcement: A Theoretical Analysis*, New York: Appleton-Century-Crofts.

Skitka, L.J. (2000), The moral mandate hypothesis, Paper presented at the International Society for Justice *Research*, September, Rishon LeZion, Israel.

Slocum, J.W., Jr. (1997), Unlearning to learn, *Academy of Management Journal*, **40**, 1429–31.

Sobieraj, S. (2002), Bush seeks new penalties for 'cooking books', *San Francisco Chronicle*, 10 July, A1, A9.

Turillo, C.J., Folger, R., Lavelle, J.J., Umphress, E.E. & Gee, J.O. (2002), Is virtue its own reward? Self-sacrificial decisions for the sake of fairness, *Organizational Behavior and Human Decision Processes*, **89**, 839–65.

Velasquez, M.G. (2002), *Business Ethics: Concepts and Cases*, 5th edn, Upper Saddle River, NJ: Prentice Hall.

Vroom, V. (1964), *Work and Motivation*, New York: Wiley.

Watson, D. (1988), Intraindividual and interindividual analysis of positive and negative affect: their relation to health complaints, perceived stress, and daily activities, *Journal of Personality and Social Psychology*, **54**, 1020–30.

Watson, D., Clark., L.A. & Tellegen, A. (1988), Development and validation of brief measures of positive and negative affect: the PANAS scales, *Journal of Personality and Social Psychology*, **54**, 1063–70.

Wayne, S.J., Shore, L.M. & Liden, R.C. (1997), Perceived organizational support and leader-member exchange: a social exchange perspective, *Academy of Management Journal*, **40**, 82–111.

Weber, M. (1947), *The Theory of Social and Economic Organization*, trans. and ed. A.M. Henderson & T. Parsons, New York: Oxford University Press.

Weick, K.E. (1999), That's moving: theories that matter, *Journal of Management Inquiry*, **8**, 134–42.

Whitley, B.E., Jr. & Keith-Spiegel, P. (2001), *Academic Dishonesty: An Educator's Guide*, Mahweh, NJ: Lawrence Erlbaum.

Wright, T.A. (1999), An eight-step approach to enhance the application of organizational research, in Larwood, L. & Gatticker, U.E. (eds), *Impact Analysis – How Research Enters Application and Makes a Difference*, Hillsdale, NJ: Lawrence Erlbaum, pp. 137–43.

Wright, T.A. (2004), When a student blows the whistle (on himself): a personal experience essay on 'delayed' integrity in a classroom setting, *Journal of Management Inquiry*, **13**, 289–303.

Wright, T.A. (2005a), The role of 'happiness' in organizational research: past, present and future directions, in Perrewe, P.L. & Ganster, D.C. (eds), *Research in Occupational Stress and Well-Being*, Vol. 4., Amsterdam: JAI Press, pp. 225–68.

Wright, T.A. (2005b), Much more than meets the eye: some troubling ethical consequences of the consumer metaphor in management education, Manuscript submitted for publication.

Wright, T.A. & Cropanzano, R. (1998), Emotional exhaustion as a predictor of job performance and voluntary turnover, *Journal of Applied Psychology*, **83**, 486–93.

Wright, T.A. & Cropanzano, R. (2000), Psychological well-being and job satisfaction as predictors of job performance, *Journal of Occupational Health Psychology*, **5**, 84–94.

Wright, T.A. & Cropanzano, R. (2004), The role of psychological well-being in job performance: a fresh look at an age-old quest, *Organizational Dynamics*, **33**, 338–52.

Wright, T.A. & Hobfoll, S.E. (2004), Commitment, psychological well-being and job performance: an examination of Conservation of Resources (COR) theory and job burnout, *Journal of Business and Management*, **9**, 389–406.

Wright, T.A. & Larwood, L. (1998), Another view on reaffirming our scholarly values: A response to Richard Mowday, *Academy of Management Review*, **23**, 9–12.

Wright, T.A. & Sweeney, D. (1990), Correctional institution workers' coping strategies and their effect on diastolic blood pressure, *Journal of Criminal Justice*, **18**, 161–9.

Wright, T.A. & Wright, V.P. (1999), Ethical responsibility and the organizational researcher: a committed-to-participant research perspective, *Journal of Organizational Behavior*, **20**, 1107–12.

Wright, T.A. & Wright, V.P. (2000), How our 'values' influence the manner in which organizational research is framed and interpreted, *Journal of Organizational Behavior*, **21**, 603–7.

Wright, T.A. & Wright, V.P. (2001), Fact or fiction: the role of [in]civility in organizational research, *Academy of Management Review*, **26**, 168–70.

Wright, T.A. & Wright, V.P. (2002), Organizational researcher values, ethical responsibility, and the committed-to-participant research perspective, *Journal of Management Inquiry*, **11**, 173–85.

Wrzesniewski, A. (2003), Finding positive meaning in work, in Cameron, K.S., Dutton, J.E. & Quinn, R.E. (eds), *Positive Organizational Scholarship: Foundations of a New Discipline*, San Francisco, CA: Berrett-Koehler, pp. 296–308.

Wrzesniewski, A. & Dutton, J.E. (2001), Crafting a job: revisioning employees as active crafters of their work, *Academy of Management Review*, **26**, 179–201.

Zammuto, R.F. (1984), A comparison of multiple constituency models of organizational effectiveness, *Academy of Management Review*, **9**, 606–16.

Zell, D. (2001), The market-driven business school: has the pendulum swung too far? *Journal of Management Inquiry*, **10**, 324–48.

16 Conclusions
Mustafa F. Özbilgin and Olivia Kyriakidou

One of the taken-for-granted ideas in organisational studies is that organisational reality can be studied by dissecting it into its key components and studying them in isolation. The outcome of this has allowed for sociologists, psychologists and other social scientists to remain in their methodological and philosophical silos when examining organisational reality, allowing for objective and subjective aspects of organisation as well as individual and institutional concerns in organisations to be studied in isolation from one another. It is our contention that this approach to organisational reality has caused a gap to emerge between rich lived experience in organisational settings and academic theorisation of organisational reality in the mainstream. It was also this belief that motivated us to devise an edited volume which will serve to bridge the gap between theorisation and the reality of organisational life by specifically exploring relationality between a wide range of constituents in and of organisational settings.

The approach we adopted was an inclusive one, seeking to reveal relationality – which manifests itself as intersubjectivite, interdependent, co-generative processes – between a range of organisational constituencies, including individual, group and intra- and inter-organisational contexts and processes. Holding the belief that an understanding of organisational reality will require an understanding of a wide range of permutations of relationality within and among these constituencies, we have organised and designed a number of academic activities. The first of these activities was a conference at the University of Surrey, School of Management, on relational perspectives in 2003. The ambitious aim to explore relationality calls for creative designs for academic activities that transcend the designs of conferences organised in the camps of organisational study that we were seeking to critique. Reflecting on our understanding of relational thinking, we devised a conference that welcomed interdisciplinary and multi-method contributions. We tried to increase interdisciplinarity by purposely inviting speakers from divergent methodological as well as disciplinary perspectives. The conference organisation also sought to engender relational engagement between researchers and end users, including organisation studies scholars, consultants and practitioners. The multi-party engagement was adopted in both presenting and discussing papers as the academic papers were discussed by consultants and practitioners. Fostering a common language, teasing out threads of common themes, and scoping for collaborative learning and researching opportunities were some of the key outcomes of this conference which adopted relationality not only as the theme but also as a marker of its design.

Drawing on the success of the conference in spring 2003, we have edited a special issue for the journal *Career Development International*, with the contributions at the conference. The special edition has encouraged us to carry our idea to an international conference. We have chosen the European Academy of Management as a platform for our track. With Dr Costanzo, we have organised two tracks with the same title as this edited text at the European Academy of Management (EURAM) Conferences in 2004 and 2005.

The first track that we ran in the EURAM conference in 2003 attracted papers that focused on relationality at micro, meso and macro aspects of organisational life. The discussions that ensued have uncovered the diversity of approaches that are termed as 'relational'. Some of the papers explored relationality of dyadic nature whilst others explored relationality in multi-level and multi-party contexts. Although our initial formulation for relationality resided at the level of relations between the individual and the organisation, some of the papers explored relationality between organisations, such as relational strategizing, or relationality in the microeconomic context of the firm.

The second track in 2005 has furthered our understanding of relational perspectives, widening its scope even further with presentations on relationality reified as inner psychological dialogue, and as interplay of micro-individual, meso-institutional and macro-structural aspects of organisation.

Although the journey we have taken in studying relational perspectives has introduced us to a broad spectrum of perspectives, it also has raised further questions that we hope to answer. This volume answers a number of questions in each of its contributed chapters. Some of the key questions that the collection of contributions in this book provides answers for are:

1. How can we envision organizational reality in relational terms, if we believe that this reality is more complex than can be captured by approaches that ignore relational processes within it?
2. What is the significance of a situated, interdependent and co-evolutionary understanding of self and circumstances in improving equity, fairness, equality and quality of work and life?
3. How do we reconcile and bridge the gap between traditional dichotomies of organizational study between objective and subjective reality, the micro and macro perspectives, the academic and practitioner

knowledge, the positivist and interpretivist perspectives and the qualitative and quantitative methods?
4. How do we formulate theoretical and methodological alternatives to the orthodoxy of studying organizations and individuals as phenomena that are independent of each other?
5. Finally, how do we move relational philosophy to the level of method and practice and yet retain its anti-reductionist ambitions?

Although we believe that this volume addresses the above questions, there are still questions that remain unanswered. The future of relational perspectives, we believe, rests very much with the ability of organizational studies scholars to attend to a new set of questions that arise from the ongoing debate:

1. What are the methodological and theoretical markers and demarcations of relational perspective in studies of organizational phenomena?
2. If we believe that relational methods allow us to study organizational reality in a way that is true to its nature, are there relational methods which are more conducive to deliver on this promise?
3. How can relational perspectives be moved from the margins of organizational research to the mainstream? What are the methodological and theoretical challenges that this endeavour may bring to bear? How can these be addressed?

It is our expectation that relational perspectives will survive the test of time and establish themselves as a cognate alternative in the main of organizational studies. We would therefore like to thank all the contributors of this text for embellishing it with their insights into new possibilities of thinking of organizational issues in relational, dynamic and processual terms and for helping us get a step closer to realizing our ambitions to describe organizational life relationally.

Index